THE POPULAR HISTORY OF

GRAFFITI

THE POPULAR HISTORY OF

GRAFFITI

FROM THE ANCIENT WORLD TO THE PRESENT

FIONA McDONALD

Skyhorse Publishing

This book is for Julie Matysik, with many thanks. —F. M.

Skyhorse Publishing books may be purchased in bulk at special discounts for sales promotion, corporate gifts, fund-raising, or educational purposes. Special editions can also be created to specifications. For details, contact the Special Sales Department, Skyhorse Publishing, 307 West 36th Street, 11th Floor, New York, NY 10018 or info@skyhorsepublishing.com.

Skyhorse® and Skyhorse Publishing® are registered trademarks of Skyhorse Publishing, Inc.®, a Delaware corporation.

Visit our website at www.skyhorsepublishing.com.

10 9 8 7 6 5 4 3 2 1

Library of Congress Cataloging-in-Publication Data is available on file.
ISBN: 978-1-61608-868-2

Printed in China

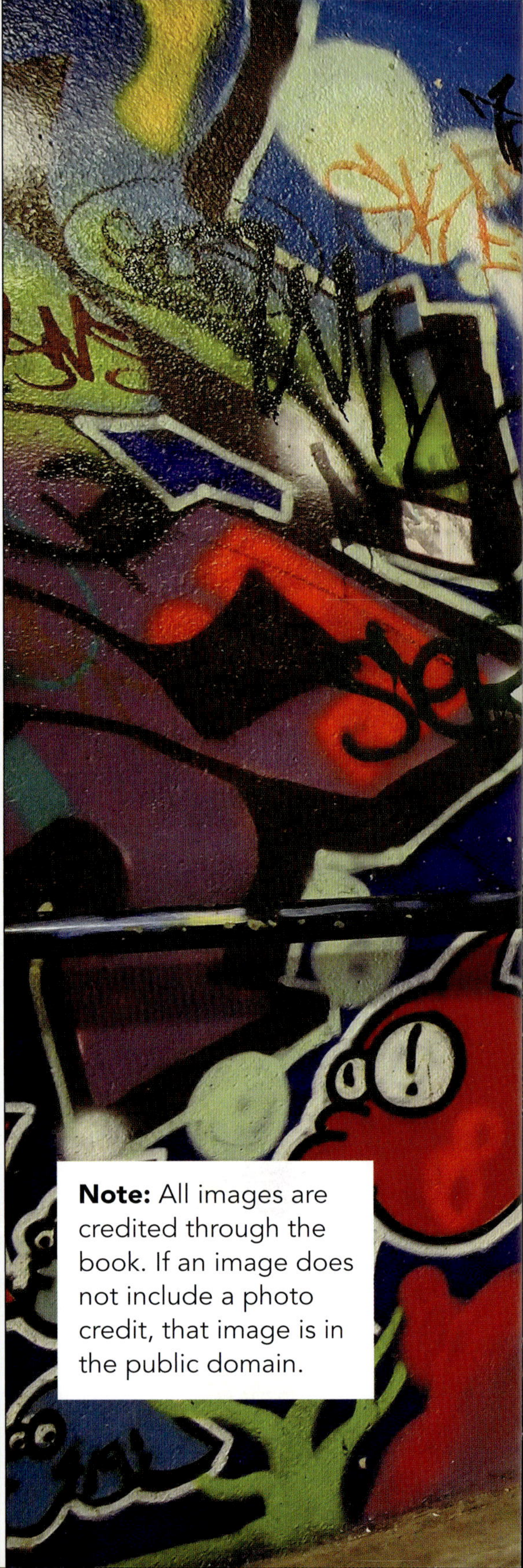

Note: All images are credited through the book. If an image does not include a photo credit, that image is in the public domain.

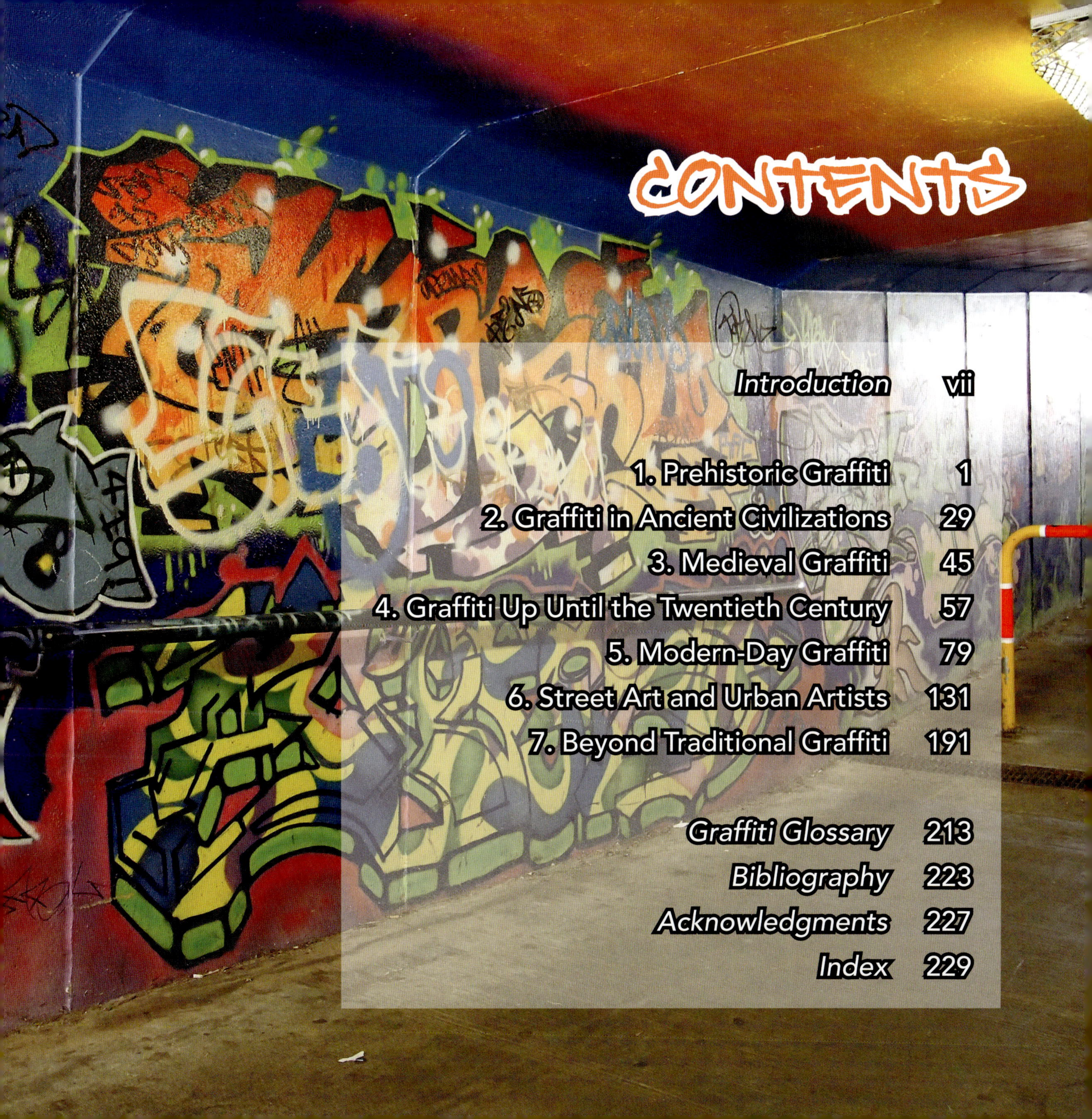

Contents

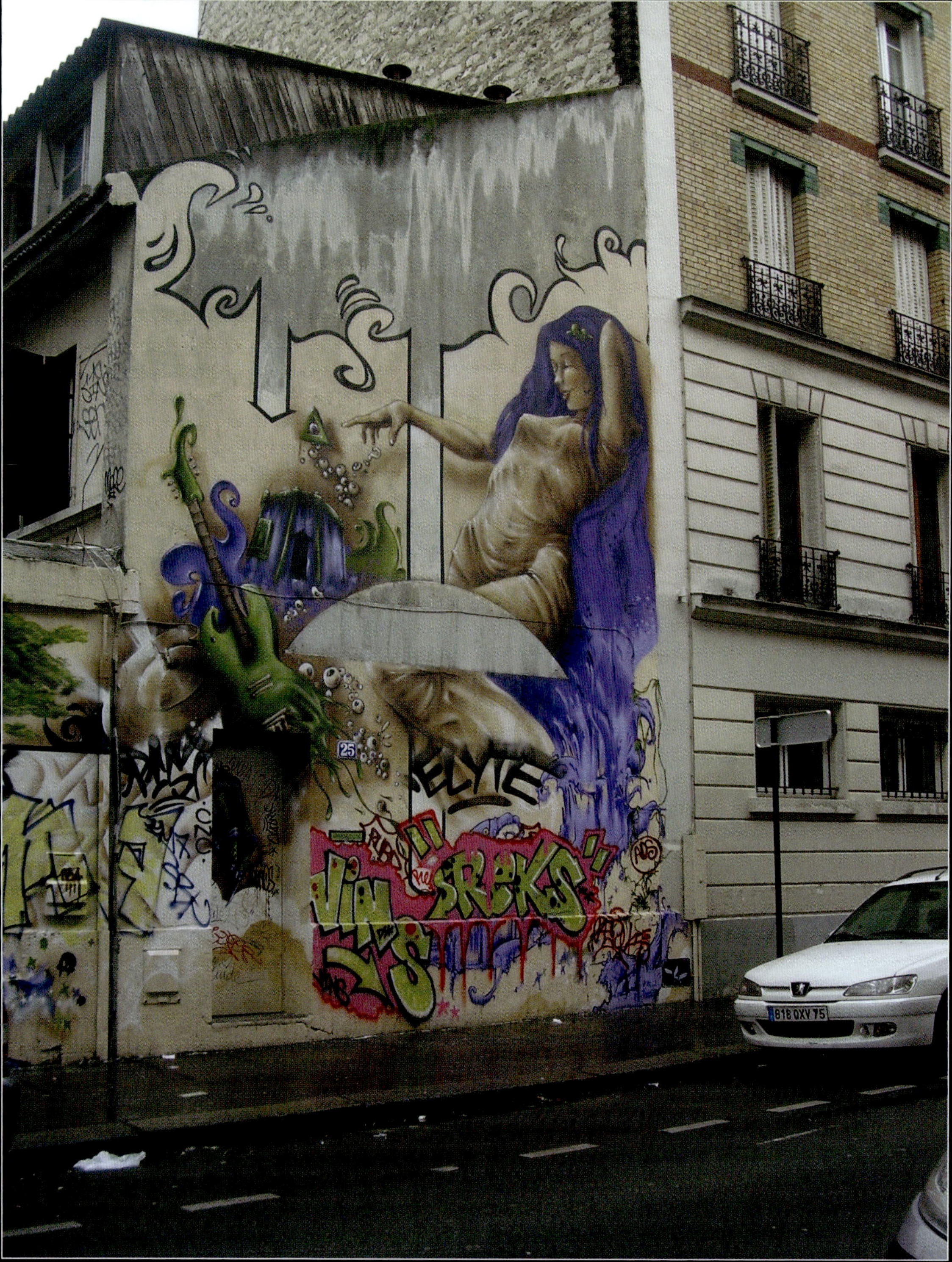

Sophie Masson. »

INTRODUCTION

When we think of graffiti today, we usually conjure images of multi-colored patterns and cartoon characters that are found on abandoned factory walls or underneath grungy bridges. We think of tags and stylized writing and the often rude scribbles on the backs of public toilet stall doors. Some of us may even remember graffiti political slogans calling for peace, war, freedom, or the incarceration of certain members of society. Perhaps hearing the word "graffiti" makes us reminisce about scratching our initials into a desk top during interminable math lessons. Or perhaps it's that old heart with an arrow through the middle carved into a tree trunk, immortalized with two sets of initials.

But what *is* graffiti exactly? Is it limited to political ideals, personal initials, spray can art, or discussions about bodily functions? If graffiti encompasses only unsolicited text and images, then where does cave art fit in? Or pieces that have been commissioned by school or city councils? And who should say if graffiti should be illegal, painted over, or not? And in the same vein, we must ask if the graffiti that sells for thousands of dollars through art galleries is really, in effect, graffiti or some new art form.

And why do we feel the urge to leave an unsolicited mark on the objects that surround us? Is it so we'll have a personal memorial for generations to come—a kind of immortal residue? Or is it a secret knowledge that we have left a bit of ourselves somewhere we shouldn't have? How old is this phenomenon we've termed "graffiti"? When did we make our earliest scratching as a human race? Where do you find graffiti, and why does it seem to have such appeal for us?

It is also important to ask, in addition to why graffiti came about, where graffiti is headed? Is the spray can becoming redundant in favor of laser projections or flash drives jammed into walls for the passerby to plug into their iPads? The hows and whys of graffiti have been studied by academics across the globe, and while their research may at times be obscure, particularly to the lay person, the one thing they all agree on is that graffiti is a worldwide practice. One journalist suggests it is so common that it can almost be classified as a human characteristic. It is both an anonymous voice and a public one; executed when no one is looking but there in full view for all to see. The subject matter ranges from toilet humor to philosophical musings. Graffiti can mark territory or provide relief from dreary bricks and mortar that are in need of a facelift. Graffiti can be painted, etched, pasted, knitted, stenciled, carved, or even projected onto a surface. Its scope is so broad that it is hard to decide where to draw the line (excuse the pun) on what actually constitutes graffiti.

This book will try to look at as many aspects and types of graffiti as possible, from the distant past to the most up-to-date practices. It may not answer all the questions about graffiti's history and its future, but hopefully it will provide a wider window into an activity (and art form) that affects us all and that many of us may never give a second thought.

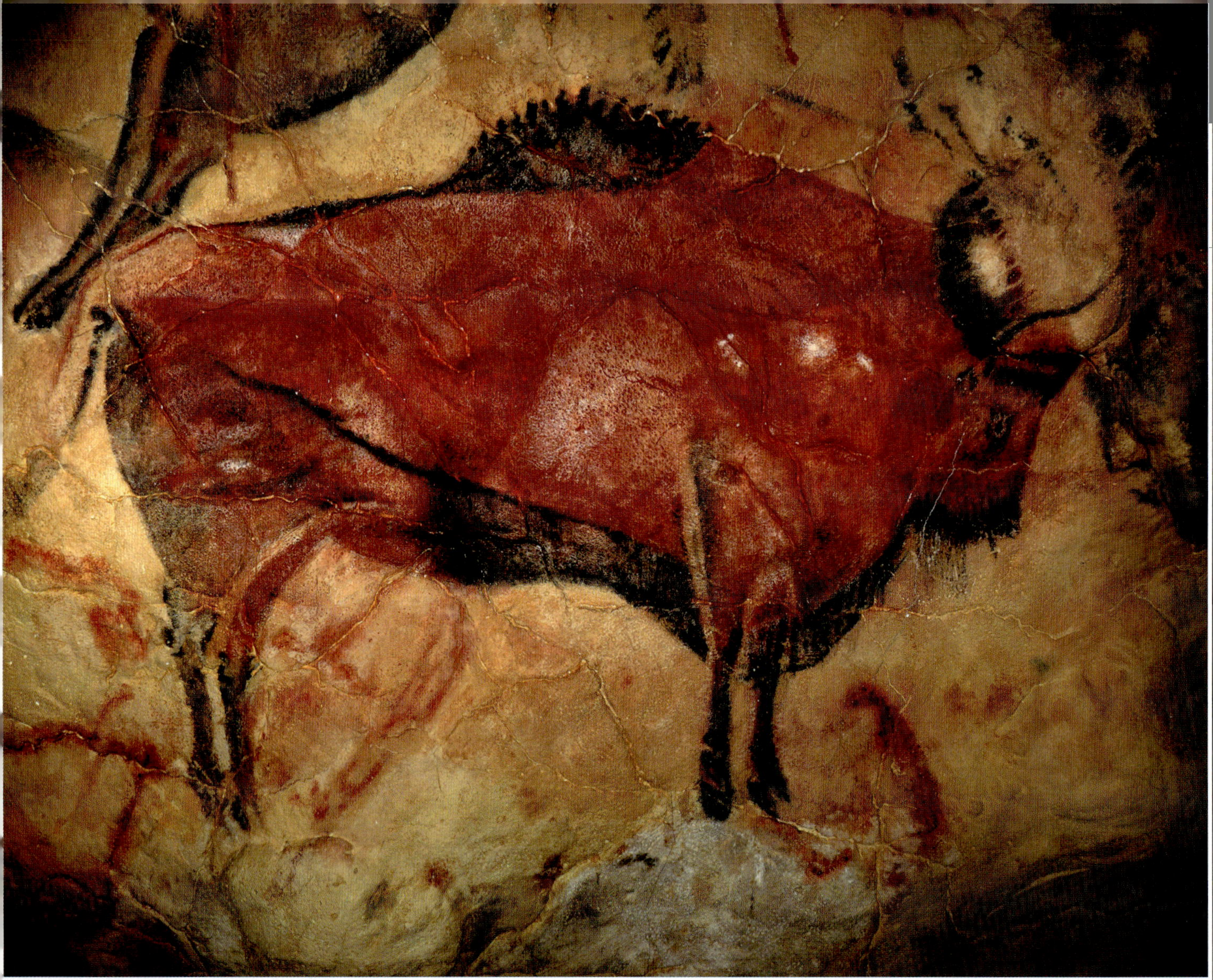

This is one of the most famous images from prehistory—a magnificent red bison from the Cave of Altamira in Spain.

CHAPTER ONE

PREHISTORIC GRAFFITI

At some point in mankind's early history, probably after we learned to stand upright and possibly about the same time as we discovered fire, we picked up a sharp object or a lump of charcoal and made a mark on another object or surface. Perhaps it was an accident, perhaps a hunter who was chipping away at a piece of flint to make a stone tool found that he was making scratches, not just a sharp edge. Maybe someone cooking meat on a fire rubbed a sooty hand over her brow and realized she'd left a black smudge. We will never know how it happened, but when it did, leaving marks on cave walls, stones, and other surfaces became an integral part of human life. Soon, drawing and painting were used to help hunters learn how to track down and kill essential meat. Tallies were used to keep track of numbers, pictograms evolved to leave messages for others, and finally cuneiform and other types of markings emerged, leading our species to

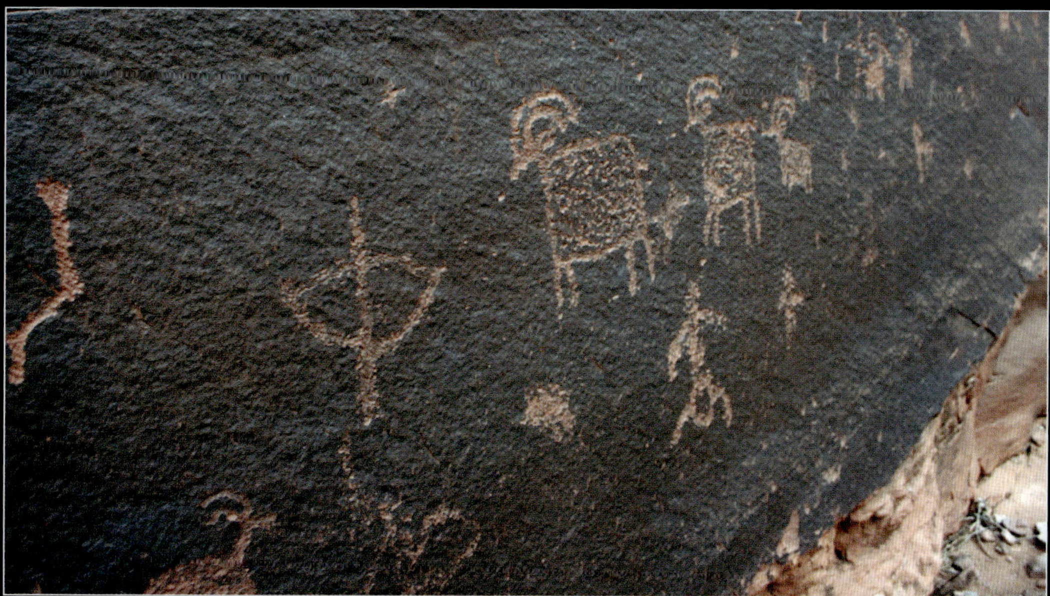

«
Like the Coso people of the Mojave Desert, the ancient Pueblo people of the Colorado plateau held the bighorn sheep central to their culture.

writing as we know it, in its various scripts and alphabets of today. But let's begin at the very beginning and find out where and when our first scratching and scribbling took place.

PETROGLYPHS

If we take the word "graffito" right back to its etymological origins, insisting that it refers to something being scratched onto a surface, then the best place to begin our discussion of the history of graffiti is through a particular form of rock art from prehistoric times known as *petroglyphs*.

Petroglyphs can be found all over the world, except in Antarctica. While most petroglyphs consist of paintings on rocks, there are some instances of images scratched into rock, though this seems less frequent. Perhaps that is due to the fact that the effort required to cut images into stone was much more laborious than simply mixing pigments and wiping or brushing them onto rock. And while petroglyphs most certainly date back more than 40,000 years, there are sadly not many cave paintings left from that long ago. The bulk of these forms of rock art begin around 27,000 years ago—many of which are found in Australia—while others are only 10,000 to 12,000 years old.

While cave paintings do not tend to depict landscape motifs, petroglyphs are thought to illustrate maps and landmarks to facilitate and communicate to other ancient humans about travel or to show where tribal boundaries were. When a petroglyph pictures a landform—a river, hill, or the like—archeologists call this a *geocontourglyph*.

Across the globe, petroglyphs show many similarities in style and content, even when found on continents that are far apart. One's natural surroundings, it has been argued, provides an immediate source of inspiration—a rock is a rock whether it is in Russia or South America; a river is the same in China or Scandinavia—so the depictions of these natural landscapes don't alter significantly from area to area. On closer examination of the glyphs, some scientists feel that the closely-related artistic

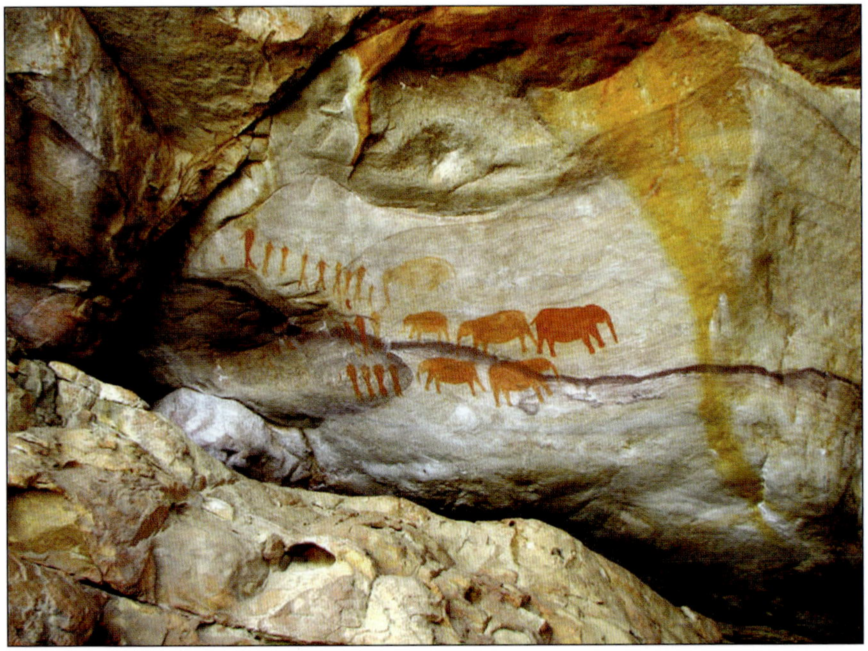

» A non-prehistoric cave painting made by the San people of the Kalahari Desert, whose culture has been studied with the hope of shedding light on our early ancestors.

styles (excluding the subject matter) might well be attributed to human migration across the continents, but there are others who see this as evidence of the "genetically inherited structure of the human brain."

Many petroglyphs are thought to be the precursor of a written language system; many seem to use symbols to represent things and ideas, not just pictures of those things (which we term *pictographs*). Furthermore, for some scientists there has been much debate about whether petroglyphs were made consciously or whether they were the result of a person in an altered state of consciousness, such as that brought on by hallucinogenic drugs. Scientists at the Rock Art Research Institute have studied the modern day San people of the Kalahari Desert region. This culture believes that the artists of the tribe actually go into and beyond the rock face (in a trance-like state). On the other side, in the spirit world, these artists capture images that they bring back to etch into the rock. It is thought that perhaps ancient mankind may have been in a similar hypnotic state while making their incised drawings.

European Bronze Age Petroglyphs

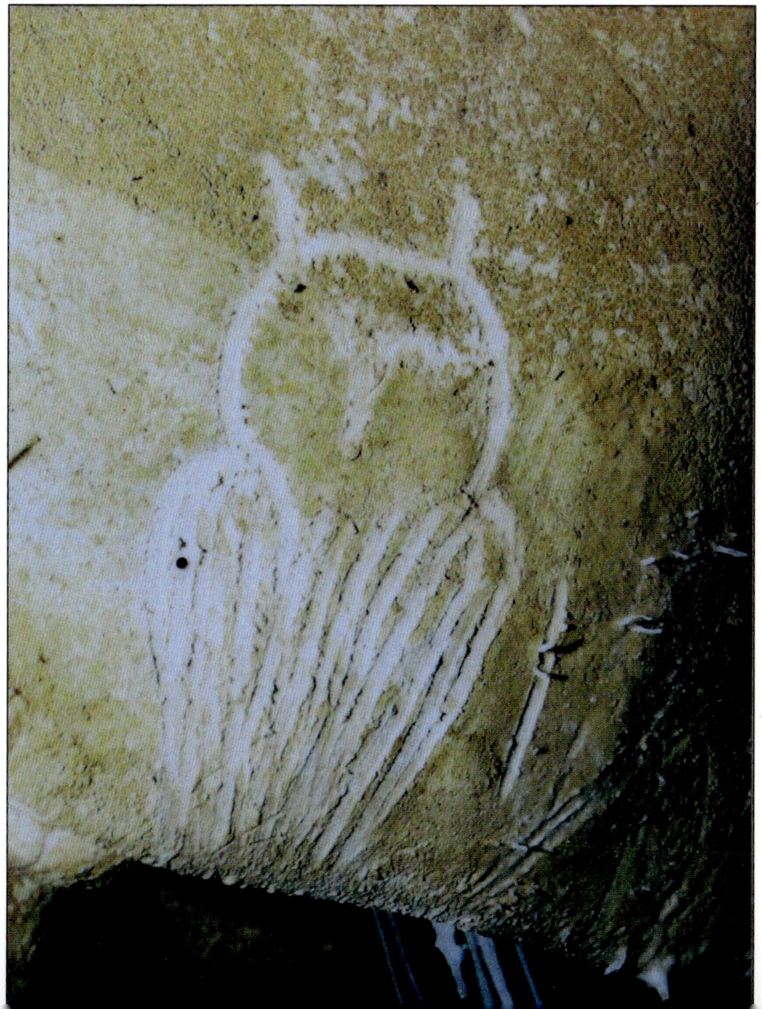

The Vallée des Merveilles in Southern France is home to the largest collection of outdoor petroglyphs on the European continent. The majority of the markings found here are from the Bronze Age and feature tools, daggers, axes, spears, and scythes alongside horned and anthropomorphic animals, suns, stars, and a selection of geometric designs, some of which have been identified as symbols for the earth itself.

The petroglyphs at Vallée des Merveilles were discovered in 1881 by Clarence Bicknell, an amateur archeologist from Britain. Bicknell spent about five years studying the glyphs, recording them, and making drawings of them. He noted more than 10,000 of them. But it wasn't until 1967 that a professional study was conducted of the drawings.

The overseeing archeologist for this study, Henry de Lumley, thought the glyphs were primarily the work of a Bronze Age people who worshipped a bull god.

« An engraving of an owl originally found in the Chauvet Caves in France, but now only seen as a reproduction in the Caves' replica museum.

America's Petroglyphs

A major petroglyph area in America spreads across the Coso Range, which is situated between the Sierra Nevada and the Argus Range, covering an area of 400 square miles. Throughout this region, there are approximately 20,000 images made by Paleo-Indians, or the Native Americans. Within the Range are a number of canyons, two of which are named the Big and Little Petroglyph Canyons, and these are the galleries featuring the most extensive and well-preserved petroglyphs. These glyphs are divided into six categories: human figures (which includes anthropomorphic figures); bighorn sheep; a mixture of other

Coso figure of a stylized human accompanied by a snake and lizards.

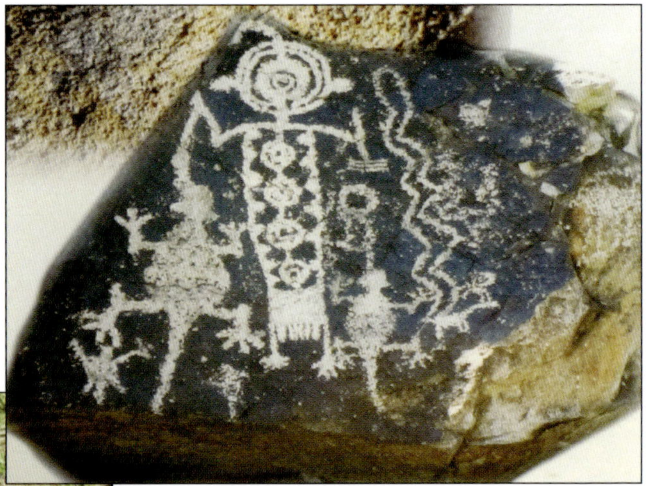

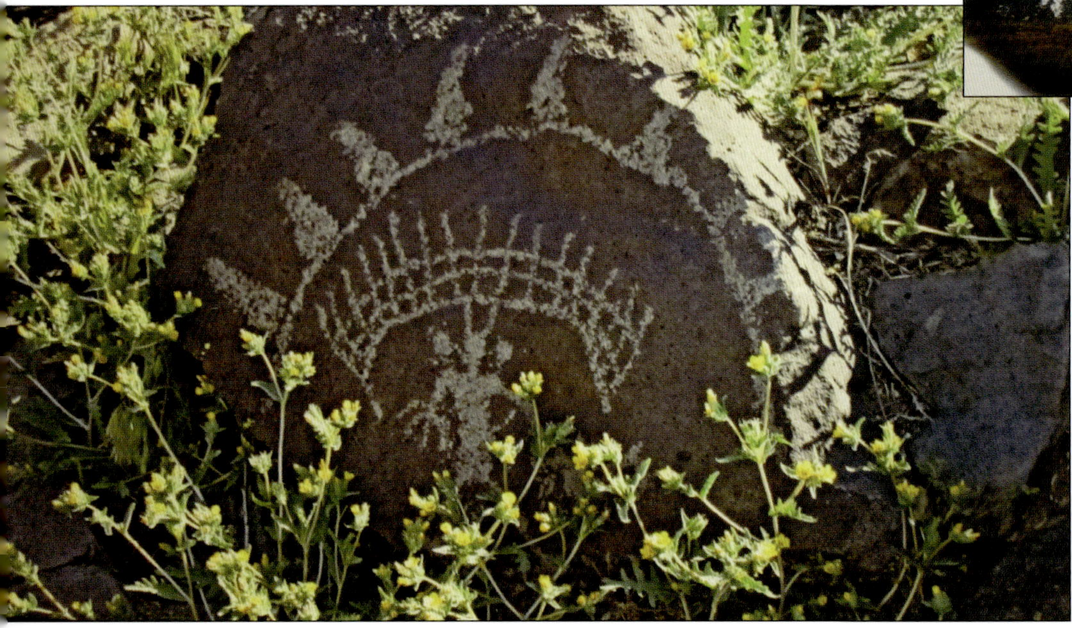

Petroglyphs made by the ancient Coso people on a rock. It is a highly stylized piece but looks as though it might be a human figure with an elaborate headdress underneath an arch that may represent the sky.

Bighorn sheep with lambs inscribed into rock by the Coso people.

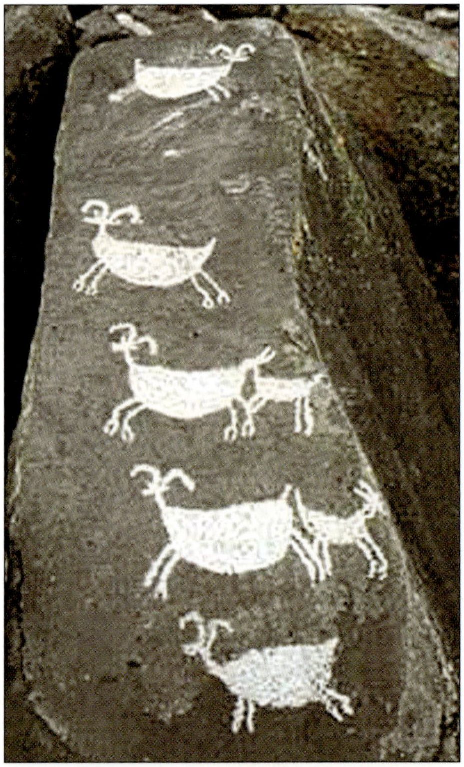

More bighorn sheep, two with horns locked in combat, made by people » living in the vicinity of the Columbia River Gorge in the United States.

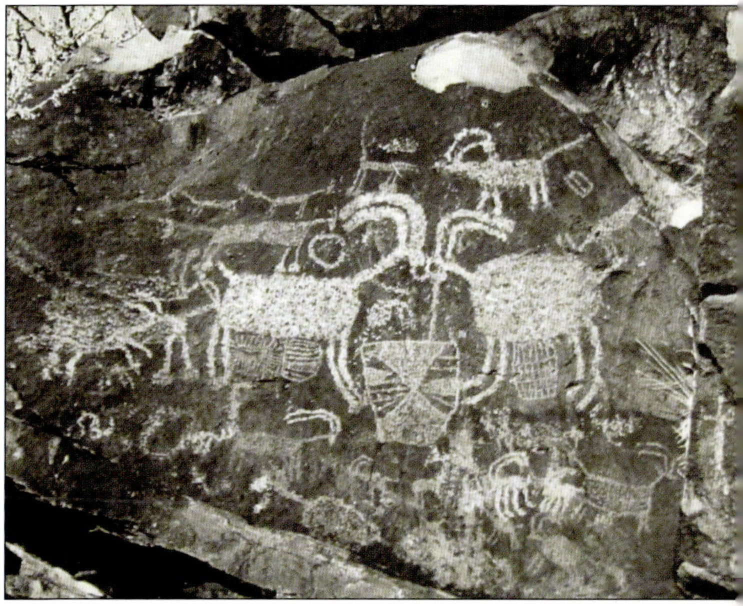

animals including deer and antelope; weapons; tools; and entopic or "medicine bag" images. The glyphs are thought to be about 10,000 years old. Why they were made is not known for certain, but various theories abound. One theory proposes the glyphs were part of some magical hunting ritual, while another posits the idea that they are linked to various shamanistic rituals.

Nazca Lines

The geoglyphs in the Nazca Desert in Southern Peru, covering a massive area of 190 square miles, are believed to have been made somewhere between 400 and 650 AD, and are therefore relatively young compared to some of the petroglyphs found in Europe and Australia. These images are made not as etchings in the rock, but in the same way that the chalk drawings in the United Kingdom have been made. To achieve this type of rock art, the top layer of the earth is removed (in the United Kingdom it is grass, but in Nazca it is the red pebbles of the desert) and a trench 10 to 15 centimeters is dug. The ground beneath, heavy with lime, is revealed in contrast to the surrounding top layer and helps make the design stand out better. When condensation falls on the exposed lime, the mineral hardens and becomes more difficult to wear away.

These Nazca Desert petroglyphs in Peru were discovered by archaeologist Toribio Mejia Xesspe in 1927, but it wasn't until some ten years later that any serious examination of them was made. Then, in the early 1940s, a historian from Long Island University, Paul Kosok, on a trip to study ancient irrigation systems, viewed the drawings as he flew over them in a small, low-flying plane. Of the hundreds of pictures in the desert, many of them are geometric designs, but there are also numerous depictions of living things: birds, monkeys, spiders, and plants, to name a few.

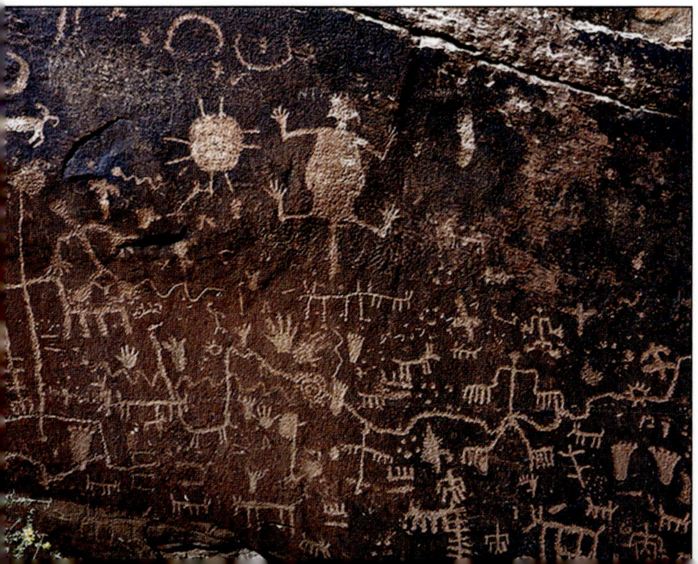

« The petroglyphs on Newspaper Rock in Eastern Utah are so closely rendered that from a distance they appear to be like newsprint, hence the name. Newspaper Rock and its surroundings feature the largest known collection of petroglyphs in the world. The first are thought to have been made 2,000 years ago. The place is called Tse' Hone in Navajo and means "a rock story."

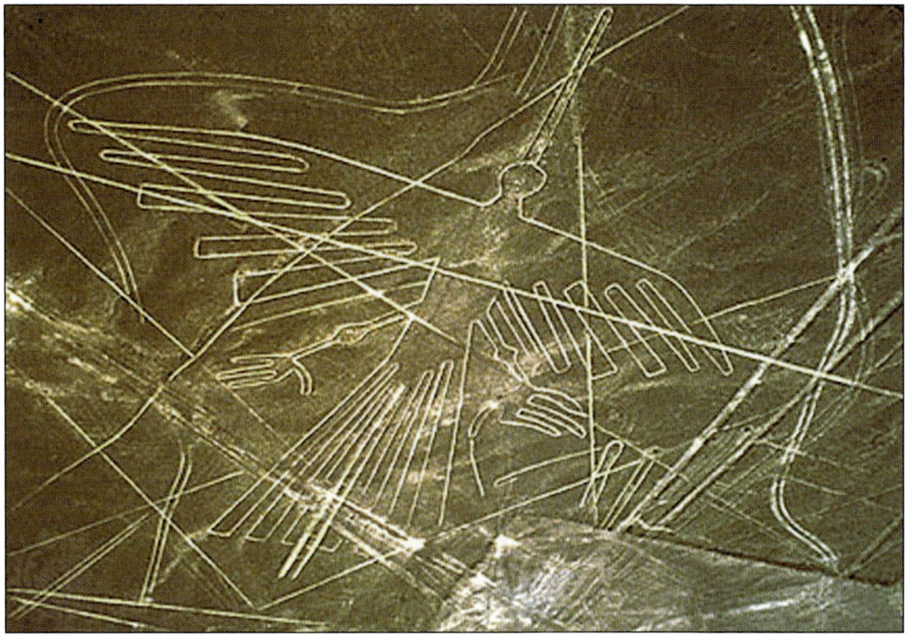

« The precision with which this huge eagle and the other giant figures found in the Nazca Desert were made is astonishing when you realize the limited technology available to the artists. It has led to the speculation, by a limited few, that the indigenous people were given extraterrestrial help.

Kosok and the German mathematician and archaeologist Maria Reiche worked together to try to discover the purpose behind the Nazca Lines. They hypothesized that some of the lines pointed to positions on the horizon where the sun, moon, and various stars rose at particular times of the year—the solstice and equinox, for example. Reiche thought that some of the figures might also have represented constellations.

Apart from why the lines were made there remains the enigma of how they were made with such accuracy. At the end of some of the lines, the remains of wooden posts have been discovered. It is thought that these may have been anchors to tie strings to and then used to measure out the dead straight line in the manner of early surveying tools. Besides offer-

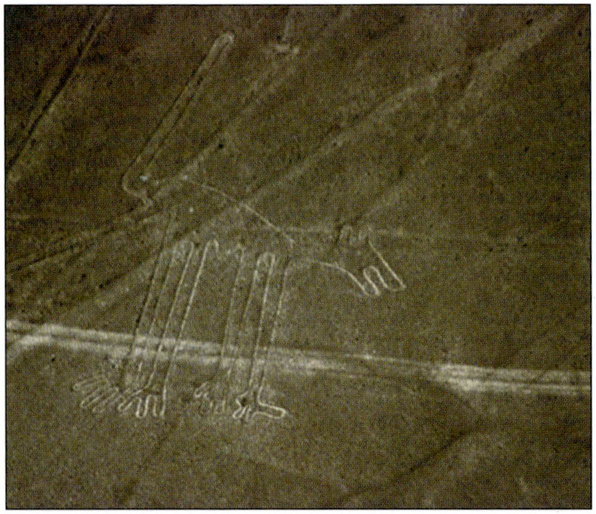

« Nazca Lima

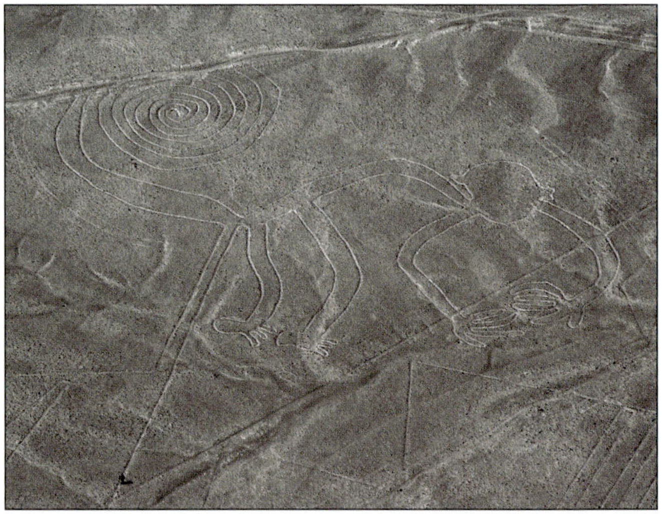

» Nazca Monkey

Yet another example of modern petroglyph graffiti. You can make out a love heart towards the bottom. There appears to be some Korean signatures on the left-hand side and a fairly recent visitor has carved the name "Jacko" to the right. »

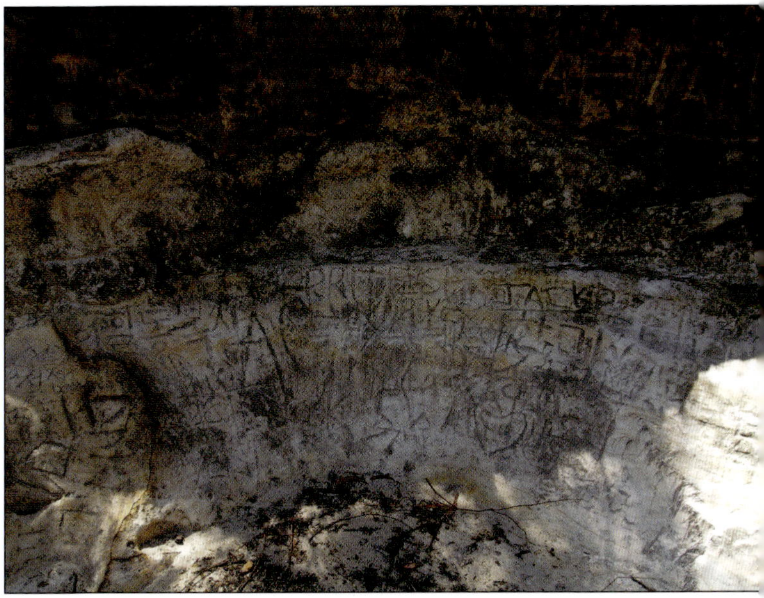

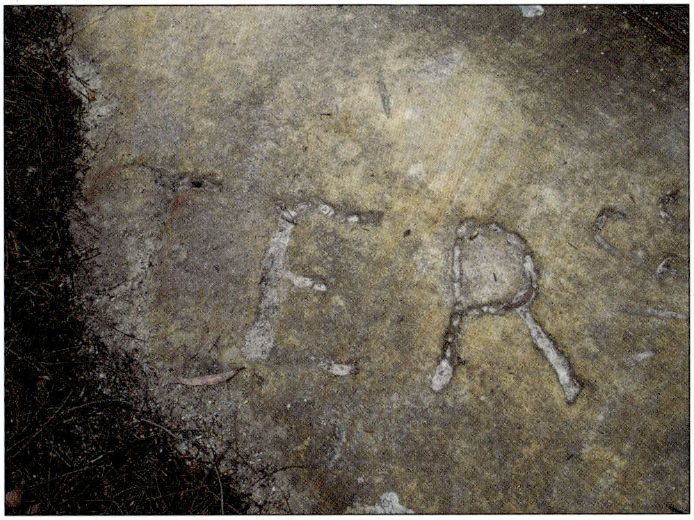

⮝ Modern-day petroglyphs scratched into rock in the popular tourist area of the Blue Mountains just west of Sydney, Australia.

Further along the same trail is an area where the graffiti is so densely carved that the whole surface is worn away. ⮟

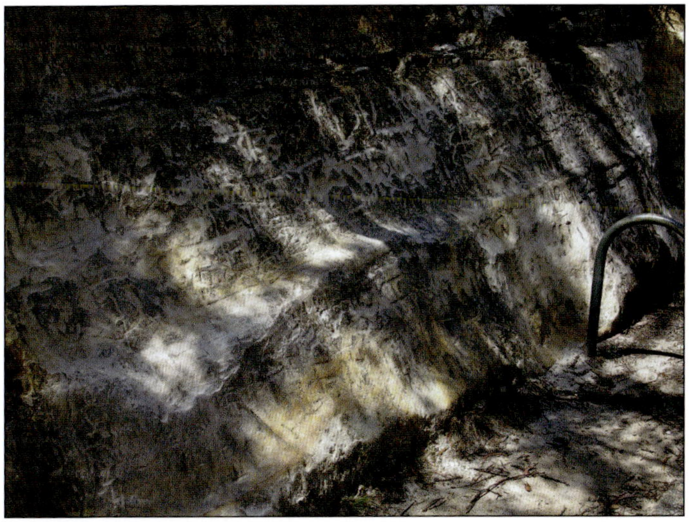

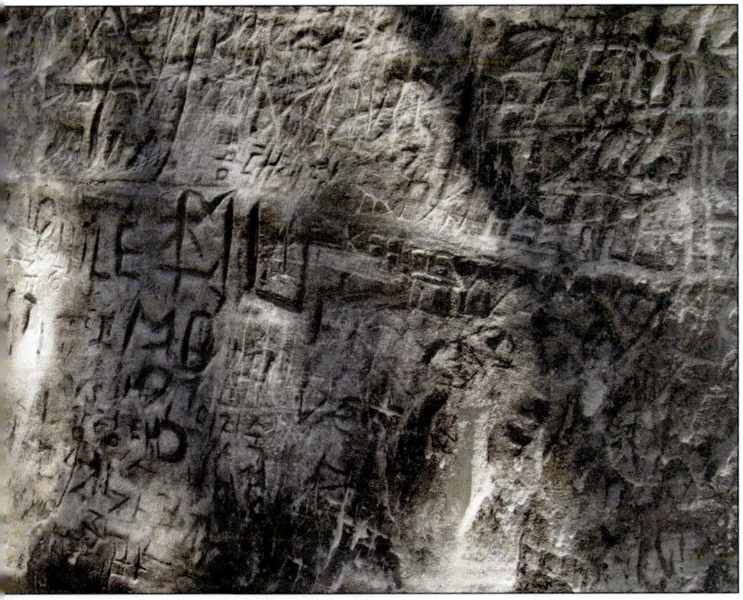

« More petroglyphs found on walking trails in the Blue Mountains. Note how they overlap and how some are obviously in languages other than English that use different characters.

ing an explanation to the lines' construction, the wooden posts have also helped scientists pinpoint possible dates of the creation of the lines through carbon dating.

Later scholars have argued over the theories of their earlier colleagues about these drawings, stating that there just is not enough evidence in the lines of geoglyphs alone to make such assumptions. And even one of Reiche's own pupils took her mentor's constellation theory a step further, suggesting that the lines were not the constellations themselves but the spaces between them.

Yet another theory put forward was that the lines were part of the Nazca Indians' spiritual belief system that was influenced by landforms such as rivers, mountains, and other natural structures. There has even been a theory that links the lines to the woven motifs on funeral shrouds, suggesting that the trenches were some kind of giant loom for the weaving of these very long textiles. Other speculations are a bit more fanciful in nature. One scientist believes the ancient makers of the geoglyphs could have constructed them only with the aid of an aircraft and thinks a hot air balloon would have been a possible option. The notoriously unreliable but imaginative Eric von Daniken believed they could have been made only with the help of beings from another planet.

We may never know the truth behind the Nazca geoglyphs, especially as the lines are now very much in danger of complete eradication. Climate change and erosion brought on by deforestation is beginning to wreak havoc on them. While they were able to withstand the minute rainfall of the area over centuries, more recent downpours have caused flooding and have damaged many of the lines.

Geopglyphs may have been one of mankind's earliest forms of graffiti, but they are also a practice that is still being implemented to this day. Caves, rock faces, and monuments all pose an enticing surface to scratch in one's initials and a date. The picture shown here illustrates a popular tourist area in Blue Mountains National Park, Australia, where visitors from decades ago have made records of their visits. In the Jenolan Caves, an hour or so further west of the mountains, visitors in the early part of the twentieth century would venture into the caverns equipped with candles, oil lamps, and knives, their main purpose being to carve their names and the date of their stopover into the rock's surface.

Rongorongo and the Petroglyphs of Easter Island

In the nineteenth century, some interesting artifacts were found on Easter Island. They were pieces of wood with symbols and little pictures on them. It is thought they represent a type of ancient writing. These pieces are called *rongorongo*, but the full title was supposedly *kohau motu mo rongorongo*, meaning "lines inscribed for chanting aloud." The glyphs are written in a system called *boustrophedon*, which means they are read from left to right and then the following line is read right to left.

In addition to the rongorongo, Easter Island is well known for its extensive collection of various petroglyphs. Even the huge heads for which the island is most famous have been covered in engravings, some of which have been painted red and white. The motifs used on these rocks include animals, mainly of the marine variety, domestic fowls, canoes, anthropomorphic bird figures, and the face of Makemake, their creator god.

Throughout the centuries, the glyphs on these rocks have been altered and carved over. The earliest were made when the Polynesians inhabited the island, somewhere between 700 and 1100 AD. The first Europeans set foot on the island in 1722 and colonized it right away. Buildings were put up over areas featuring glyphs that have since been rediscovered. Among the 4,000 recorded glyphs, there are several that are very similar to some motifs in the rongorongo tablets.

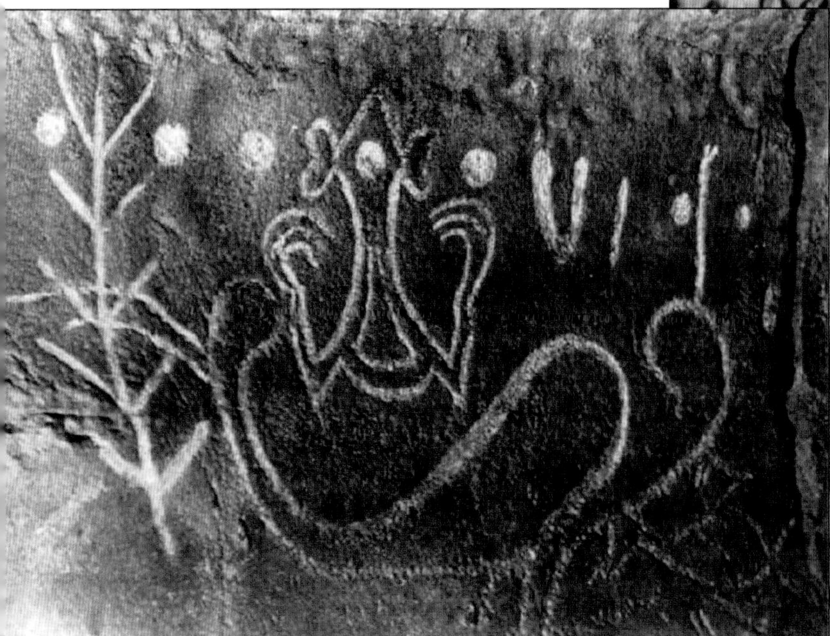

≈ Glyphs on Easter Island.

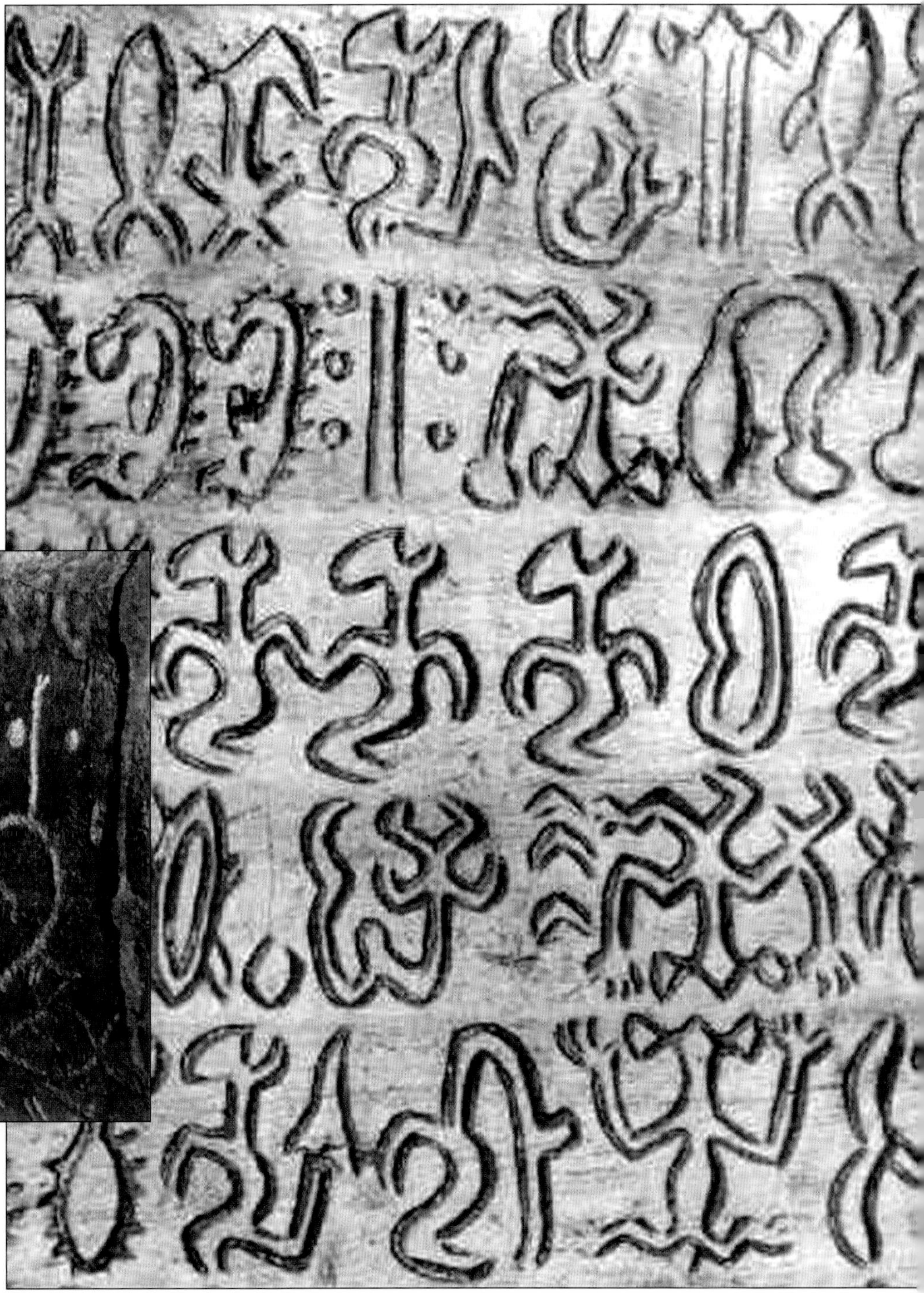

Rongorongo script »
found on Easter Island.

CAVE PAINTING

While modern-day graffiti is considered by some to be a blight on urban buildings and is also seen as a form of vandalism, this was clearly not the case in prehistoric days. Scientists have found markings on walls, stone, the trunks of trees, and elsewhere from centuries ago. And while these ancient forms of art are quite different from our modern spray-painted tags, I have decided to include ancient cave painting in this book as a form of graffiti because it illuminates what appears to be a timeless obsession throughout mankind: drawing and painting on stone and making one's presence known through images. The paintings rendered on cave walls in ancient times were the forerunners of the modern graffitist's in our culture today. Hands were used as reverse stencils and the mouth blew the liquefied paint over them to form an image of a hand, the same principle as spray can stencil art today. A hand may also have been a kind of tag, a personal and/or community identity marker such as the stylized initials graffiti crew use to mark their turf.

As mentioned at the beginning of this chapter, the oldest cave paintings yet discovered throughout the world are around 40,000 years old. Australia has a number of sites where the indigenous people have painted images of the now extinct mega fauna that they hunted, such as kangaroos and wombats as big as oxen. One such painting found on the Arnhem Land plateau, in the territory of the Jawoyn people and rendered in red ochre, features two creatures that are thought to be giant emus—*genyornis* as archaeologists have called them—with their long necks stretched out in front of them. Scientists believe the birds represented in these images to have died out more than 40,000 years ago, which suggests the painting predates their demise and coincides with the estimated date of the beginning of human habitation in Australia. It has also been suggested that firsthand knowledge of genyornis would not be necessary for an artist to depict one, but experts say that the detail on the paintings could only come from great familiarity with the animal and would not be obtainable through the oral tradition of storytelling. Of course, another argument put forward against

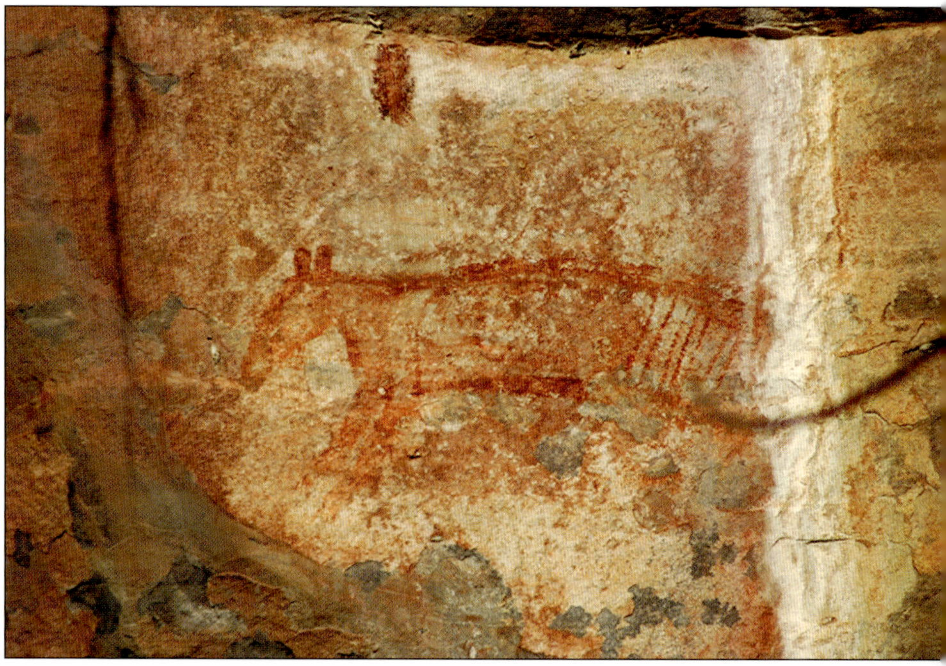

A painting of an Australian Thylacine, popularly » known as a Tasmanian tiger and extinct since the 1930s, made by indigenous Australians at Ubir.
Photo image used with permission of the Northern Territory Tourism Authority.

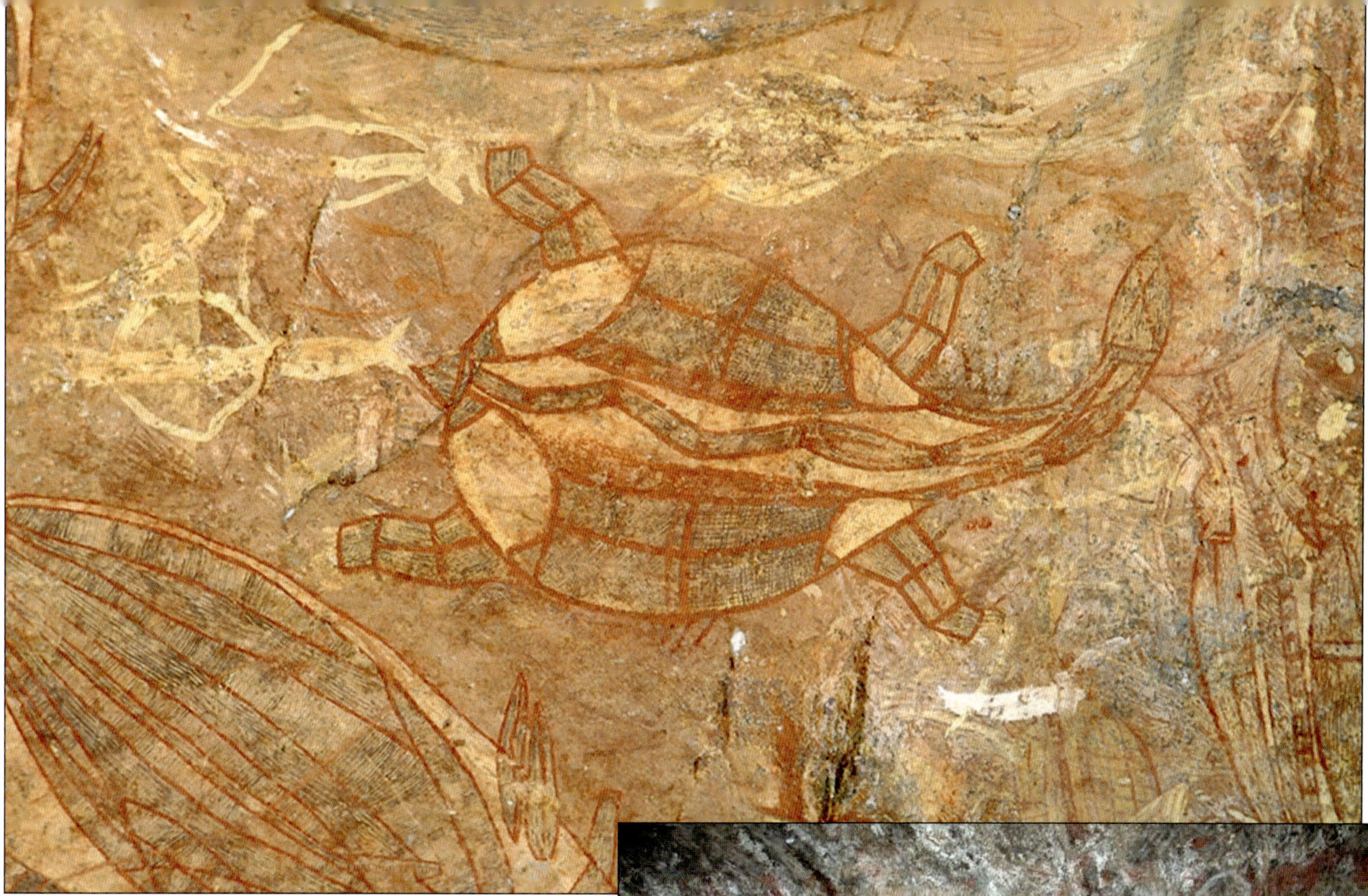

≈ An Australian Aboriginal painting of a turtle, also found at Ubir. These paintings, although not ancient, are typical of the much older style of the giant animals.
Photo courtesy of the Northern Territory Tourism Authority.

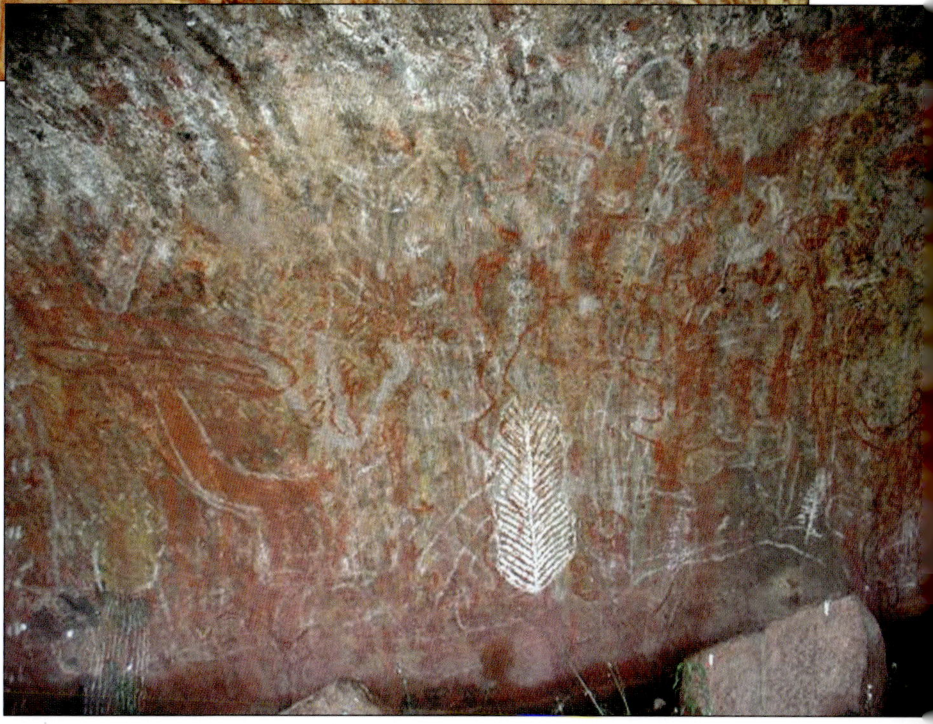

As we have seen with the modern-day petroglyphs, » overlaying of images is common even in cave or rock art. This rock at Ubir shows multiple images placed over one another to the point where the earlier ones are practically obscured. The ochres, chalks, and charcoals used in painting are ephemeral media that can be rubbed off, blown away by wind, and washed off with water. The surprising thing is how long they sometimes last.
Photo courtesy of the Northern Territory Tourism Authority.

the age of the painting is that the birds actually enjoyed a much longer life as a species, but there is little other evidence to support this.

One of the problems archaeologists face in trying to date ancient art is the fact that mineral pigments that were used in many of the paintings, like ochre, are not organic and therefore cannot be carbon dated. However, archaeologists have found that some of the paint contains traces of organic material, such as soot from a campfire, that *will* respond to carbon dating, so scientists are able to make at least a rough estimate of its age. Other ways of dating cave art can be deduced by examining the pictures themselves and what they represent, as we have seen in the case of the giant emus; artifacts might also be found at the site that are in keeping with the subject of the picture, such as animal bones.

European Cave Art

At the beginning of 2012, an important cave art discovery was made in the Cave of El Castillo in Spain. The cave paintings found included one small red dot and several hand stencils, which were effectively dated back to 42,000 years ago, making them the oldest recorded cave paintings in Europe, if not the world.

Just as the Australian representation of the giant emus seemed to have been made at the time Australia first became inhabited by humans, so the Spanish red dot is thought to have come about at the time Europe saw its first settlers. This important discovery has led to a heated discussion about whether the paintings were made by Neanderthal man. If Neanderthals were actually the artists of these drawings, then this suggests that they were the first human-like creature to paint on cave walls, hence their intellectual and cultural development was as advanced as that of their near contemporaries who we call our direct ancestors, Homo sapiens. Such an argument leads us to the further surmise that perhaps Homo sapiens and Neanderthals were not so different after all and may have even been two sub-sects of the same species rather than two completely different animals.

The ongoing debate over the existence of Neanderthal symbolic art and its relationship to Homo sapien cave paintings provides yet another illustration as to the importance of studying phenomena such as graffiti, whether it be thousands of years old or only two weeks old.

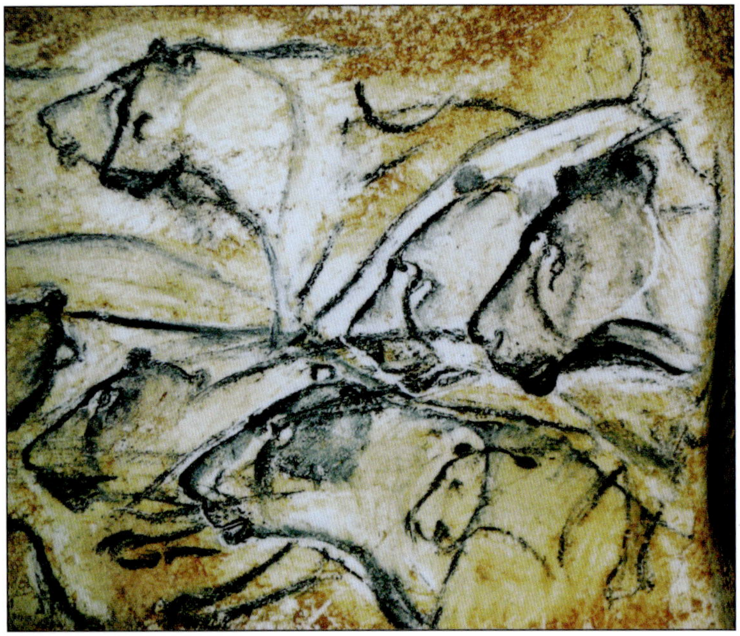

« Drawings of lions reproduced for the replica caves at Chauvet in France.

Chauvet Caves

From Spain, we move to France and the Chauvet Caves that had been thought, until the recent discovery of the El Castillo paintings, to house the oldest cave art in Europe. The art at Chauvet is thought to date back to around 35,000 years ago. The images at this site have been carbon dated using samples taken from the accumulated smoke on the roof and walls made from torches, as well as the remnants of charcoal and animal bones on the cave floor. The radiocarbon dating process has been very thorough and the results are felt to be reliable enough to classify the Chauvet paintings into two distinct periods and dates: the first being 35,000 years ago; the second 30,000 years ago. Interestingly, it has also been noted that many of the paintings have been retouched or repainted over the millennia. It is thought that a landslide blocked the entrance to the caves about 25,000 years ago and kept their treasures inside untouched until their discovery in 1994.

The paintings at Chavet, done in ochre, hematite, manganese oxide, and charcoal often over engravings in the rock, depict mostly large animals, such as bison, deer, and horses, which are the most numerous subjects. It is interesting to note that the animals painted here are not actually the same species hunted by the painters who rendered them, as evidenced by animal bones found in the caves. Additionally, human figures are rare in these paintings and, when they do appear, are highly stylized compared to the naturalistic drawings of the animals. One theory for this difference in style between animals and humans is that there may have been religious reasons for not realistically depicting humans.

Again, there is heated debate over these paintings: Why were they painted and by whom? One argument is that they are the work of shamans who painted while in a trance-like state; therefore, they may be the result of dreams or visions (perhaps in ways similar to those of the San people in the Kalahari Desert). Another theory suggests that the works are by a variety of people of different ages and even genders. Larger animals (one of which may have a bull or bison head giving it the appearance of a Minotaur) and Venus-like figures (voluptuous females named after the famous Venus of Willendorf figurine) were possibly the work of young adult males, while many of the hand stencils were conceivably made by women and children.

It is typical to find little emphasis on human figures in early European Cave art. In cases where humans are depicted, it's common to find body parts represented by themselves: heads, hands, and genitalia are the most common. Other exclusions in the artwork include small animals, such as rodents, insects and reptiles, and landscapes. Throughout cave paintings the world over, there are no depictions of plants, hills, water features, or everyday living quarters; these seem to have been the exclusive subject matter of geoglyphs.

One unusual feature of the paintings at Chauvet is the inclusion of animals such as hyenas, panthers, and lions alongside the more usual suspects: cattle, mammoths, horses, and bison. Some of the figures appear to be part of a larger picture, as they fight or interact with each other, making these paintings quite different to others dated from a similar age.

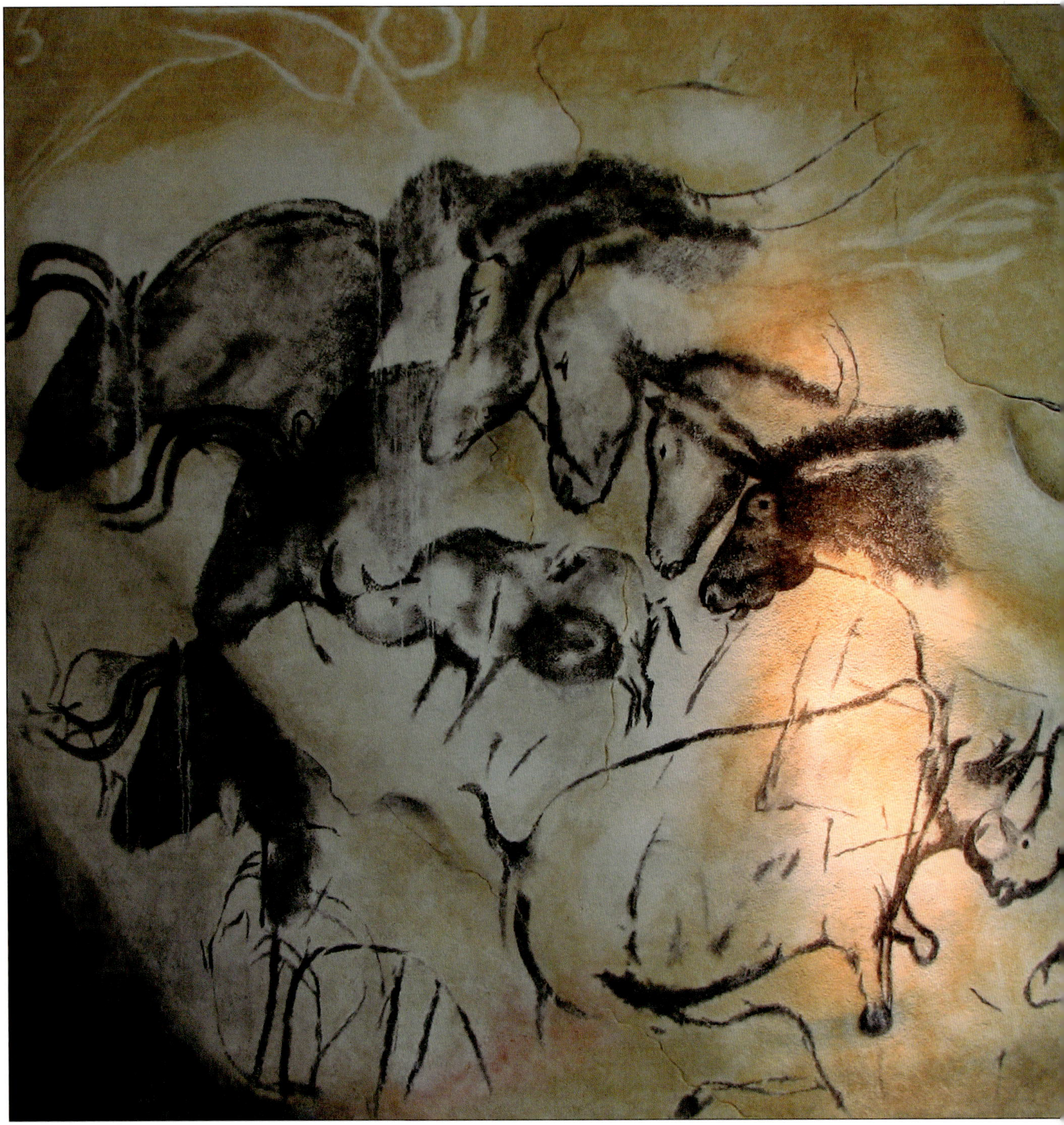

» Beautiful detailed renderings of bison, horses, and rhinoceroses, two of which are engaged in fighting, presented as faithful reproductions in the replica caves at Chauvet, France. There is nothing primitive about these drawings—the proportion and animation are excellent and would not look out of place in any modern art gallery.

A close-up of a reproduction » drawing of horse heads at Chauvet, France.

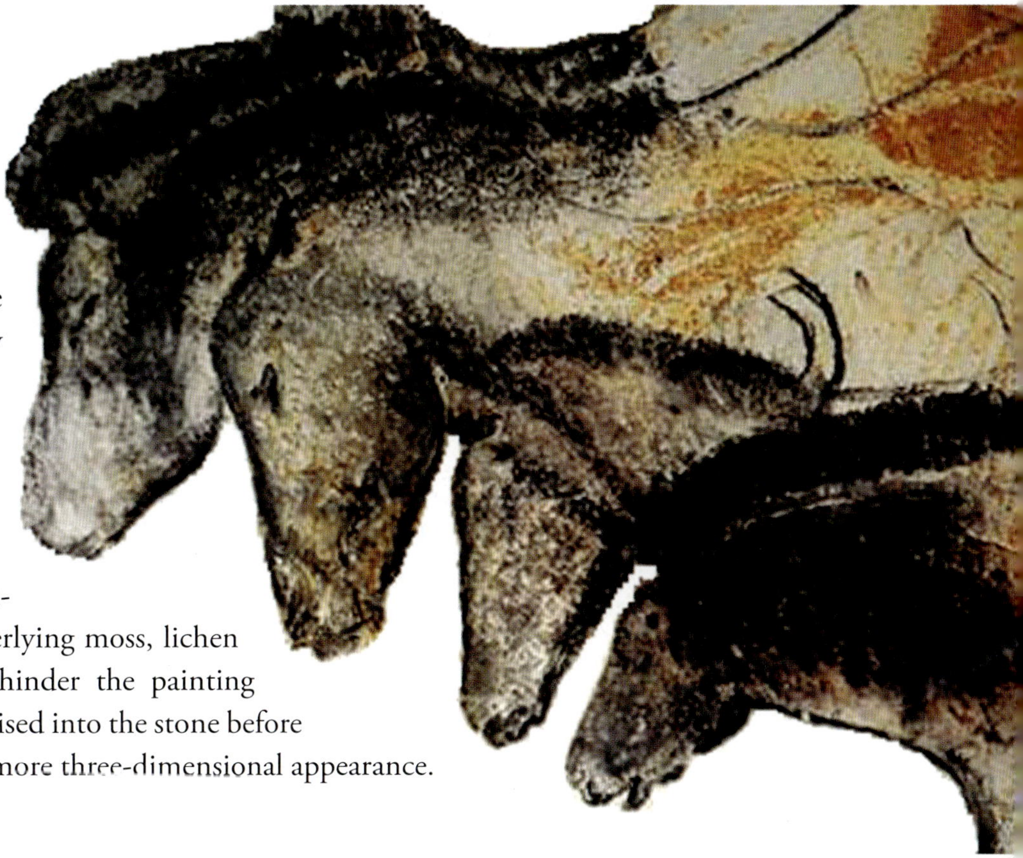

In other areas of the cave there are hand stencils, possibly done by the women and children of the tribe. There are also a series of dots and lines. Two drawings look a bit like butterflies, but they have not been positively identified as such.

Archaeologists have been able to uncover another fascinating aspect to the Chavet cave paintings and that is the preparation that was made to the walls prior to the paint being applied. It seems as though the walls were actually scraped down, clearing them of any underlying moss, lichen growth, or any rough patches that would hinder the painting process. And some of the images have been incised into the stone before or after the painting was done, giving them a more three-dimensional appearance.

Altamira

Altamira in Spain is another famous site of European cave paintings. The Bison from this Upper Paleolithic site is one of the best-known examples of ancient art we have today. The cave's discovery in 1880 makes it the first prehistoric cave to have been found that housed paintings. The cave system was closed by a rock fall 13,000 years ago and was only discovered after a tree fell in a storm, reopening a part of its entrance in the late nineteenth century. When it was first discovered, many scholars doubted the authenticity of these works, holding the then popular belief that prehistoric man

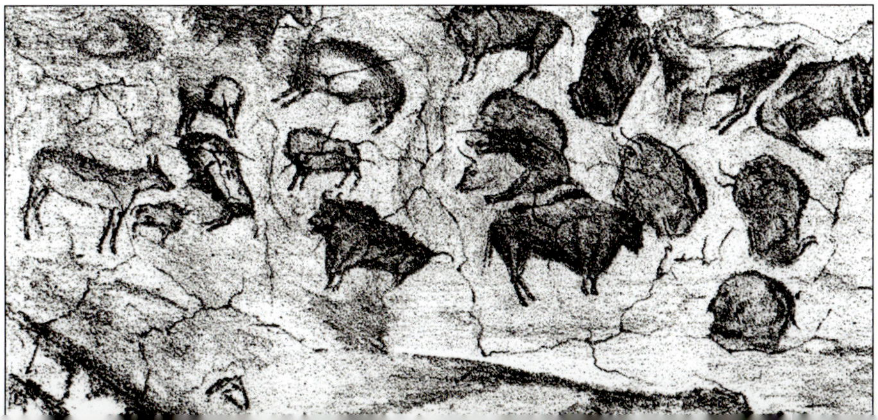

« This is a nineteenth-century picture documenting the drawings as they appeared in the cave at Altamira, Spain. Note how the cracks and other surface formations of the cave have been rendered to show the whole representation of the cave paintings in situ.

could not have made such intricate and beautiful images. But by 1902, this thinking had changed and it was generally accepted that the paintings were indeed made by ancient man.

When discovered, the cave contained many artifacts strewn across the floor. These have been dated from as early as 18,500 to 14,000 years ago. And not only were the Altamira paintings the first to have been discovered in modern times, but the skill and detail of the renderings is of a very high (and rare) artistic quality. Ochre, charcoal, and haematite were used to paint images of animals, handprints, and abstract shapes, and the paint has been thinned out in sections. This has been spread as a wash over the cave wall and it appears that lightening and shading was also attempted, which is quite unique to the drawings in this cave.

The painting of the bison, as mentioned before, is one of the most famous cave paintings in the world, and it has influenced several modern artists, much like modern graffiti influences contemporary artists today. The bison has been used on Bisonte cigarette packets as well as in the logo for the tourism department of the Catabrian government. In 1965, a Spanish cartoon of a prehistoric people was invented and was called Altamiro de la Cueva. It is even said that the great Spanish painter Pablo Picasso once noted that after the Altamira Bison painting, everything else is decadence.

TAG THIS!

The archeologist who discovered the Altamira paintings, Marcelin Sanz de Sautola, and his twelve-year-old daughter were accused of forgery by some of Sanz de Sautola's colleagues and fellow scholars, one of whom claimed that they knew the identity of the artist. Unfortunately, Sautola died less than ten years after his discovery and fourteen years before similar cave findings helped prove his hypothesis correct and before his critics published an article admitting their mistake.

Lascaux Caves

The Lascaux Caves in the South of France are home to some of the most well-known cave paintings in the world. The paintings were discovered by a group of teenage boys and their dog in 1940, and by 1948, the system of caves was opened to the public, receiving a staggering 1,200 visitors per day ten years later. Unfortunately, the constant tramping in and out of people through the caves, breathing and producing carbon dioxide, began to take its toll on the paintings. To stop further deterioration of the artwork, the caves were closed to the public in 1963. The paintings were then restored and are now kept under close observation for signs of further deterioration.

The cave system contains a number of galleries filled with ancient art: the Passageway, the Shaft, the Apse, and the Chamber of Felines. The paintings themselves number almost 2,000 and have been organized into three basic types: animals, humans, and abstract designs. The images are mostly painted on the surface of the cave wall using mineral pigments, such as ochre, but some have also been incised.

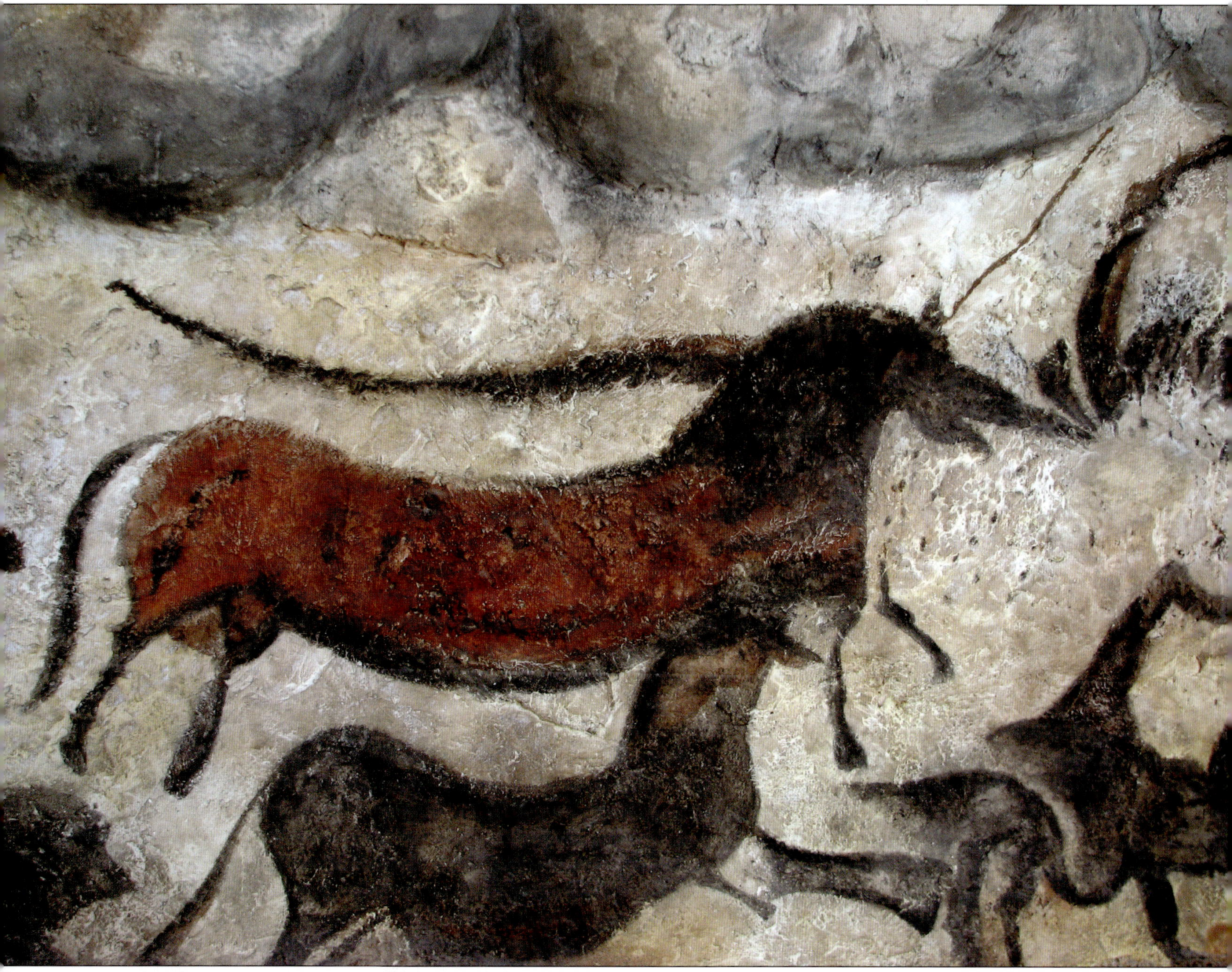

Horses in motion, seen in reproduction at the replica caves of Lascaux, France.

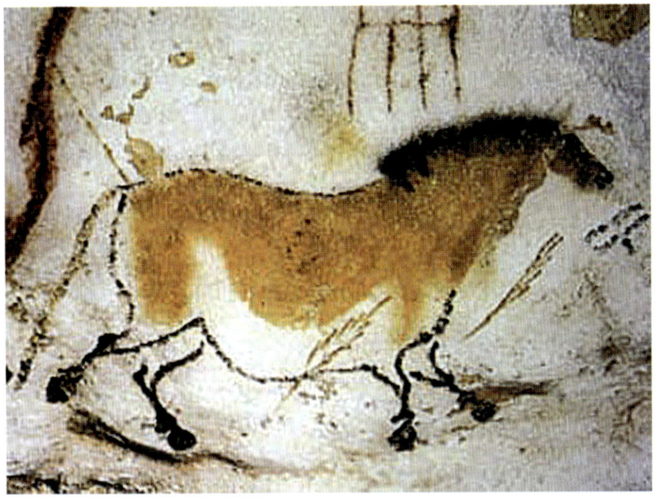

A magnificent horse showing a lighter underside and lovely detail in the drawing of the hooves. The large belly possibly indicates a pregnant mare.

Of the animal paintings, of which there are approximately 900, two-thirds of them belong to identifiable species. More than 350 of the animals are definitely horses; the other animals comprise ninety deer, cattle, bison, felines, and one each of a bird, a bear, and a rhinoceros. In the Hall of the Bulls, as would be expected, there are paintings of four large impressive bulls. One of these images is about seventeen feet long and it the largest painting of an animal ever found in cave art. Besides bulls, this hall also features horses and stags. It is interesting that there are no representations of reindeer in the cave system; these animals were one of the main sources of meat for the people who painted in the caves, as evidenced by bones found in and around the site.

One of the most noticeable features of the paintings at Lascaux is the skill of the artists in representing these various animals. Bison are painted in such a way as to render a certain element of perspective, while other animals have been painted running and leaping. The animation of the works is beautiful by any art standard. However, putting the aesthetic value aside, these paintings also begin to reveal all sorts of secrets to researchers about ancient man. One such finding, still very much in the theoretical stage, posits that many of the abstract paintings, comprised largely of dots and human-type figures containing dots, may very well be representations of constellations, specifically Taurus and the Pleiades as well as the Summer Triangle. Another scientist has built upon this idea and claims that not only do the images represent these constellations, but they are also part of a whole map of the night sky. Another significant discovery was the Apse, a chamber about five yards across and spherical in shape. The whole surface, including the ceiling, which is almost nine feet high, is covered in incised drawings. It is thought that the painters would have had to use some kind of scaffold to draw so high up.

After the caves were closed to the general public, archeologists and scientists were still able to access them for research purposes. Unfortunately, a fungus—believed to have been present in the soil of the cave—

TAG THIS!

Sometimes good intentions prove worse than the problem they attempt to solve. A seventy-member youth group was invited to the Mayrieres Cave in France to help get rid of modern-day graffiti that was scrawled over some of the walls. Unfortunately, in their ignorance, they accidently destroyed some of the cave's ancient paintings of bison that had been estimated to be 15,000 years old.

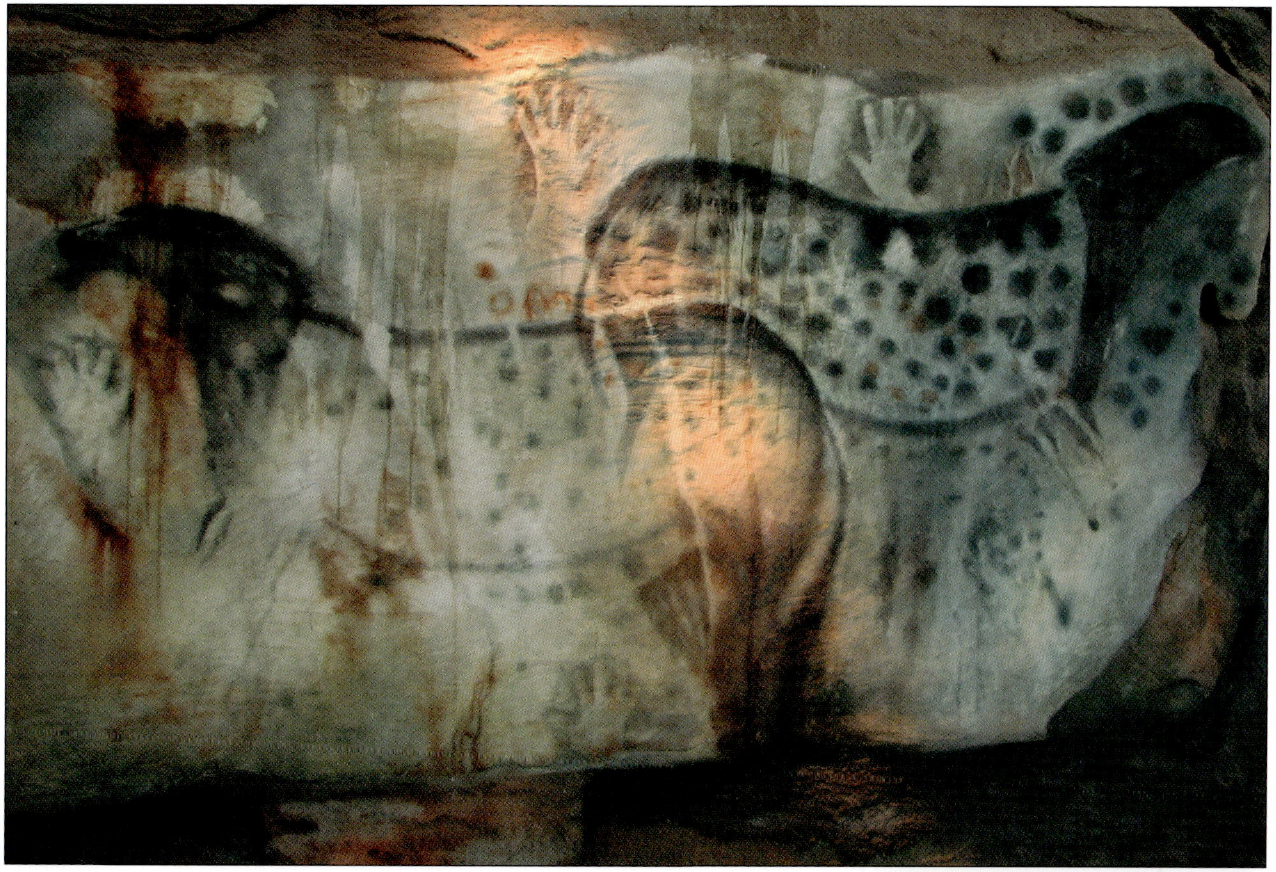

At another site, » the Pech Merle Caves in Midi-Pyrenees in France, there are wonderful spotted horses accompanied by hand stencils. It looks as though some of the spots may have been spray painted on due to the softer edges around the spots.

established itself inside after the installation of a new air conditioning system in 2001. While this infestation was treated efficiently with quicklime, a subsequent fungus appeared and spread rapidly in 2007 and 2008, leading the cave to be completely closed to all but one person a week who enters to monitor the problem. The fungus has not been entirely eradicated and some attempts at removing it have left dark stains on the walls. This situation has led to detailed discussions about the the delicate nature of caves and ancient art and who may enter them and for how long.

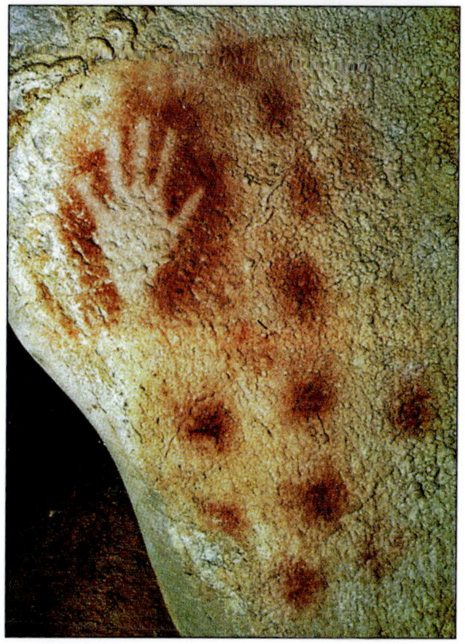

A close-up of a hand stencil and sprayed » spots at Pech Merle, France. These caves are one of the few archeological cave sites still open to the public.

Britain's Cave Art

Europe has a number of spectacular caves full of paintings rendered tens of thousands of years ago. Britain, on the other hand, is not known for its prehistoric art. The one exception is Creswell Crags, a limestone gorge dotted with caves situated halfway between Derbyshire and Nottinghamshire in England. Evidence has been found within the gorge that the caves were once used by ice age people at various times between 43,000 and 10,000 years ago. The caves were also used during recorded history: during the Neolithic Age, the Bronze Age, the Roman Occupation, and even as late as the Middle Ages.

The caves, discovered in 2003, hold incised drawings similar to those that constitute not only the most northern cave art in Europe, but also the only known specimens of cave art in all of Britain. Incised into the cave's walls are pictures of birds and animals, including bison and reindeer, although the birds are thought by some to actually be female anthropomorphic figures. In dating the art, the uranium-series disequilibrium method was used (where uranium in water seeping into the caves flows over the artwork trapping the uranium beneath the surface then turning into thorium). By using this method, a minimum age of 12,800 years has been established for the cave paintings.

India

Bhimbetka

In the Indian state of Madhya Pradesh, there is a place called Bhimbetka, where distinctive rock ledges form natural shelters. It is here that archaeologists have found evidence pointing to it being one of the first inhabited areas of what is now classified as India. Although the shelters were home to human beings for at least 100,000 years, it seems that the earliest rock paintings only date to about 30,000 years ago. From the Mesolithic period until the Middle Ages, the people who lived in the

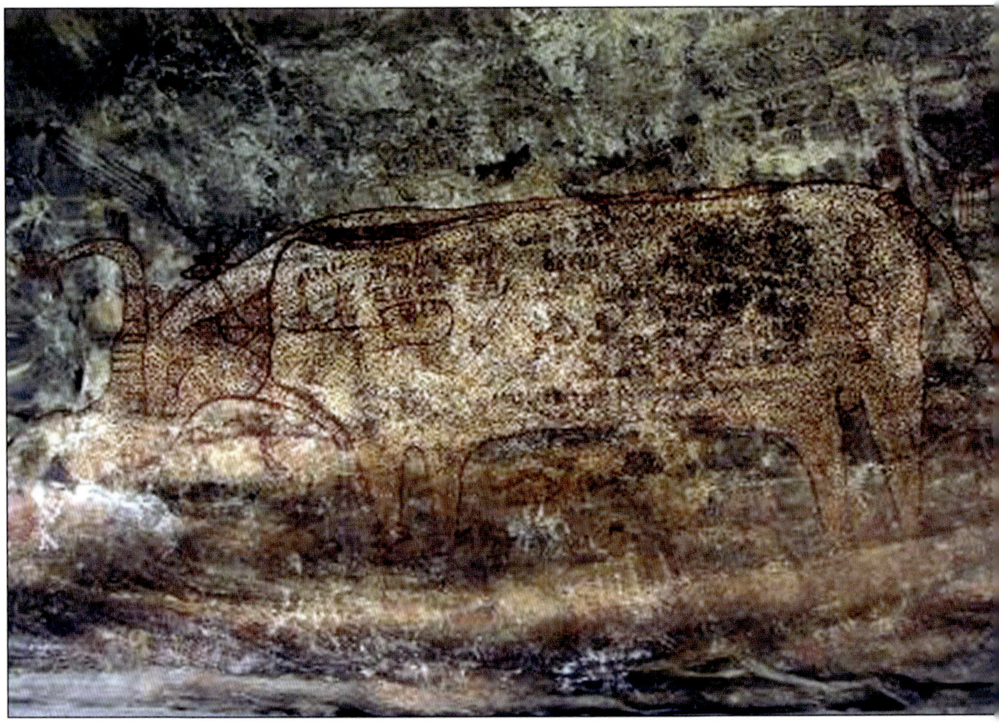

A horned animal, possibly » a buffalo, painted in red at Bhimbetka, India.

area recorded scenes from their everyday life—from childbirth to funeral rites, dancing, horse and elephant riding, gathering honey, and an abundance of animals.

As with modern graffiti, many of the paintings at Bhimbetka have been made over previous paintings. Seven distinct periods of painting have been identified. The first period shows the earliest paintings and is thought to be from the Upper Paleolithic era. The works are generally rendered in a dark red and green and are line drawings of large animals, including tigers, bison, and rhinoceros.

The next period of paintings are from the Mesolithic era, are quite different in style, and have the added content of human figures interacting with each other in activities such as hunting, dancing, and drinking. The pictures are fairly stylized and go into detail illustrating the types of weapons used and even human body decorations. The Chalcolithic period, which comes next, depicts further social development of the inhabitants of the caves, showing them trading with people from other areas.

The next two periods are grouped together and form the early historic period, which is so called because it sees the beginning of identifiable writing. The paintings from these eras are distinctively rendered in red, white, and yellow and contain detailed and decorative elements. It is from this period that animal riders appear, both those riding elephants and horses. Another interesting development is the representation of deities.

The sixth and seventh periods are from medieval times and artistically they show a decline in skill. Perhaps this was because there were other media to use for fine work: papyrus, silk, paper and ink, pens, and fine-haired brushes. Those who still painted on the rock walls may well have been from lower socio-economic classes and therefore self-taught artists. The paint used by these last artists was generally made from manganese, hematite (which is a soft, red stone), and charcoal. These ingredients were mixed with animal fat to make them stick to the rock surface. Throughout the ages, various pigments and media, such as the animal fat mentioned above, were used to help the artist paint. There have been traces of plant material found in the paint suggesting the use of vegetable dyes. Tools for applying the paint were made from plant fibers, maybe in the form of twigs with their ends chewed or pounded to form a paintbrush.

Bhimbetka, with its multi-layers of paint from thousands of years of use, is an excellent example of why the study of graffiti (ancient and modern) is important. If previous layers of art had been removed or totally obliterated, then it would not have been possible to see the development of an entire culture. Not that this should be an excuse for the preservation of every tag, throw-up, or stencil art, but it does show why we should be careful before we remove images and text without documentation from our current cities.

North and South America

Indian Painted Rocks

There are many significant rock art sites in the United State that were made by its indigenous peoples. Indian Painted Rocks, near Yakima, Washington, is one such site and features paintings that are now believed to be at least 1,000 years

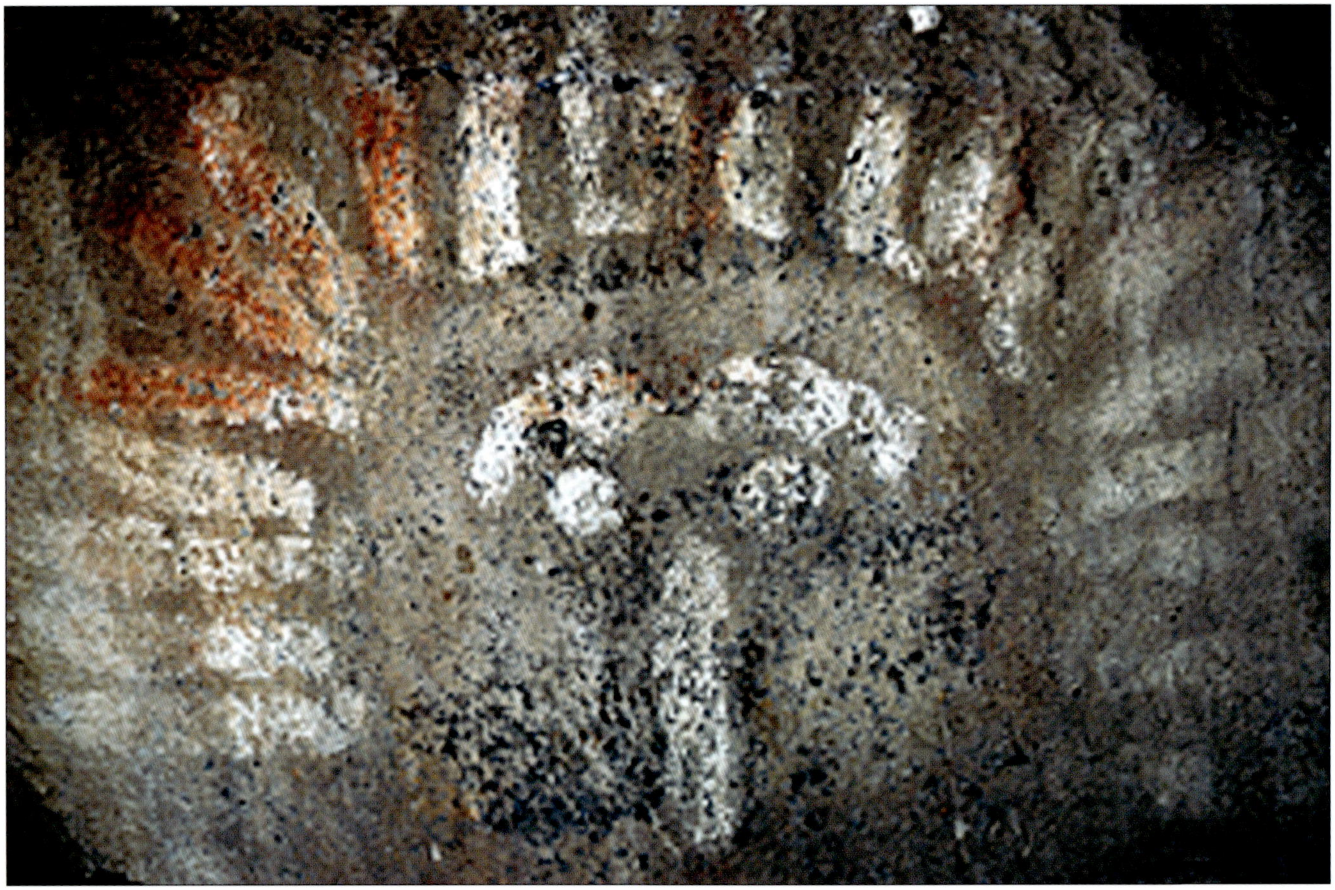

≈ A close-up of the highly stylized face painted on a rock at Yakima, Washington, in the United States.

old. The paintings are done in red, white, and black using organic pigments. At the time of their painting, the cliff had a large lake at its foot, which meant that the only way to access the rock face was by canoe and it was from their boats that the people must have made their marks.

The paintings at Indian Painted Rocks are not currently understood by Native Americans who have lived in the area in fairly modern times, so the pictures' origins can only be guessed at. They appear to show hunting scenes and perhaps meetings with other tribes; however, the pictures are quite stylized. The faces as pictured here are simplified and all have

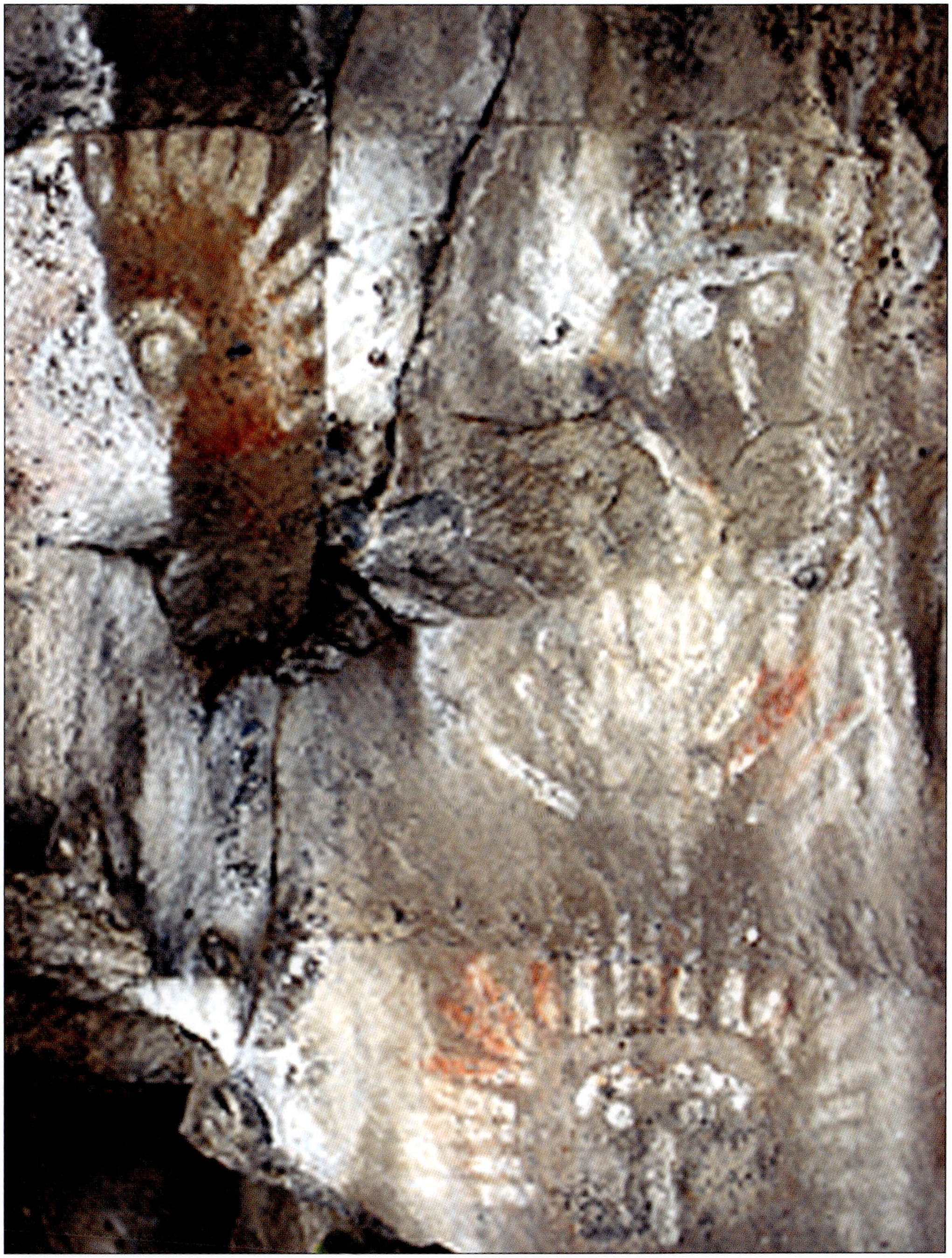

« Here is the face seen in position, lower right-hand corner, surrounded by similar faces.

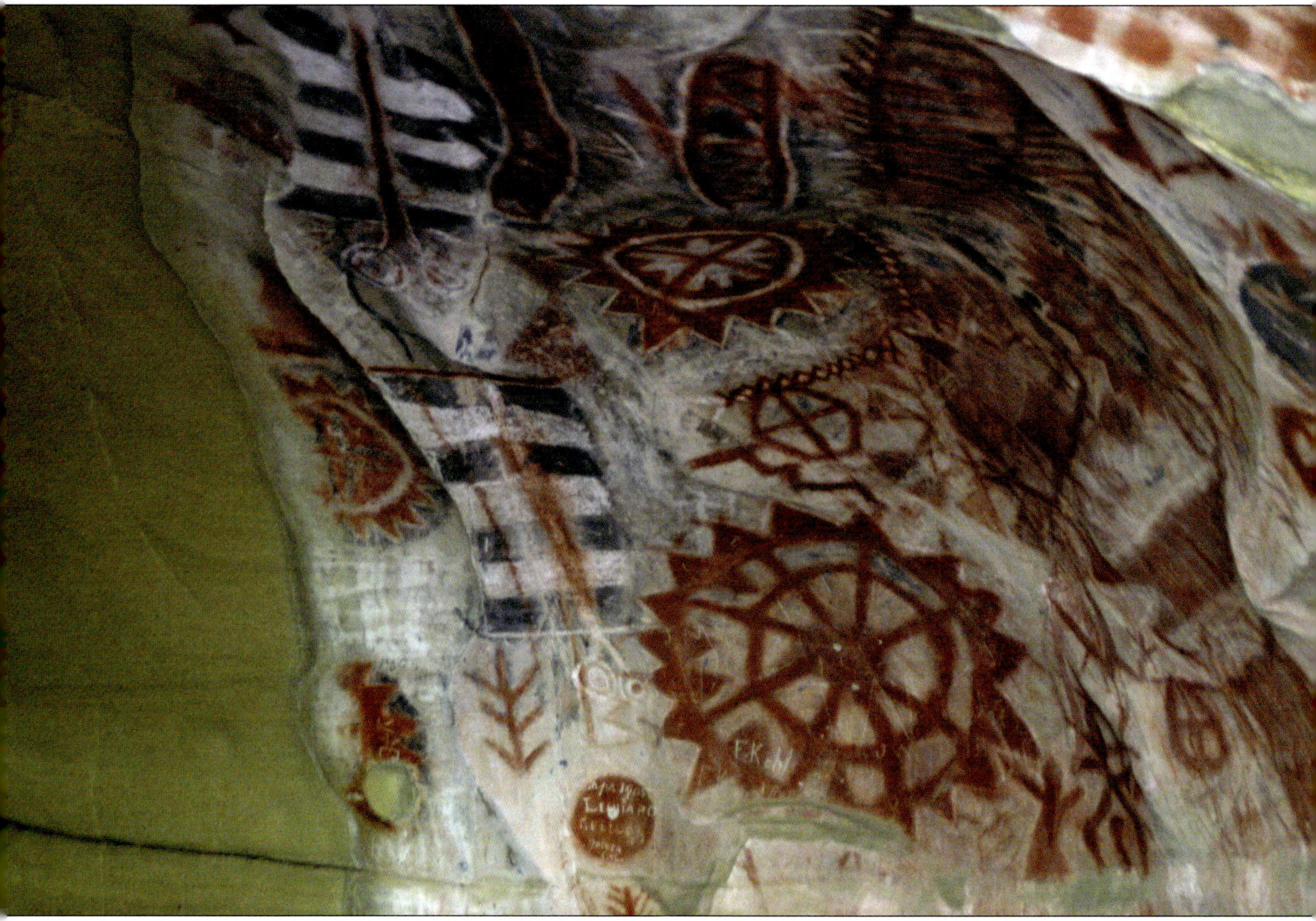

≈ This piece of cave art is quite different to anything we have seen so far. The background has been covered to form a sophisticated whole with the pattern of decorative red and blue circles and other abstract elements. From a distance, it looks like a piece of fabric rippling in the wind. If you look closely, there appears to be writing of some kind in the small red circle towards the bottom.

radiating elements coming from the tops of their heads as though signifying headdresses. The rather startling effect of the faces suggests they were not meant to represent human figures, but rather supernatural deities.

Chumash Art

The Chumash people of Southern California were prolific painters and rock engravers. Their work can be seen throughout their region of the state. The Chumash also continued to paint their traditional works up into the nineteenth century. Living in the areas that now constitute Santa Barbara, Ventura, and San Luis, the Chumash were hunter-gatherers who relied heavily on produce and animals from the sea. Their rock art is as enigmatic as any other early pictographs, although they seem to have connections to astronomy as well as having some sort of spiritual significance.

It is thought that many of these paintings were made by shamans, called *alchuklash* by the Chumash, who were typically in a trance-like state. Trances were induced by the use of hallucinogenic drugs, either a native tobacco or jimsonweed. As we have seen with the San people of the Kalahari, the Chumash believed that in such a state the shaman was able to enter the spirit world and enlist the help of spirits who were often seen in animal form, particularly grizzly bears and rattlesnakes. Likewise, the magic doorways to the spirit world were often situated in caves.

Stone and water were also important sources of power and the caves were chosen that were close to these whenever possible. Sites of Chumash art can be found in the Ventureño area as well as in the Cuyama Valley and at the Painted Cave State Historic Park in Santa Barbara. Painted Rock itself is an odd horseshoe-shaped free-standing rock. Its inner surface is covered in paintings not only by the native Chumash tribes, but also by other tribes (and includes later graffiti made by non-indigenous people).

The pigment used by the Chumash was mostly mineral based, to which was added an organic mixer or binder. This may have been animal blood or fat or even seeds, possibly linseed oil from the flax plant. The colors include yellows, reds, white, and black, as well as blue, green, and orange. Some works are monochrome, but others were multicolored. Images are of animals and human figures, geometric patterns, and identifiable astral bodies. Apparently where tribes lived in villages there was a proliferation of abstract and geometric designs, while the hunter-gatherers tended to make pictures showing recognizable animals and people. Fingers were the common tools for applying paint, but brushes were used, as well.

Burro Flats Painted Cave

There are two human figures of particular interest on this site, which is situated on private land containing Chumash art. They are only simple stick figures, but they are wearing elaborate headdresses. Four-fingered stick figure animals, a circle with a star shape inside, and an ear of corn are also part of the group and have led researchers to speculate on the meaning of the paintings. Theories include the following: they are images that have come to unmarried girls in their dreams;

they depict a celebration of the winter solstice; or they are the result of collaboration between the Chumash and another tribe, the Gabrielino, five or six hundred years ago as a sign of their ongoing friendship. The paintings are estimated to have been made between 500 AD and when the first white people settled in the area.

WHEN WRITING BEGAN

From cave etchings and paintings, we move to actual writing. When did the change from pure image to an abstract squiggle that corresponded to a spoken sound exactly take place? It was a very gradual and complex process, but it also appears to have been a wide-spread phenomenon.

One of the earliest forms of writing found in caves is the pictogram, or pictograph. As the name suggests it is a picture that is used to carry the meaning of the article it represents: a picture of a mountain means a mountain, for example. Pictograms differ from pictures of an object in that they are often stylized or drawn in a stereotypical way so that they represent the idea of a mountain rather than a particular mountain; thus, there is no individualizing detail. We still use pictograms today: public toilets will feature a stylized but recognizable picture of a male or female, wildlife signs will show a picture of the animals whose habitat you are entering, disabled facilities will have a simplified picture of a wheelchair, to name a few. The reason behind using pictorial signs like these rather than word-based signs is to make them universally understandable.

Of course, over time, humans felt the need to write more elaborate messages and in a much quicker manner. Many of the pictograms seen in cave art became so stylized that they were no longer recognizable to the common person. Ideograms appeared in which abstract ideas were conveyed via drawings. These were harder to give a universal image to and from these pictograms symbols written language began to evolve. The problem with using symbols for whole words and ideas was that you had to learn an awful lot of them, thus limiting the art of reading and writing to a select few characters. When alphabetic writing came on the scene, it meant that only a set amount of letters needed to be learned and from this number all words, phrases, and ideas could be formed.

An important discovery was made by archeologists in 1998 who had been examining graffiti made by Semitic soldiers on a cliff wall in Egypt. The writing has been dated to about 2000 BC. The implications of the find are that alphabetic writing may have arisen at least 200 years earlier than previously thought. The graffiti found consists of what is thought to be a man's name and a reference to God.

TAG THIS!

The Safaitic language, a precursor of Arabic dating from the first century BC to the fourth century AD, is only known through the remnants of graffiti found incised into rocks in the desert of Southern Syria, Eastern Jordan, and Northern Saudi Arabia.

Evidence such as this leads researchers to believe that Egypt may have been the birthplace of the alphabet rather than Syria, Lebanon, or Israel, which hold samples of text that had been previously thought to be the oldest examples of alphabetic writing. This idea is supported by the link between the graffiti and Egyptian hieroglyphics.

When we think about the impact that these studies of ancient forms of graffiti have made on our current understanding of ancient cultures and peoples, it is interesting to imagine what our distant descendants will think about our late-twentieth-century and early twenty-first-century graffiti 40,000 years from now.

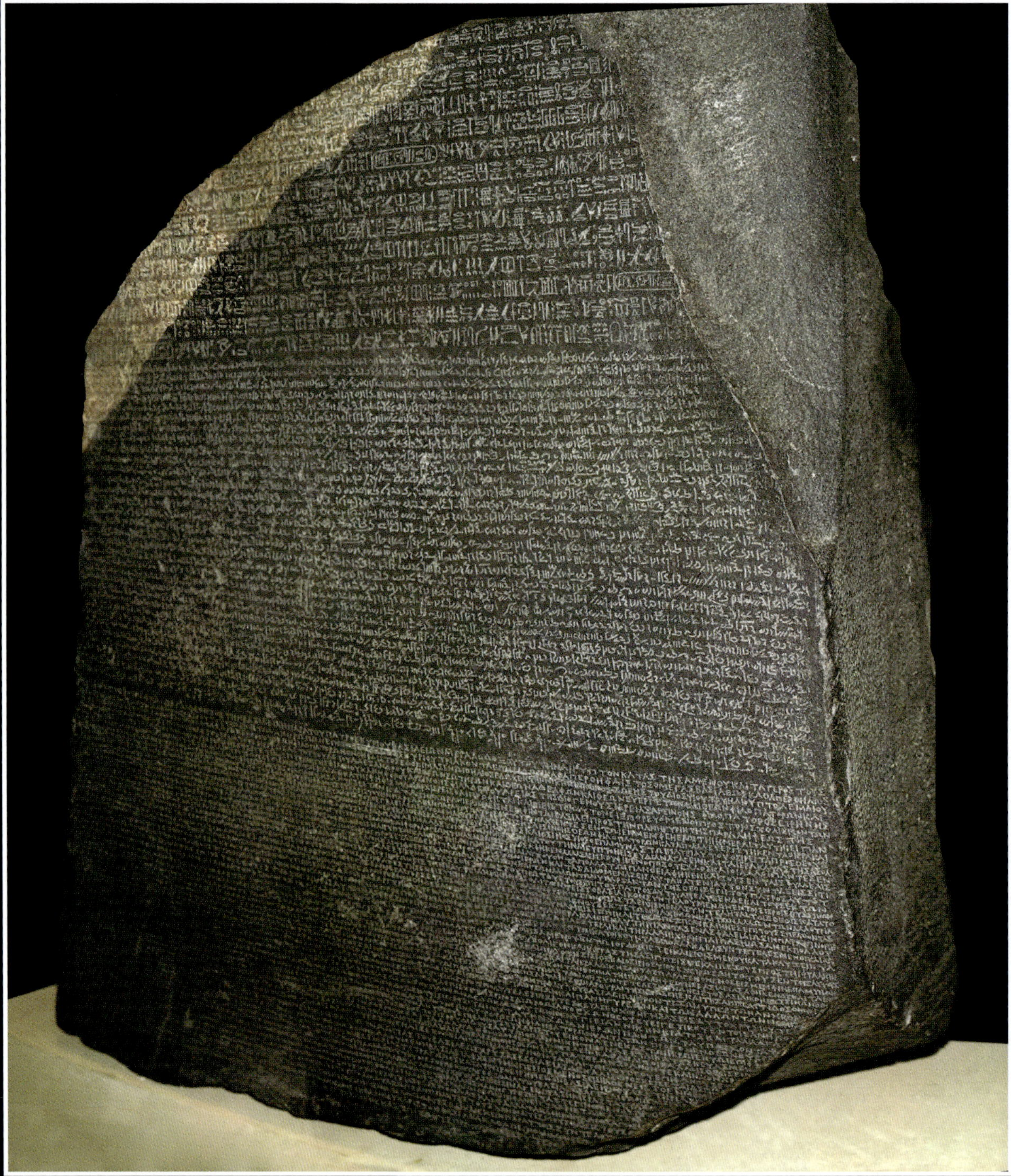

»
The Rosetta Stone.
Photo courtesy of
Hans Hillewaert.

CHAPTER TWO

GRAFFITI IN ANCIENT CIVILIZATIONS

ANCIENT EGYPT

We owe much of our knowledge about life in ancient Egypt to the inscribed texts left behind. Papyrus did become a popular vehicle for making documents but, for centuries before its discovery, scribes chipped away at the walls of temples and tombs, leaving information about everything from prayers for the dead pharaoh to personal messages and insignia.

It has taken decades to decipher the hieroglyphics used by the ancient Egyptians, but they have slowly formed into intelligible words. Other bits of writing have also turned up that have helped in the process of understanding this ancient written language; *ostraca*, for instance, are bits of discarded pottery or stone on which inscriptions were made. These were rather like notebooks, kept for jotting things down that were only for temporary use. The writing on these shards is a variation of hieroglyphics called *hieratic* and it looks a bit like cursive writing and was often written in ink.

The Rosetta Stone has been fundamental to the process of deciphering ancient Egyptian hieroglyphics. The stone was discovered by a French soldier, Pierre-François Bouchard, in 1799 when the inscribed fragment was set to be used as building material for Fort Julien. When British troops defeated the French in 1801, the Rosetta Stone passed into their hands and it was taken to London and deposited in the British Museum.

Upon its discovery, it became apparent that the stone contained texts in three separate languages: Greek, Demotic, and Hieroglyphic. In 1803, the Greek had been deciphered, but it took another twenty years for the hieroglyphs to be translated and understood, and even once the basics of the Rosetta Stone were worked out, it was still years before other separate Ancient Egyptian texts could be accurately deciphered.

The Book of the Dead

While the *Book of the Dead* has not typically been viewed as a type of graffiti, and especially not the graffiti as we know it today, this is nonetheless an example of a long-standing tradition of writing on tomb walls and monuments and is linked to the whole development of writing in Egypt. *The Book of the Dead* was not a single object; it was not even a book, but rather a number of texts, including spells, written onto the walls of the tomb of the dead pharaoh (and later the queen) so they could have help crossing over into the land of the dead to be reunited with the divine father, the god Ra. The tradition dates back to the Old Kingdom, about 2400 BC; the earliest known text was found in the burial chamber within the Pyramid of King Unas, who was part of the fifth dynasty. Medieval Europeans knew of the existence of such books, but at the time equated them with the Christian bible.

The texts showed unfinished hieroglyphics thought to represent incomplete humans and animals, because in that state they didn't pose a threat to the dead king. By the time the Middle Kingdom emerged, the tradition had changed so that any high-born or high-ranking person could have these special texts placed in the tomb with them. They were not written on the inner walls of the pyramids, but on the insides of the burial casket. The tradition continued and evolved further as the Middle Kingdom period came to an end. Funeral texts became increasingly more available to anyone who could afford them, and they soon began to be written on linen shrouds (although they were still sometimes found on the inner surfaces of coffins and even on tomb walls).

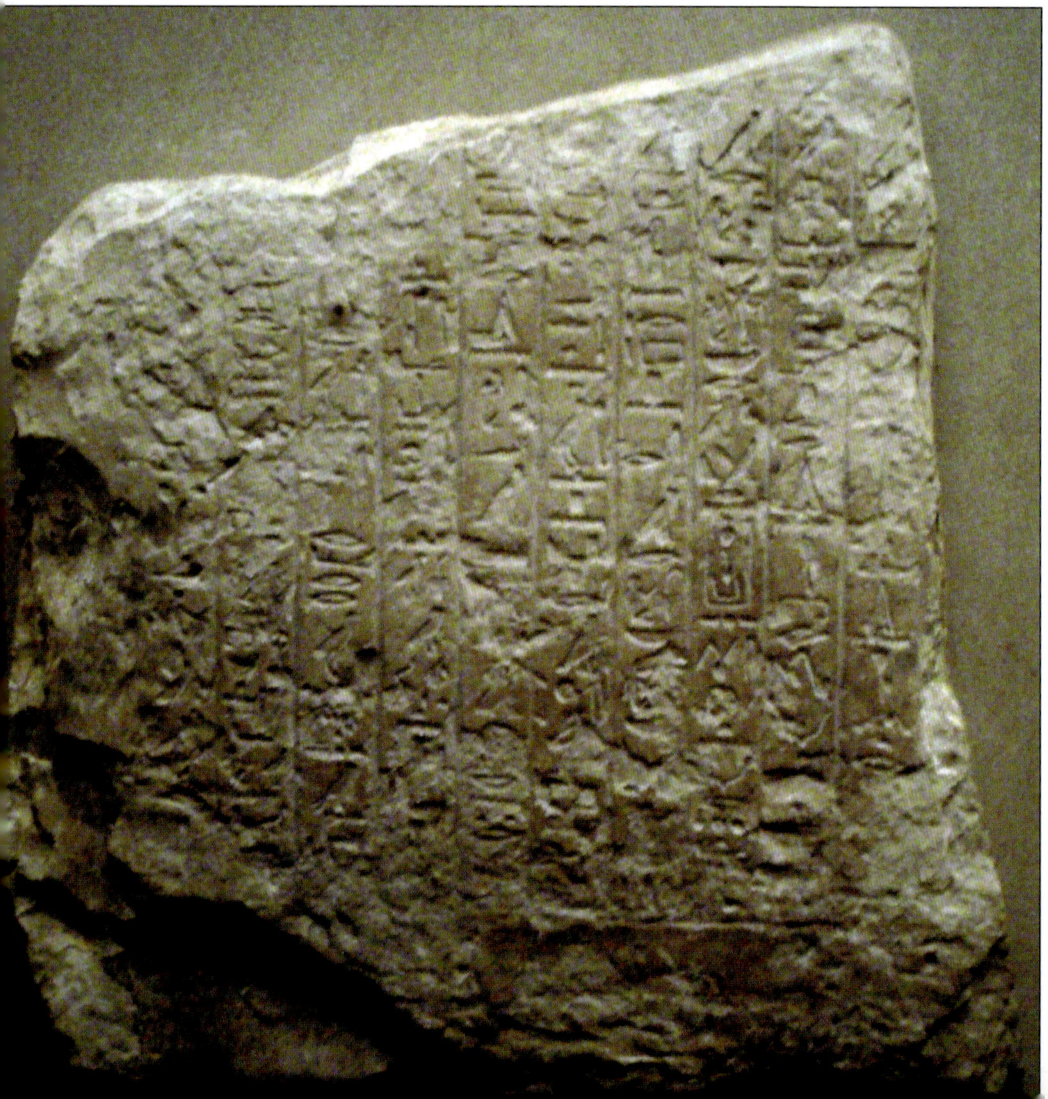

For the ancient Egyptians, both the written and spoken word were believed to hold supernatural powers. Hieroglyphs were considered a divine invention; therefore, to make them was to tap into that divine power. The idea that funerary texts like *The Book of the Dead* was a magical tool to help the deceased cross into the afterlife and join the gods is not dissimilar to the images that cavemen and the San people of the Kalahari painted.

« A decree made by Pharaoh Pepi II of Egypt (circa 2246–2152 BC), granting immunity to the Temple of Min from official exactions, is now housed in the Metropolitan Museum of Art in New York City. *Photo courtesy of Keith Shengili Roberts.*

In Ancient Egypt, there was a tradition of writing graffiti on monuments, in doorways, and on walls of sacred places such as pyramids and temples. It was not a case of people leaving a mark purely for fun; rather, scholars believe it was a sign of respect to the gods by pilgrims who were often scribes.

Evidence, in the form of an ostracon from the tomb of Senenmut, shows that graffiti was a practice that had its rules and regulations and was part of the work of a scribe. Writing graffiti on sacred walls was quite a competitive venture. A scribe would write his graffiti in clusters to keep it distinguishable from that of other scribes. Prayers would make up a large bulk of the graffiti about which the individual scribe would also make commentary.

TAG THIS!

Mesoamerica is the name for the early-inhabited American continent. Many technological developments were made in the distant continent from the western part of the world in a similar way and around the same time. Writing was one of them. A stone slab was found in Veracruz, Mexico, that contained writing thought to be 3,000 years old.

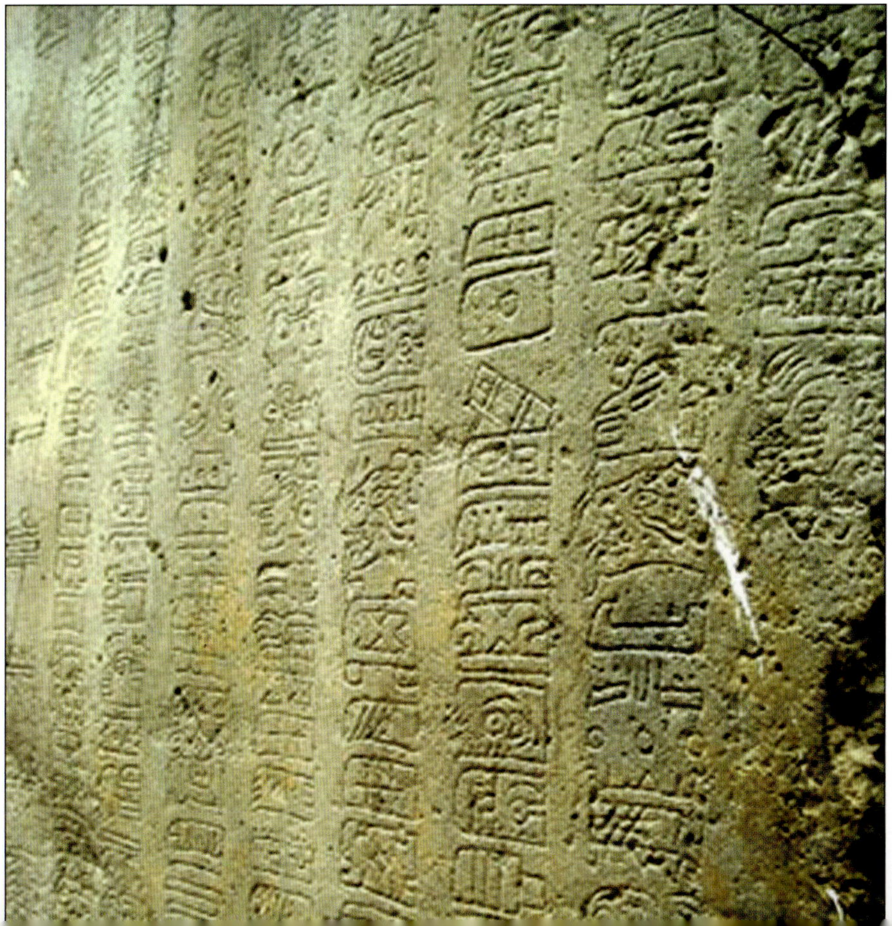

« Lamojarra script from Mesoamerica. Mesoamerica developed writing independently of any other writing system and was one of the five places to do so.

TAG THIS!

In thirteenth-century Italy, it was forbidden to make legal or official documents on paper (a relatively new invention) because it was not seen as sturdy enough; vellum or parchment had to be used in most cases.

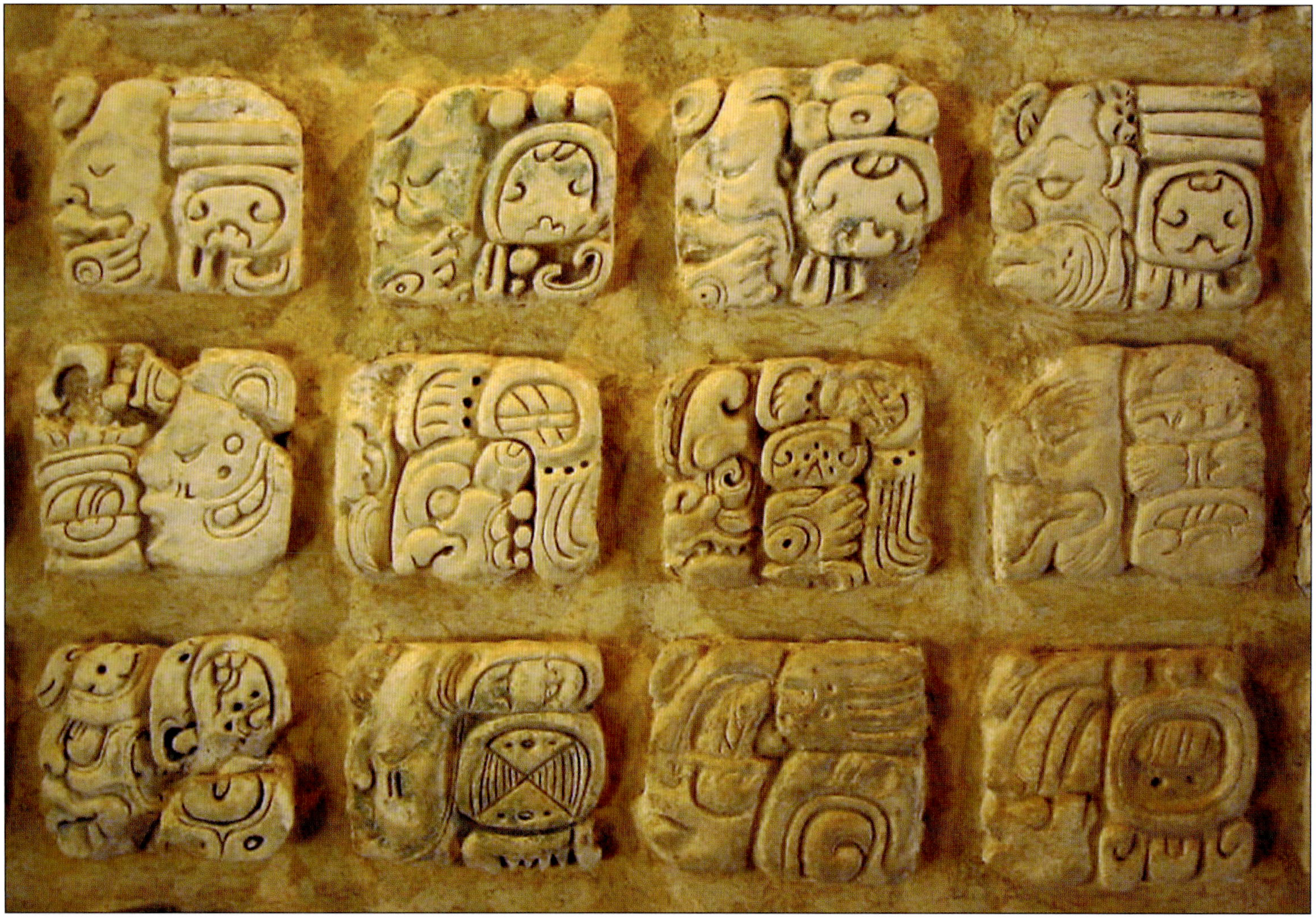

Mayan Script using Palenque glyphs. Palenque was one of the early sites where Mayan writing has been found and the area produced some of the most elaborate forms. The earliest Mayan scripts date back to between 300 and 200 BC and are the earliest of all Mesoamerican writing systems.

Most of humans' oldest writing was done incised onto stone, though sometimes it was also etched into metal. These were enduring materials and were therefore seen as being of such permanence that they suited the making of important documents.

The importance of including a history of writing on tomb walls, whether solicited or not, is to show that there has been a history throughout mankind of making marks on rock or wall since language began—and this persists to this day in what we call graffiti. There is a definite link between recording life, religion, and rituals on walls, as pictures or abstract symbols, and the advent of writing. Modern day graffiti, with its urgent messages of territorial boundaries, warnings for others, and the desire for fame and recognition, albeit ever so brief, is easily linked to our ancient ancestors' practices of spraying paint over their hands (a kind of tag) or making drawings of the type of giant beasts they would have liked to hunt, perhaps to show off their manhood among other things.

ANCIENT GREECE

The ancient Greeks were great practitioners of graffiti. They used it for a variety of things including toilet humor, sexual messages, and even insults. The earliest forms of Greek graffiti to have been found come from about 800 BC and the later ones were made in the early Christian era. Greeks wrote graffiti on their own city walls, such as "Sydromachos has a

This broken tablet shows some of the earliest Greek writing, dating to 1450 BC. It shows what is known as Linear B script, as well as examples of an even earlier form of Greek, the Minoan Linear A script, which has been adapted to fit with the more modern text form. The subject matter of the tablet is nothing more than a documentation of animal hides sold to saddlers and shoemakers. The tablets were baked and therefore preserved when the Mycenaean Palace of Pylos caught fire around 1200 BC.
Photo courtesy of Sharon Mollerus.

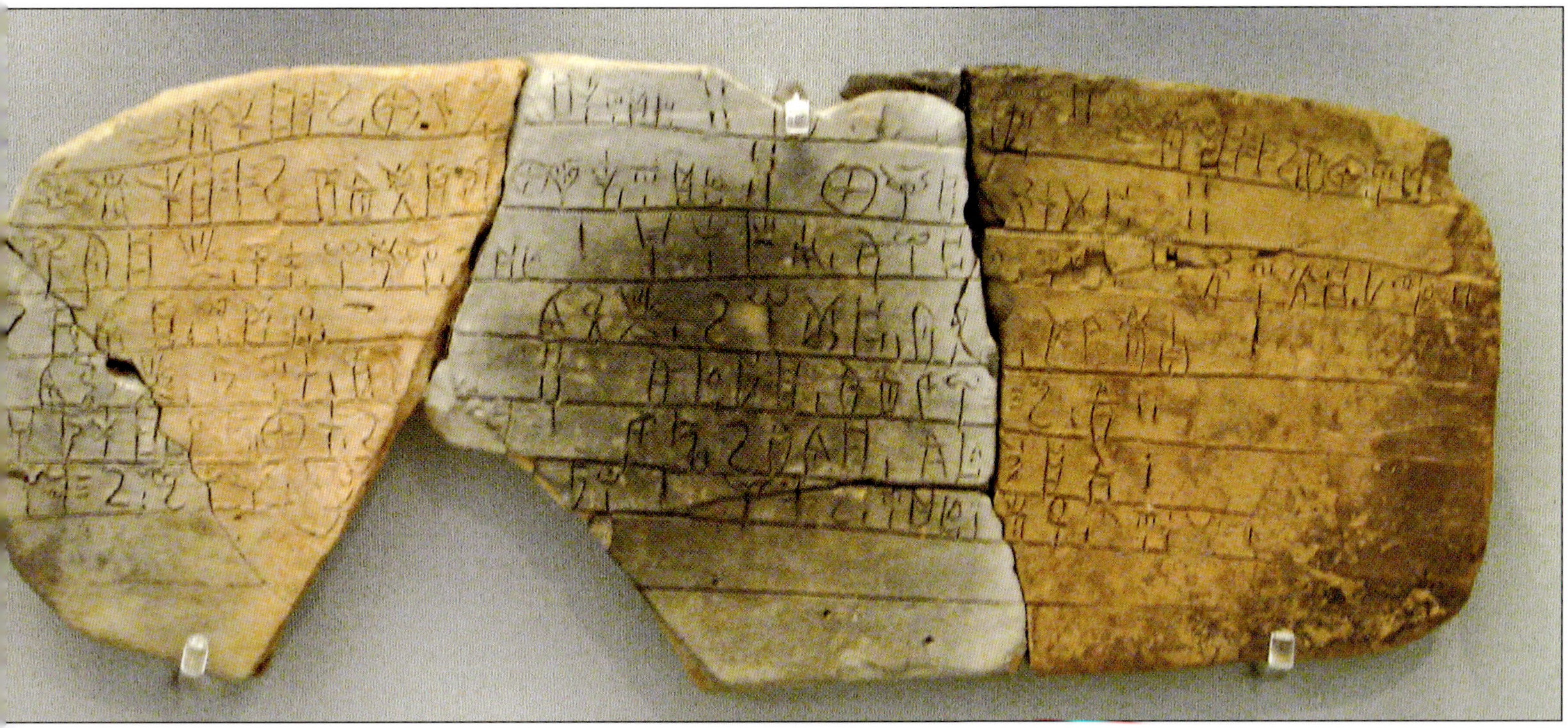

backside as big as a cistern," which was written about 1,500 years ago. They also left their mark across the known world, leaving all sorts of inscriptions on natural formations, rocks, and cliffs, as well as on temple walls, tombs, and other important places that didn't belong to them.

One of these places was the rock face at El Kanais in Egypt. This site is covered with graffiti made over a 3,000-year period and by many visitors from different countries and different cultures. Greek graffiti is prominent and ranges from mere scratching to detailed carvings in the rock and was created within 400 to 500 years of the earliest and the latest. Some of the graffiti records return visits by the same person and is noted by the person's name and the date. Not only was a name given, but quite often a patronymic was provided as well to identify that particular person by his ancestry. Other pieces of writing graffitied onto the rock face include prayers for safe travel through the desert.

Garrisons of soldiers were stationed near the temple at El Kanais and they too left their mark as they did nearly everywhere they went. Other travelers, both Greek and not, also liked to leave a record of why they were traveling through the inhospitable desert. Possibly the last Greek graffitist at El Kanais was a Cretan called Leonidas Lychounes who visited the area twice, once in 1843 and the other in 1846. Interestingly, he wrote in French.

THE ROMAN EMPIRE

Pompeii

Graffiti was a popular form of communication in ancient Rome and it was not necessarily seen as a form of vandalism (although if it was offensive enough, and in the wrong place it probably would have been condemned and removed). Subject matter ranged from politics, poetry, and gladiators to sex, love, and obscenities. In 79 AD, when the volcanic mountain Vesuvius erupted and blan-

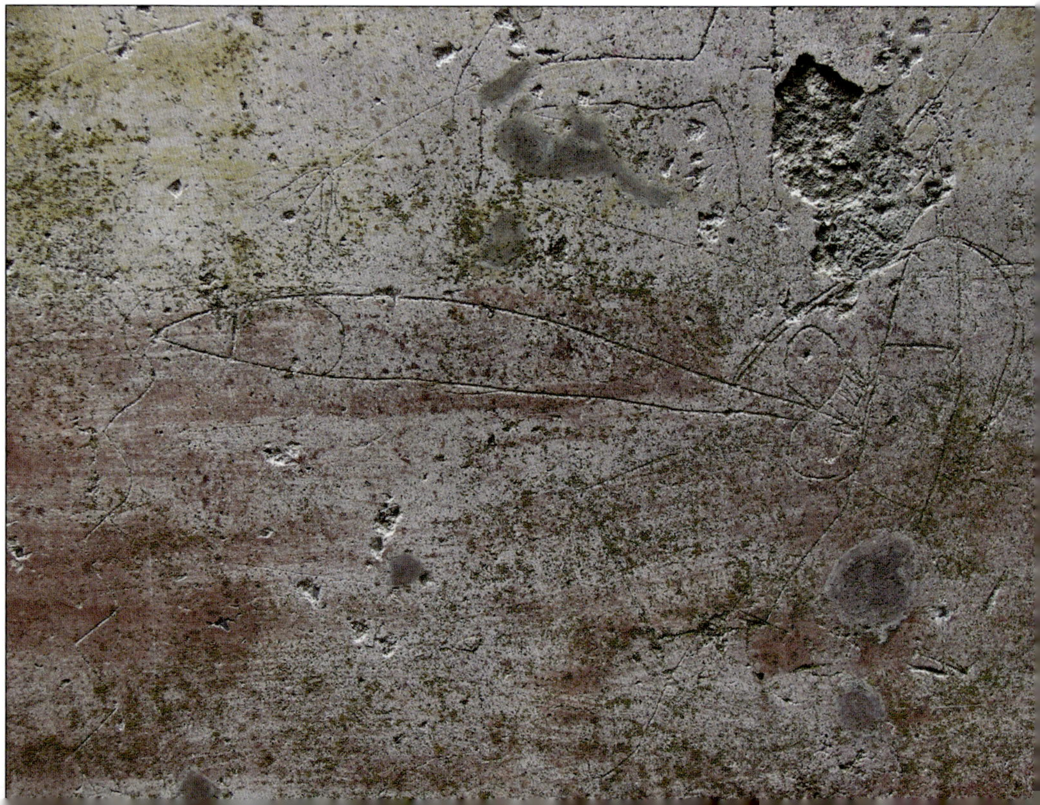

Graffiti as we know it today—a penis » is scratched onto the surface of a wall and looks just like those drawings made by school boys on the undersides of their desks.

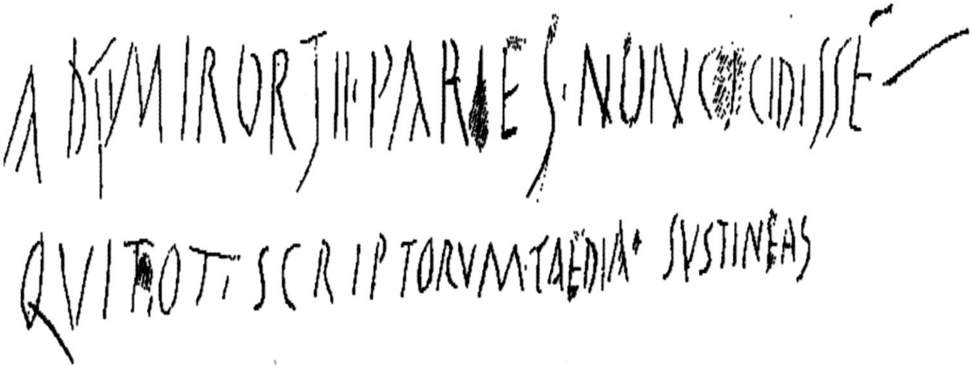

A copy of a piece of graffiti found at Pompeii and registered as C.I.L. IV 2487. The piece reads: "Admiror te paries non cecidisse Qvi tot scriptorvm taedia Svstineas." Note that in Latin "v" is used in place of "u" and takes its sound. The English translation is: "I marvel, at you wall that you haven't fallen, you who bear the scribblings of so many writers."

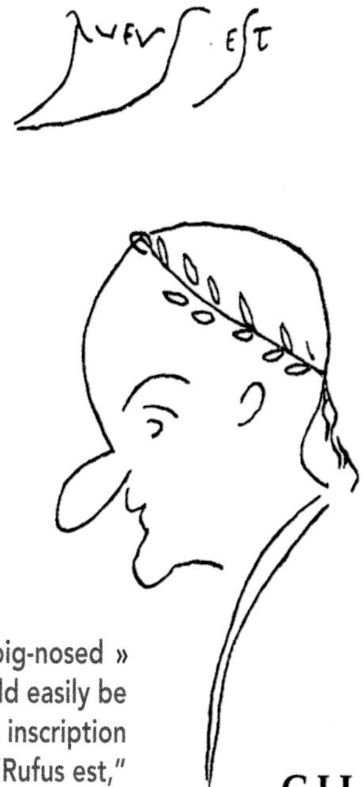

This little caricature shows a big-nosed man with a bald head; he could easily be a version of Mr. Magoo. The inscription above the drawing reads "Rufus est," which means "This is Rufus."

C.I.L. IV 9226

An elaborate scene showing gladiators fighting while musicians blow trumpets. On the left-hand side are figures such as spectators, although the details are rather obscure. Note how the numerals have been scratched out.

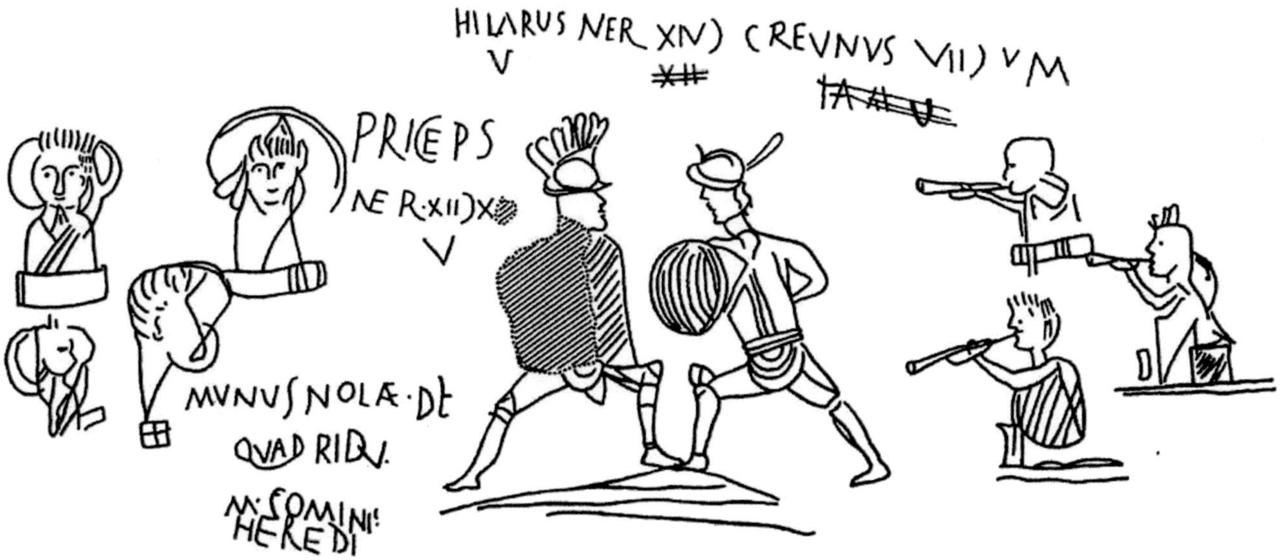

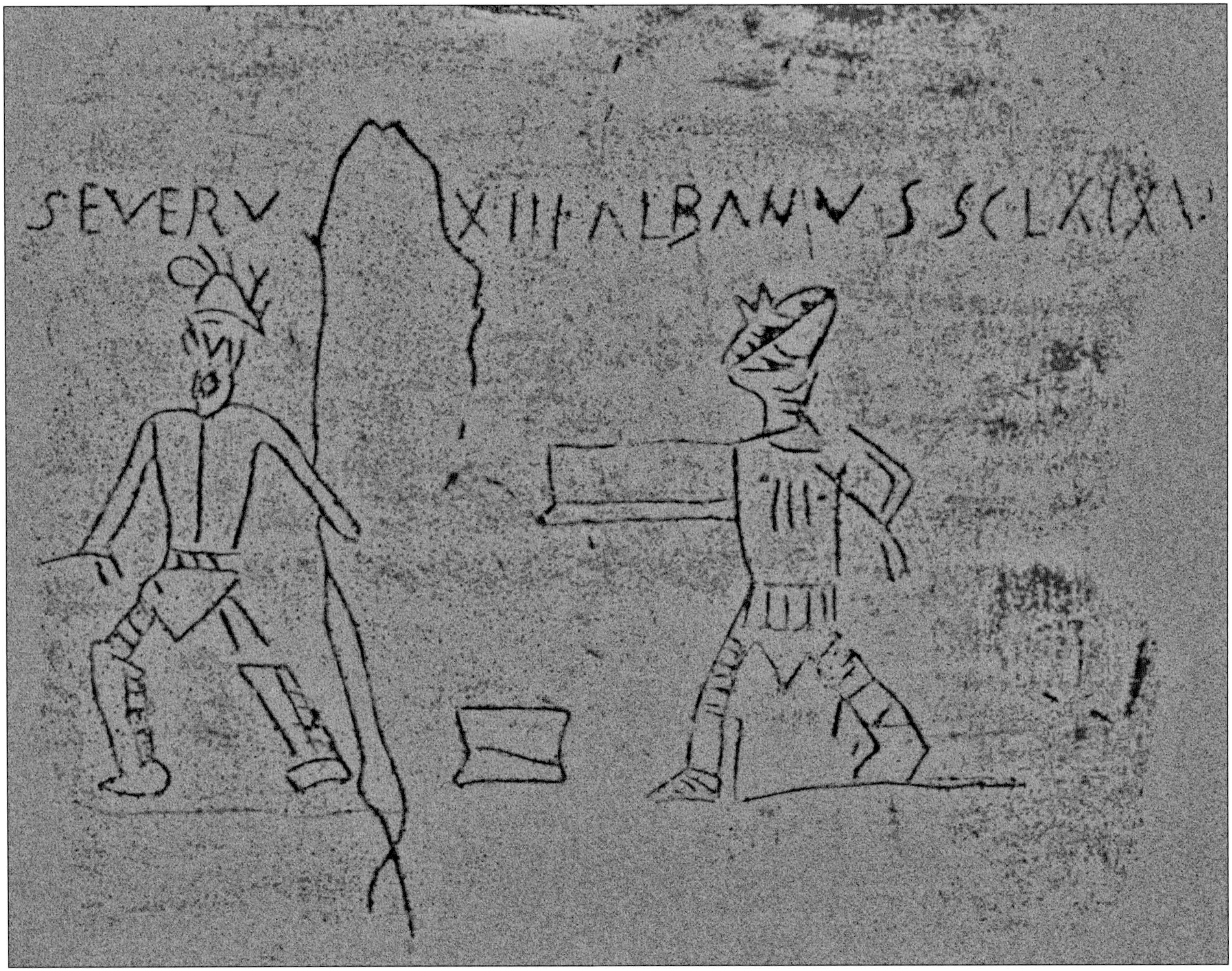

Another gladiator fight showing only the opponents. Pictures of gladiators and writings about them were among some of the most popular forms of graffiti in Pompeii.

keted Pompeii in ash, it preserved a whole way of life in the very midst of its business—including the graffiti throughout the town.

In fact, there have been about 15,000 pieces of writing discovered on walls along the streets of the decimated city. Walls in Pompeii were largely made of plaster, which was a most amenable surface to scratch graffiti into. People used anything available to do so: nails, bits of wood, sharps stones, or even bone. The earliest writing has been dated to the very beginning days of Pompeii. This is known because of the language used—Oscan. There are samples of painted graffiti, as well. It has all been kept in a state of suspended animation thanks to Vesuvius—graffiti that would otherwise have been lost to the modern world, as it was common practice for the writing to eventually get painted over.

Roman graffiti is scarce in other parts of the once mighty empire. Britain retains some fragments, as does Egypt, but when seen how prolific it was in Pompeii, it is easy to assume that much of the Roman Empire's graffiti must have been destroyed over the centuries.

Despite the fact that a lot of Roman graffiti is not all that dissimilar to what we find scribbled in urban areas to this day, we still find ourselves fascinated by it, perhaps for the very reason that it is *not* so different. Another surprising deduction made from the huge amount of graffiti found in the Pompeian ruins is that a larger percentage of the population was literate, more so than had been previously thought. Alphabets have been found written at child height along several walls, suggesting that this was one way of teaching children to read and write. There is even one case of words being written not only backwards, but also upside down. From this it would seem that even in those ancient times, people liked to play word games.

A lot of the graffiti in Pompeii can be found inside bathing complexes. It is mostly of a sexual nature, often relating to conquests and stamina. Inns were another popular place for the crude type of graffiti that is now known as *latrinalia*. Alcohol would have surely inspired much of it and again there are numerous sexual references as well as references to drinking and prostitutes.

One scholar formed a theory about the graffiti that appeared outside in the street. After studying it carefully, he decided that the walls where there was the most graffiti tended to be thoroughfares that saw a lot of traffic and therefore had both numerous authors and readers. The bulk of the graffiti refers to gladiators. Men and women wrote about their favorites and related exciting matches; they drew pictures and wrote names underneath, sometimes accompanied by declarations of love and lust. This type of graffiti was most prevalent near the arena, of course.

The following are a few examples of the types of graffiti written by the good citizens of Pompeii before they were buried under mountains of ash, most of it of a sexual nature. "Weep, you girls. My Penis has given you up. Now it penetrates men's behinds. Goodbye, wondrous femininity!" This piece was written on the wall of a brothel. And on the wall of a tavern was written a charming piece about Restituta: "Take off your tunic, please, and show us your hairy parts." The next was written on the wall of a private house: "Amplicatus, I know that Icarus is buggering you. Salvius wrote this."

Sex was not the only subject of graffiti in Pompeii, however. A comment on the food at the house of Cuspius Pansa by one of Nero's finance officers suggests it is poison. And there was always the common phenomenon of writing "[name] was here"; in one case it was Satura on September the third. Or, written in the barracks of the gladiators, "Antiochus was here with his girl Cithera." Or "Romula hung out here with Staphylus." And in the street of Mercury: "Publius Comicius Restitutus stood right here with his brother."

And then there were the usual plethora of toilet related items: "To the one defecating here. Beware of the curse. If you ignore it may you have an angry Jupiter for an enemy," which was found written on the left-hand side of a house doorway. Obviously people had a habit of answering this particular call of nature anywhere they felt like. Here is one posted outside the city gate: "Defecator, may everything turn out okay so that you can leave this place." And it was not just the commoners who did it: "Apollinaris, the doctor of the emperor Titus, defecated well here." Or at least someone thought he did. And a warning to all would-be defecators at the water tower: "Anyone who wants to defecate in this place is advised to move along. If you act contrary to this warning, you will have to pay a penalty. Children must pay . . . silver coins. Slaves will be beaten on their behinds."

It was not only defecating that was the problem, though, as this little note suggests: "We have wet the bed, host. I confess we have done wrong. If you want to know why, there was no chamber pot."

And of course, love had plenty written about it: "Lovers are like bees in that they live a honeyed life"; "Whoever loves, let him flourish. Let him perish who knows not love. Let him perish twice over whoever forbids love"; "Marcus loves Spendusa"; "Cruel Lalagus, why do you not love me?" And even married women wrote, "I don't want to sell my husband, not for all the gold in the world."

They graffitied about the consequences of love, too: "Atimetus got me pregnant."

Not everything was crude, though. There are some very ordinary occurrences being written onto the stone, such as "on the 19th April I made bread." And even the laundry was noted down on a wall in public: "On April 20, I gave a cloak to be washed. On May 7, a headband. On May 8, two tunics."

Wisdom and good advice were often offered, such as, "Remove lustful expressions and flirtatious tender eyes from another man's wife; may there be modesty in your expression."' And age-old good sense: "A small problem gets larger if you ignore it."

Graffiti also served as advertisements to rent apartments or to provide information about stolen goods. Some contain nasty curses ("Chie, I hope your hemorrhoids rub together so much that they hurt worse than they ever have before!") and some statements of fact ("It took 640 paces to walk back and forth between here and there ten times"). And some were public displays of grief for dead friends. To sum it all up and to see how little things have changed in the history of graffiti, there is one piece that will resonate with many modern citizens: "O walls, you have held up so much tedious graffiti that I am amazed that you have not already collapsed in ruin."

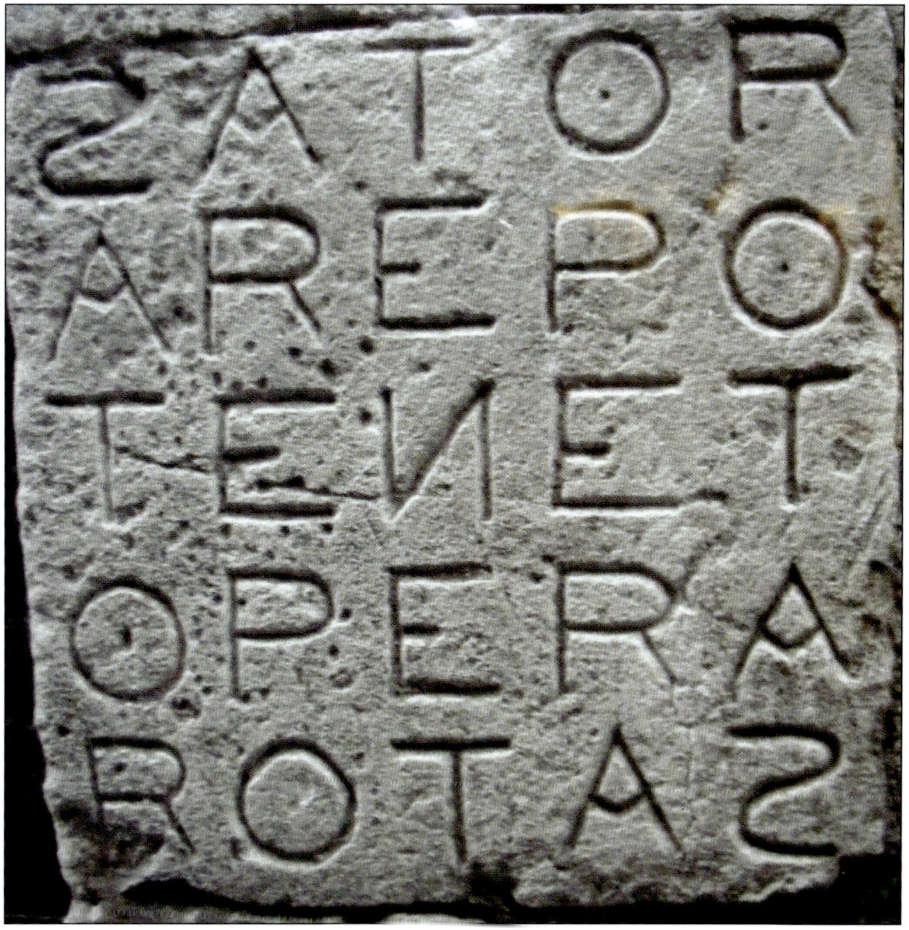

A Sator Square carved » into a stone block and set into a wall.

The Sator Square is a bit different to the run-of-the-mill graffiti found in Pompeii and other parts of the Roman Empire. This particular graffiti was found carved into a plaster column and has set a puzzle for scholars ever since it was unearthed:

SATOR
AREPO
TENET
OPERA
ROTAS

When written in a square it is easy to see that it is the same read across, up, down, and back to front. There have been many attempts at trying to decipher its meaning and the popular one is along these lines: The farmer, Arepo, uses wheels for his work, presumably to plough the field. The word *Arepo* is most probably a proper noun and may well have been invented for use in the square. It has been hotly debated among scholars as to who may have invented the square and why. In translating it, various ingenious methods have been used to come up with fitting theories. The most likely explanation is that it was the product of Latin-speaking Jews living in Pompeii at the time.

The earliest example of the Sator Square is believed to have been written onto a Coptic papyrus in the fourth or fifth century AD. The first graffito of the Sator Square was only a fragment found in the house of Publius Paquius Proculus in Pompeii, but by the mid-1930s, a more extant version had been uncovered, which is the second one found in Pompeii. It is now believed that these two specimens of this graffiti that were found in Pompeii are the earliest examples. However, there were four more such squares uncovered in a dig between 1931 and 1939 conducted by Yale University and the

French Academy of Inscriptions and Letters. They were found carved into the wall of a military headquarters that had previously been the temple of Azzanathkona at Dura-Europus on the Euphrates. These squares have been dated to a time before the Persian destruction of Dura in 256 AD. And another square was found in Cirencester, in Gloustershire, United Kingdom. It is thought to have been medieval in origin but the findings at Dura opened the debate as to whether the British example was from Roman-occupied Britain many centuries earlier.

Twenty years later, a Sator Square was discovered in Altofen, Budapest, on a roof tile and it has hence been dated to the third century during the Roman occupation. It is likely that it was the Pompeian square that sparked off the writing of all the others, though it's hard to know this for certain. In any case, it became popular as a superstitious charm for both black and white magic and is a fine early example of copy-cat graffiti, which we find across the world to this day.

Graffiti of Smyrna

In 2003 an archaeological dig uncovered the basement of the basilica in the agora of Smyrna. The building, which had been converted into a Roman style basilica in the first or second century AD, was severely damaged by an earthquake that hit the region in 178 AD. There was enough sound structure left after the earthquake to rebuild and it was used for several hundred years more. The basement area was, however, left untouched, filled with the rubble of the fallen masonry from the quake. This did, in fact, allow the contents of that area to be largely preserved until the dig in 2003. Unfortunately, with the opening of the site, the outside exposure led to quick deterioration of the wall surfaces, some of which collapsed almost immediately. Other parts of the underground area were covered in thick grime and, when it was removed, it too destroyed the unknown underlying graffiti.

What was discovered, however, was a layer of plaster housing large amounts of graffiti that had been applied over at least another layer of plaster. When portions of the top layer were removed, it was found that the underlying layer was also heavily covered in graffiti. One of the extraordinary things about the find was that the writings and drawings were mostly done in ink. This is unusual for the fact that the nature of the graffiti seemed to comprise of spontaneous scribbling from tourists and vandals—"I was here"-type messages. To write this in ink suggests a certain amount of forethought because the ordinary citizen did not travel around town with a bottle of ink and a pen in his or her pocket. The ink used on the walls was tested to see what it was made of. While one of the most common types of ink at the time was made from carbon black, some of the ink from the Smyrna basilica site contains traces of oak gall, which is not thought to have been used much before the Middle Ages. Another surprising find was the use of red pigment for highlighting as well as charcoal.

There was evidence of incised graffiti discovered at the site, but the finding of graffiti written in ink overshadowed that of the more ordinary kind. The fact that a second layer of graffiti-laden plaster was covering another suggests that even in ancient times graffiti was considered an undesirable public nuisance—unless, that is, the fresh layer was to provide a new surface for the graffiti because the old was just too used up. This is something we can only conjecture.

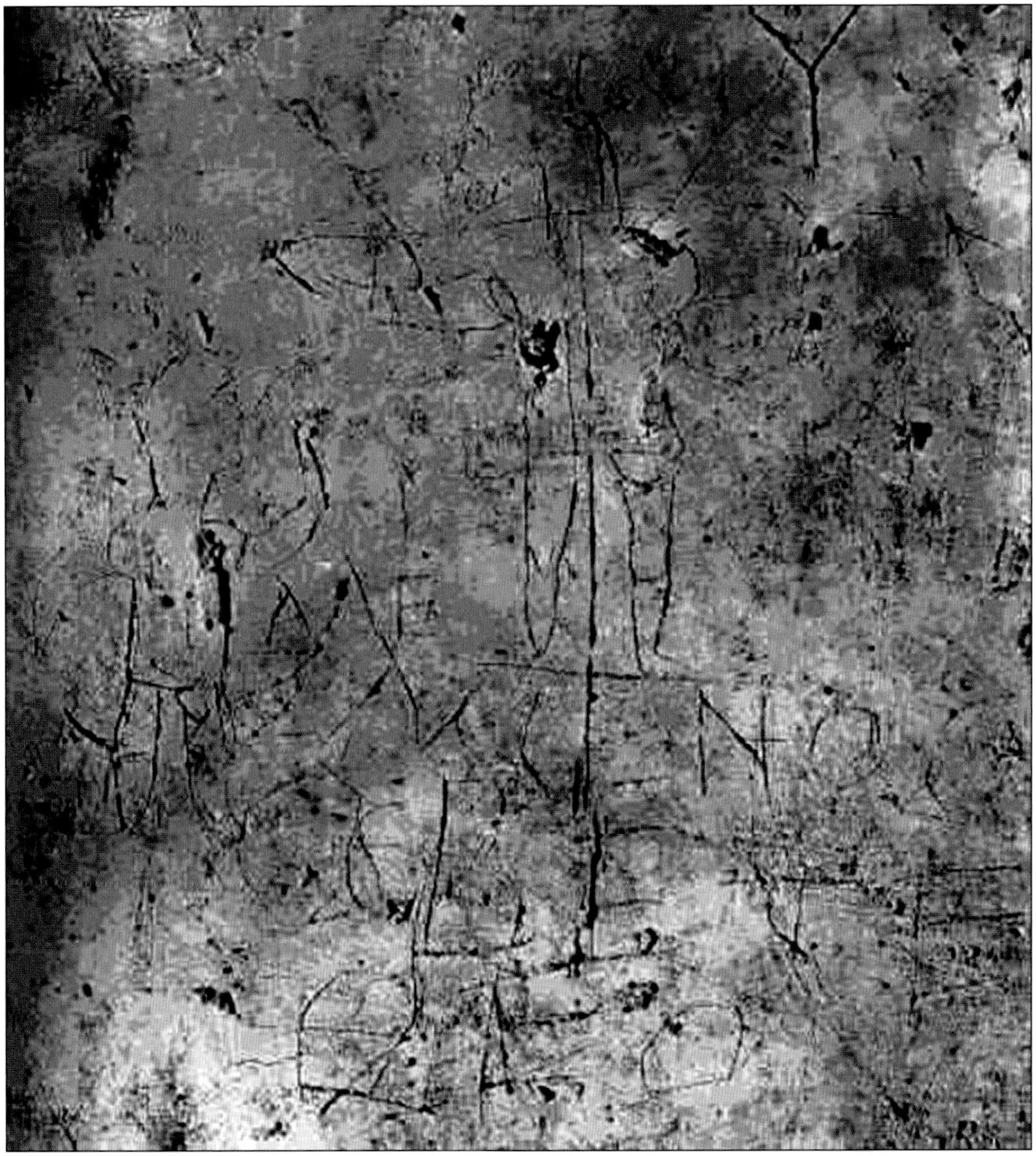

« The Alexmanos graffiti.

Some of the graffiti on these walls is several lines long; others are made up of single words and pictures. Graffiti covers graffiti, and there is graffiti that has been crossed out. A lot of the text is similar in content that what we might find today tagged on the underside of a bridge or on a building: personal messages of a sexual nature or unrequited love, political messages, and insults. Some of these are accompanied by drawings; one shows a set of testicles over which a young man's head was drawn; the inscription reads "I am being buggered." Another example suggests the writer knew someone who killed an adulterer; the plaster is broken off before the identity of the person was discovered. Another suggests that a loved one, or even the writer himself, has had a safe voyage home under the auspices of Isis. There are even examples of those kinds of silly riddles in which the answer is contained in the question, such as, "Who was the father of Priam's children?" There are a number of pieces giving thanks for the healing of sore eyes and the restoration of sight. There is also graffiti referring to sporting achievements and gladiatorial shows, barracking for particular fighters and downing others. Besides these crude writings there were a fair number of drawings of ships.

Additionally, there was evidence of early Christian writing among these rather trite tags. Isopsephisms, the practice of attributing numerical values to letters, and therefore whole words, was a popular activity among Christians, although by no means exclusive to them. The way this code works was something along the lines of "alpha equals 1." The symbol for omega was used to denote the equal sign. Several bits of graffiti were found where a woman's or man's name was found to equal a number and it's possible that this was written by an early Christian.

Roman graffiti has been found wherever the Empire occupied land. And even in Rome there were numerous scrawls on the city walls. A famous piece of graffito, the Alexmanos, which has also been called the graffito blasfemo, was unearthed at a site on Palatine Hill in 1857. On the plaster in a house called the domus Gelotiana—which belonged to Caligula before it was turned into a boarding school of pageboys of the court—and buried under newer buildings for centuries, this inscription is thought to be the earliest pictorial representation of Christ on the cross.

The graffito depicts the figure of a human figure on a cross, but it has been given the head of a donkey, which is believed to be ridiculing the Christian religion. Many non-Christians thought that Christians and Jews worshipped a god with an ass's head. Although this reading of the graffito offers a rational and believable explanation, there are other theories circulating among scholars. Some have suggested the drawing isn't of Christ, but of Anubis or Seth, Egyptian gods with animal heads, or that the figure is a Gnostic rite with a horse headed and that the top of the cross is actually the Greek letter upsilon. And yet another theory has been put forth that the graffito is the product of a heretical group set apart from the main church. Further controversy has risen over when the crucifixion became part of the iconography of Christianity. It has been suggested that this didn't come into practice until the fourth or fifth century AD. To further complicate matters, an adjacent room has the inscription "Alexamenos is faithful," which had been interpreted as a defiant answer to the previous blasphemous cartoon.

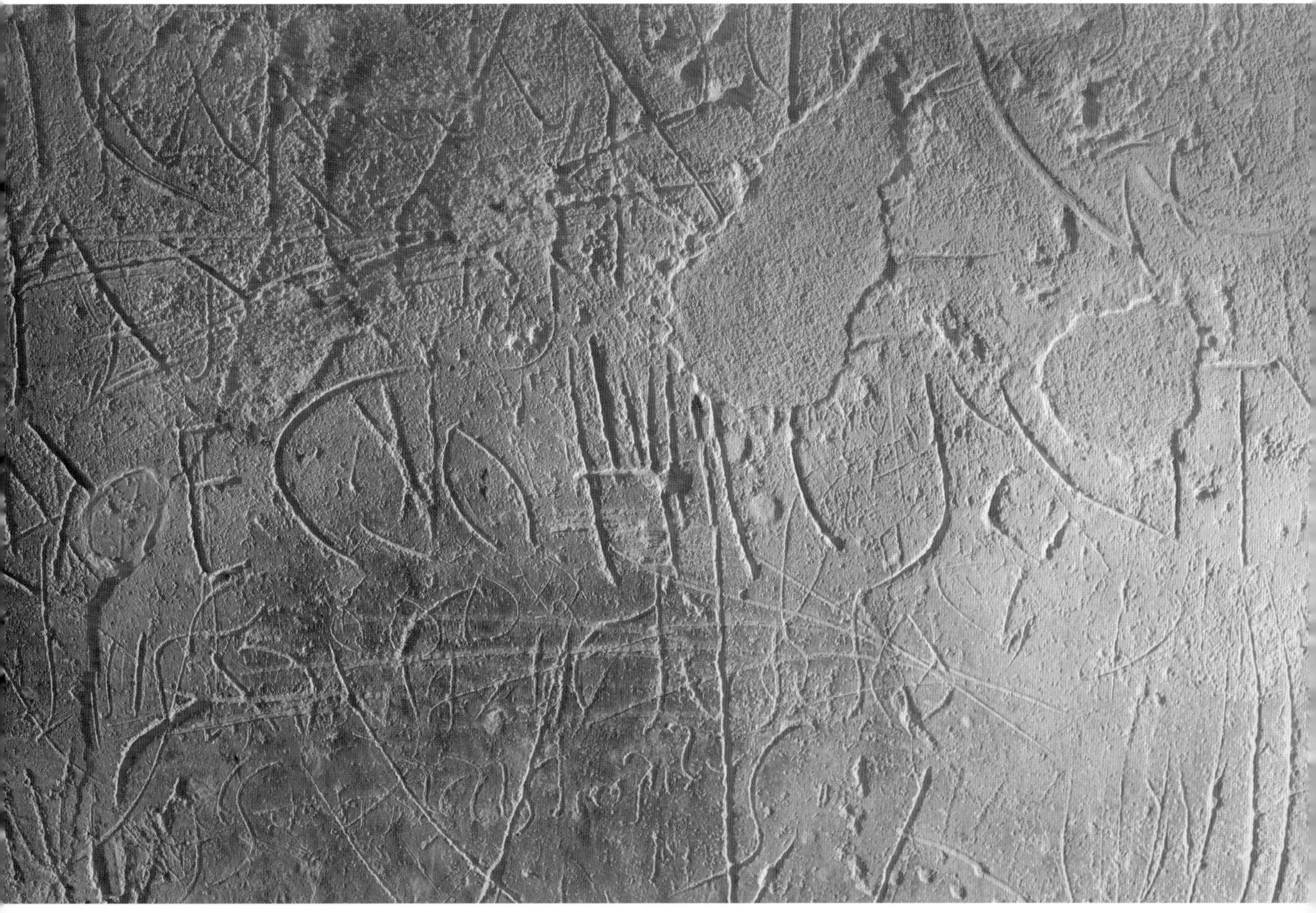

≈ An example of ancient graffiti.

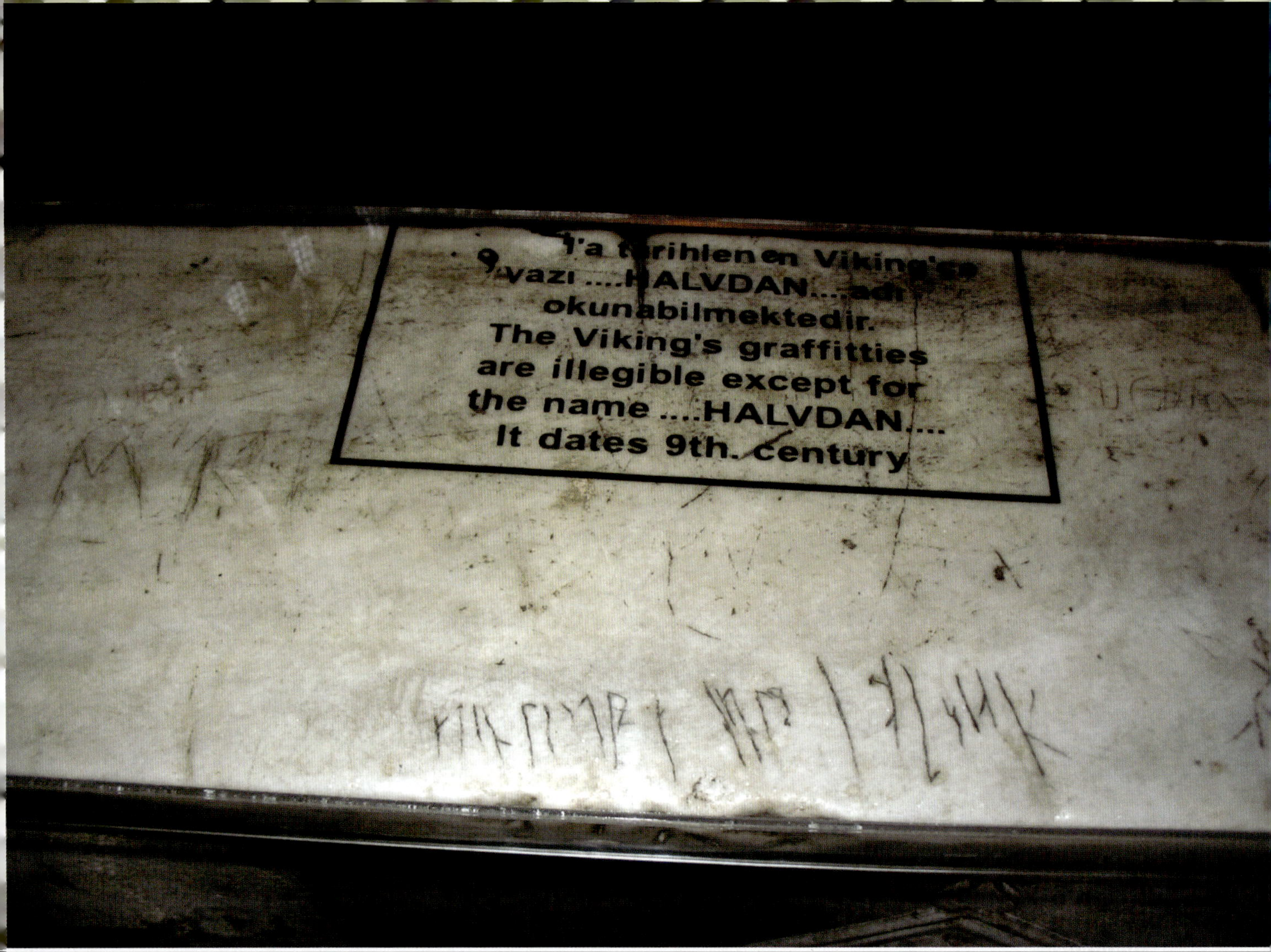

The marble block on which a Viking member of the Varangian guard to the Emperor of Byzantium scratched his runic initials

CHAPTER THREE

MEDIEVAL GRAFFITI

THE GRAFFITI OF THE VIKINGS

A Viking in Constantinople

The Vikings weren't only raiders and invaders, as history has often portrayed. A select fighting outfit made up of handpicked Viking warriors was once employed by the Byzantine emperor between the tenth and the fourteenth centuries AD to act as his personal bodyguards. From the frozen north of their native land, the Vikings, with their long flaxen hair and beards, were an unmistakable sight in the exotic and glittering city of Constantinople. The Vikings kept true to their own beliefs and their own gods, so to carve one's initials onto the marble parapet of another people's temple, the church of Hagia Sofia, was probably nothing more than a simple "so and so was here" marking, possibly made during some ceremony that needed relief from boredom.

Runes are the letters of alphabets that were used in Germanic and Scandinavian countries before the adopted use of the Latin alphabet. The earliest examples we have of runic writing date to 150 AD. Various runic alphabets were developed, used, and declined. The last general use of a runic alphabet was around 1500 AD.

The runes have been deciphered to reveal the name Halfdan and it is presumed that the original inscription meant something along these lines: "Halfdan carved these runes." Incredibly, the markings weren't discovered until 1964. They are located on the top floor of the southern gallery of what is known as the Empress's gallery.

A second lot of runes were found just over ten years later in the same section of the building as Halfdan's runes. The find was made by Folke Högberg from Uppsala. Högberg was sure the runes were the name of a man called Arni, but another archeologist argued that they should be interpreted as "Ari made these runes." There have been more runes found in other parts of the building, indicating that the Vikings left their mark while in Constantinople.

Viking Graffiti in Britain

Five thousand years ago, the Orkney Islands at the very top of Scotland were a thriving center of Stone Age life. Part of the rituals of the Orkney Islands' dwellers involved interring their dead in underground tombs. There are quite a number of these multi-roomed burial chambers in the Orkneys. In 1861, a keen antiquarian by the name of James Farrer led an expedition to open up a burial mound at Maes Howe. Farrer's approach was fairly unsupervised and there were no

The fenced-off entrance to Maes Howe in the Orkney Islands of Scotland.

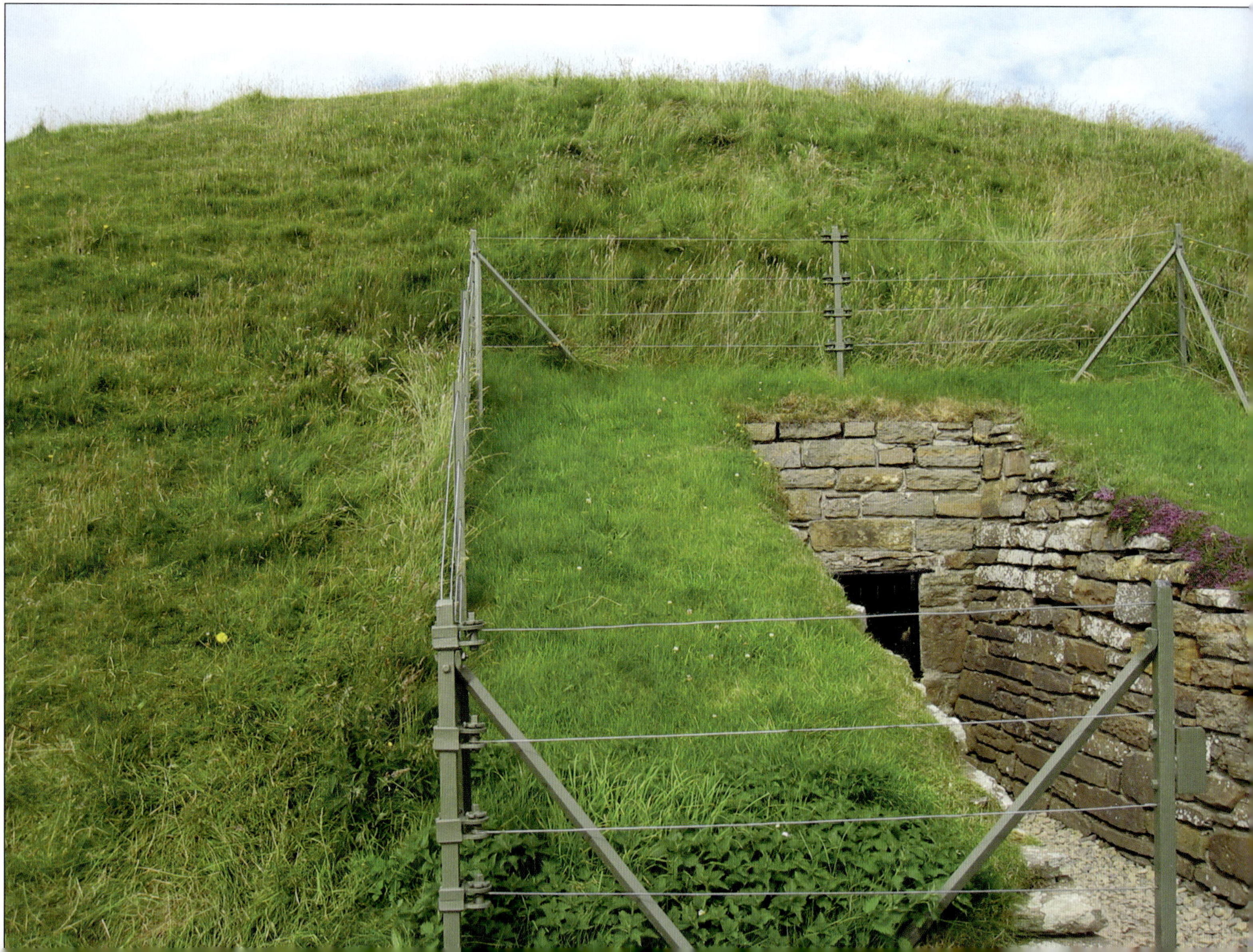

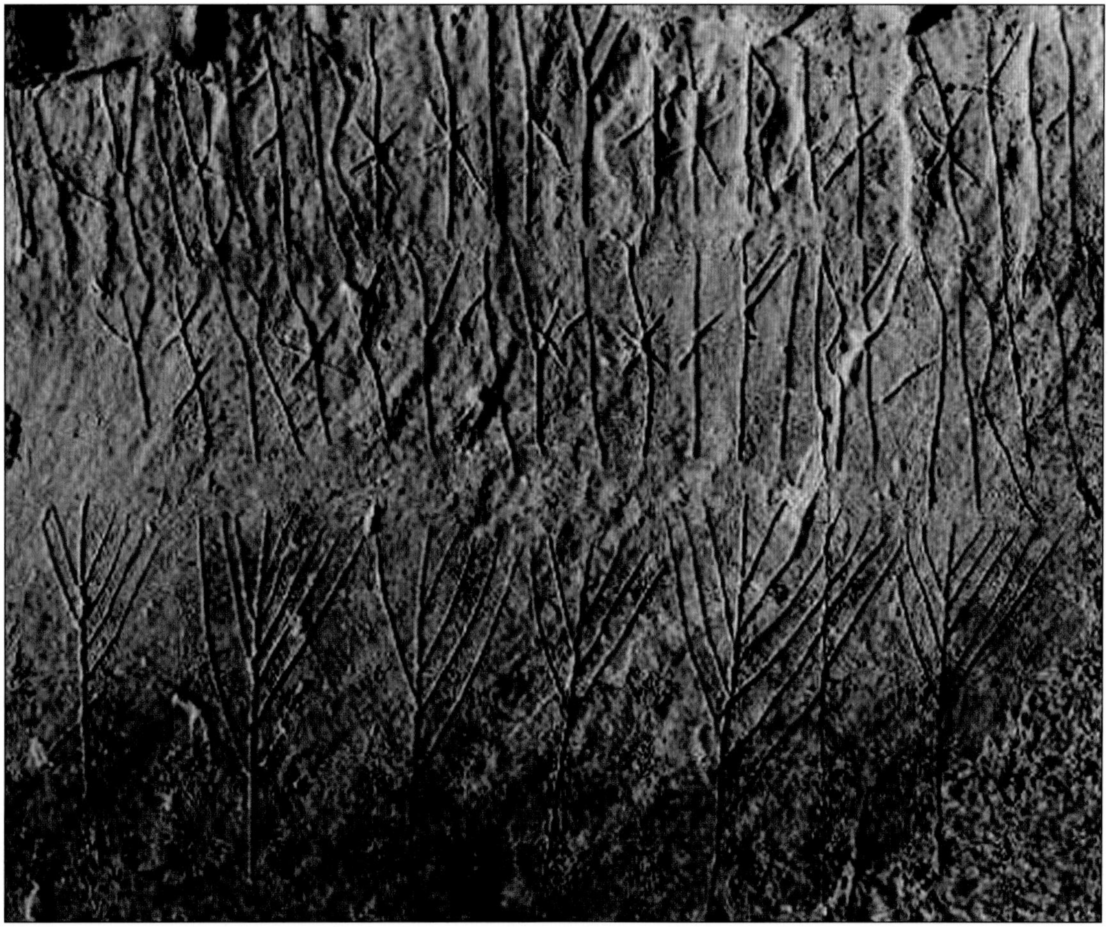

The runes found within the burial » chamber and thought to have been made by Vikings, who were either seeking buried treasure or were seeking shelter from a storm.

attempts to limit the damage done to the site as he and his team broke through the roof of the entrance tunnel. But the tunnel being full of rubble, they were unable to get into the tomb that way. Consequently, Farrer then dug through the roof of the howe and eventually made it into the main chamber. What the group discovered was not actually a burial chamber full of treasure, but rather an empty cavern full of Viking graffiti that had been placed there in the mid-twelfth century. It appears the Vikings had been on the Orkney Islands, as well.

Indeed, the dates for the early Viking raid are supported by a report in the *Orkneyinga Saga*, written about 1230 AD, that a band of Vikings, on their way to the crusades, sought shelter in the tomb when they were forced ashore during a storm. The saga claims it was on Christmas Day, year 1153. Thus, writing on the wall was merely a way to pass the time until the storm abated and their important quest could be resumed. Upon further inspection, the real dates of the graffiti may be a couple of centuries earlier than claimed in the *Orkneyinga Saga* and are probably from the ninth century.

The Vikings wrote various phrases onto the rock, including the following: "Trygg carved these runes"; "Lyf the Cook made these runes"; and "Tholfr Kolsseinn's son carved these runes high up" (written near the chamber roof). Also present are what we've found to be the standard musings about love and lust: "Ingigerth is the most beautiful of women" (although the sentiment is rather spoiled by the fact that it is accompanied by a cartoon picture of a slavering dog). One man carved his name and boasted that he was the best at writing runes in all of the Western Ocean.

The writing of runes was considered as a fine art in Viking culture and not many Vikings had perfected it. Those who had studied runeship—the making of runes—were known as Runemasters. In the tomb, explorers also found a drawing of a dragon and a serpent knot that are quite elegantly rendered, even by today's standards. And besides these carved phrases are graffiti relating to a speculation that the tomb had once been filled with the treasure of a long-dead king. Scientists believe it may have been this rumor of buried treasure that led the Vikings to the tomb in the first place. The surprise and disappointment at finding nothing is obvious in the statements that were left: "It was long ago that a great treasure was hidden here. Happy is he that might find that great treasure."

The dating of the runes is rather difficult to determine. It does seem most likely that at least two if not three visits were made by the Vikings to this spot in total. There is evidence of Vikings having been in the tomb as early as the ninth century due to the dating of the messages left within. Then there were the Viking Crusaders who only went into the mound to get out of the rain. Another source suggests two years before the "Jerusalem men" visited the tomb another two Viking travelers sheltered in the tomb but went mad. One of the later Vikings, Simon Sirith, states that "Hakon alone bore treasure from this mound," and we are left to wonder how he knew that.

Another bit of important Viking graffiti that's been discovered in recent years is the drawing of an oared ship inside the church at Stow Minster, Lincolnshire, England. It is the earliest example of Viking graffiti in England that has been discovered, dating back to the tenth century.

LATER MEDIEVAL GRAFFITI

As we get closer to the modern day, graffiti from the Middle Ages onward becomes more prevalent. Many more buildings from the late Medieval period are still in existence around the world, and although much of the graffiti on them has faded, it is still present if you are able to look closely enough.

Graffiti made by the Crusaders fighting for the Holy Land of Jerusalem on the stairwell of the » Chapel of Saint Helena in the Church of the Holy Sepulchre in the Old City of Jerusalem.
Photo courtesy of Guillaume Paumier.

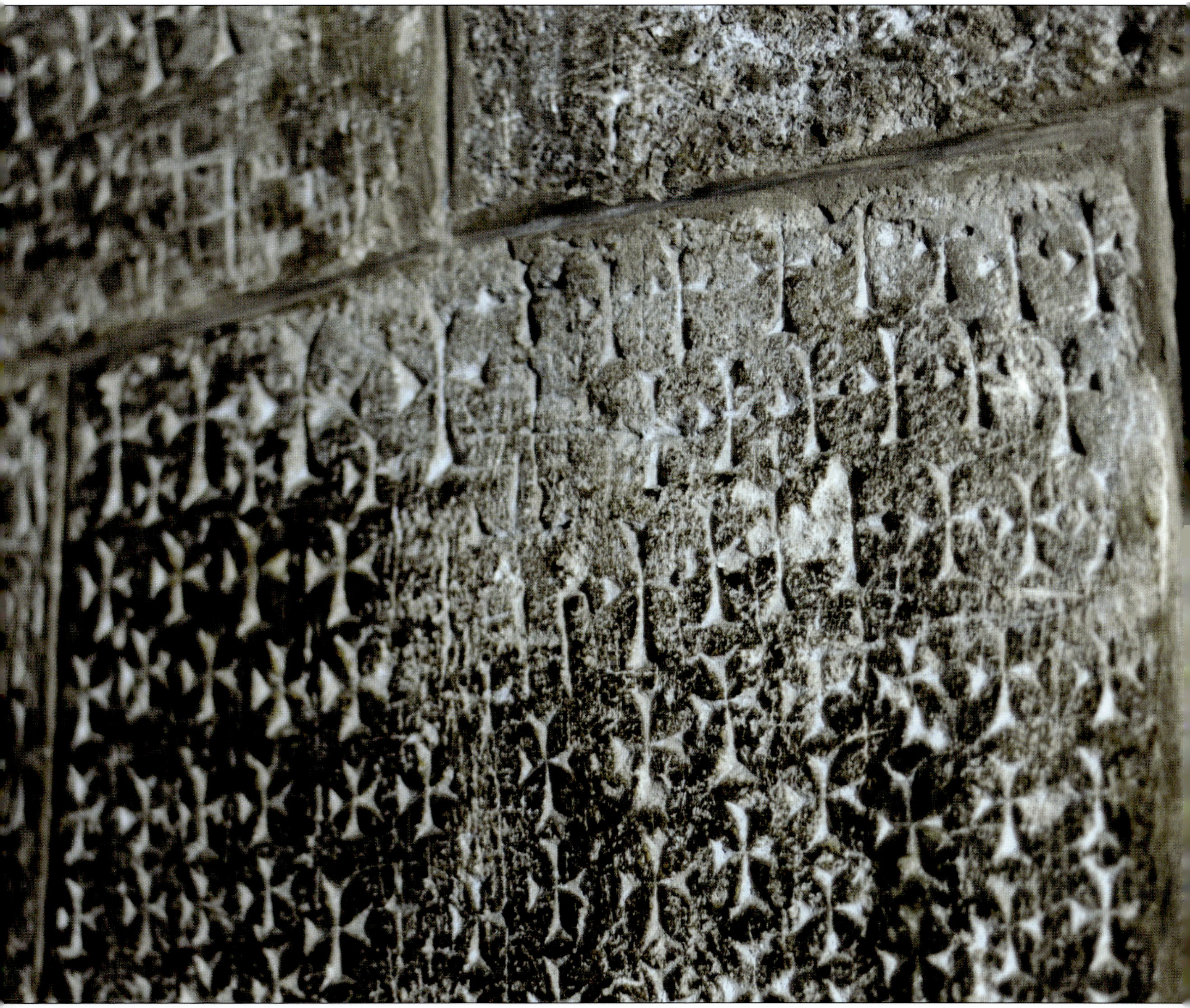

There are some pieces of graffiti that have been known for a long time, and although the true origins and meanings of them have been lost, a kind of folklore has grown to help explain them to modern-day enthusiasts. One such example is a drawing on a pillar in All Saints Church, Leighton-Linsdale, England. It is a rather crudely scratched picture featuring two figures that have been named by the locals as Simon and Nell. It is said that this couple is having an argument about the best way to make a pudding. Simon is holding a lump of dough in his hand, which looks as though he is about to throw it at Nell, who is likewise holding a spoon in a very threatening manner (or so the story goes, as the pictures are really too roughly made to support this). However, as legend has it, they don't actually have a food brawl, but decide to cooperate and make the pudding together. The result is the Simnel cake, a light fruit cake with two layers of marzipan icing. Slices of cake are toasted before eating. The cake is made and eaten at Easter throughout Great Britain.

TAG THIS!

Stone Masons' Graffiti

Stone masons typically marked their work with their own initials, insignia, or symbol into one of the stones of the building they had worked on. These markers are useful today because they allow us to identify who worked on what building and when, which also provides clues as to how various building techniques spread across a given country.

Graffiti in the Cellar

An important find in the history of graffiti came to light when Blackfriar's Barn, once a Guild Hall in Winchelsea, was cleared of centuries of garbage. The graffiti that the cleaners found is of a number of ships drawn on a large scale. They have since become known as Winchelsea's Lost Fleet.

The building, which houses the collection, was built in the early fourteenth century when the town was an important seaport. The town had actually been rebuilt when the encroaching sea had started to demolish it and it sadly did not survive long, as towards the end of the century the French made a series of naval raids on it and it reverted to being a quiet village in the process of which the Guildhall also quietly sank into decline and then disuse. For more than a hundred years, and continuing into the nineteenth century, the villagers had used the cellar of the building as a garbage dump, until the clean up and then discovery of the graffiti. It opened to the public for the first time in 2013.

Graffiti and the Plague

In Ashwell Church in Hertfordshire, England, there is graffiti relating to the Great Plague, which killed as many as 25 million people in the fourteenth century. The plague came in two great waves, the first from 1348 to 1349, and the second approximately ten years later in 1361.

The graffiti found in Ashwell Church is rendered in Latin and believed to be the work of the monks of the church. The graffiti seems to have been made by two or three different people. The first graffito states the date of the plague:

"Primula pestis" (the start of the plague) "in M ter CCC fuit L" (in 1350 was) "minus uno" (less one, meaning the year 1349). The next one farther down on the wall reads: "Pestilencia –I—quinque" (Plague that is five). The third one translates as "1350 wretched fierce violent" and is followed by "1350 live to tell the tale the dregs of the people." Then comes "in the end of the second plague—A great wind—This year—Maurus in heaven thunders 1361."

A demon's head has » been scratched into a church wall, perhaps by a church goer during an overlong sermon.

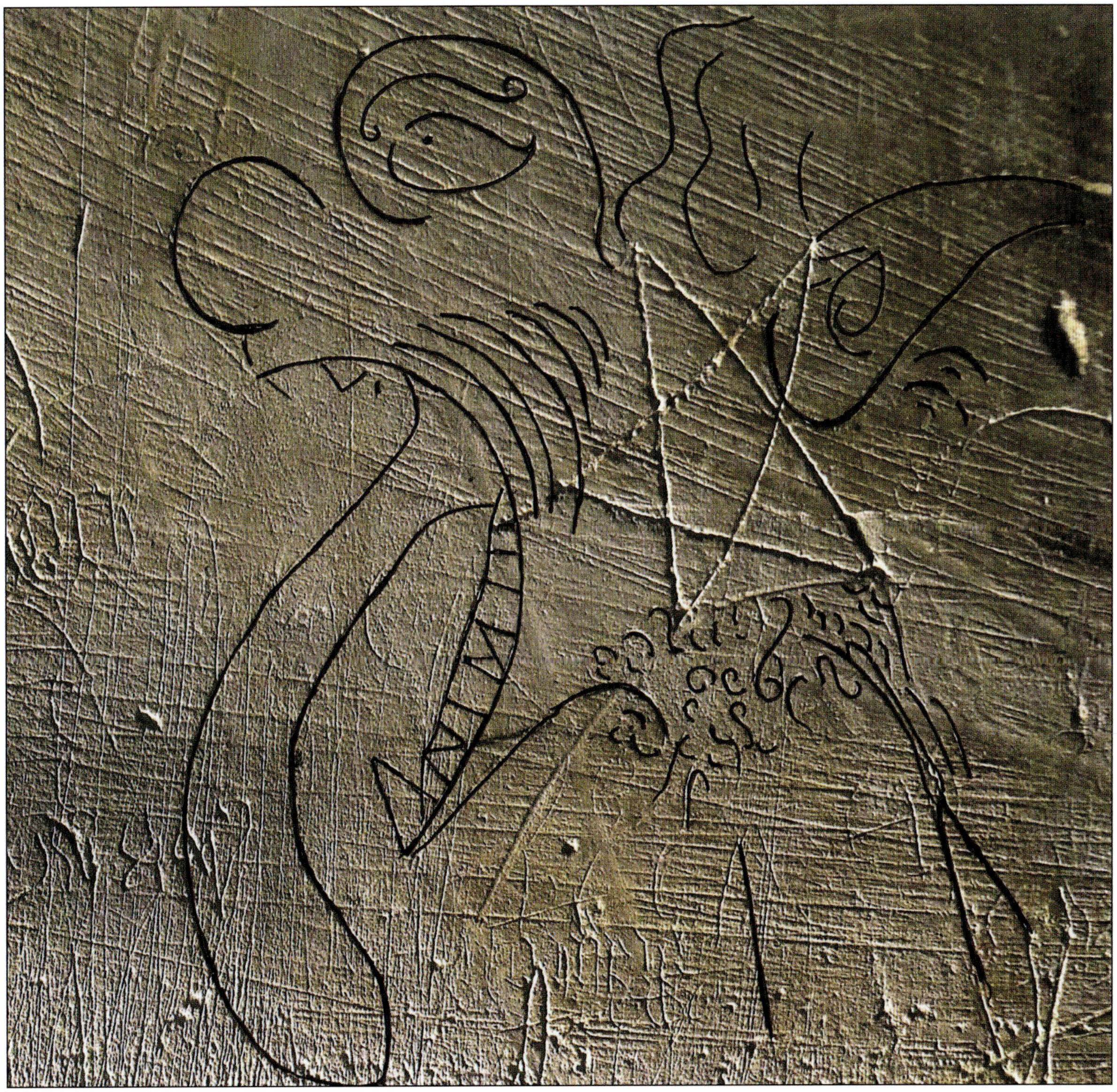

A drawing of an incised graffito also found on a church » wall. It has been done with precision and appears to be a detailed diagram of a church window.

« Graffiti of the Christian symbol of a fish inside of a church.

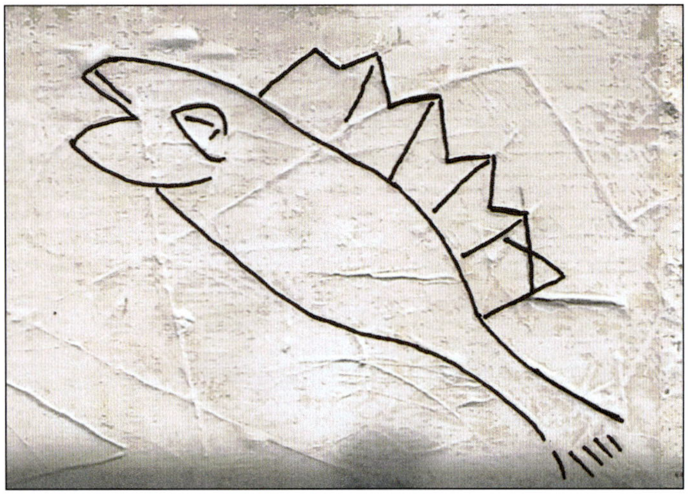

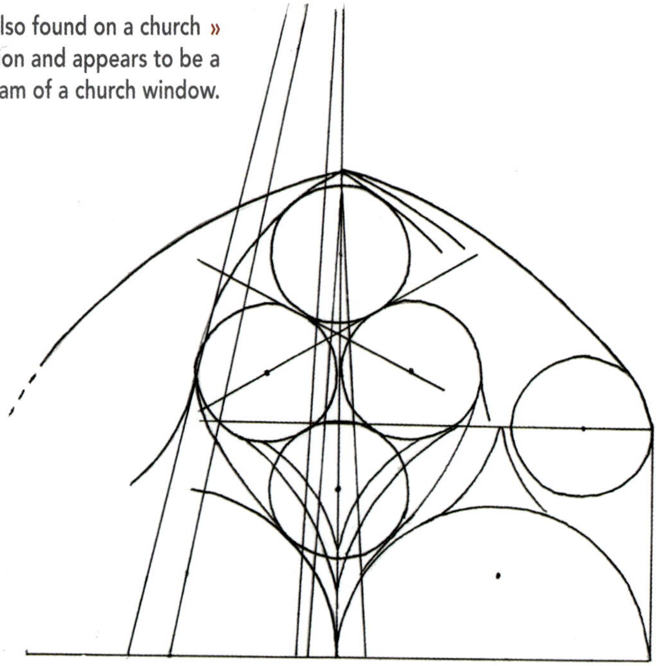

Ship Graffiti

Drawing ships was not an uncommon pastime in the history of humankind, and there are images of ships drawn all over coastal areas of the world, from the cellar of an old guildhall to the slave quarters of the Bahamas. It is with the aid of these graffitied sketches that archeologists have since discovered a lot about ship design and shipbuilding throughout the Middle Ages.

One of the most important examples of ships marked in stone was found in bricks that were discovered in Elsinore, Denmark, in an old friary. After the friary burned down in the fifteenth century, it was rebuilt using hand-made, sun-baked bricks. While the bricks were drying, the workers seem to have carved images of ships that were passing in the channel below them into the hardening surface. Many of the images are fairly rough and without much detail, but they provide a general shape and style of the ships. One or two, however, are drawn very carefully, giving the impression that they were made using a real ship as a model, probably one that was moored just below where the building site lay.

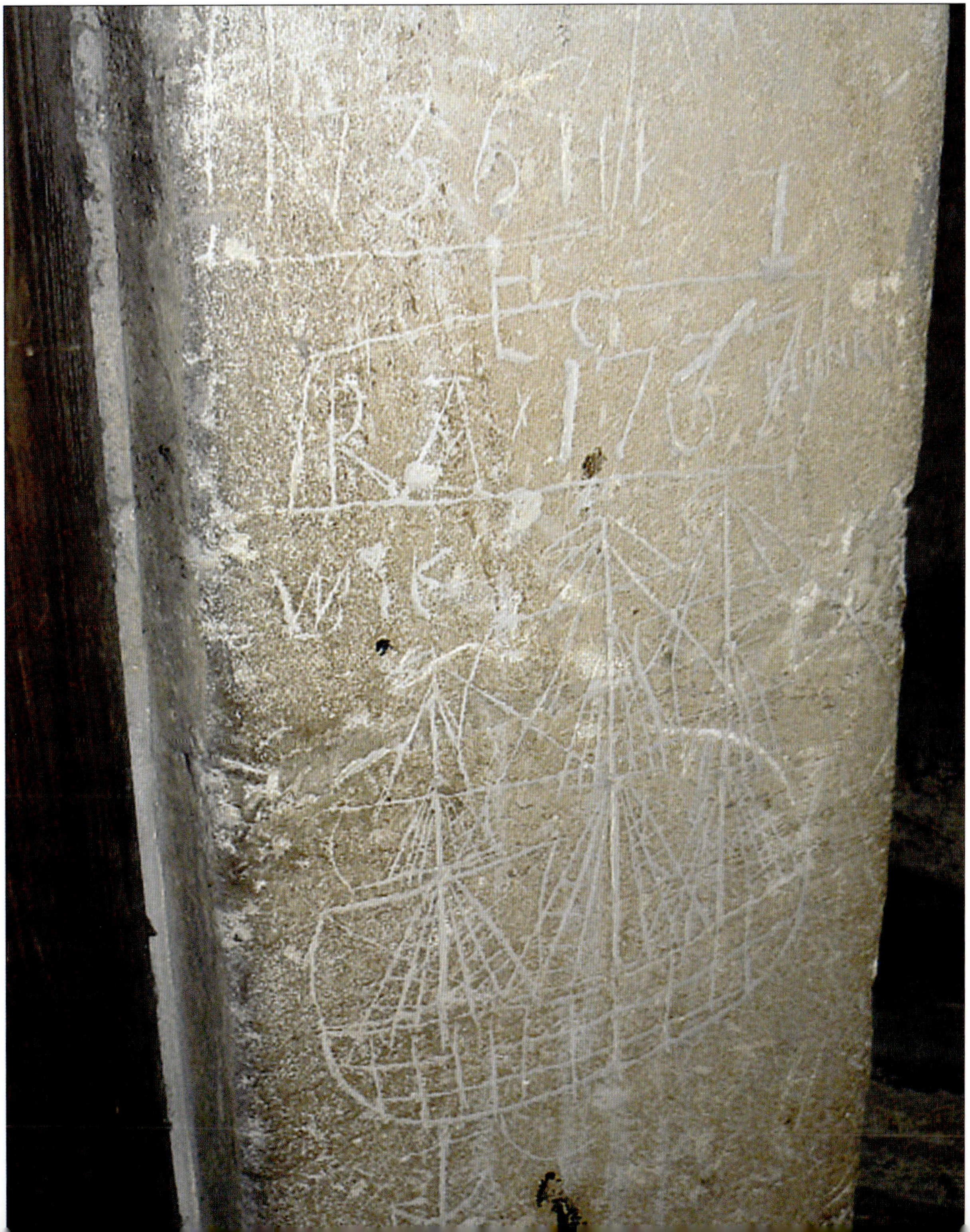

Graffiti of a ship with » three masts, full rigging, and anchors carved into stone at St. Sampson's, Cricklade.
Photo courtesy of Brian Robert Marshall, Geography Org, United Kingdom.

New World Ship Graffiti

In the Bahamas, there are several sites featuring ship graffiti that were most likely made by slaves. This is not an isolated occurrence, though, as ship graffiti can also be found in Puerto Rico, the Dominican Republic, on the Turks and Caicos Islands, and in Martha's Vineyard in Massachusetts. The drawings are of different ships, drawn in different styles with varying skill, and are believed to be made over a period of years, perhaps decades or even centuries.

One grouping of graffiti was found in the Jose Maria cave system in the Dominican Republic. These drawings were made using a mixture of clay and charcoal and seem to represent food and other produce loaded onto a Spanish ship. It is most probably the work of the indigenous population showing the early dealings between them and the unscrupulous Europeans. The graffiti in San Cristobel in San Juan, Puerto Rico, on the other hand, appears to be the work of an artillery captain held at the fort there. He used red, yellow, and black paint for his work and the details on the ship, especially its rigging, suggest he knew the anatomy of his ships well. Scientists have put the age of the graffiti before the early eighteenth century.

Old graffiti at Thornton Abbey showing simple ships but with quite complex rigging.
Photo courtesy of Miranda Hodgson, Geography Org, United Kingdom.

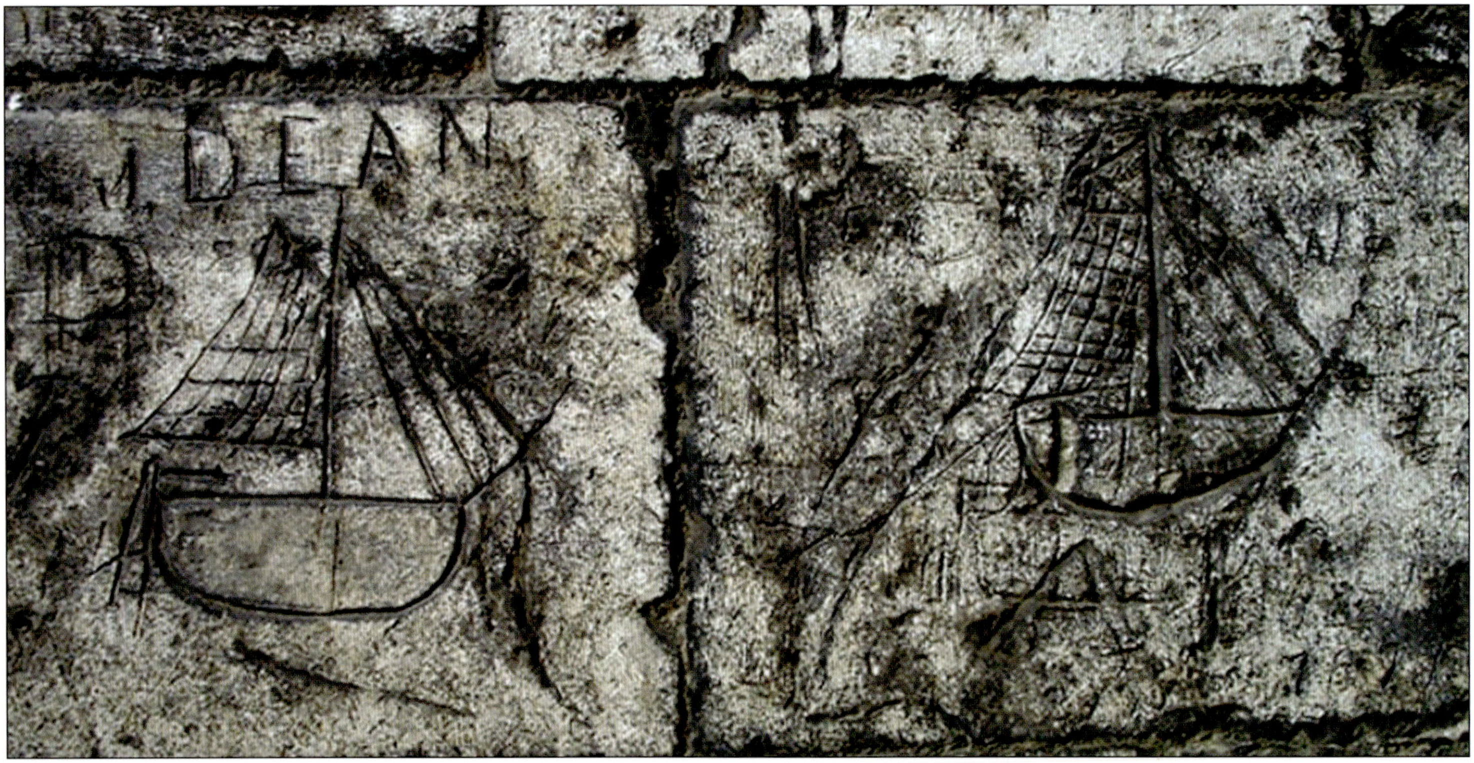

At Martha's Vineyard, graffiti has been found engraved into the wooden beams and posts of the houses that date from the seventeenth to the eighteenth centuries, and these pictorials also show a professional knowledge of ships by the amount of detail in them. They were compared with contemporary illustrations of ships of the same time and were immediately identifiable.

Graffiti is not a modern phenomenon. We have seen Viking mercenaries and raiders leaving their names on the monuments of other peoples in far-off countries, for what other reason than to leave a trace of their presence after they left. What began as images on cave walls—which may have been made with the idea of taking control over the animals they represented—soon began to form into written language. The need to communicate, to tell a story, is an inherent trait of the human race. All people tell stories. Writing and drawing are extensions of this need to impart ideas from one mind to another.

The history of graffiti, which began as its etymology suggests from scratching made in stone, developed quickly as writing emerged and soon became a way of letting others know who went where and when—and even why and what they thought about. As we leave the early history of graffiti and enter the modern era, we will see that things did not necessarily change but morphed in some surprising ways. Modern-day graffiti split into different types, but it continues to retain a fundamental element linking it to graffiti throughout the ages.

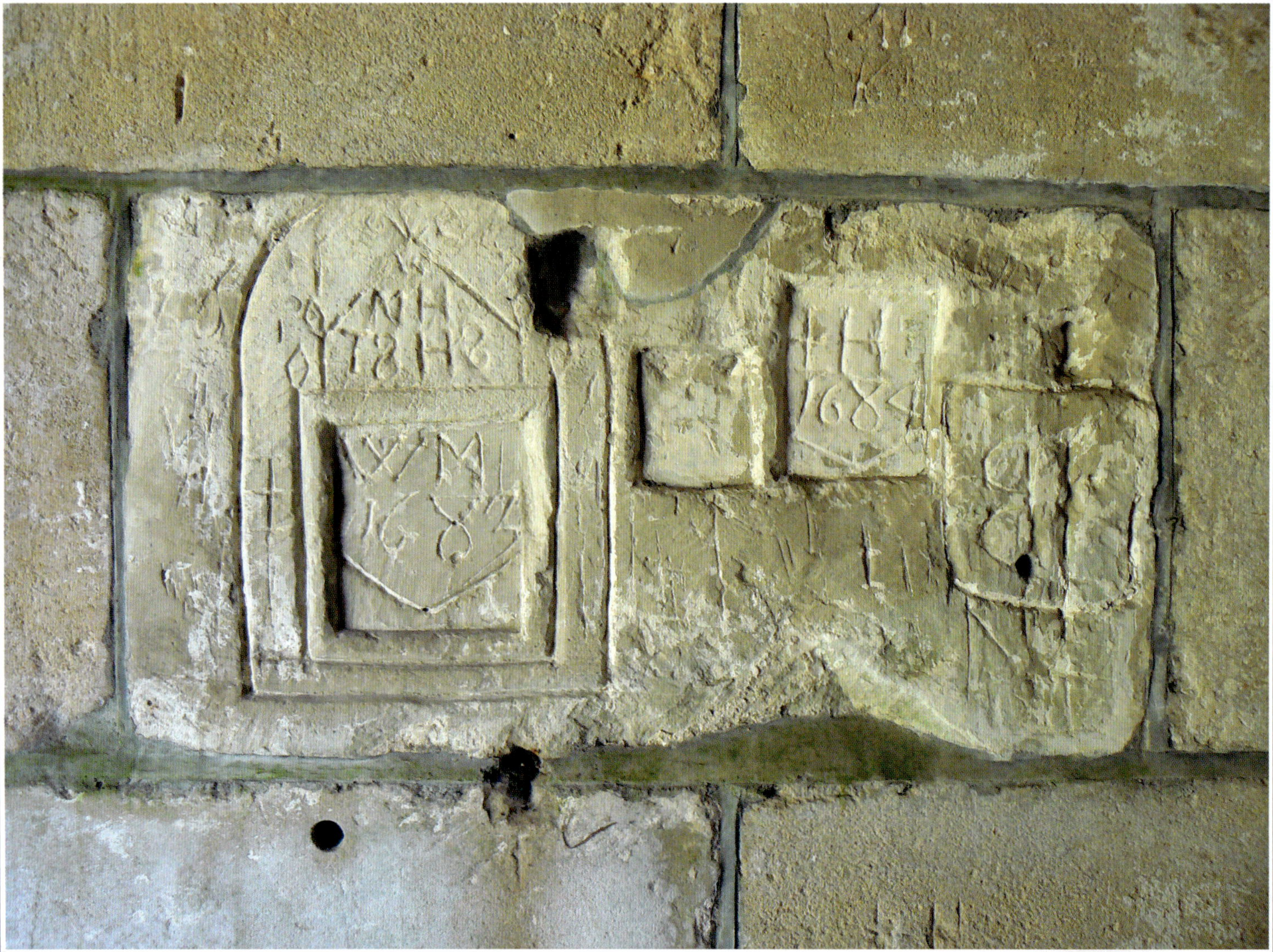

≈ Graffiti carved deeply into stone or plaster over stone in a church. The dates 1683 and 1684 can be seen.
Photo courtesy of Brian Marshall.

GRAFFITI UP UNTIL THE TWENTIETH CENTURY

CHALK AND HILL FIGURES

In the hillside of Britain, large figures—primarily horses and men—have been cut into the turf. Who made them and why has long been a puzzle for historians and archaeologists alike. Some of the graffiti can be dated to prehistoric times, but others, once thought to be thousands of years old, are now considered to be only a few hundred years old at most. It has also been noted that many are actually political satire.

There are examples of hill drawings in other parts of the world, such as in Peru where the desert is the canvas for the Nazca Lines. The stony, barren conditions in which these lines were made were more conducive to the longevity of the drawing and thus we are able to study them in more detail. Conversely, several large images documented in Britain have now become so overgrown that it is impossible to identify them any longer. The remaining and best-known of the chalk drawings have been maintained over the

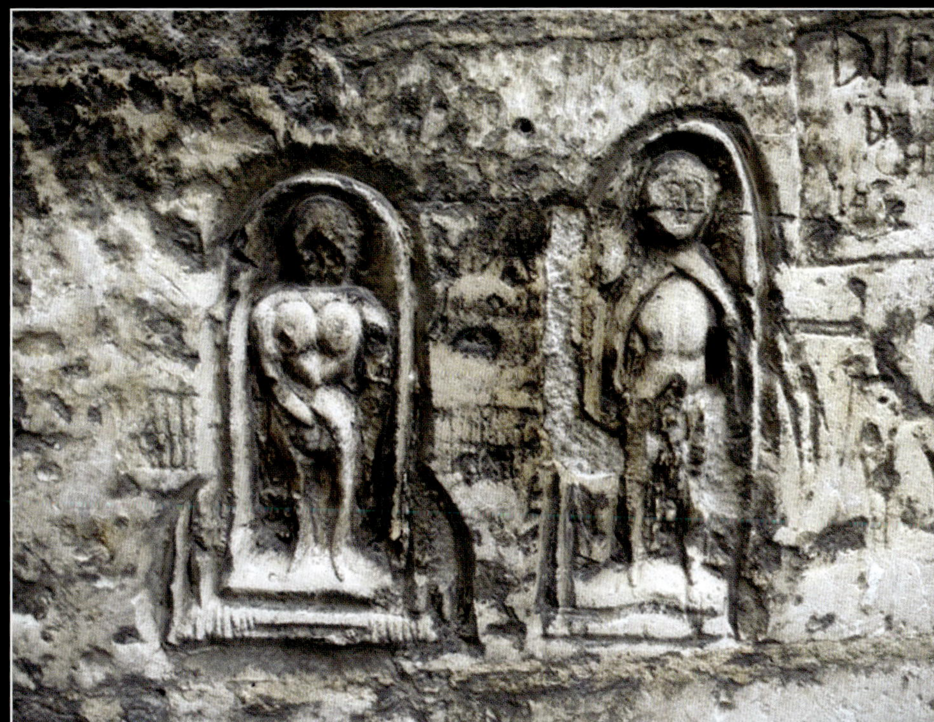

Similar graffiti is found across the English Channel in France, as can be seen in this piece featuring two human figures. It is hard to make out who they are, probably saints.

Photo courtesy of P.D. Lecron.

Uffington White Horse

In the Berkshire Downs lies what is perhaps the most well-known chalk figure in the world, dating back to the Bronze Age, somewhere between 1400 and 600 BC. The image, which is considered by most to be a rendering of a highly stylized and animated horse (though this is questioned by some) had been considered, until recently, to be the creation of Anglo-Saxons. But through a number of modern methods of dating, it is now definite that the figure is far older than the Dark Ages and coins from the time of pre-Roman Britain show horse figures that resemble that of the Uffington chalk horse, which also affirms its Bronze Age dating.

Although it was made in the trench method discussed previously, the Uffington Horse still required regular clearing of plant material that constantly threatened to obscure it throughout the ages. The process was held every few years, it seems, and was accompanied by a fair and other festivities held in the immediate area.

Because of its old age, intrinsic beauty, and general air of mystery, the Uffington Horse is considered an important cultural icon for the British people. Therefore, when members of the Real Countryside Alliance added a rider and three

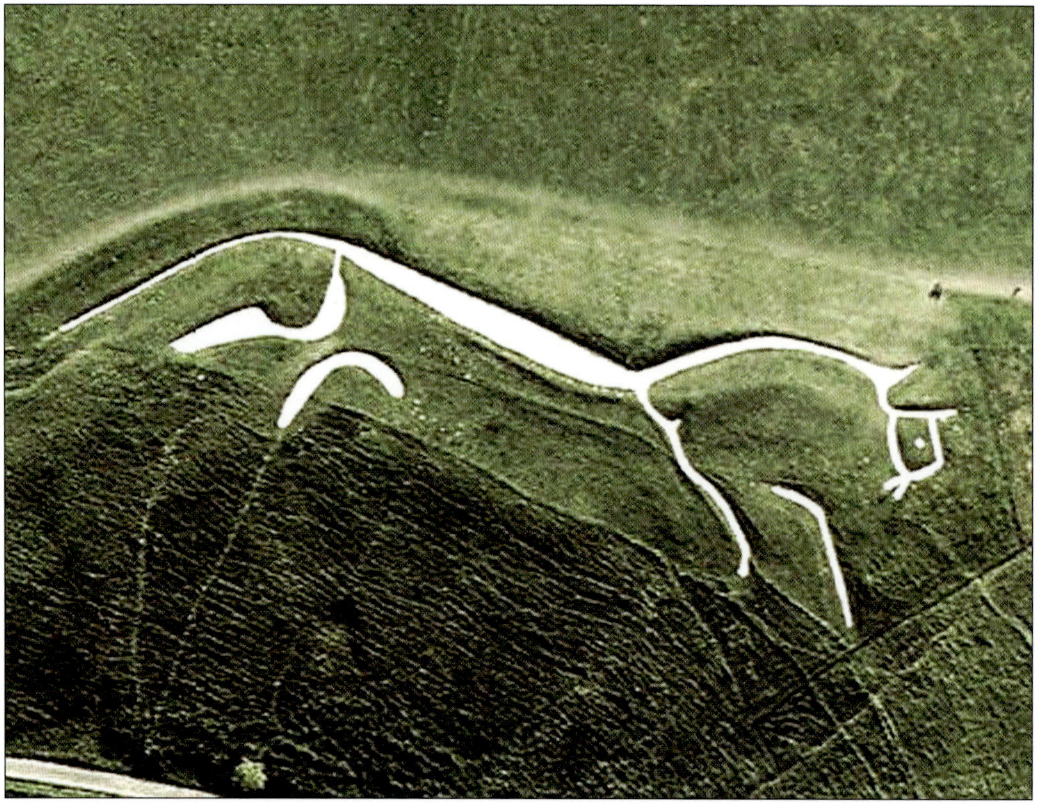

« The White Horse at Uffington in the United Kingdom prances across the hillside and has probably done so for 2,000 to 3,000 years. The animal is highly stylized and its form may well have changed over the years as the locals work to keep it visible. It may not have even been a figure of a horse to begin with, but some other creature; however, it has been called a horse for a long time.

hounds to the running horse, there was a general outcry and the act was condemned as vandalism. Ten years later, a similar addition was made to the horse in the name of a publicity stunt by a bookmaker. Presumably, the jockey was a very temporary addition and the bookmaker had obtained permission from the authorities to add the drawing. This is a good example, though, of the ongoing debate about graffiti and it being an act of vandalism, which we will come to later in the book.

Westbury White Horse

Another British chalk horse, whose age is more dubious than the Uffington Horse, is the Westbury White Horse, which is situated on a hillside rising up from Salisbury Plain. This animal is stationary and more realistic in style, but in its present form only dates back with any assurance to its restoration date in the late-eighteenth century. The earliest documentary evidence of a horse in this location, however, is from 1742, and a drawing made twenty years later shows a different horse facing in the opposite direction.

Legend has it that the Westbury White Horse was carved into the hillside after King Alfred's success at the Battle of Eðandun in 878 AD. The problem with this theory, though, is that the legend does not appear in historical record before the eighteenth century, calling into question its authenticity. Also, the site of the battle has never been definitely placed

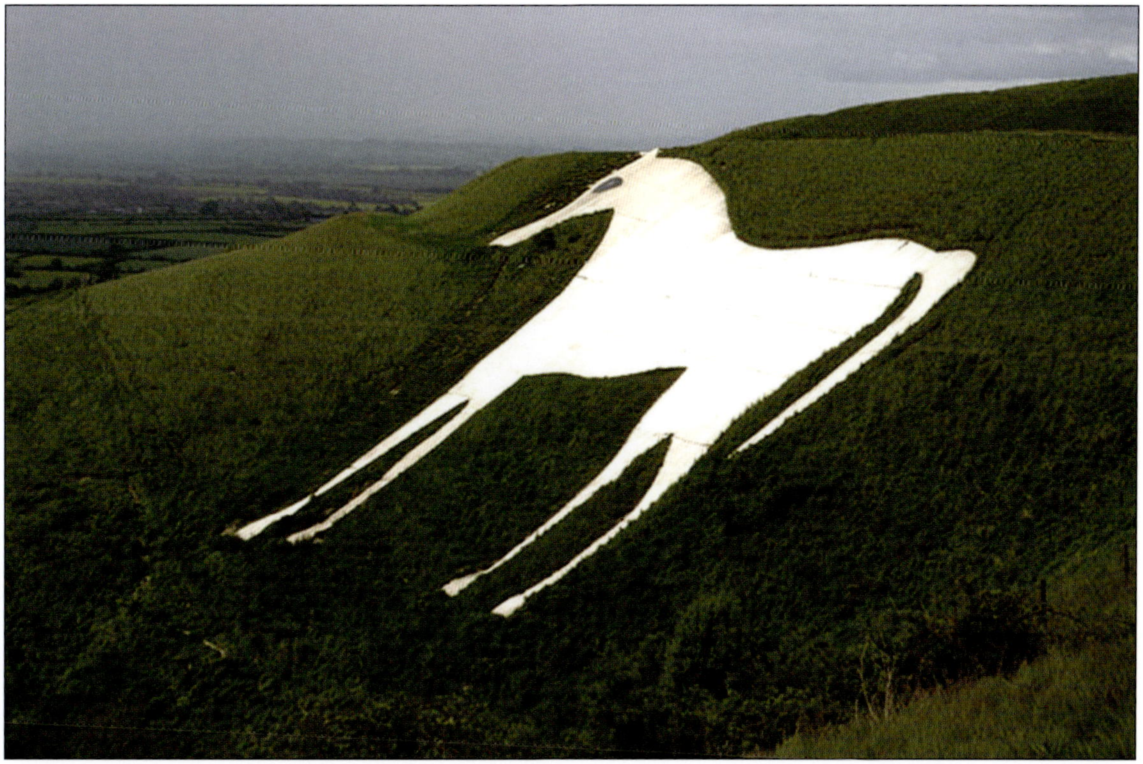

This is a much more realistic » representation of a horse than the animal of Uffington. It is also a static figure and does not have the life or joy that its much older cousin offers.
Photo courtesy of Roger Gittins, Geography Org, United Kingdom.

There is a vast difference between the two versions of » the Westbury chalk horse. The original animal may not have been a horse; its one Cyclops-like eye and forked tail suggest a mythical beast. The eighteenth-century revision of the work has completely remodeled it, turning it to face the opposite direction and making an unmistakable rendition of a horse.

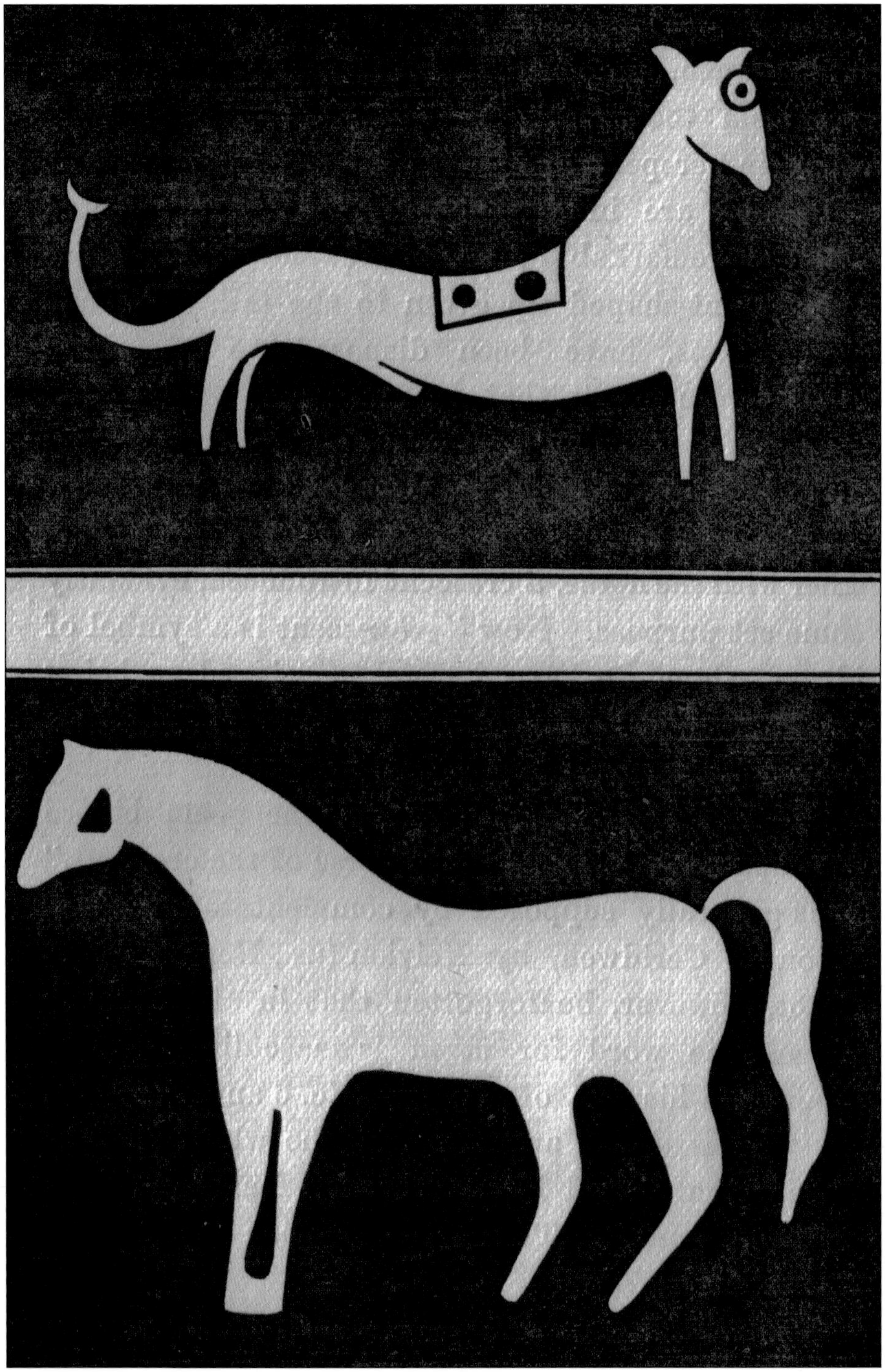

at this location either. So the age of the horse still remains somewhat of a mystery.

The use of the horse as a motif in graffiti in general is often linked to the Anglo-Saxon invasion of Britain and the importance of the horse to those peoples. As seen with the Uffington Horse, the image of the horse has also been found on much older coinage from before the Christian Era. Thus, it is reasonable to link the Westbury White Horse with the time in which the Uffington Horse was created, but it is more likely that its creation was closer to the eighteenth century—and it was at this time that the House of Hanover, who used a white horse as its symbol, became the new Royal House in England. So it is possible the Westbury White Horse was simply a byproduct of this new royal family.

Cerne Abbas Giant

Apart from horses, of which there have been sixteen or seventeen (both ancient and modern) cut into the English countryside, there have also been several large humanoid figures that are popularly known as "giants" created throughout the country.

An enormous picture of a crude and naked man wielding a massive club presides over the village of Cerne Abbas in Dorset. His primitive demeanor and highly prominent, upright penis have made many people assume this giant is of ancient origin. However, to pinpoint a realistic date of creation for such an image, it is important to look at historical documentary evidence. To begin with, the first written mention of the giant appeared in the churchwarden's accounts for the village only in 1694, referring to payment made for repairs done to the figure. This suggests that the giant had been in the vicinity long enough to require maintenance. However, a land survey performed in 1617 makes no mention of the giant whatsoever. And it wasn't until well into the following century that written references were more frequently made concerning the Cerne Abbas giant. Even though it was suggested as early as 1774 that the giant had only been carved in the previous century, on research undertaken by a well-known antiquarian, John Hutchins, the idea that the giant was from deep antiquity persisted among many. The Somersetshire Archaeological and Natural History Society

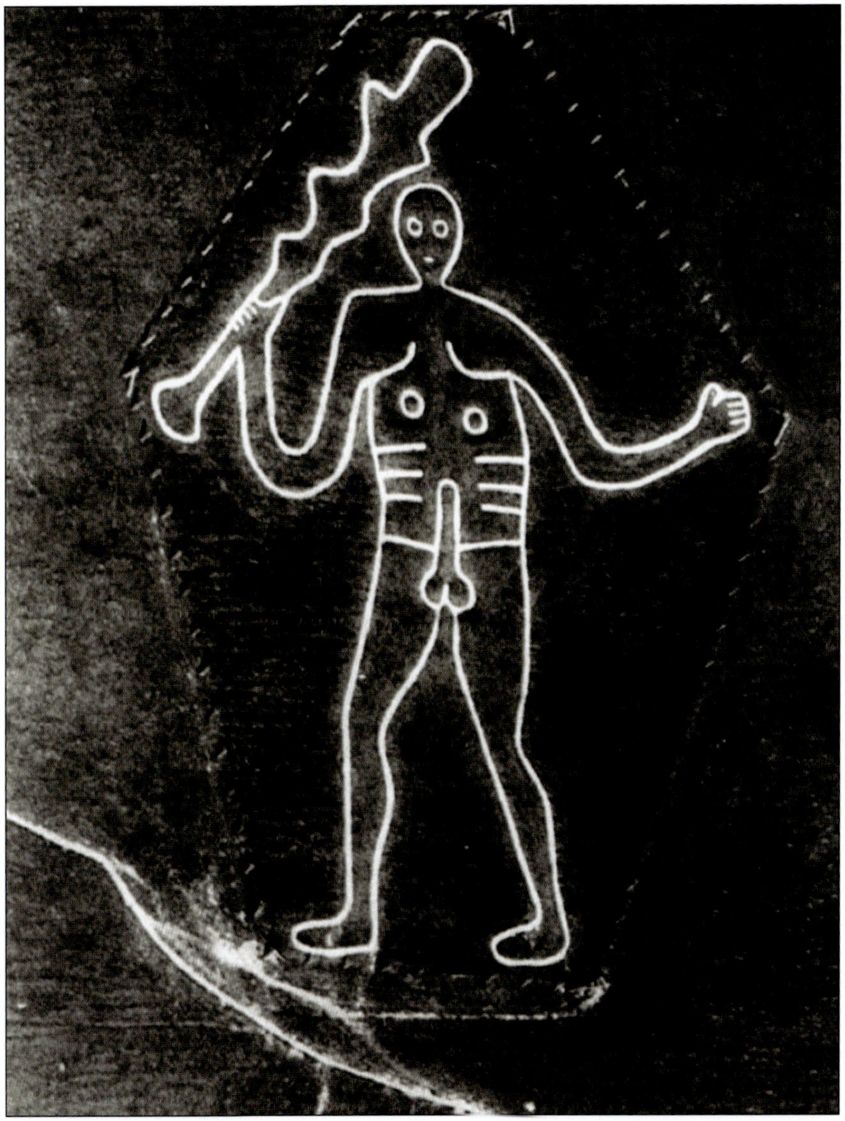

The giant man of Cerne Abbas » suggests a primitive giant from a distant era, but there is no evidence that it was made any earlier than the mid- to late-sixteenth century if that.

were convinced that the giant was of ancient origins, but this was based solely on the physical appearance of the giant and not any precise documentation.

One of the strongest pieces of evidence against the giant having ancient origins, though, is the fact that there is no mention of this "giant" before the seventeenth century. Surely, as the argument goes, such a distinctive landmark would have been the talk of the area from its earliest inception. Post-seventeenth-century legend has named the giant a fertility figure from prehistory and has also coined it a version of Hercules, which would place its origin at the time of Roman occupation of the country, but again, without evidence of earlier descriptions of the painting, it is difficult to be certain of its date of creation.

Archaeological research from the last twenty years has brought to light features of the giant that have changed or disappeared over time. One of these was the addition of a cloak slung over his arm that is not holding a club. A cloak would fit in well with the theory that the giant is indeed a depiction of Hercules and that the cloak is actually the skin of the Nemean lion with which he was commonly depicted. The overlarge penis may have also been the result of maintenance that re-cut the navel with a much more modest appendage.

Stories from the locals abound about the origins of the giant as well, giving it somewhat of a legendary past. Some people state that he is the outline of a real giant who had been lying on the hillside or who had even died there. Another persists that he was a Danish giant invading the English and was killed while he lay sleeping. Then there are others who prefer the theory that the giant is connected with fertility magic and sleeping, or better still, that making love on top of the giant's phallus would cure infertility.

If the giant was indeed made as recently as the mid-seventeenth century, then the question as to why it was made is particularly intriguing. Why would someone in the relatively civilized seventeenth century want to make such a primitive-looking figure in such a prominent position? Some now believe that the Cerne Abbas giant was actually a piece of political satire and was in fact a parody of the Parliamentarian Oliver Cromwell. Cromwell was also known as the British Hercules, which furthers this supposition.

The Cerne Abbas Giant has received a number of additions just as the Westbury Horse has over the years. None of the extras have caused any significant damage and all have been done in humor and goodwill. The figure has been used to promote a variety of modern-day commodities and has even been used to promote the wearing of blue jeans, the use of condoms (an obvious one), and even the Olympic Games.

HILLSIDE LETTERS

Hillside letters is a modern phenomenon particularly prevalent in the United States. The extra large letters and texts are classified as geoglyphs and first emerged in the early part of the twentieth century. The first recorded letter was an uppercase "C" made from concrete and placed on a hillside overlooking the University of California, Berkeley.

There is a myth that this and other letters placed in prominent positions were created so that airplanes delivering mail would know where to mail drop. However, the real reason for the construction of letters and slogans has nothing to do with this bogus story. Hillside letters as a form of graffiti began at UC Berkeley where rival classes had been displaying outrageous behavior toward each other. The construction and placement of a giant C was decided upon by the classes of 1907 and 1908 as a joint project that would bring an end to these class animosities.

The C at Berkeley set a precedent and was soon copied by the placement of a letter "U" at the University of Utah in Salt Lake City. The next to follow suit was Brigham Young University at Provo, Utah, which placed a letter "Y" on a nearby hillside. Soon Colorado School of Mines in Golden, Colorado, placed a letter "M" on a hillside—a precursor to the famous Golden Arches—to stand for the miners that made up the community. This letter has been floodlit since the 1930s.

Letters soon began springing up across the country. Universities were emulated by schools and other places of higher learning who started placing letters on hillsides near their establishments. To date, there are at least five hundred super-sized letters and slogans across the United States—a unusual form of graffiti.

GRAFFITI AND THE GRAND TOUR

Today, if someone attempted to initial a monument or to scrawl a message on a natural wonder, that person would most likely be arrested. But just a few centuries ago, it was considered the popular thing to do and many tourists visiting great cultural and historical sites left their marks, which can still be seen to this day.

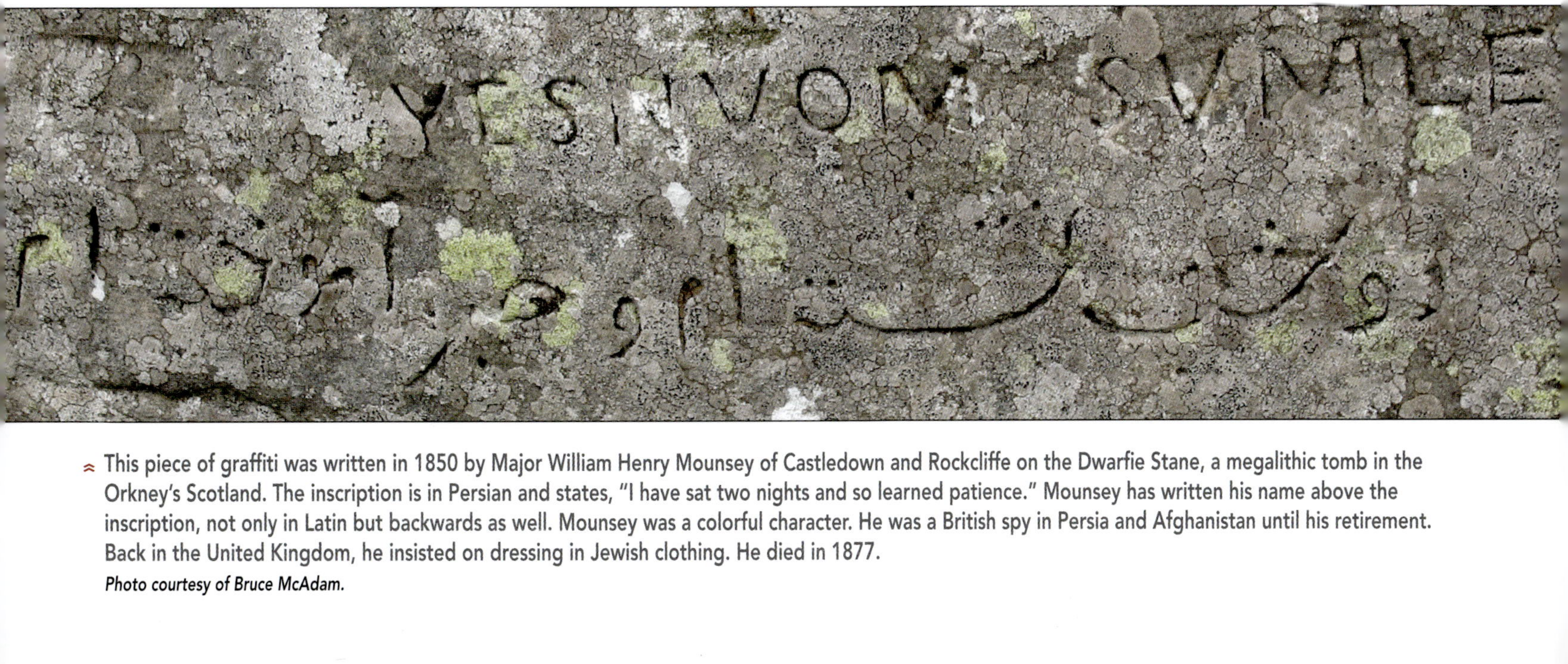

This piece of graffiti was written in 1850 by Major William Henry Mounsey of Castledown and Rockcliffe on the Dwarfie Stane, a megalithic tomb in the Orkney's Scotland. The inscription is in Persian and states, "I have sat two nights and so learned patience." Mounsey has written his name above the inscription, not only in Latin but backwards as well. Mounsey was a colorful character. He was a British spy in Persia and Afghanistan until his retirement. Back in the United Kingdom, he insisted on dressing in Jewish clothing. He died in 1877.
Photo courtesy of Bruce McAdam.

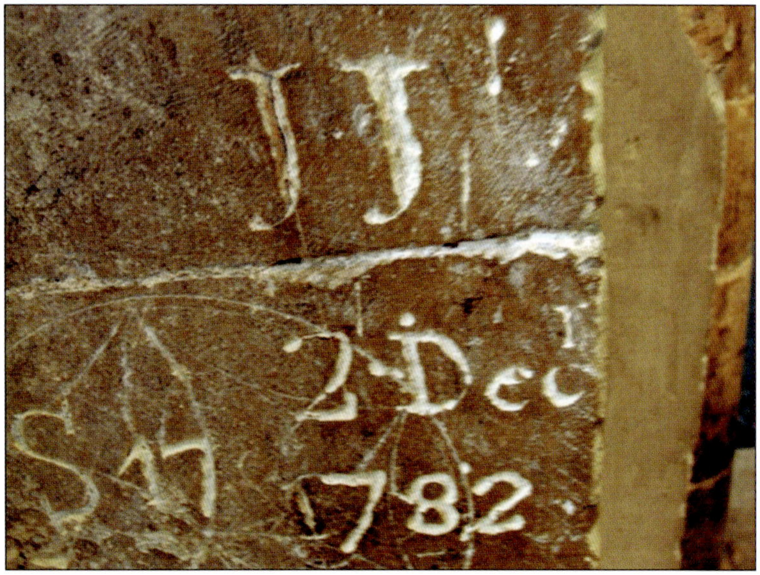

≈ A close-up of graffiti etched in the stone of Rochester Cathedral in 1782.
Photo courtesy of Chris Whippet, Geography Org, United Kingdom.

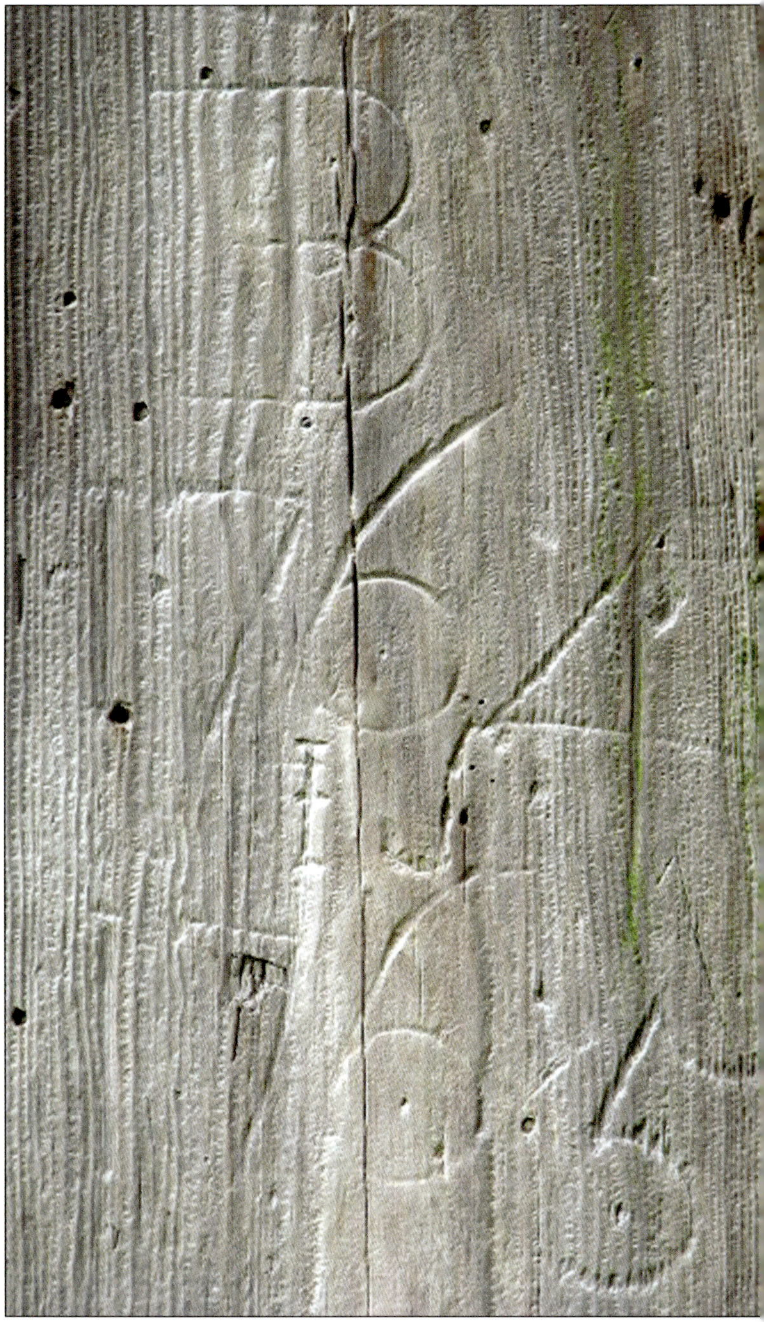

St. Michael's Church shows graffiti carved into wood. There are two dates: 1764 and another under it showing 1765. »
Photo courtesy of Evelyn Simak, Geography Org, United Kingdom.

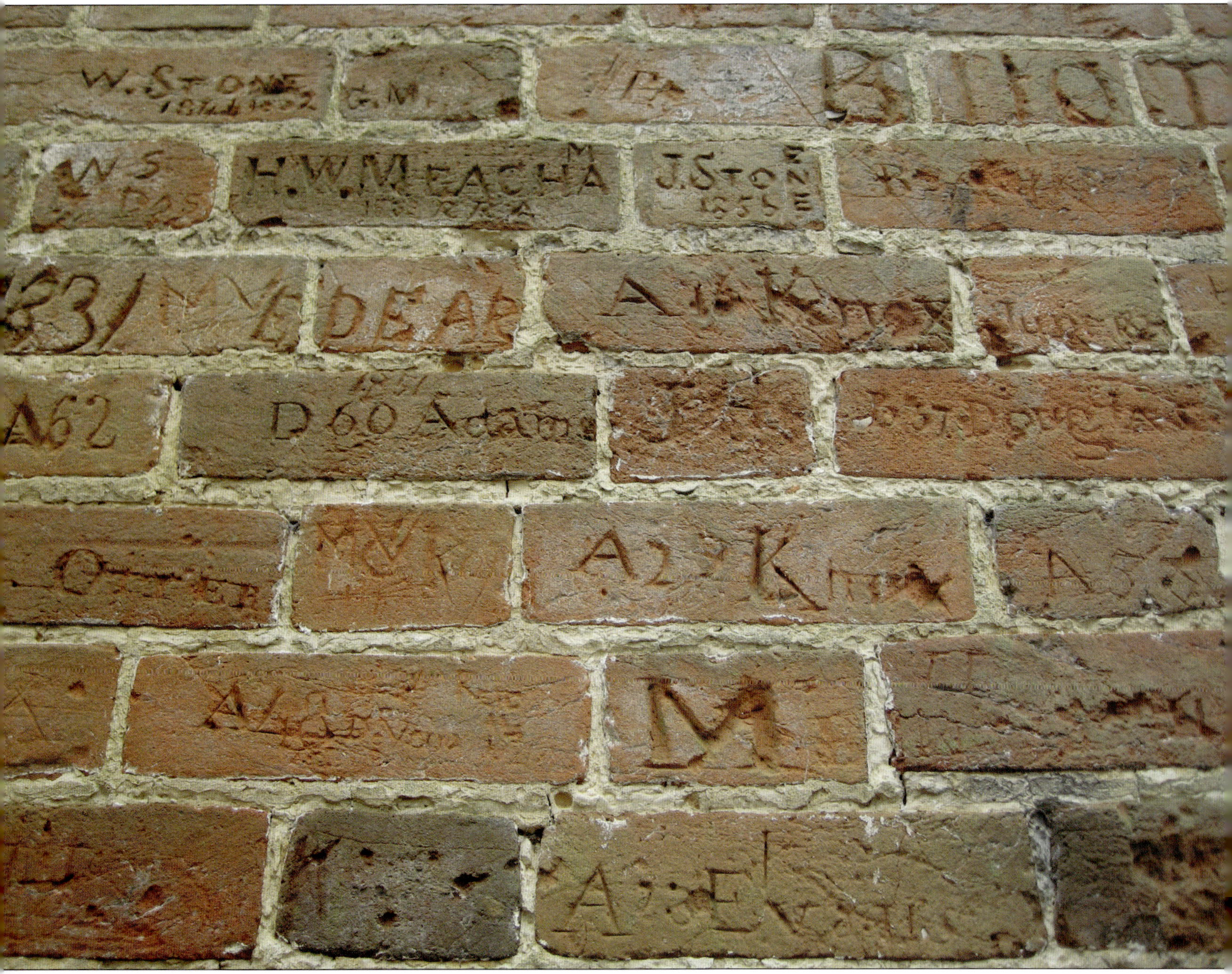

Many carefully-made names and dates are found on Norris's Obelisk.
Photo courtesy of BabelStone.

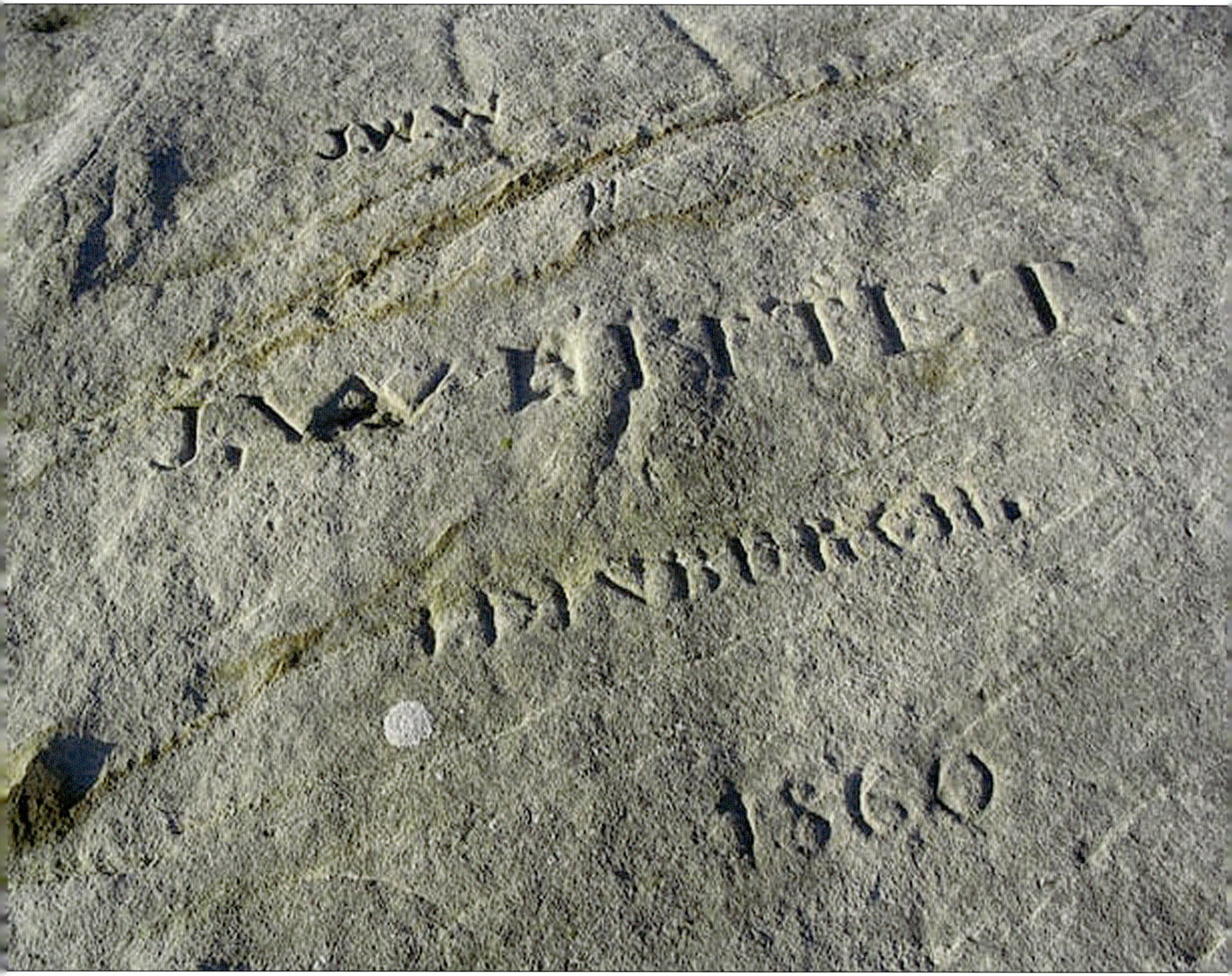

Petroglyphs made in 1860—simply a name and a date but carved quite meticulously. It would have taken time and patience to do this.
Photo courtesy of Walter Baxter, Geography Org, United Kingdom.

Many well to-do Englishmen and women used to embark on the culturally weighty task of touring Europe, known as the Grand Tour. Among the destinations, Italy was an essential spot, as were the places where great painters, poets, and thinkers had lived and were buried. Petrarch's tomb and the villa in which he had lived were prominent on the list and it had been the practice of tourists during these pilgrimages to scrawl their initials, full names, and the dates of their visit onto the walls of Petrarch's house (but never on the tomb itself). To remedy this vandalism, which made quite a mess, it was decided in 1787 to provide a visitors book at the house instead. The original book is now on display in the house and is called the Codici di Arquà.

No new graffiti has been noted on the structure for many years, but some of the earlier work is also now part of the visiting experience. There is a piece written by a group of Austrian students back in 1564 on one of the fireplaces that remains to this day. In fact, for a long time, the house was actually occupied by a family who seemed to welcome the visitors and who took no issue with the graffiti they left.

VICTORIAN GRAFFITI

Graffiti was no means a dying art by the time of the reign of Queen Victoria, although attitudes to its practice were not always as tolerant as they had previously been. Newspapers reported incidents they thought newsworthy, or amusing, in conjunction with graffiti, such as the event that occurred on the fence surrounding the premises of Mr. Keaton's house. A father and son team had written in chalk all over the fence the following: "Warren's Liquid Blacking." This was not an attack on Mr. Keaton, but rather it was the unauthorized use of his fence as an impromptu billboard.

A similar case of guerrilla advertising—as it is called today—was undertaken by William Simpson Lawson, who was an agent for a tea company. He was charged a number of times with having hired the services of William Jones, John Smith, and Joseph Thomson to paint or chalk up advertising for his business on private property.

One of the offended parties was Mr. Webb, who rented the railway arches between the city and Blackwall specifically for advertising purposes. Mr. Lawson employed these men to write up the following slogan: "Use the London Tea Company's famous pure teas." But when the man were caught with paint in hand and apprehended, the magistrate told the court that it was the instigator of the graffiti who should be charged and not his lowly henchman. So Lawson was summonsed and when found guilty of the charge of defacement of a wall, he was fined ultimately twenty shillings and made to have the wall lime washed.

A different type of graffiti was chalked on a wall in Regent's Park, London, at about the same time in 1861. The man charged for the crime was Edward Bambrook and he had written the words "What nation can fight?" Bambrook, it was discovered later, had already been in trouble over vandalism to statues of Queen Victoria and Prince Albert. But when brought before the magistrate a second time, Bambrook claimed that he wrote those words in response to his

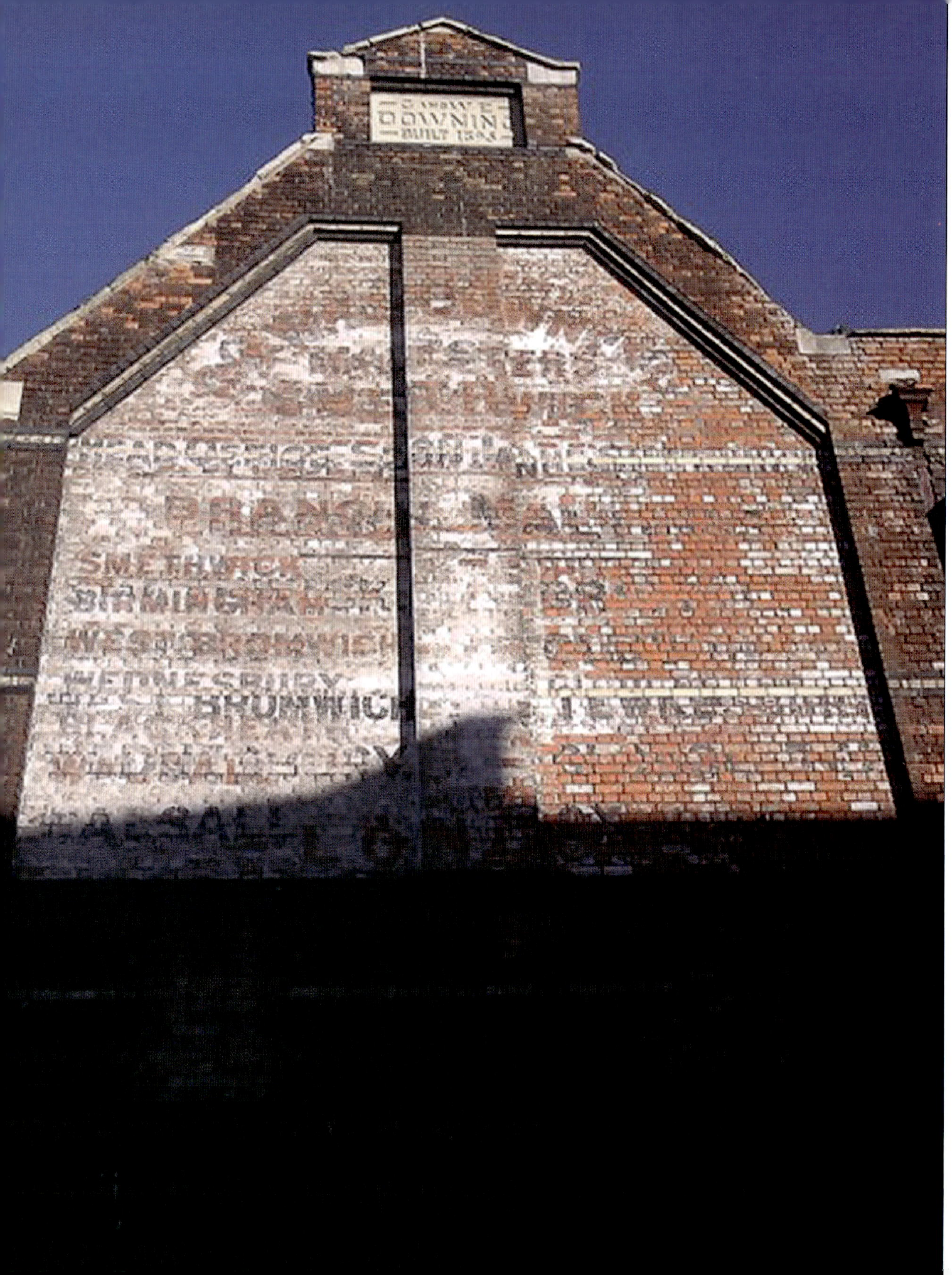

« Lettering was written on the sides of buildings to advertize goods sold at those premises or an address would be given for goods sold at another location. This type of graffiti was legitimate and paid for just like advertising billboards today. This building shows the faint remnants of previous advertising with layers showing through layers.
Photo courtesy of Brian Marshall.

reading the Book of Daniel and was trying to fulfill the various prophecies he found there and in other Old Testament books.

Another act of religious verve or moral indignation was made by a young, eighteen-year-old woman named Elizabeth Fairbanks, who was also found to be inciting a much younger girl to act with her. Fairbanks and her accomplice were found busily defacing the wall of a private house with obscene words. When asked why she was doing so, she claimed that the house was a brothel and needed to be shamed. Whatever the intentions behind the act, Fairbanks was found guilty and fined ten shillings (or she would have to face imprisonment for seven days).

What we have come to know of as "modern" graffiti was not exactly unknown of in Victorian times, either. There is written evidence that scribbles and words, not necessarily offensive, were found in great numbers among certain streets in Glasgow. It was considered an eyesore, though—much like some of today's graffiti is considered—and a letter to a newspaper in 1859 demanded that something be done about it.

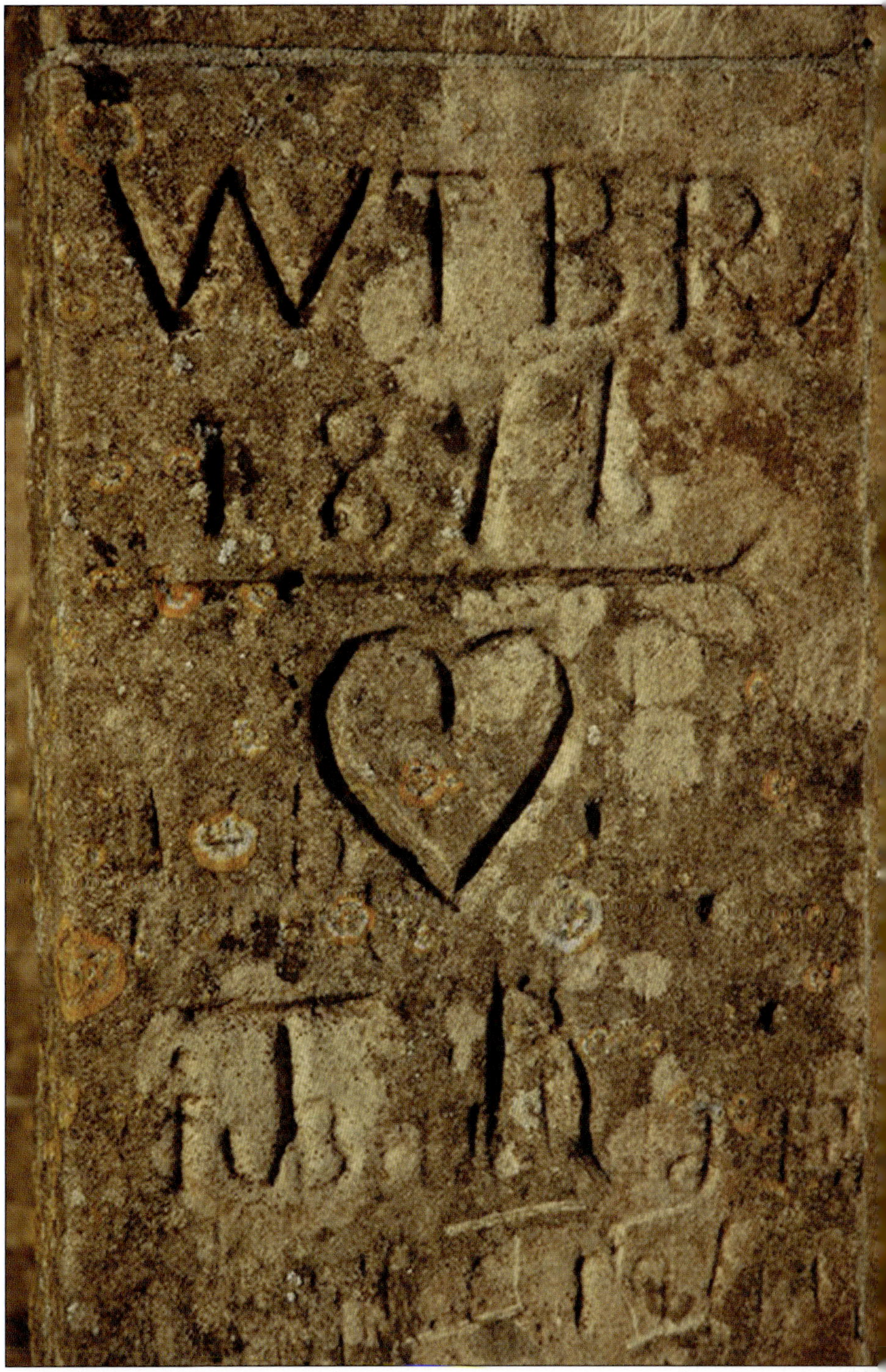

Hearts were popular in the nineteenth century » and here is a lovely example of one carved in stone with the date 1876 and initials above and below it. It is also possible to make out previous graffiti underneath, but not carved as deeply or as expertly as this monument to eternal love.
Photo courtesy of Philip Halling, Geography Org, United Kingdom.

In fact, graffiti was such a common crime during the rule of Queen Victoria that it was mentioned in the handbook for trainee police at the turn of the twentieth century in London, explaining to officers how to deal with the matter:

> 43. *A gentleman complains to you of rude and indecent words being chalked on the outside of his premises, by children from a neighbouring street. Having before complained to the police of similar nuisance, with no effect, he now wishes strong measures to be taken. What steps would you take?*
>
> P.C . . . . *(No.)* . . . . *(name)*, reports that at . . . . AM . . . . inst., a gentleman . . . . *(name)* . . . . *(occupation)* . . . . *(address)*, complained of great annoyance caused by children from . . . . Street (adjoining) chalking rude and indecent words on the outside of his walls and shutters; and also stated that having before complained of similar nuisance, he now wished strong measures to be taken to prevent a recurrence.

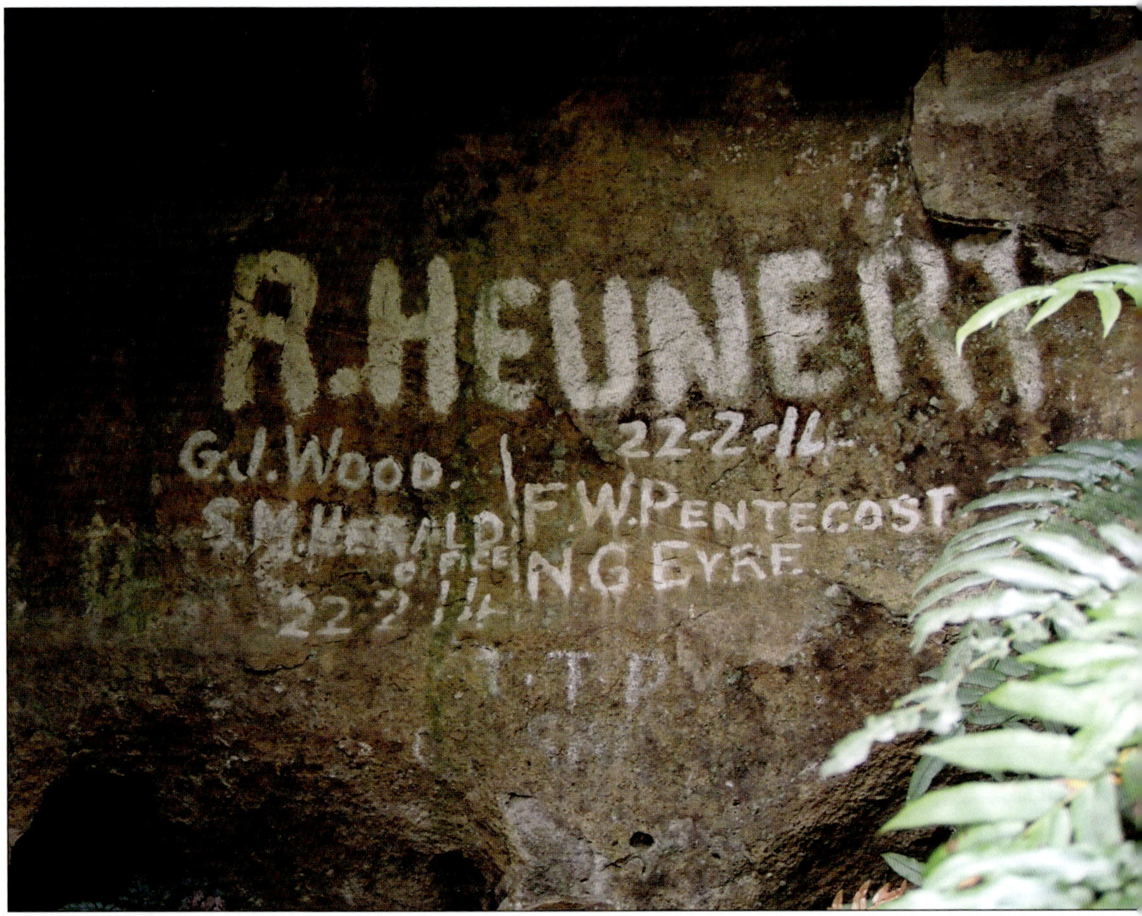

The rather ugly white paint was » splashed onto this popular tourist spot in the Blue Mountains in 1914. It may well be the initials and surnames of young men who went to fight in the First World War. One wonders if they came back or lost their lives overseas.

P.C. at once obliterated the words complained of, and informed complainant that he would duly report the matter so that it should be read out to each relief; and in the meantime he would keep strict observation to detect the offenders.

Graffiti was certainly showing signs of its modern self in Victorian times. The notion that it could be offensive and that a perpetrator could be prosecuted for it is certainly a forerunner of what cities were going to be facing a hundred years in the future. Up until the late-nineteenth century, it seems that leaving graffiti was not strictly thought of as an act that required punishment. Countries didn't discourage visitors from leaving their calling cards in the form of initials and dates incised into ancient monuments; rather it was encouraged and viewed as a means to pocket tourists' cash. It appears that trouble came about only when someone tried to get something for free, like advertising space, at a time when it was becoming the norm to charge people rent for it.

As we look at the twentieth and twenty-first centuries, and the graffiti made then, we see how the viewpoint changed radically from something that was once quite acceptable to something that is often seen as an abomination that should be scrubbed out beyond recognition.

LATRINALIA

Latrinalia is derived from the latin "latrine" plus "alia," which means a worthless collection of something. This term was coined in 1966 by eminent folklorist Alan Dundes specifically in reference to the scribbles found more frequently in toilets and bathrooms around the world.

We have seen that graffiti in public bathroom stalls is by no means a modern phenomenon and that the scrawling of initials, names, and often sexually-explicit messages on the walls and doors of toilets and other public places has carried out for at least two thousand

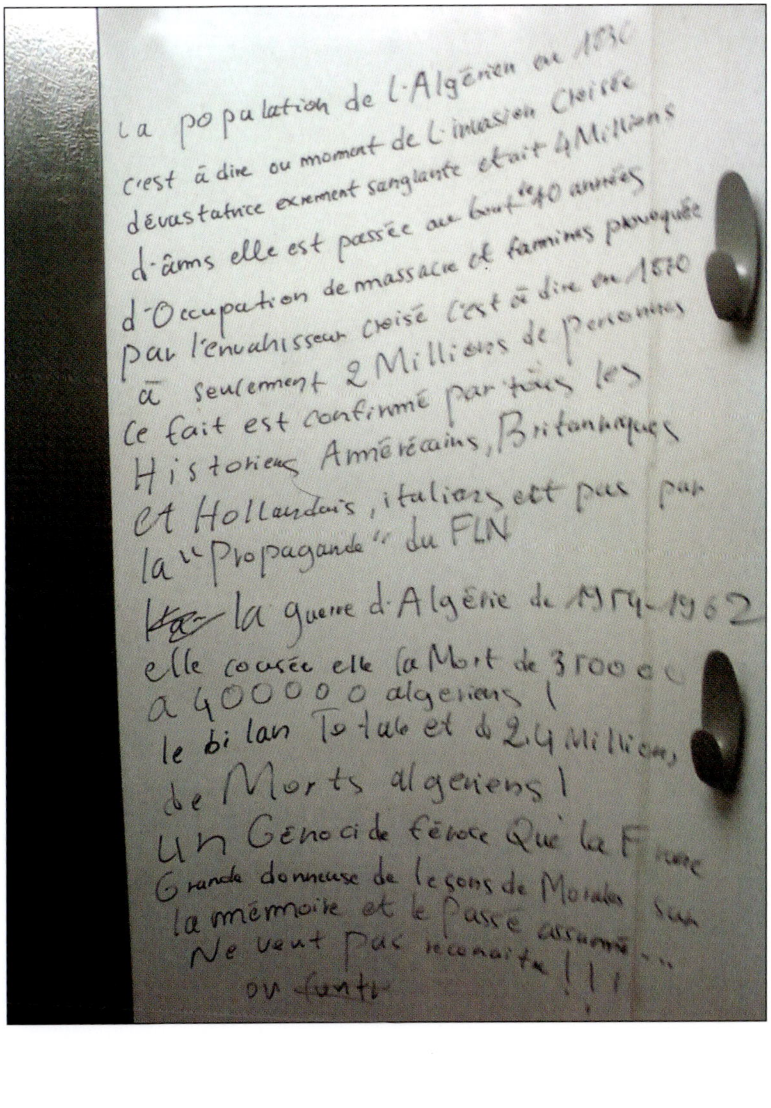

Writing in French on a restroom wall » showing not the usual toilet humor, but rather a political statement. *Photo courtsey of Mickael Denet.*

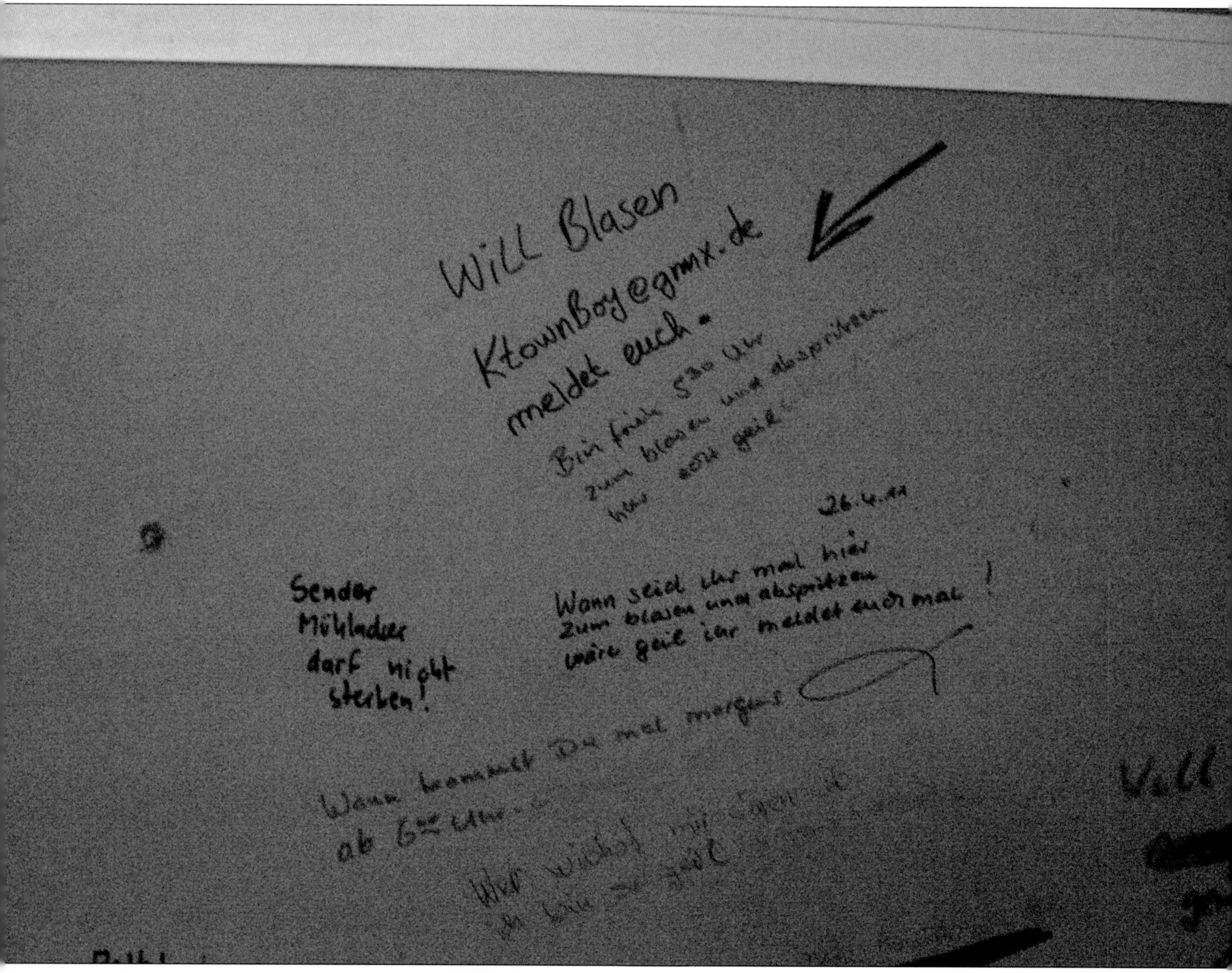

≈ This German piece, on the other hand, is typical of the writing found in public restrooms the world over and can be deciphered by anyone.

years. And we still giggle at the wittier ones and cringe at the outright vulgar and malicious ones, such as this one: "Here I sit, broken hearted, tried to shit but only farted."

Not only has latrinalia graffiti been around for thousands of years, but it has also sparked a desire to collect choice pieces and publish them. Hurlo Thrumbo (a pseudonym) put together *The Merry-Thought: or the Glass-Window and Bog-House Miscellany* in 1731 and was, by all accounts, in very poor taste and not suitable for ladies or gentlemen of polite society. At the time the collection was made, men and women did not have separate public toilets to use, so there was the opportunity for a lot of banter between the sexes to take place in their various graffitied phrases. Not only did men and women write crude ditties on toilet walls, but they also scratched them onto window panes in public houses. There were even rings available with diamond points made just for this purpose.

The Merry-Thought collection, at its best, makes for fascinating reading; at worst, it offers more of the same old vulgar crudities that we encounter today in public bathrooms. It demonstrates that graffiti in these often low-brow places would often spark responses from subsequent patrons and even returnees so that quite a dialogue would be recorded, although it was rarely of any great intellect or insight.

The difference between the latrinalia of men and women, however, is demonstrated in the pieces to do with love and lust. Men find women are insatiable where sex is concerned, while women bemoan the fact that the usual consequence of a night of passion is pregnancy. Men show little or no compassion for women who complain about having babies. It is a natural state and not nearly as dangerous or unpleasant as women make out. And, if women really didn't want more children, then they shouldn't indulge in the passion in the first place.

The following demonstrates the woman's point of view:

A poor Woman was ill in a dangerous Case,
She lay in, and was just as some other Folks was:
By the Lord, cries *She* then, if my Husband e'er come,
Once again with his Will for to tickle my Bum,
I'll storm, and I'll swear, and I'll run staring wild;
And yet the next Night, the Man got her with Child.

As is pointed out by Maximilian E. Novak in his introduction to the 1983 edition of *The Merry-Thought* collection—which you can find at Gutenberg.org—the book would offer a very lopsided view of eighteenth-century society if it were the only source available for study of that era. There are serious pieces, he acknowledges, and points out that the Flask tavern in Hampstead contains at least one philosophical musing scratched into a toilet wall: "Nothing so certain as the Uncertainties of this Life, *says one of the Greek Philosophers*."

The identity of the collector of *The Merry-Thought* collection was named as Hurlo Thrumbo, who was actually a character in one of Samuel Johnson's plays. One assumption is that the real person behind Hurlo was James Roberts, who actually printed the collection. One theory posits that he used the Hurlo pseudonym to ride on the back of Johnson's play's success. However, it is more commonly thought that Hurlo was Johnson himself, because the collection is just the kind of thing that he would enjoy putting together.

Here are some of the inclusions in Hurlo's collection:

The first is written on a window at an inn Cambridge:

> Is *Molly Fr*—— immortal? ——No.
> She is; and I will prove her so.
> She's fifteen now, and was, I know,
> Fifteen, full fifteen Years ago.

The next piece is found on the same window but on another pane of glass:

> At Home Miss *Molly*'s scarce fifteen.
> Mamma says she's no more;
> But if the Parish-Book says true,
> Miss *Molly*'s thirty four.
> Poor Miss *Molly*!

This flattering little piece was written in a lady's dressing room:

> *Brunetta*, I grant you, can give her Swain Death;
> But 'tis not with her Eyes, but with her—ill Breath

As fits with the subject of latrinalia, the following was written in a Bog-House (a crude slang English term for bathroom or lavatory) in Hampstead:

> There's Nothing foul that we commit,
> But what we write, and what we sh—t.

And here is another from a toilet in Uxbridge:

If a Man should breathe backwards, and happens to stink,
You may say, if you will, it is natural *Instinct.*

Underneath this piece of wit a reply was written:
You may quibble upon the Word *Instinct*, if you will; but I think 'tis better out than in, considering the Case.

Even the rich and famous had to attend to nature's call:

Good Lord! who could think,
That such fine Folks should stink?

The need to relieve oneself is universal:

Well sung of Yore, a Bard of Wit,
That some Folks read, but all Folks sh—-t;
But now the Case is alter'd quite,
Since all who come to Boghouse write.

And it seems that the desire to write about the practice is almost as universal as this answer to the above suggests:

Because they cannot eat, some Authors write;
And some, it seems, because they cannot sh—te.

Not all scribbling are found on toilet walls. It is said that the young lady who wrote these lines on a tabletop then hanged herself:

O Death! thou pleasing End of human Woe!
Thou Cure of Life, thou best of Things below!
May'st thou for ever shun the Coward Slave,
And thy soft Slumbers only ease the Brave!

Yet more is written about writing while on the toilet:

> Privies are now Receptacles of Wit,
> And every Fool that hither comes to sh——t,
> Affects to write what other Fools have writ.

Modern-day studies have come up with some interesting facts about latrinalia. One student of latrinalia found in the toilets of the university campus where he studied that humorous graffiti in toilets had different characteristics to political or sexually explicit graffiti. For a start, only the humorous graffiti was written in the public area of the toilets and not within the confines of the toilet stall. They did not invite reply or enter into any kind of dialogue with the other graffiti. The pieces were always short and usually focused on the natural purpose of a toilet, such as bodily functions.

Another observation recorded was that the grout between the tiles was also used as a space to write on. Perhaps the less porous surface was more amenable to writing on with a marker than the shiny tiles. But the outcome was a spate of graffiti makings puns on the word "grout." These included "Oscar the Grout" and "Grout Expectations," to name a few.

Novak also points out the continuance of latrinalia in our society (as well as others across the world). People seem drawn to writing this type of graffiti in public places, such as lavatories and other prominent sites, and that people are just as fascinated to read and chuckle at the scribbles as they were two thousand years ago. This goes to show just how true the saying from the Old Testament is: "There is nothing new under the sun."

After Dundes published the findings of his studies into latrinalia, he sparked off a whole separate area of study. Subsequent research has now progressed into looking at how toilet graffiti can be linked to the suppression of the writers' sexual desires. Another group of researchers undertook a study to see if men or women produced more toilet graffiti and to see if the subject matter was different or handled in a complementary or alternate way. This group came to the conclusion that there was very little to separate the graffiti on terms of gender.

Much of this research is actually taken very seriously, but there is room for some doubt to creep into the minds of laypeople that perhaps there are more worthy literary subjects to be studying. In his studies, Dundes was able to categorize toilet graffiti into five distinct types: 1) solicitations usually of a sexual nature; 2) commentary about bodily functions, particularly excretion and urination; 3) seeking directions; 4) commentary about anything relevant to the day; and 5) personal musings.

While this kind of research is almost as titillating as the graffiti it analyzes (and yes, there could be a rude pun there), it does not really answer the question of *why* this type of graffiti has persisted for so long. Why do people feel the overwhelming desire to take out a pen and scribble inanities in bathrooms? My own theory, and maybe it is only fit to be written on a bathroom wall, is not so much that people need to leave graffiti, but that they are incessant fiddlers and doodlers who can't manage to sit, or stand, for periods of time without doing something with their hands. A similar semi-automatic scribbling happens on paper scraps, the backs of old envelopes, in the margins of books, and even on bare limbs if there is nothing else to write on.

If it is not the byproduct of a need to do something with ones fingers, then perhaps it is linked to the act of reading in the toilet, which is a phenomenon that probably out-rivals that of writing on toilet doors. To read is to relax and that is always an aid to answering the call of nature.

This kind of wit involving our bodily functions has been around since the beginning of the human race and probably precedes our first cave paintings. It is considered very immature humor by many people, but one which seems totally ingrained in the human psyche.

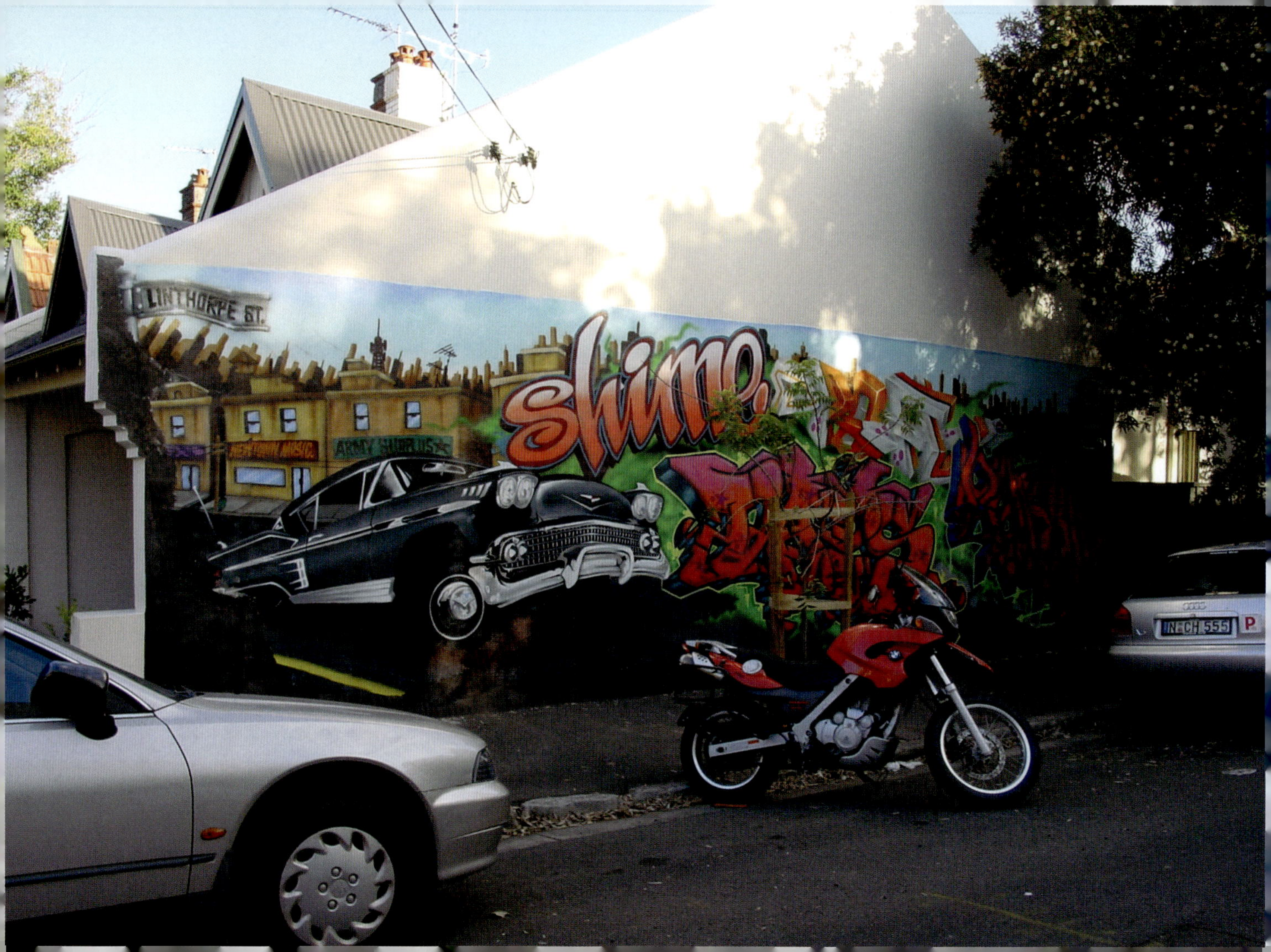
LINTHORPE ST.
shine
ARMY SURPLUS

CHAPTER FIVE

MODERN-DAY GRAFFITI

KILROY, MR. CHAD, AND FOO WERE HERE

Kilroy, known as Mr. Chad in Britain and as Foo in Australia (and who is called Smoe, Clem, Herbie, Private Snoops, Overby, and Sapo throughout the world, as well) is an odd little figure. A bald-headed man with an enormous nose, he peers over a high wall, his two hands (of four stubby fingers each) grasp the top of it almost as if he is trying to pull himself up to see over it. He is perhaps the best known, the best loved, and the most enduring of all graffiti renderings in the modern day, but where did he come from and when did he appear? As to why, that may just remain a complete mystery until the end of time.

Kilroy, a US creation, was already well known during the Second World War. He traveled far with the American troops, mainly with the air force, and left his mark across the globe. American air service men left a Kilroy doodle at every posting they were sent to during WWII. At one point, his presence was so prevalent in enemy territory that a rumor spread that the Nazis thought Kilroy was actually some kind of secret agent.

Although Kilroy rose to fame in the 1940s, there is some documentary evidence to suggest that he was already present and making his mark in 1937. A documentary made in 2007 shows a Kilroy doodle written on the inner walls of a vault at Fort Knox with the date 1937. The vault had been closed in '37 and was not reopened until an audit was made in the 1970s.

There are many theories about who Kilroy really was, several of which claim that he was James Kilroy, a shipyard inspector who started the fad when he chalked "Kilroy was here" on the bulkhead of ships he had inspected. The sailors were intrigued by the words and, not knowing their real meaning, took to writing the words themselves, claiming that Kilroy had been there before anyone else. Variations on this theme abound throughout the world and are joined by plenty of other theories, generally more bizarre than the previous one. (Authors' note: In 1946, the Transit Company of America ran a competition to find the real Kilroy. They offered a trolley car as the prize. James Kilroy, the same rivet inspector, took his fellow workers with him to the contest to prove that he was the originator of the phrase. It was decided his proof was incontrovertible, and he was given the prize. Kilroy had a brood of nine kids and the trolley car became their play house.)

A diagram of a bpf circuit showing how » similar it is to a little man looking over a fence. This may have been the origin of the English equivalent of Kilroy—Mr. Chad.

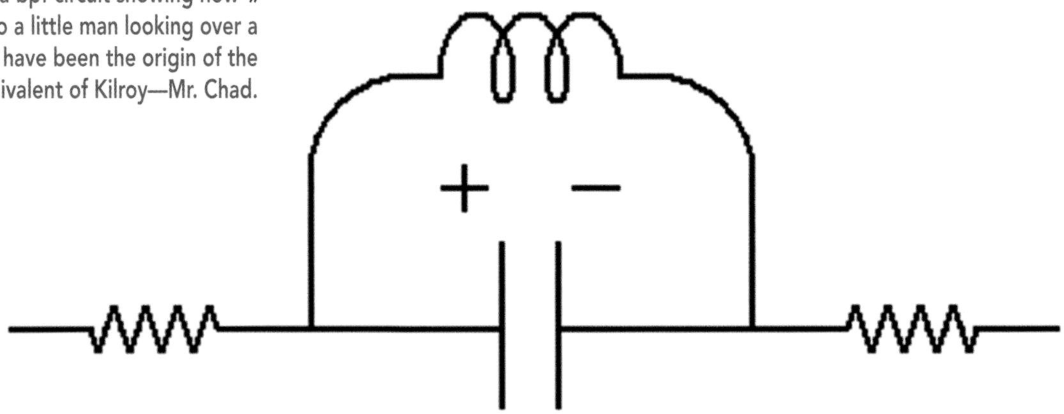

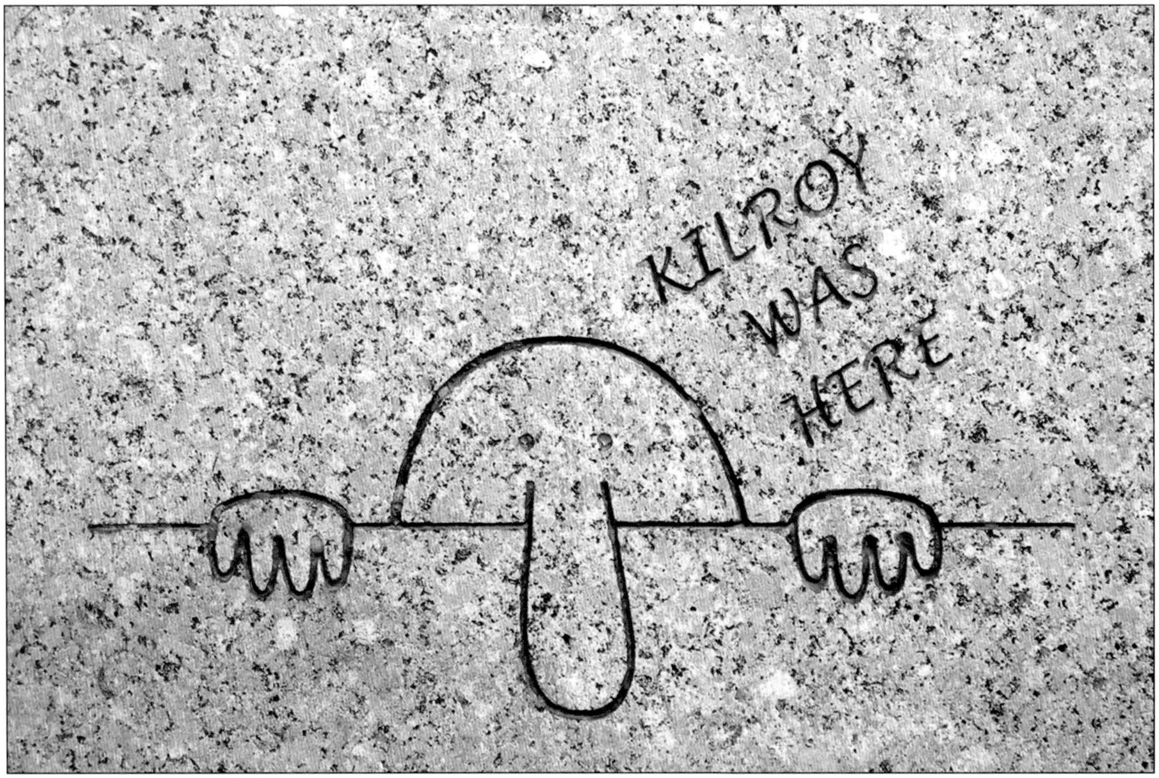

« Kilroy was here. This version was carved into the Washington World War II Monument as a memorial to the little character who took on the world in the face of war.

Photo courtesy of Luis Rubio, Alexandria, Virginia, United States.

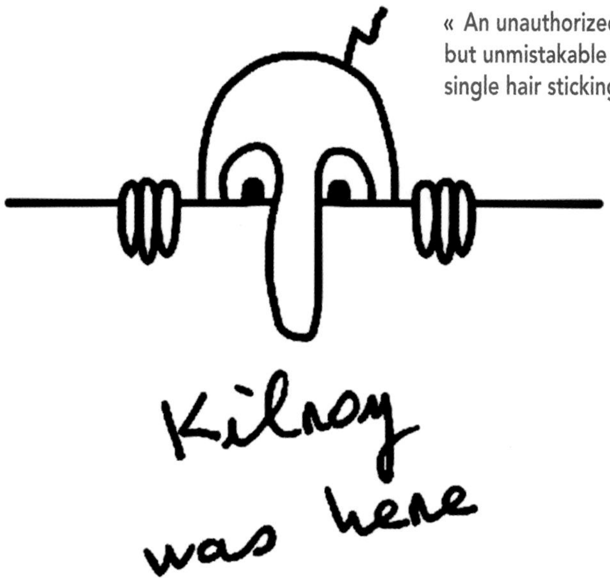

« An unauthorized version of Kilroy but unmistakable even with the single hair sticking up.

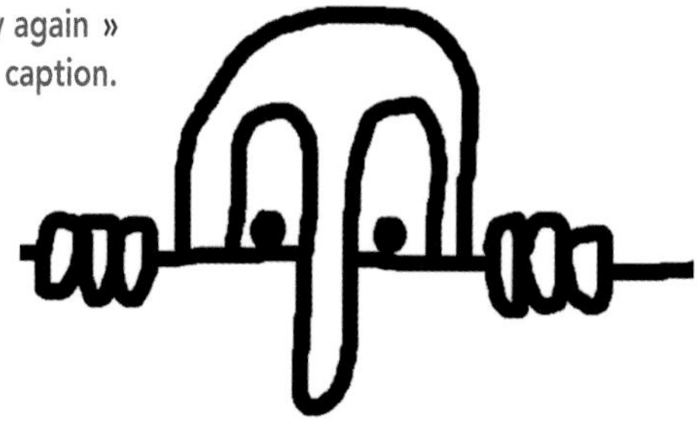

Kilroy again » without caption.

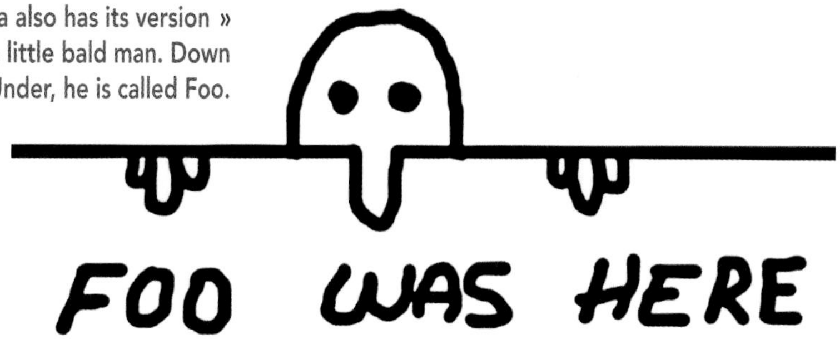

Australia also has its version » of the little bald man. Down Under, he is called Foo.

After the Second World War, Kilroy's activities lessened, but never fully ceased. Throughout the 1950s he would appear in all sorts of unlikely places, much to the amusement of the general public. It is also possible that elements of the Kilroy graffiti doodle go back as far as the First World War. "Foo was here" was a graffito that appeared in common usage in Australia during World War I. It was also the word used by a cartoon character from the 1930s.

Furthermore, the little bald guy who accompanies the phrase may have originated from just before the Second World War, when members of the Royal Australian Air Force connected him with the gremlins that led aircraft astray and made things go wrong in the engines of planes. Foo was a good one to blame, as he couldn't object. And yet another theory is Foo is actually an acronym of Forward Observation Officer.

The British version, Mr. Chad, also has a number of theories about his invention. First, it has been suggested that Mr. Chad was a character created by the British cartoonist George Chatterton around 1938. Chad could be a corruption of Chatterton's nickname Chat. It is possible that Mr. Chad originated as the letter omega (Ω), which was used as the symbol for electrical resistance during the 1930s. Mr. Chad would have been, so this theory goes, the creation of an electrician and taking into account his strong links with the RAF (Royal Air Force—United Kingdom) and the RAAF (Royal Australian Air Force in Australia), it may well have been an electrician with the ground crew of a fighter plane.

To back up this theory, there have been many people who claim that Mr. Chad looks just like the diagram of an electrical circuit.

Mr. Chad would often appear accompanied by sayings such as "Wot, no sugar?" It is also possible that Mr. Chad preceded Kilroy and that the busy little US airman was influenced by his British cousin.

Just as graffiti is a worldwide phenomenon, transposing time and space, so is the figure of Kilroy. The name changes but the character and sentiment do not. It is also interesting to note that there seems to be a more lenient attitude toward Kilroy, Foo, and Mr. Chad than there is to other tags or more personalized graffiti. Is it his innocent appearance (has anyone ever seen a sinister Kilroy?) and naive character that invites empathy by the viewer towards him? Or is it that he has been around during some very tough times and weathered it through with everyone else? We may never really be able to explain it, but the fact is that Kilroy will most likely be around for years to come.

POLITICAL AND SOCIAL GRAFFITI

Statements made about ruling bodies are almost as ancient as writing itself. Graffiti in Pompeii and also in Athens would make accusations against rulers, or they'd support them or make rude suggestions for them. Today, the same thing continues. This is political graffiti at its

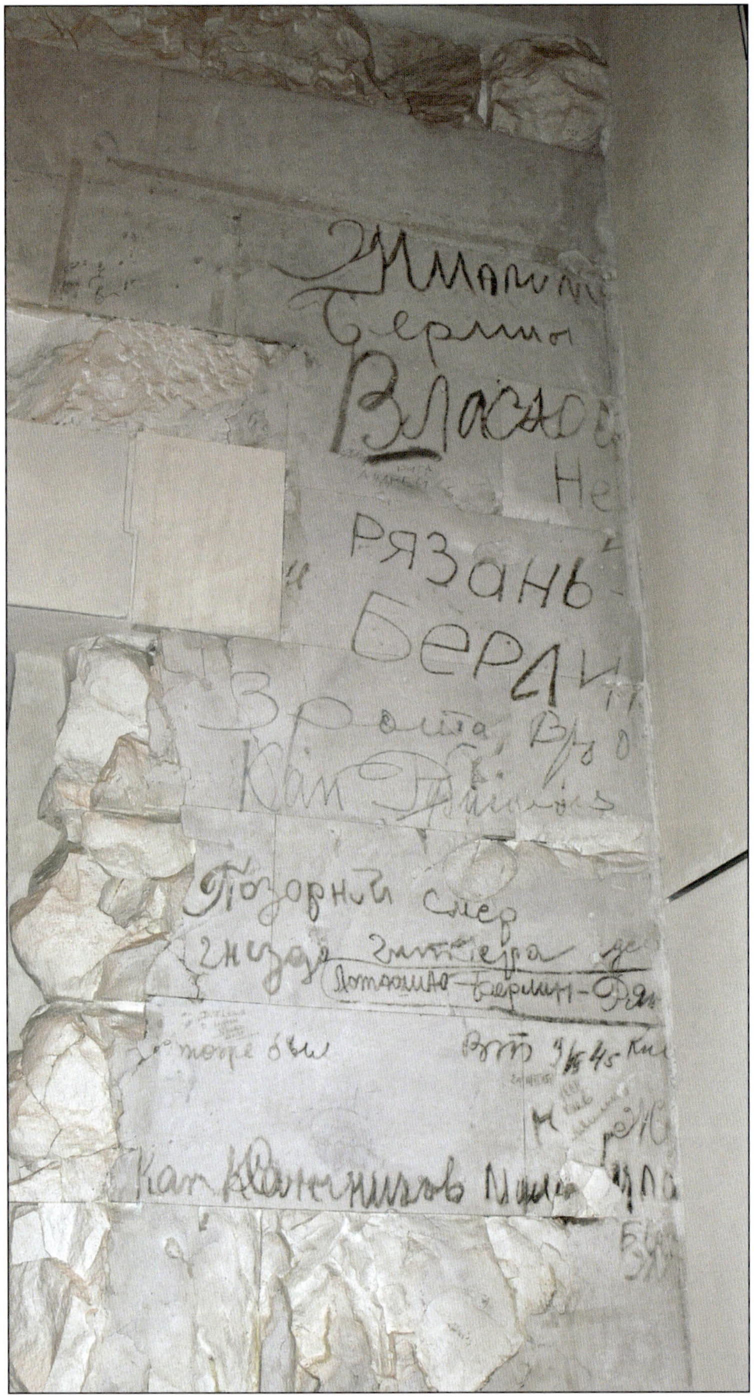

A close-up of a wall in the Reichstag, » Germany, illustrating the Russian graffiti made by the soldiers who took over Eastern Germany after the Nazi defeat.

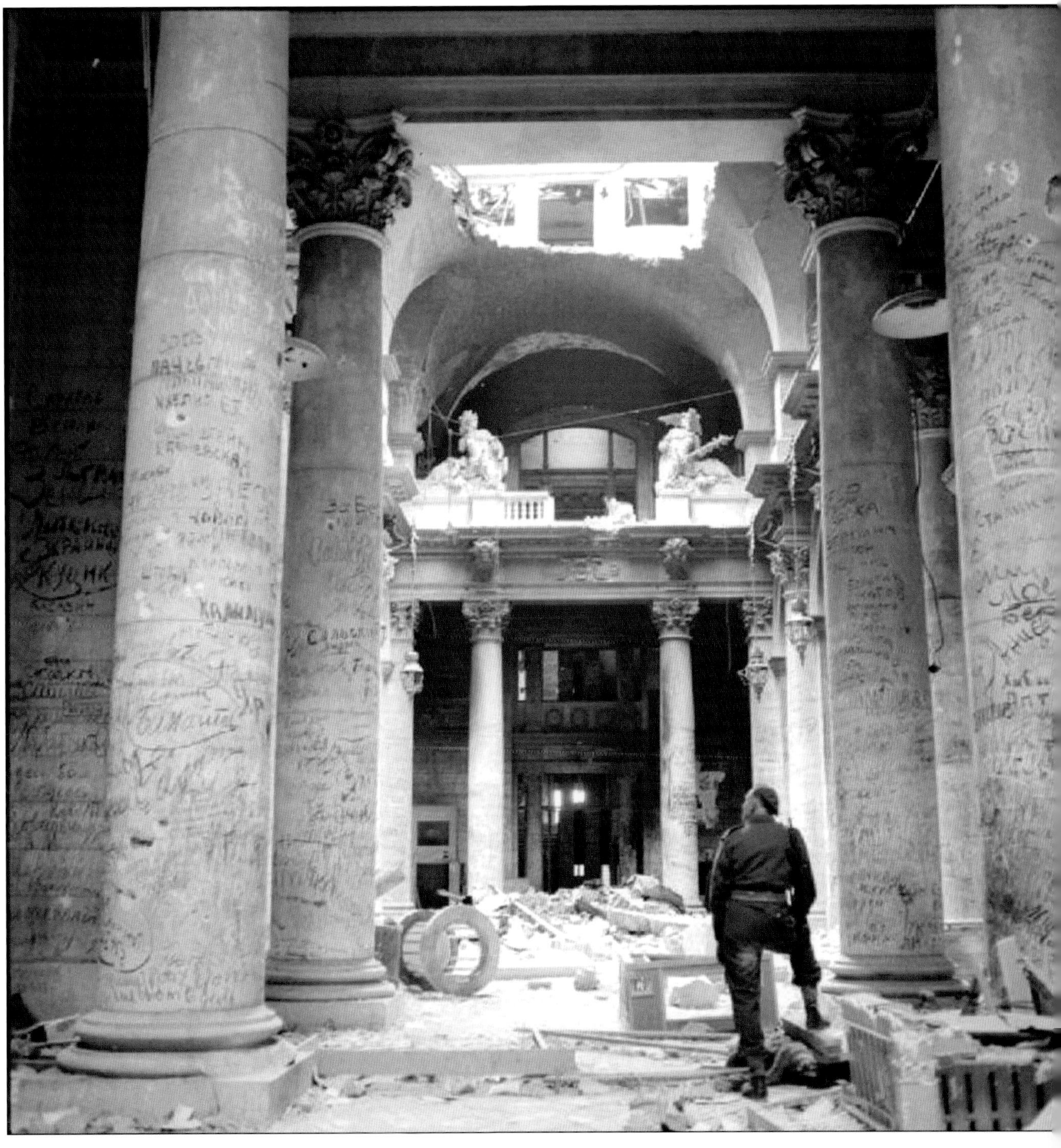

Reichstag in Germany » after it was taken over by the Russians at the end of World War II. The graffiti is all in Russian.

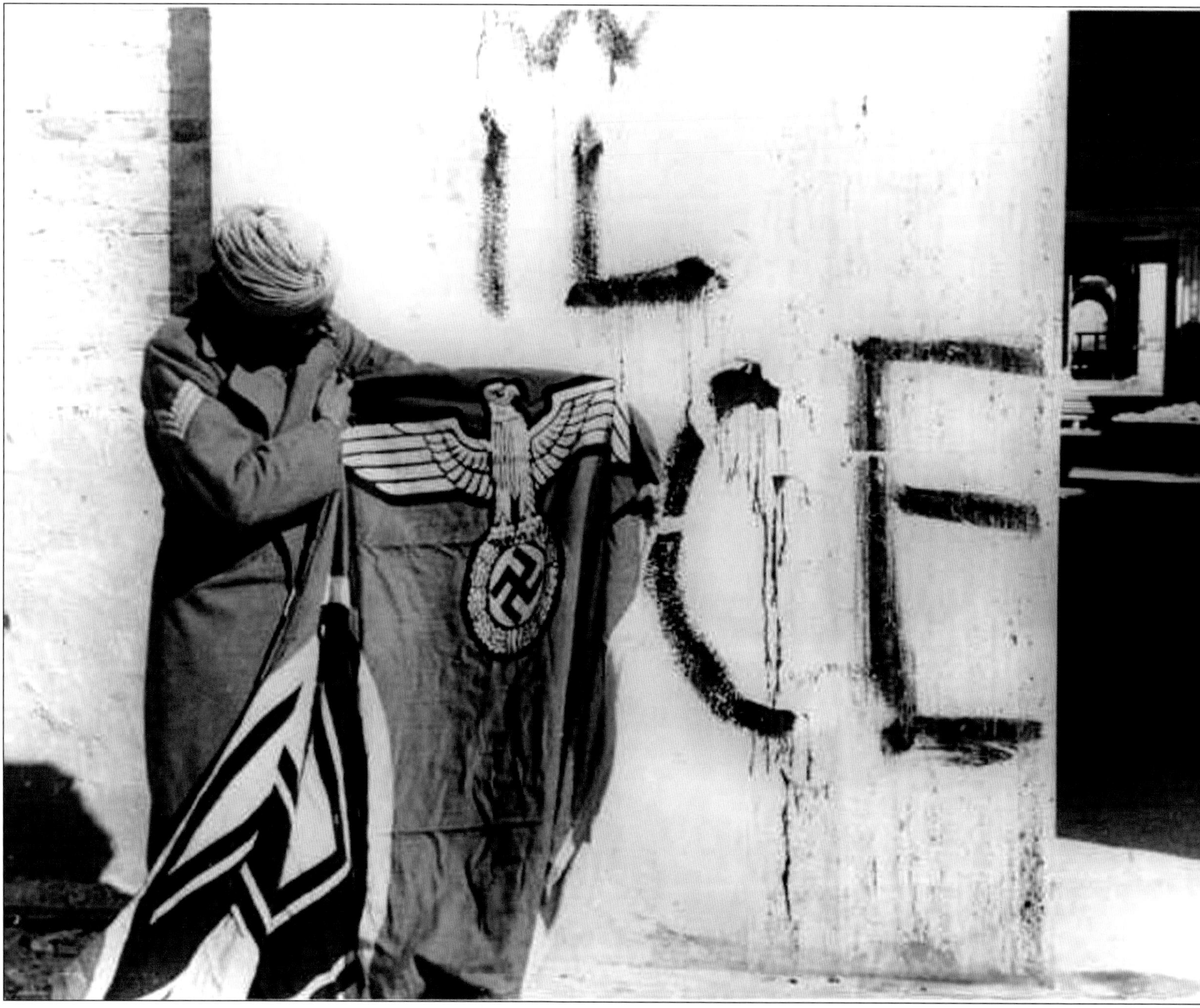

≈ A Sikh soldier shows off a captured Nazi flag for the camera—in the background is a graffiti-covered wall.

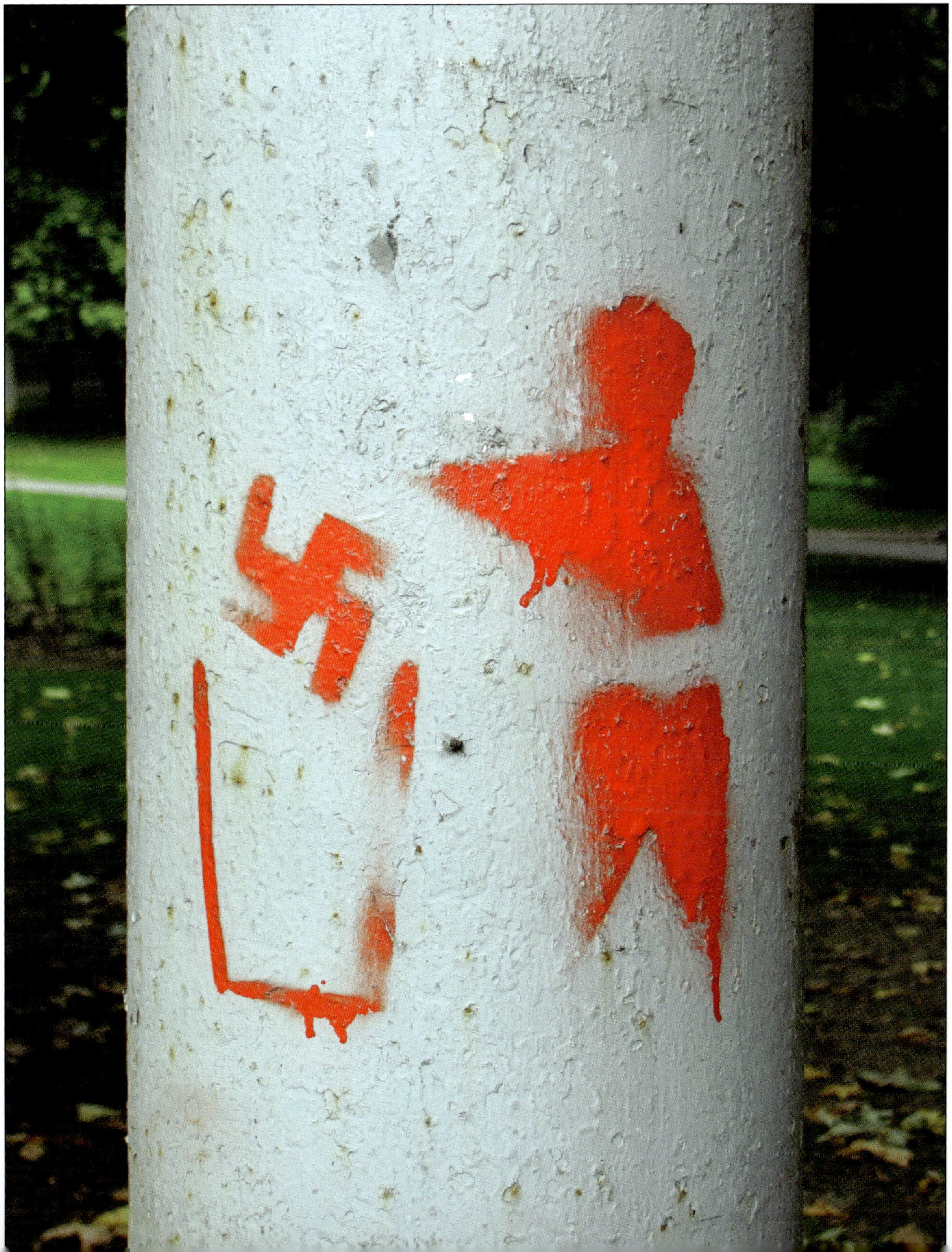

The Swastika is still used » as a political symbol and represents Fascist organizations. The message is clear in this small piece of graffiti where a protestor throws it into the trashcan.

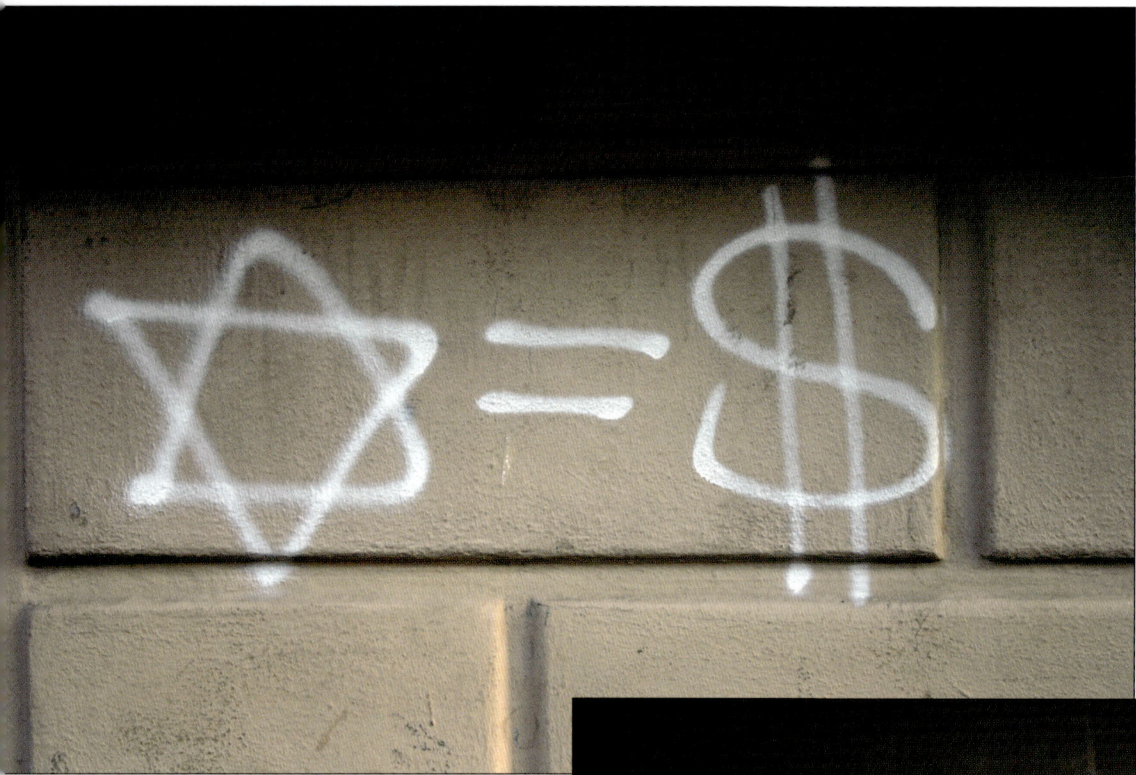

« The Jewish people have been persecuted for centuries and one of the bones of contention is the idea that Jews are only interested in money. This is illustrated by this unmistakable piece of anti-Semetic graffiti showing the Star of David equaling dollars.
Photo courtesy of Giovanni Dall'Orto.

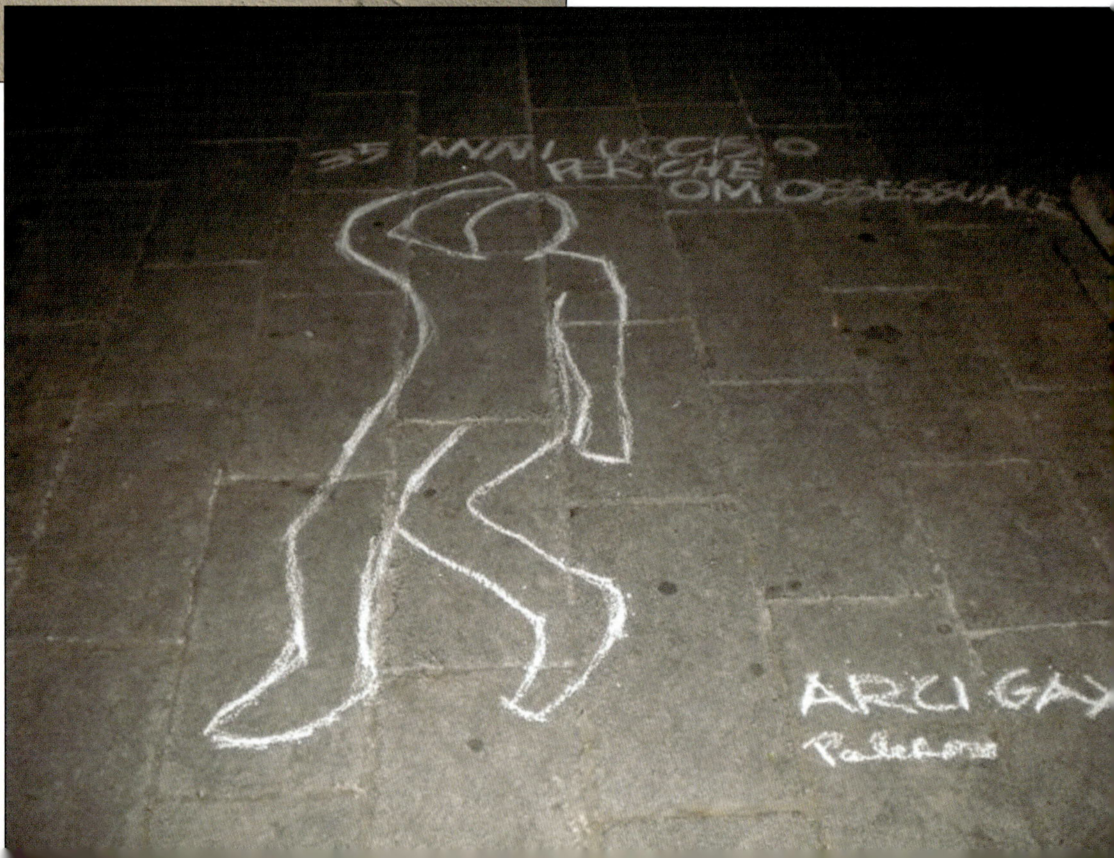

Political graffiti also encompasses the » persecution of many minority groups. Homosexual men are not only common targets of unpleasant graffiti, but also of violent assaults, as shown in this anti-homophobic graffito showing the chalk outline of a dead body.

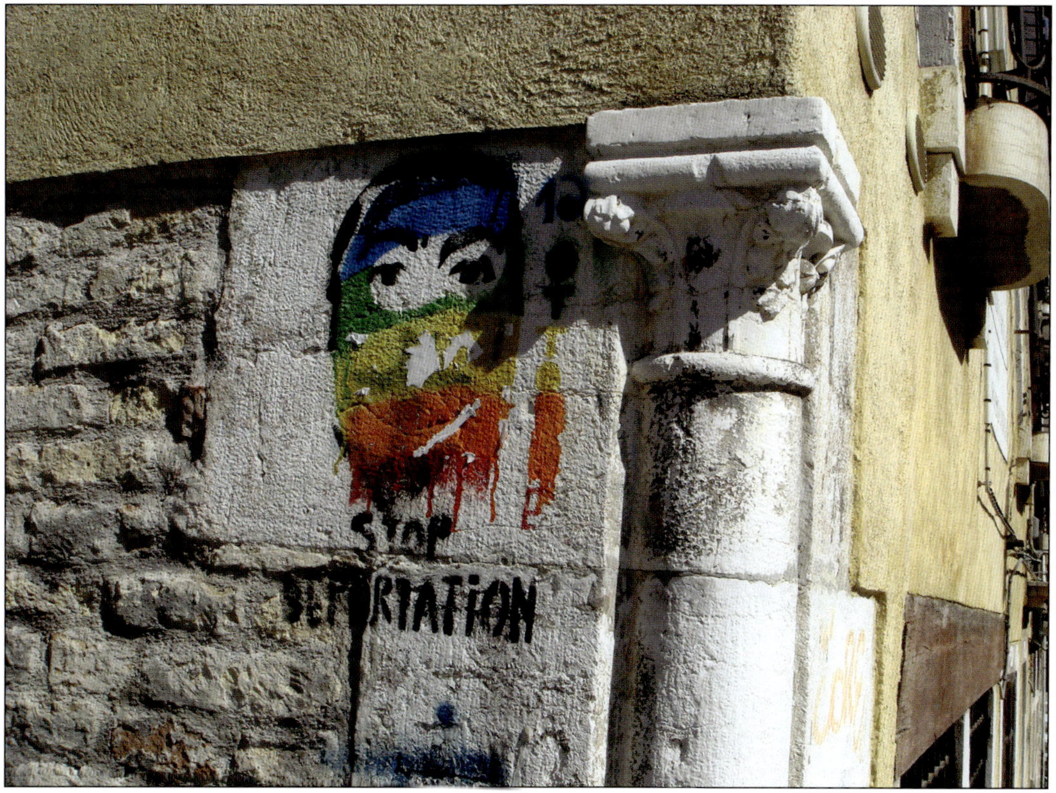

A stencil directing » people to stop the deportation of asylum seekers in Venice. *Photo courtesy of Giovanni Dall'Orto.*

least effective. In countries where there is much oppression against the people, graffiti tends to take on a more serious tone and to be painted in a more organized way. Lately in Egypt there has been a spate of anti-government, anti-dictator graffiti and messages calling for true democracy. These images are picked up by foreign news crews and broadcast to the world.

During World War II, Italy was being held under a fascist regime and the resulting anti-Mussolini graffiti have influenced the stencil graffiti artists of today. Stencils are a good way to reproduce a face plus add a politicized message. It is quicker than doing each graffito freehand and the likeness to the target of the message is more realistic. Furthermore, stencil campaigns provide a sense of unity to the message and give the feel that an organization is behind a given cause.

Then there is the type of graffiti that has been scrawled by conquering troops. The Reichstag graffiti in Berlin—made by the Russians as they took over the city—functions as a tagging of a particular territory. The marks are not considered beautiful like some artforms, and they are written in either pencil or chalk. Some of the pieces are just initials, but others

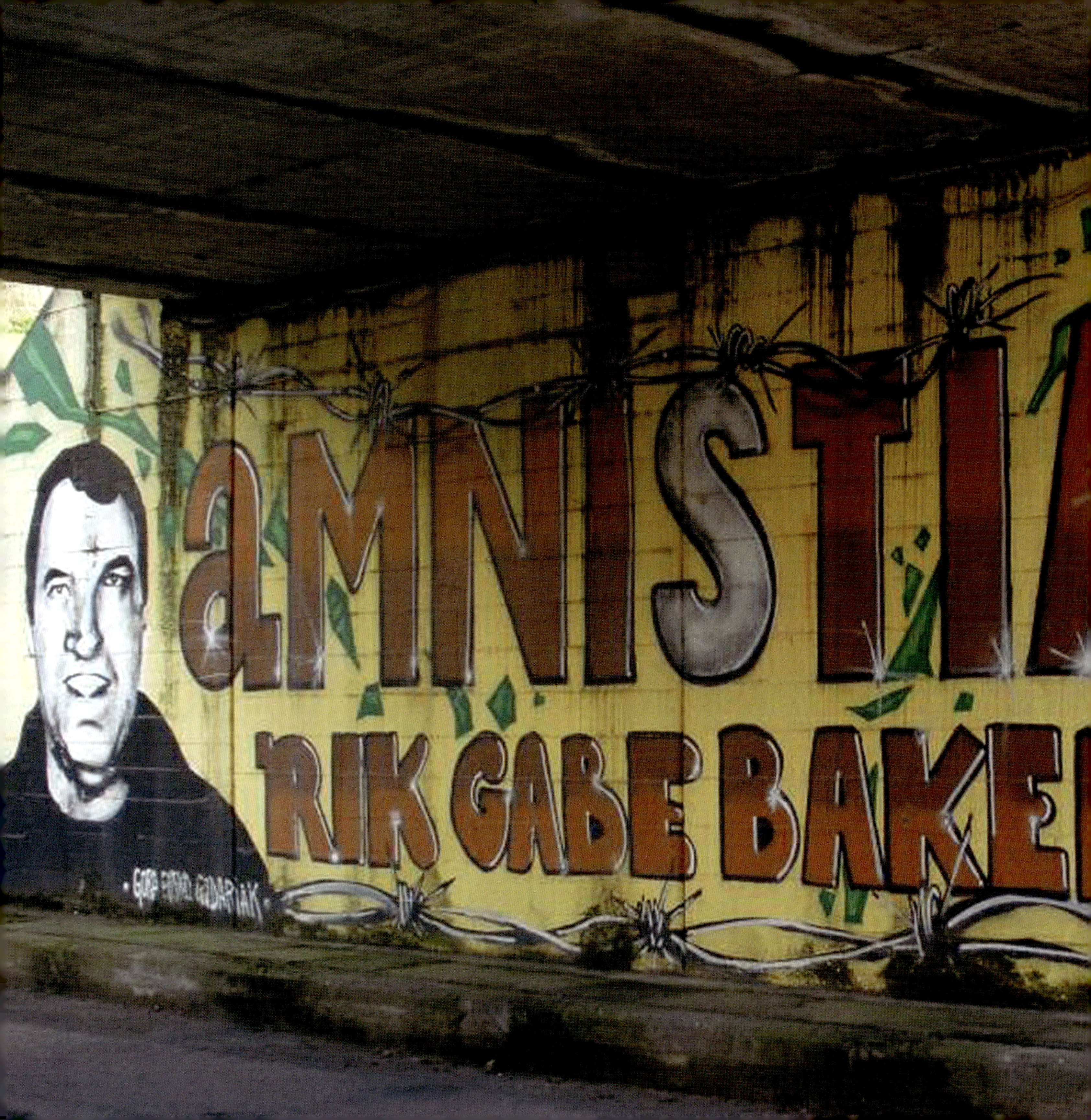
aMNISTIA
'RIK GABE BAKE

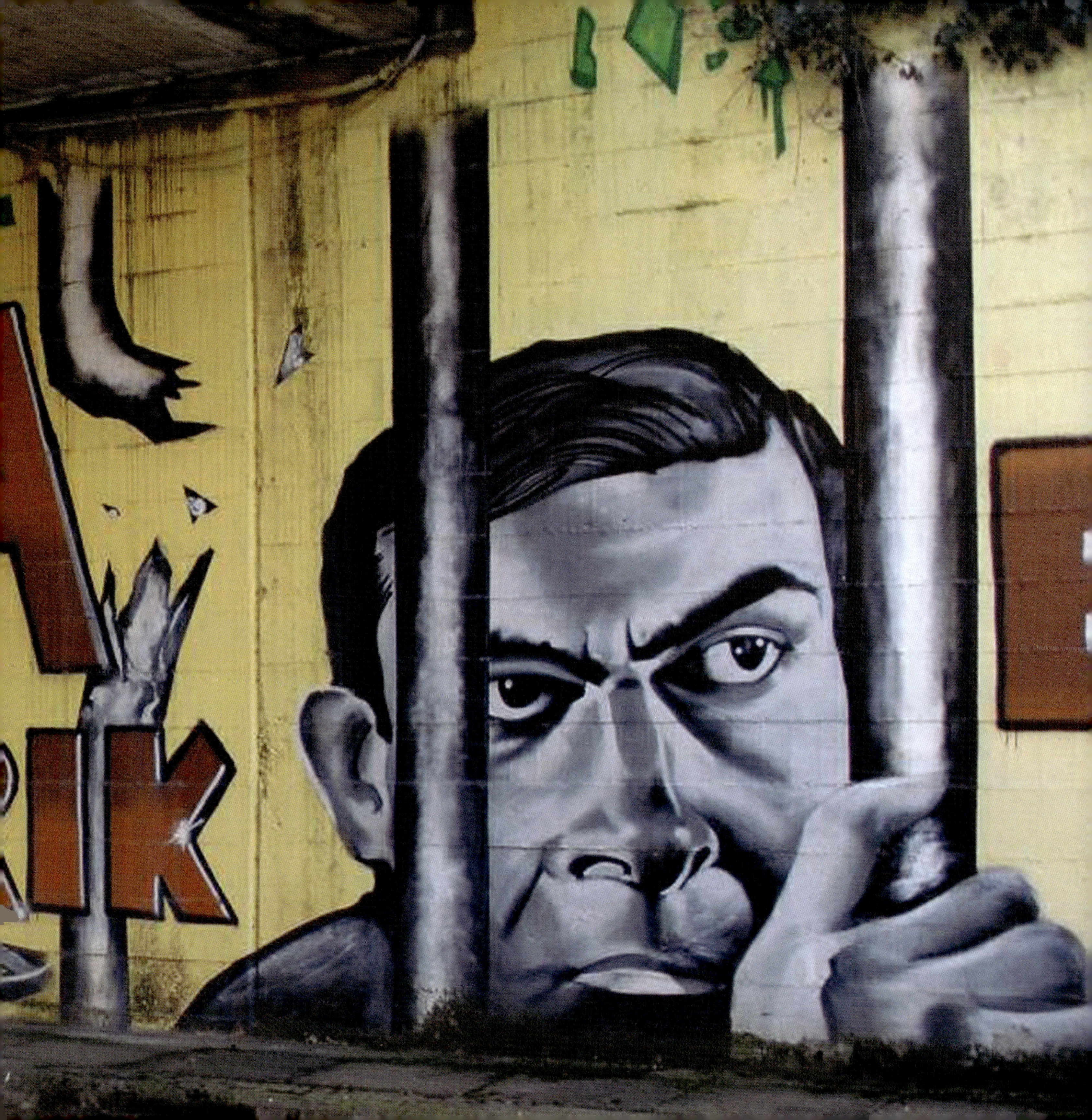

make statements of victory: "Glory to the heroes who hoisted the banner of victory over Berlin!" The Reichstag graffiti has been preserved rather than destroyed, which has been the fate of political graffiti in other cities that have been invaded and marked by the intruders. It is as though the Germans have decided to keep these pieces as a sort of memento to show what really happened in the city's past, rather than to resort to replicas and dioramas in museums.

Political graffiti also includes racist comments and hateful messages written by ignorant people. This type of graffiti gives out a written message, supposedly with the aim to drive out the other party out of fear. The intent is clearly of intimidation and to spread fear and mistrust throughout a community. In the past, Jews have been a prominent hate target for this type of graffiti, and in some places they are still equated with money misers, as can be seen in the piece shown on page 86.

Homophobia is another major factor in targeting a group with vindictive graffiti that often implies violence. In male bathrooms, a large proportion of graffiti that is present consists of mentions about gay people and how they should be dealt with (usually negatively). On the other hand, there is also graffiti made to help build awareness of the problems and prejudices that homosexuals endure, as can be seen in the illustration of a graffiti piece showing the chalk outline of a dead body on page 86.

In some ways Kilroy can also be considered a type of political and social graffiti. It functions similarly to the graffiti of the Russian soldiers in Berlin, in that sense that an American cartoon character could make so many conquests across the globe, laying claim to places before anyone else. This, in one sense, is like staking a claim on another's property as a sort of anachronistic conquest. It is doubtful that Kilroy actually meant to be offensive in such a way, but it may very well be received like that when future generations look back on it.

Anti-Churchill Graffiti

A piece of graffiti done in the 1940s has recently been uncovered in the Bishop's Palace at Ely Cathedral in Britain. The work was found on the underside of some floorboards that had been installed between 1941 and 1942. The graffiti is in black pencil and shows a spitfire targeting a woman and two children beside a flag with a swastika on it. The soldier, turned away from Churchill, has a thought bubble with the phrase, "Hmm you warmonger Churchill" and is also muttering, "Drink and smoke while we die." Above the drawing of Churchill are the words "You stinkweed Churchill you cunt." Apparently stinkweed was the name given to Churchill when he was inebriated by Lord Halifax. Apparently when the Prime Minister was in that state he was likely to defecate in his underwear. It is further said that Churchill had a special pair of pants made with an opening at the back so he could relieve himself quickly while drunk. Clearly the artist of this graffiti was in on the reference to this.

Ely Cathedral is situated in East Anglia in Britain, and it was an area that was not naturally hostile to the German nation, believing that their counterparts in Germany had a higher standard of living and therefore so should they. Not

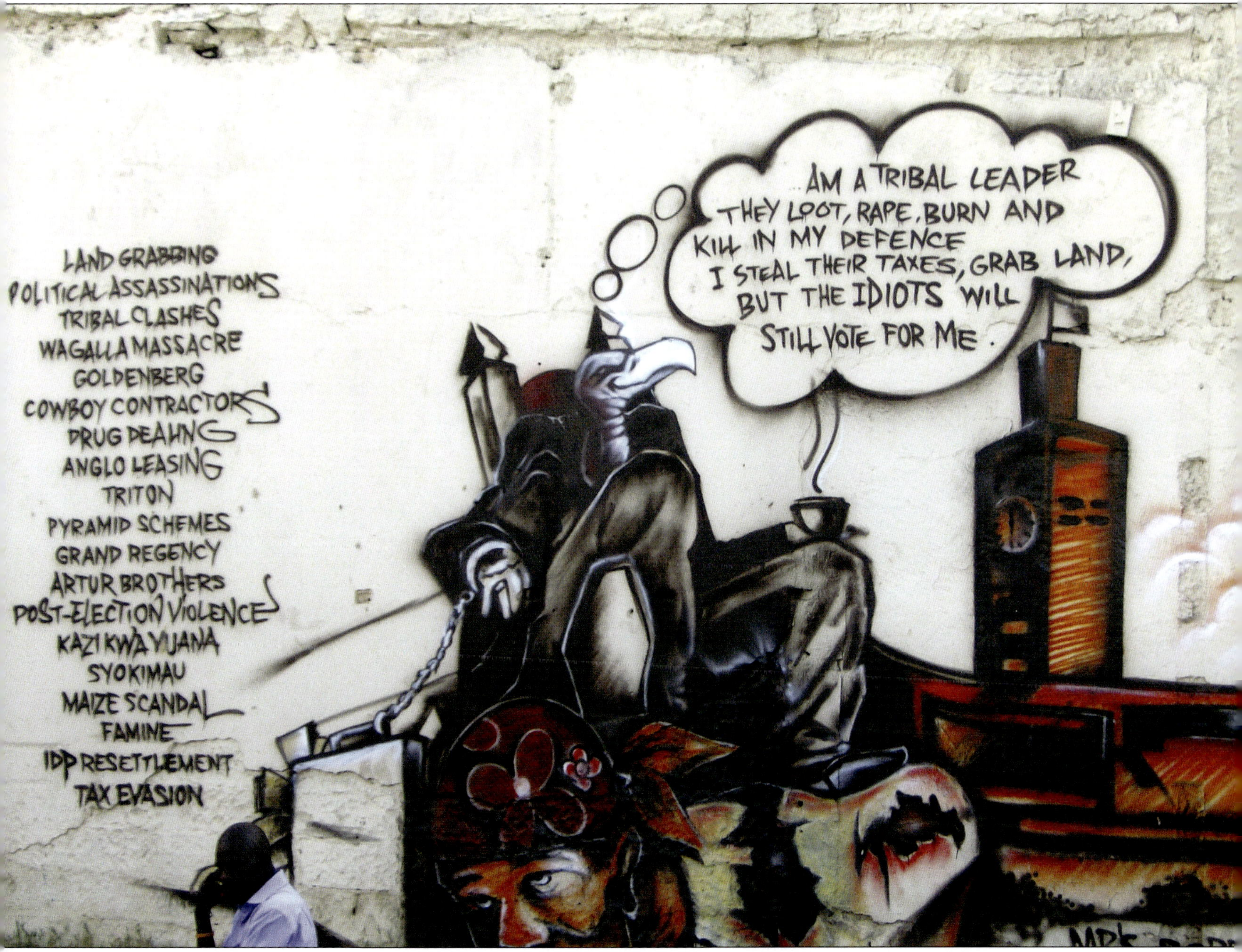

This graffito is from Africa and gives a list of all the wrongs that need to be righted with little subtlety.

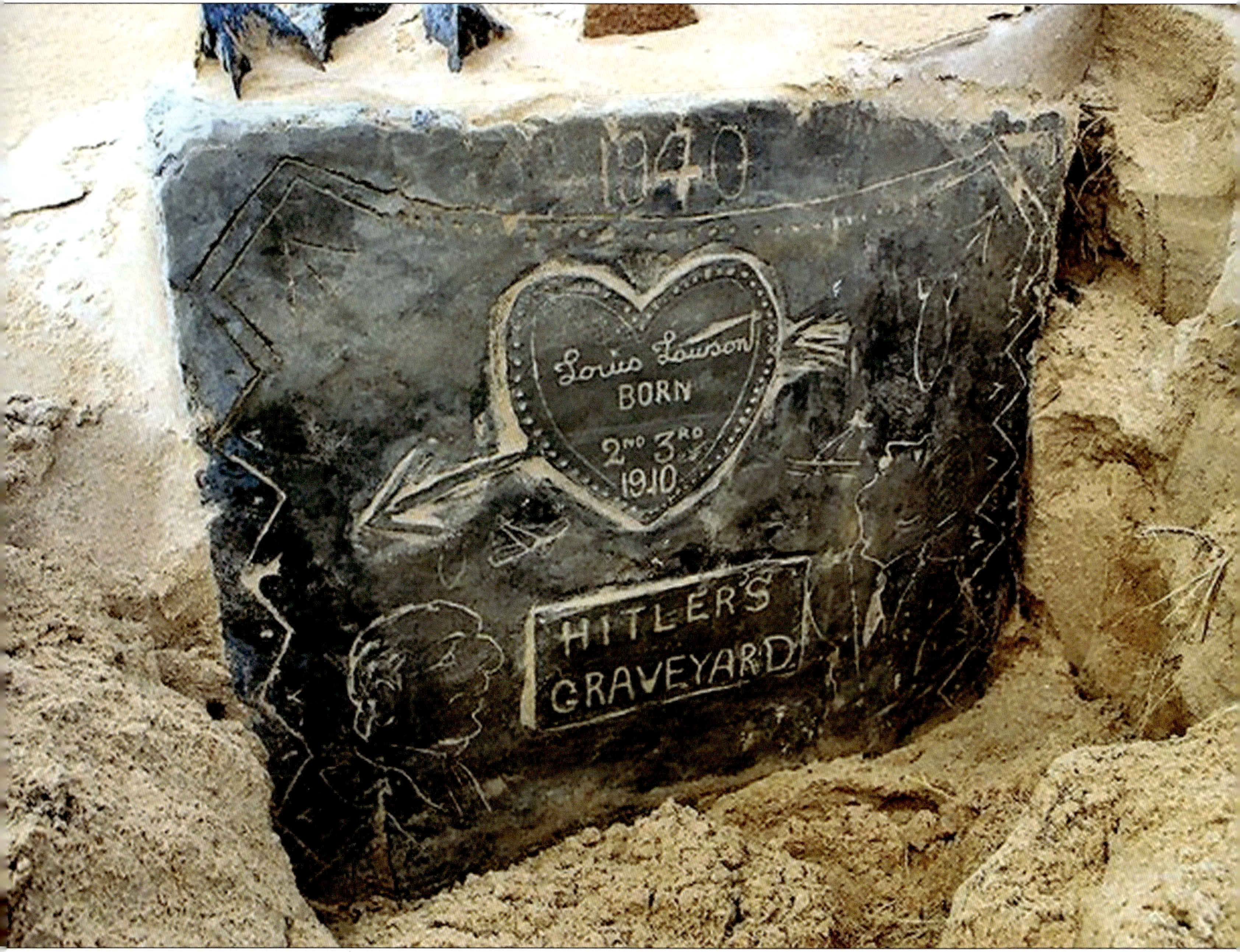

A tank trap from World War II expecting Hitler's demise with great anticipation.
Photo courtesy of Martyn Gorman, Geography Org, United Kingdom.

only that, but many of the residents of East Anglia felt they were fighting people like themselves: Anglo-Saxons. The British monarchy was full of the blood of German Royals and vice versa. There were rumors that locals were acting as spies for the German's by aiding them in hitting their targets. Whatever the reason that the graffiti under the floorboard was drawn, it was clearly hidden due to the hateful and disgusting nature it portrayed for the English Prime Minister.

The Irish Republican Army Blanket Protestors

I remember seeing a documentary on television about the British artist Richard Hamilton working on a painting of an Irish republican blanket protestor many years ago. One side of the two-panel work was covered in a brown swirling pattern. This was, the artist explained, a stylized version of the graffiti painted on the walls of the political prisoner's cell. It was executed in excrement.

The protests, which lasted over five years, were a reaction to the British government's decision to treat these political prisoners as criminals. This meant that the prisoners were required to wear prison uniforms and to participate in the usual activities demanded of ordinary criminals. The Irish republican prisoners, men and women, went on strike. They refused to wear the designated clothes, preferring to swathe themselves in their prison blankets. They refused to bathe, and they daubed the walls of their cells with their own feces. This last act was to attract media attention as well as to keep the prison guards away. It was successful on both counts.

When Hamilton exhibited the diptych in 1988 at the Fruitmarket Gallery in Edinburgh, he recreated the actual cell in which the prisoners lived. The walls of the cell were painted with the Celtic-type patterns of the graffiti and a mattress and pillow, both filthy looking, were put on the floor. The painting was hung within this installation, almost like a shrine.

Opera House Graffiti

The glistening white sails of the Sydney Opera House are an Australian icon and are known the world over. What better place, therefore, to write an internationally targeted message? That is exactly what happened in 2003, when two peace activists, David Burgess and Will Saunders, utilized abseiling equipment to help them access the curves of the roof in order to paint these words in bright red letters: No War. This was in response to the movement of the West into Iraq. The men were subsequently arrested and taken to court.

Although the pair had urged their counsel, John Doris, to plead that the graffiti was painted in an attempt to stop major bloodshed in Iraq as the result of war, it was to no avail. The court claimed that if they accepted this logic, then all terrorists could use the same argument that their activities had only been done in the attempt to try to protect their countries and their way of life. As part of their punishment, Burgess and Saunders had to serve nine months of periodic detention and pay a fine of $151,000 towards the Opera House repair bill.

CULTURE JAMMING

The term "culture jamming" was invented in 1984 by the band Negativland, who were trading on the idea of radio jamming. Although not given a proper name until this time, the practice of culture jamming is ancient. The target of this subversive practice is that of the consumerist west. The aim is to make the public aware of the manipulation that goes on through media advertising and how ads can also be politically motivated, even to this day. The movement re-manipulates the legitimate advertisements that are used by big business; they alter them subtly so that the message is inverted and the effect on the consumer is the opposite of that originally intended.

Some of the issues that are taken up by the culture jammists are topics such as the use of child sweatshop labor in third world countries so that western societies can buy expensive commodities and the companies make large profits. Any practice that is morally unsound, exploitative, or at the cost of another person, culture, or class is a target of this culture jamming. Often the primary aim is its shock value and attempts to disturb and distress consumers so they will start thinking more about the implications of the media's tactics and the bad business practices of corporations.

Graffiti has played a large part in culture jamming since the inception of the term and even before. There are graffitists who will parody popular advertisements, turning them on their head and making the message poignant in some way. Humor is another tool that makes the public think about important issues and is something that is employed with the use of graffiti in this way. Perhaps culture jamming has come to the end of its efficacy in an age where such efforts are being turned back on themselves—many advertising firms are resorting to similar styles and tactics—but the role that graffiti plays in this phenomenon is no less important or worthy of note.

Space Hijackers

The space hijackers is a group of British cultural jammers who label themselves "an international band of anarchitects." They specialize in making people aware of the space around them, both private and

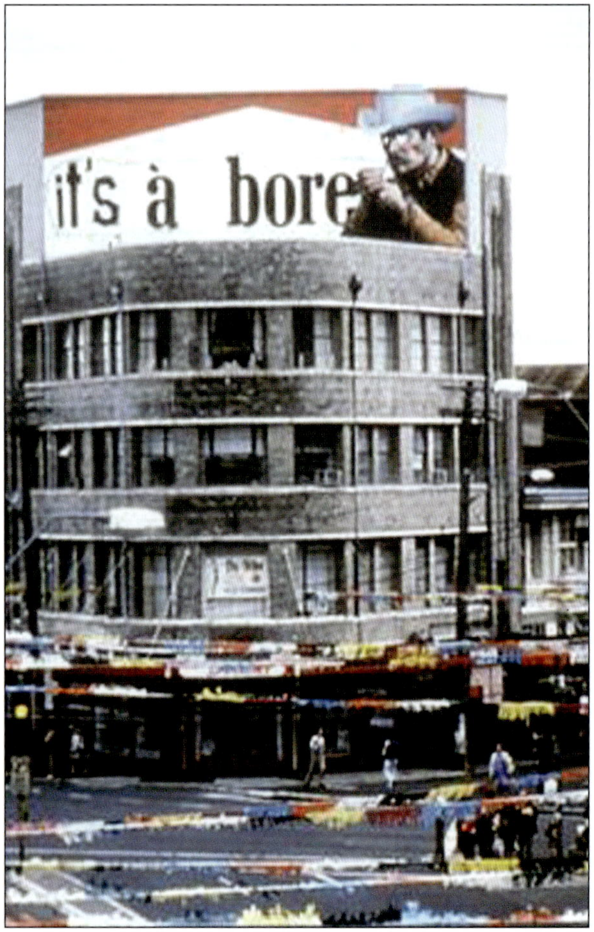

BUGAUP Marlborough »
Advertisement, Sydney, Australia.

public. They believe that the areas surrounding us are being taken over and used specifically by certain groups of people and individuals, often big business, for their gain and to the detriment of the citizens. In retaliation, space hijackers use peaceful and public-friendly methods of bringing their mission to the foreground. They use graffiti to post alternative ideas for luxury housing projects; instead of a multi-story apartment block for the wealthy, the space hijackers will graffiti alongside the pictures of the proposed development similar drawings but of parks and playgrounds accessible to all citizens in the community. In this way, graffiti is being used by this group as a social statement and to bring about a common good in these communities.

Billboard Liberation Front

The Billboard Liberation Front is a group that practices sabotaging billboard advertising campaigns by altering the wording on the ads. The group began in 1977 by Jack Napier (a pseudonym taken from a character in the Batman comics). Napier belonged to the San Francisco Suicide Club, whose mission was to perform public practical jokes. One such joke was to alter a billboard, and this type of activity became the mission of the BLF after the Suicide Club fizzled out.

There is an element of anti-corporate, anti-commercial, pro-healthy-living radicalism to the group. The kinds of ads they most frequently target are for products like cigarettes, fast food, and computer equipment. The group does not intend to offend or permanently deface the ad or to cause any kind of civic disruption. On the contrary, the main aim of the activity is to bring some humor to the communities that are forced to look at these billboards every day.

The secret of the success and longevity of the group is probably their secrecy. No member uses his or her real name, and they are not allowed to tell anyone that they are a part of the club. The fact that they try to avoid conflict, dangerous situations, and getting caught (the most important, of course) also helps the group.

The BLF have performed some daring alterations—some even under the very noses of the law. They make sure they are invisible in the public eye, dressing in the kinds of work gear that legitimate billboard workers wear. Napier, supported by other BLF members, justifies what the group does by pointing out that when newspapers and other media discover the witty alterations done to the advertisements, the extra exposure actually works in favor of the company whose ad was changed while relaying BLF's message to consumers.

Billboard Utilising Graffitists Against Unhealthy Promotions is the Australian version of the BLF. When reduced to its initials, the group's acronym spells BUGAUP (bugger up). The group was founded in 1979 by Bill Snow, Ric Bolzan, and Geoff Coleman. It targets cigarette, alcohol, and soft drink advertisements. After BUGAUP coined its name, it was added to each billboard that had been altered so that all would know the graffiti was the work of an organization and not just random vandalism. However, all a graffitist had to do to become a member of the group was to add the BUGAUP name to his or her own altered billboard, which meant that the movement spread rapidly across the country—and even across the sea. Typical members of the group are university educated and at least one prominent member went on to become a notable politician.

One of the most eccentric and colorful early members of the group was a man named Rolo Mestman Tapier (who later changed his name by deed poll to Lord Bloody Wog Rolo) who originally came from Argentina. One of his first activities that led to his joining BUGAUP was his reaction to being given a shopping bag in a supermarket that had cigarette advertising on it. In absolute disgust, he declined to go through with his purchase. This was followed by arriving at the checkout counter with a shopping cart loaded with goods and then, after having them wrung up, refusing to have them packed in the cigarette bags. An accomplice then repeated the performance at another check out counter. This eventually had the desired affect and the shopping market withdrew from using the bags all together.

Borf

The word "Borf" began to appear on walls all over Washington, DC, starting in 2004. It soon became linked to the work of a young art student, John Tsombikos, who was making a statement and tribute to his friend Bobby Fisher, who had committed suicide at the age of sixteen. Borf graffiti took many forms: tags, throw-ups, stencils, was incorporated into sentences (such as "Bush Hates Borf"), and as huge lettering on an exit sign on the Theodore Roosevelt Bridge leading to Constitution Avenue.

A while later, Borf graffiti started to appear in New York City, San Francisco, and even as far as Rome. The group working with Tsombikos called themselves the Borf Brigade and they publicly announced that their aim was to attack capitalism and our culture of aesthetics, which had such a negative impact on Bobby Fisher, who took his own life because of it.

In 2005, Tsombikos was arrested and pleaded guilty to the destruction of property. His punishment included community service, in which he had to clean graffiti around the city. The following year a member of the Borf Brigade announced, on video that was projected onto a wall, that Tsombikos was only a minor member of the group and that he had been ostracized by the others in the organization. The statement continued to say that Bobby Fisher's suicide was not an isolated incident and that more than 30,000 people kill themselves every year in the United States.

HIP HOP AND THE CULTURE OF GRAFFITI

The graffiti that is perhaps best known today and is foremost in our minds when we hear the term is that which has grown out of an important subculture known as *hip hop*. Hip hop arose in the 1970s out of a music movement that was invented and developed by African Americans living in the Bronx neighborhood of New York City. Although it began as a musical style, the term was soon used to cover four particular sections of this subculture: graffiti, hip-hop dance, rap, and DJ-ing. The music was a result of the work of Kool Herc, a DJ who made his own music, which he played on two turntables to highlight rhythmic beats.

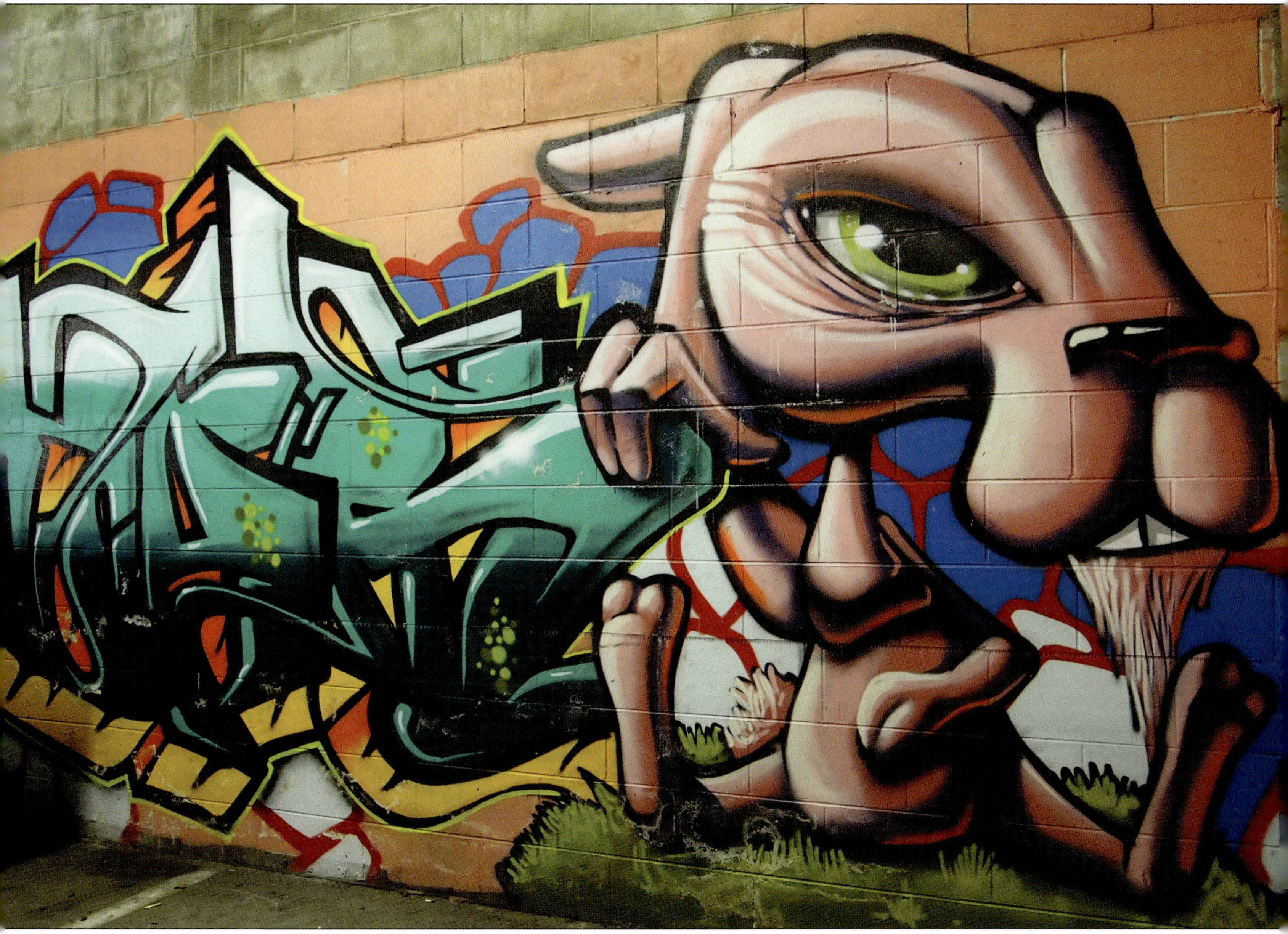

An example of the type of graffiti most people are familiar with nowadays. This piece was actually commissioned for an underground car park in an attempt to help prevent unsolicited graffiti.

Photo courtesy of Homer Alvarez.

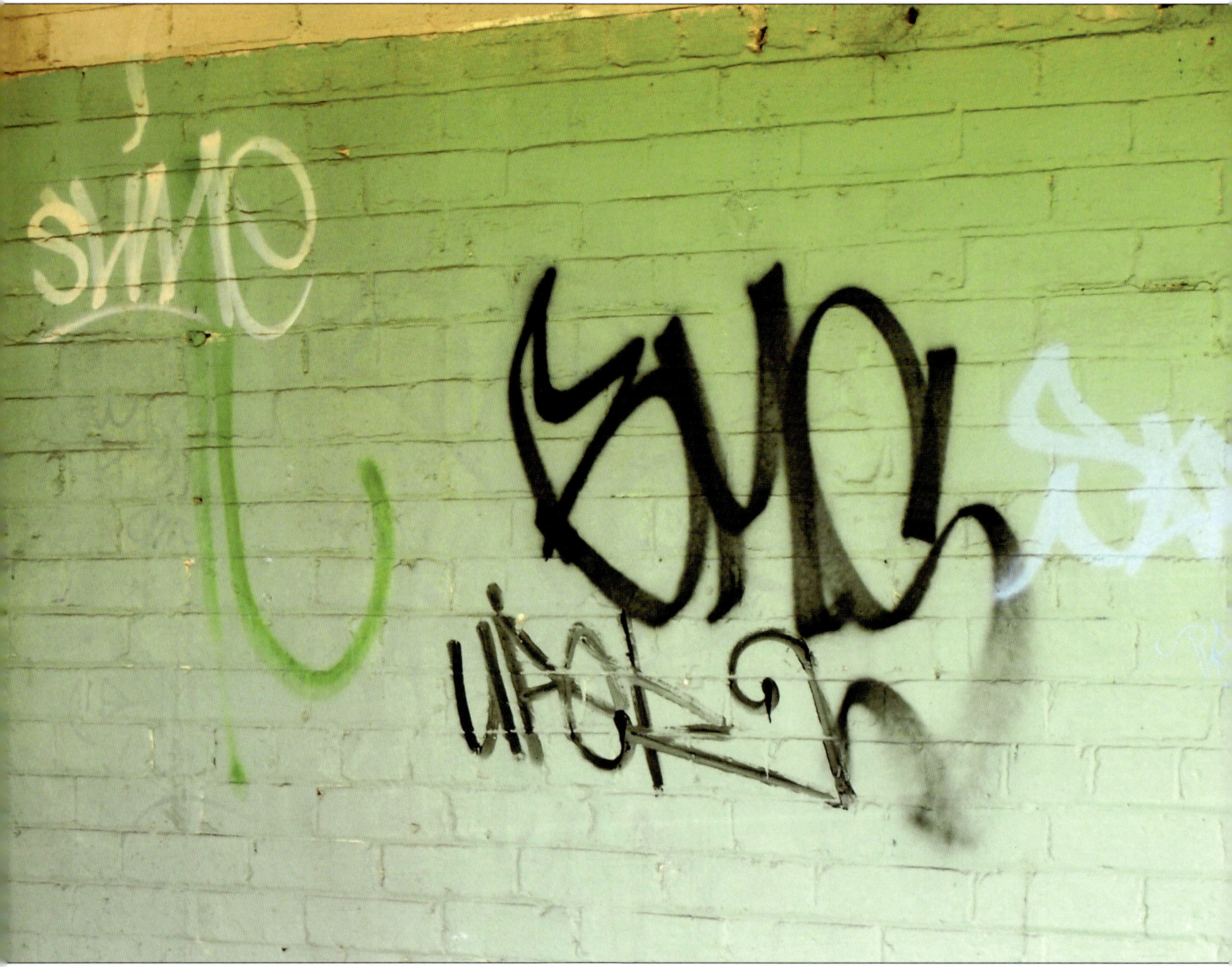

Tags are signatures used by graffitists to mark territory or to let other graffitists know that they have been and tagged there. Competitions are often carried out between individuals and groups of graffitists to see who can tag the most in a given area.

Photo courtesy of Homer Alvarez.

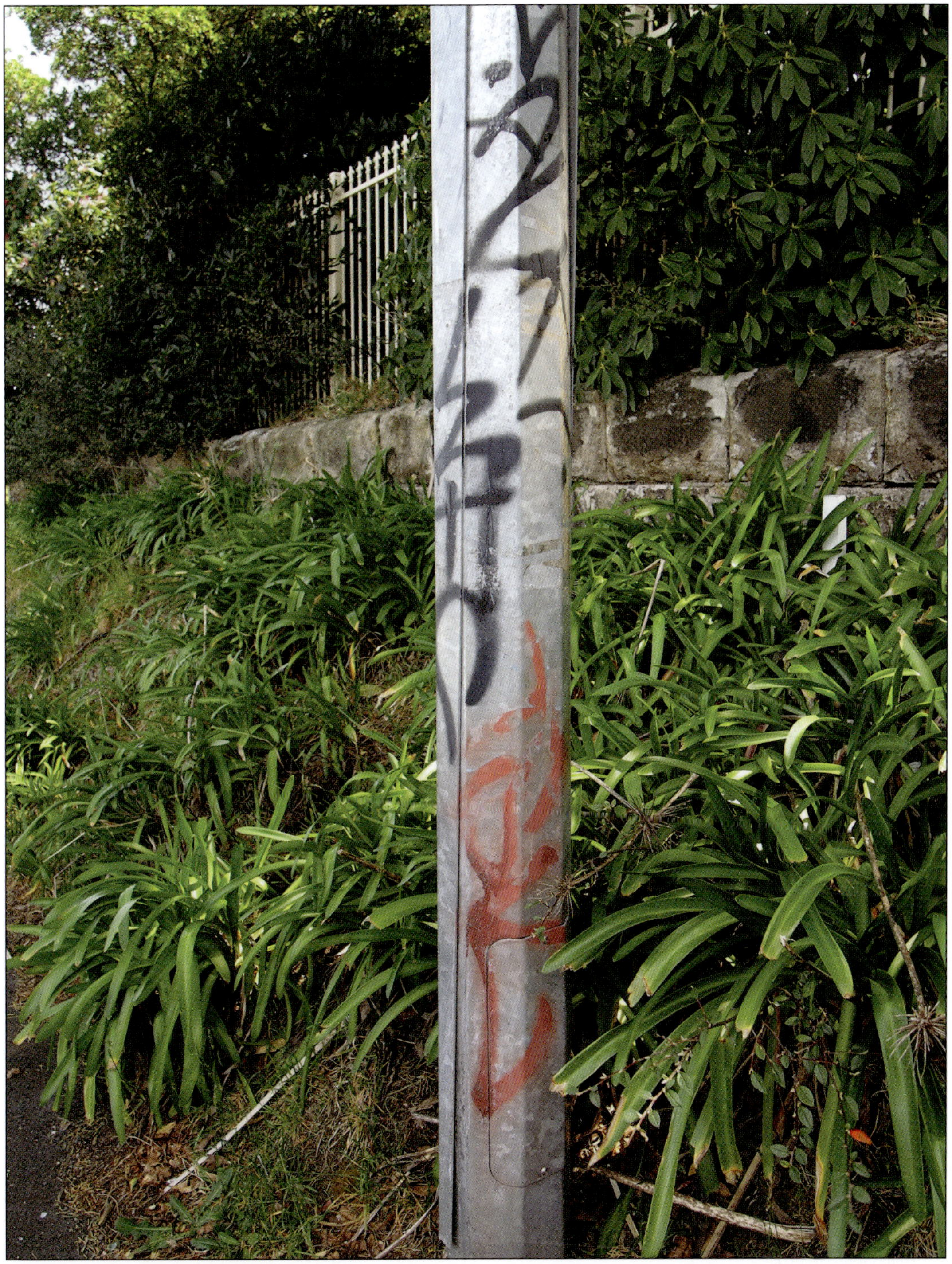

Tags are applied to » any surface possible. Here it is written down an electricity pole.
Photo courtesy of Homer Alvarez.

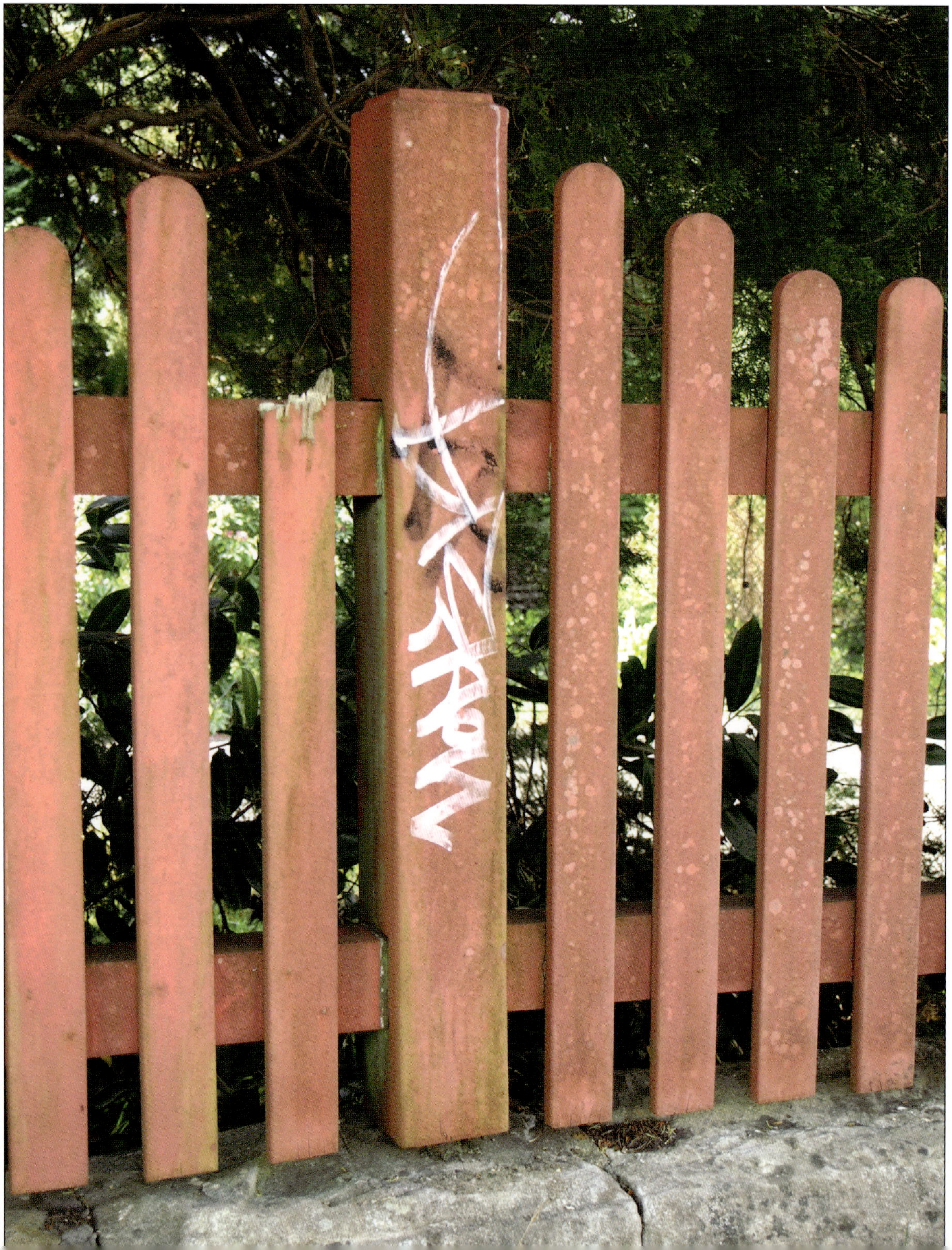

« The narrow palings of a picket fence provide a challenge to tag with an aerosol can.
Photo courtesy of Homer Alvarez.

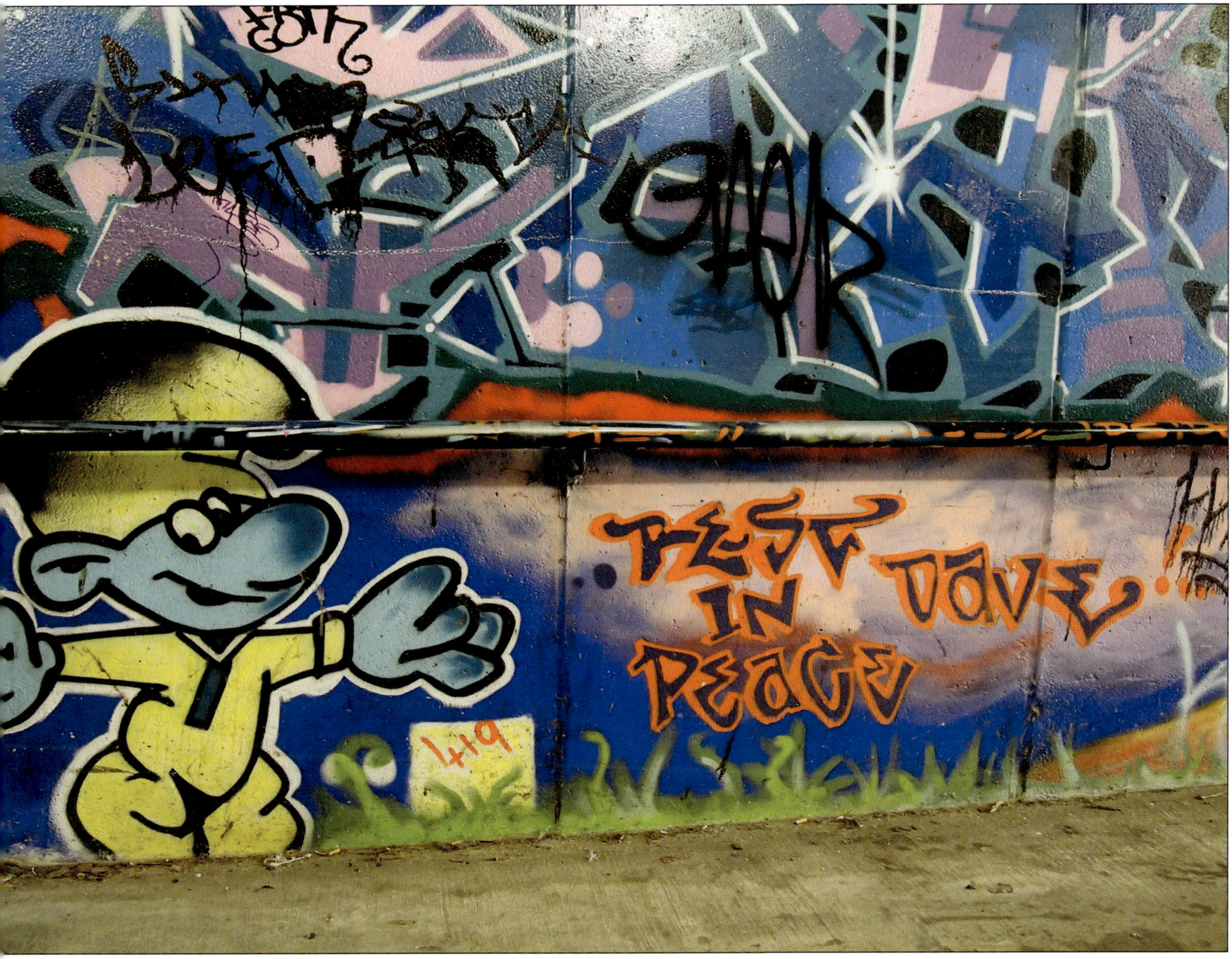

Graffiti was once considered sacred among graffitists and it was considered an insult to graffiti over someone else's work, although a major work could be placed over a minor one and tags were the lowest form of graffiti. In this instance, though, tags have been scrawled over major works, which is breaking the code of respect among graffitists and is called "dissing" (as in disrespect). Perhaps the taggers felt the painting didn't constitute real graffiti because it had been authorized.

Photo courtesy of Homer Alvarez.

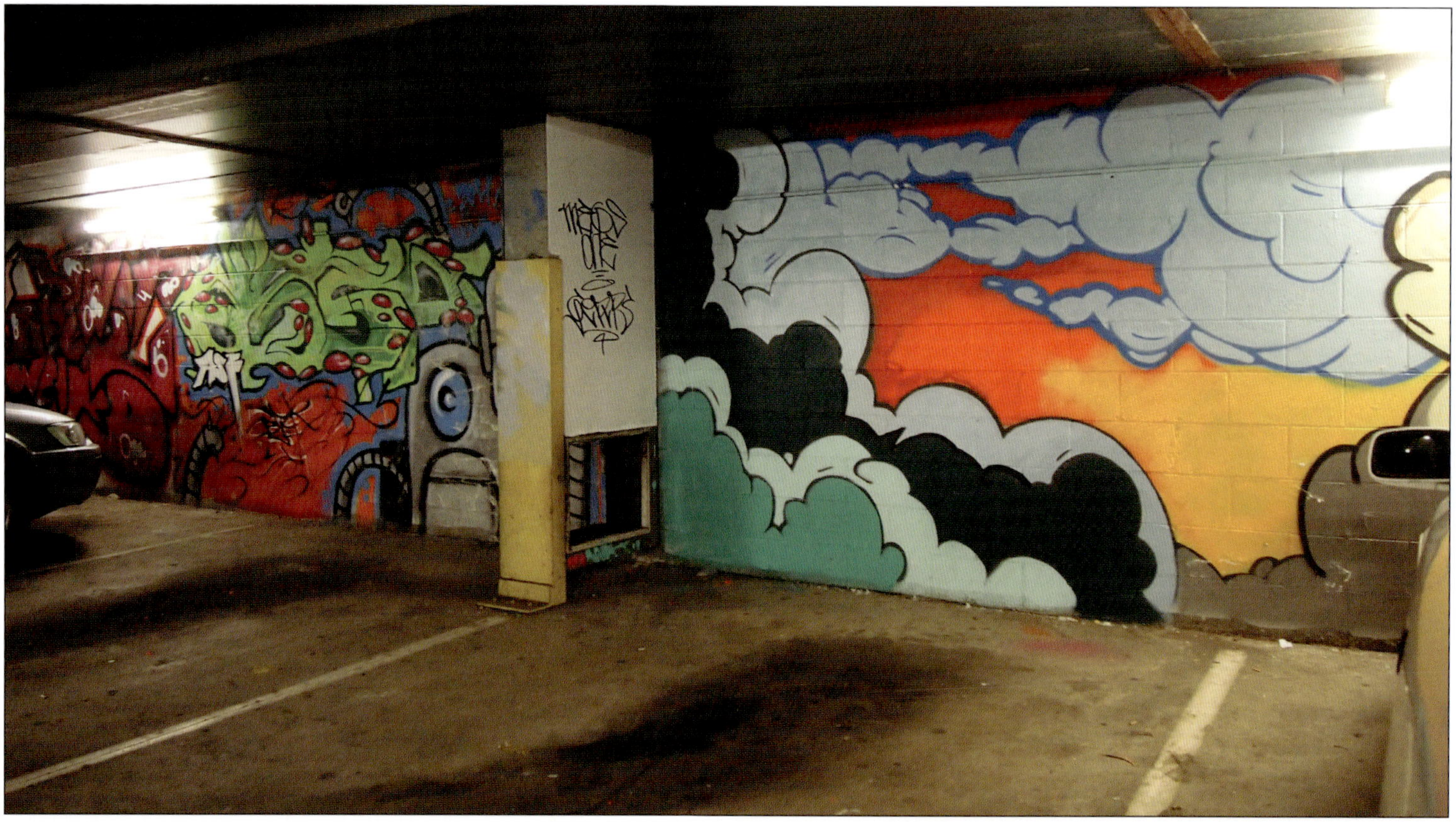

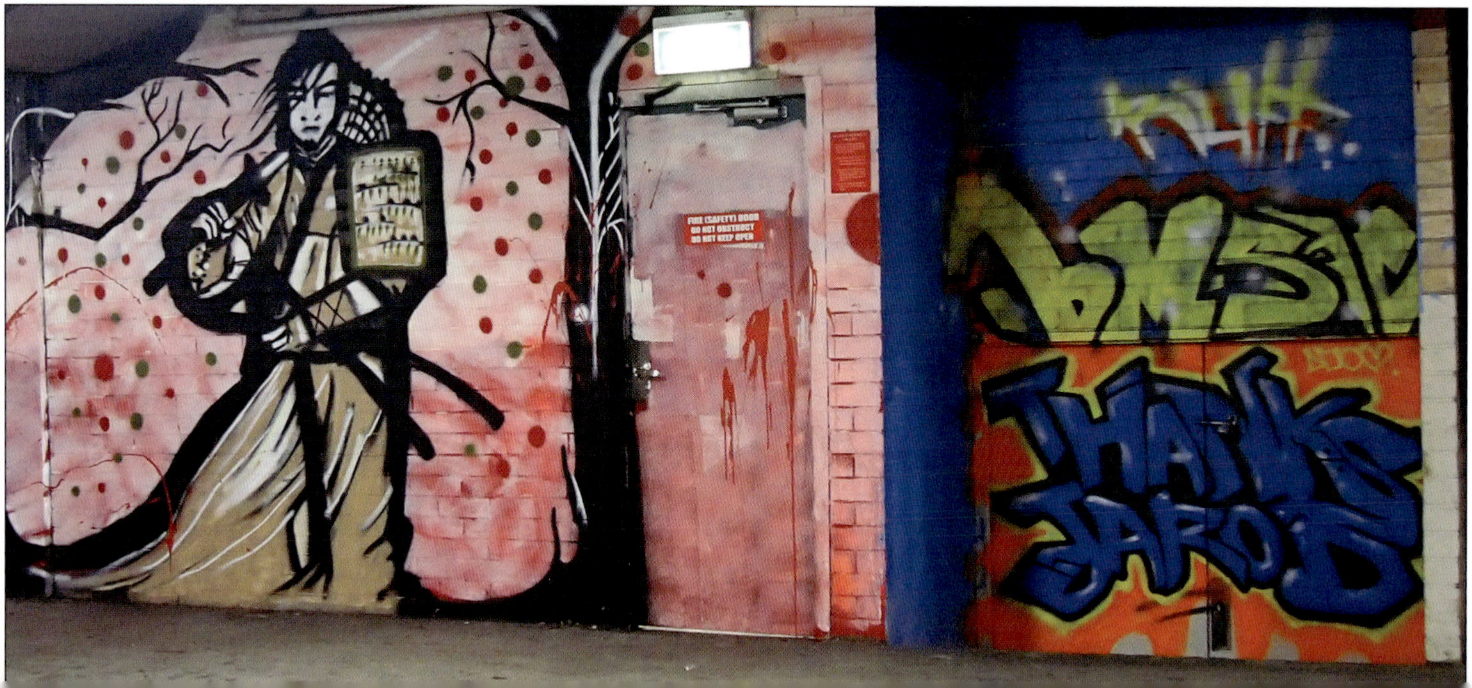
FIRE (SAFETY) DOOR
DO NOT OBSTRUCT
DO NOT KEEP OPEN
THANKS
JAROD

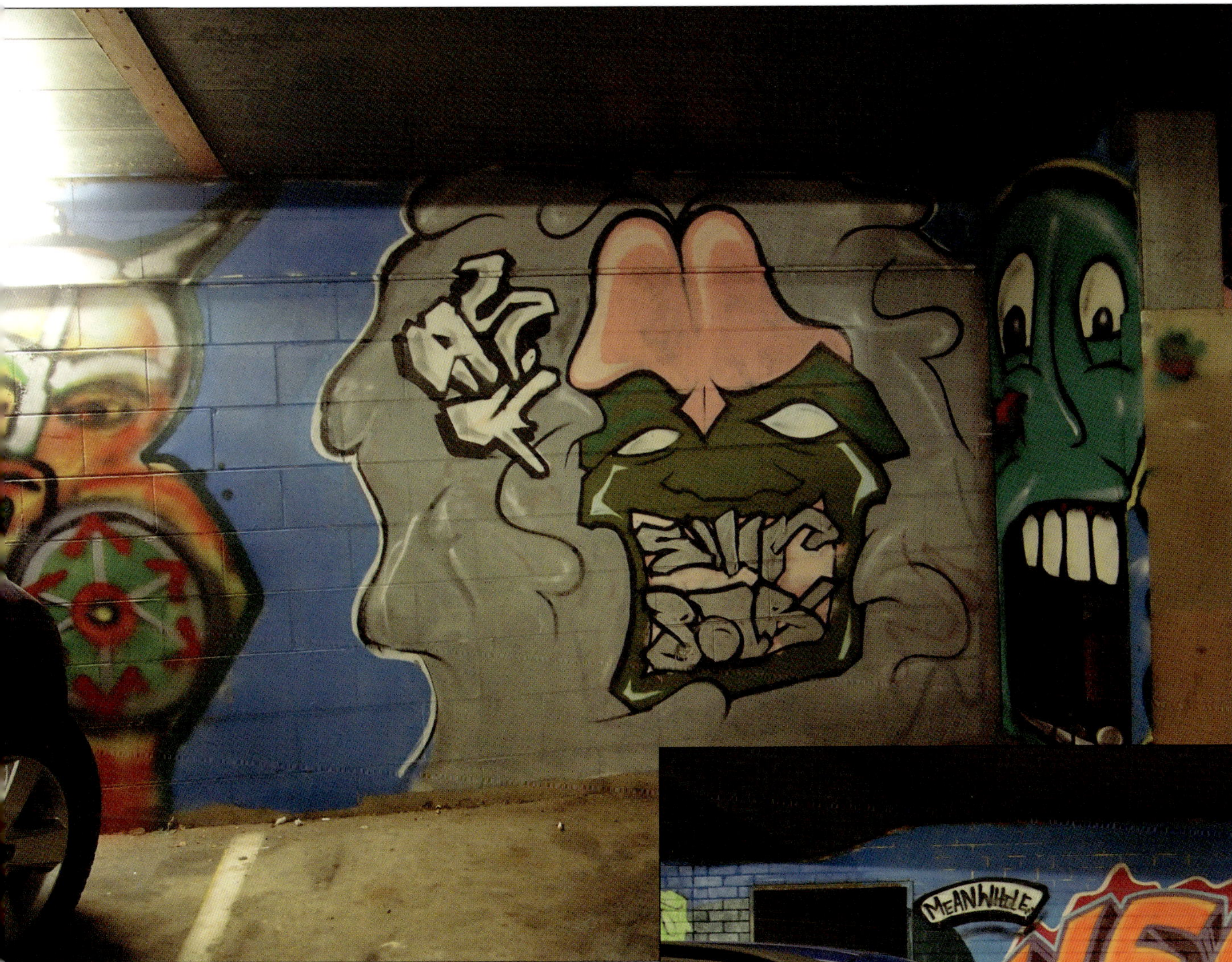

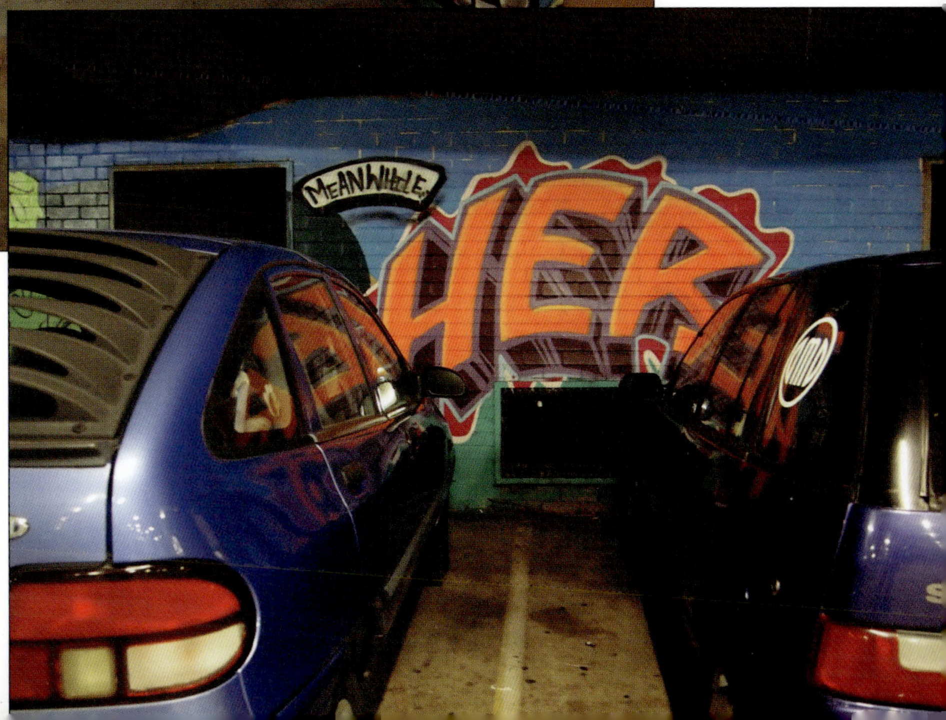

This is a series of commissioned graffiti for an underground car park in Katoomba in the Blue Mountains, NSW, Australia.

Photos courtesy of Homer Alvarez.

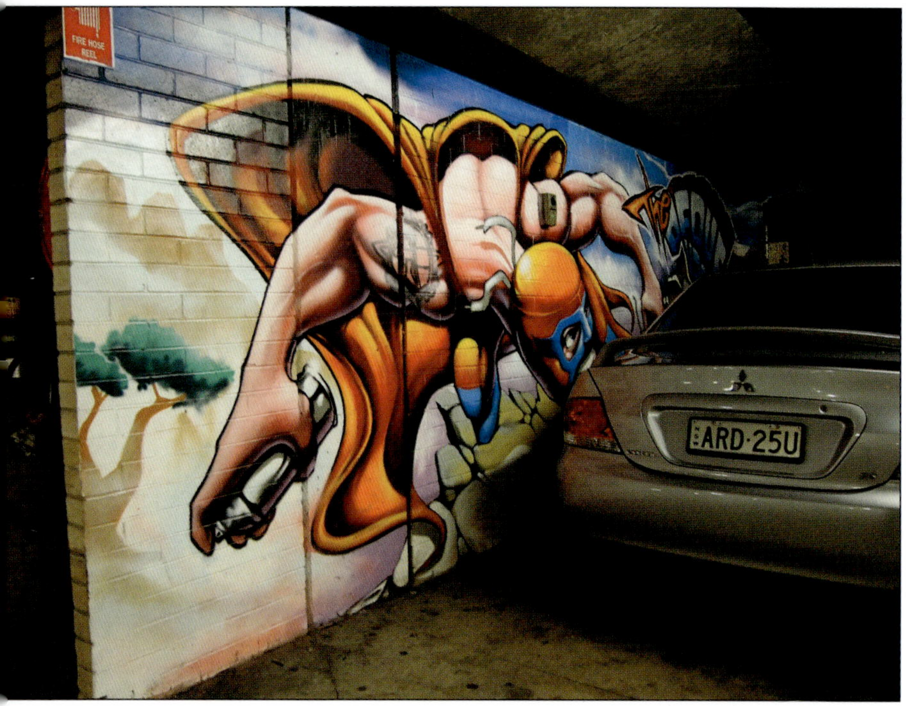

Photo courtesy of Homer Alvarez.

The term "hip hop" was not actually coined until 1978, when a member of Grandmaster Flash and the Furious Five, Keith "Cowboy" Wiggins, made fun of a friend who was joining the army. He mimicked the marching of soldiers by singing "hip, hop, hip, hop." Wiggins was so pleased with the effect, he made it part of his show, which led to other artists working with him calling the music "hip hoppers."

When it first emerged, hip hop was something new; it challenged existing ideas about sexism, racism, and consumerism. This made it the perfect breeding ground for graffiti, which had a strong history of expressing subversive social ideals, as we've seen.

The negative connotations associated with hip hop came about with the linking of the term with street gangs in the Bronx. These were the boys, and girls, responsible for graffiti-ing large parts of the city as well as indulging in turf wars, drug dealing, and prostitution. To change the violent culture of the gangs and the youth in general, Afrika Bambaataa set up the Zulu Nation. This enterprise involved dancers, musicians, and artists pooled from the gangs who were then given direction and purpose through their art.

Graffiti, as already mentioned, had been used in the modern era mainly for political slogans and protests, but in urban areas, it was also being used by gangs to mark their turf. From this culture of graffiti grew the practice of writing tags—the first of these emerged on Philadelphia city streets in the late 1960s. Within two years, the movement of graffiti had moved its center to New York City and a practice sprang up of adding the street number of a given artist to his or her tag. Tagging, or "bombing," trains became a popular pastime. The train would spread the name, and consequently the reputation, of the artist. Soon competition arose between graffiti aficionados to see who could cover the most territory with their tags.

Tagging was a good challenge for graffiti artists, but the more artistically inclined painters started to write whole words and phrases in their graffiti, making them fancy, filling them with color, and creating designs that were reminiscent of the 1970s hippies, with their psychedelic colors and wildly distorted lettering that was barely legible. This type of graffiti work is still practiced today—especially in urban centers—although stencils and figurative work are now taking over in popularity.

TAG THIS!

Tsang Tsou Choi

Like urban taggers, Tsang Tsou Choi, also known as the King of Kowloon, used graffiti to mark his familial territory. Tsang began his graffiti work in the mid-1950s and it was his belief that the area he was marking with his calligraphy had belonged to his grandfather and that he, Tsang, was just re-staking his family's claim to it, in name at least.

Tsang's method of working was to write his graffiti and let it dry, and then he would return later to touch it up. He painted his art everywhere in Hong Kong, leaving it on mailboxes and street signs, walls and cars parked in the street. Tsang's graffiti included his name, his supposed title—the Emperor of Kowloon—and the location of Hong Kong. Then he would make his family tree, which usually contained about twenty names. After this, he wrote the names of various

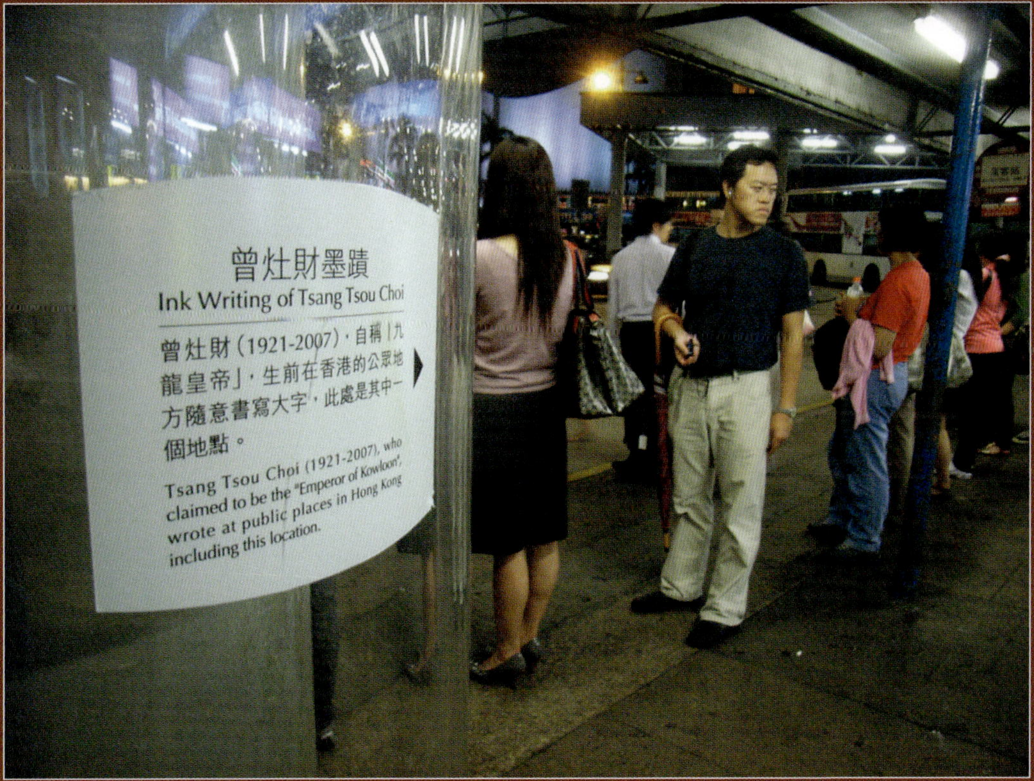

« When he was alive and writing his graffiti, Tsang Tsou Choi was considered an eccentric vandal. Now that he is dead, his work is seen as a curious part of Hong Kong's heritage and surviving work is preserved behind Perspex. *Photo courtesy of Sainfangmid.*

emperors. At the end of his lists he would conclude: "Down with the Queen of England." On occasion, Tsang would also include a demand for repatriation from the government for the loss of what he deemed his family's land.

Tsang covered whole pillars or walls with his writing, and he was arrested for doing so in several instances. He was never given a harsh punishment, though, and when fined, it was only a small amount. But the tagging had a tragic effect on his family life. His wife and the rest of his relations eventually abandoned him, claiming he was a lunatic.

Tsang was considered quite famous for his tags, and his work inspired fashion designers and other artists across the globe. But even so, one magazine put him on a list of their ten top least influential people, though it is likely they were referring to his personality and not his talent. Tsang was also featured in a commercial for Swipe, a cleaning formula that was purported to clean away most messes, where he was shown cleaning up his own inky graffiti. His participation in the commercial nearly gave him star status.

In his last years, Tsang lived quietly in a nursing home, no longer capable of wandering the streets on his own. He applied pen and ink to paper, pieces of furniture, and other domestic products, though, never stopping with his art. Tsang also told visitors of the home that he should be the chief executive of Hong Kong. And even though he was never given acknowledgment for his family's ownership of Hong Kong, Tsang found fame and a small fortune in his artistic recognition. His work was taken all over the world and sold for large sums of money. He died of a heart attack in 2007 at the age of eighty-five.

SPRAY CAN ART

Some purists will debate about whether spray paint art is graffiti or not, arguing that it is an art form in its own right. One way that spray can art differs from graffiti *made* with spray paint is that it is usually not painted directly onto a wall, but instead uses a base such as masonite or posterboard, metal panels, glass, or ceramic, which is then placed outside in public, though not always.

Just as modern graffiti comes from hip-hop culture with its big, crazy lettering and bright colors, so spray can art has its own genres and paint styles. Typical themes of spray can art include surreal landscapes, cityscapes, cosmology, and abundant forest scenes.

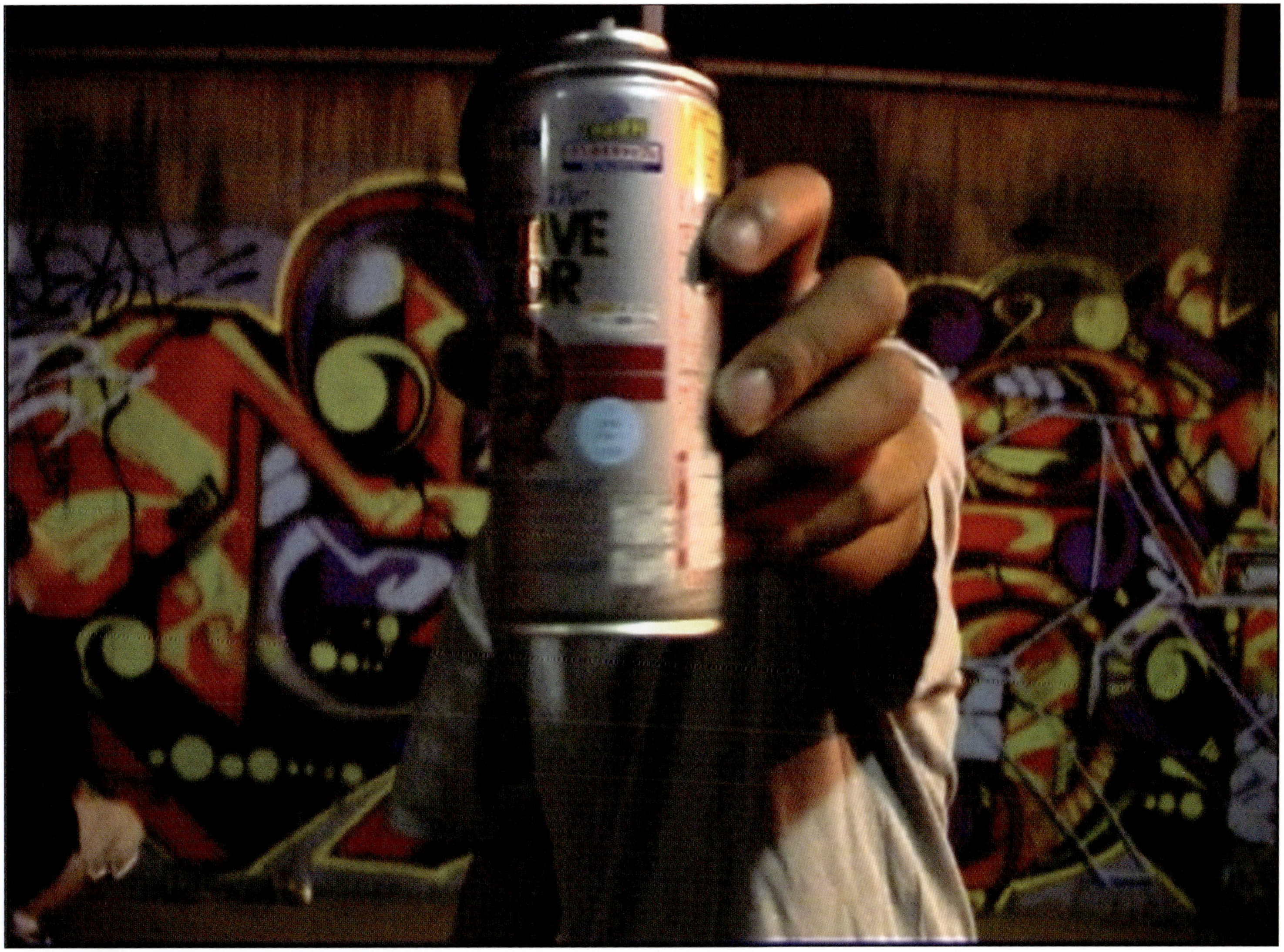

An example of spray can art found on the street.

There is conjecture that spray can art began with one particular artist, Ruben "Sadot" Fernandez of Mexico City. Frenandez would set up his workspace outside his house and begin to paint a variety of subjects using only spray paint. He then progressed to making art in more public places. His entire painting process involved accompanying music; Fernandez would listen to anything from classical to rock and everything in between. It made the act of painting a spectacle and drew large crowds to watch him work. Not only did Frenandez paint to music in public, but he also punctuated the performance with words of wisdom and philosophical musings.

Because Fernandez made both a name for himself and a large sum of money from his art, there were many people eager to follow suit. The result was a subgenre of graffiti in which graffiti-style pictures were made on transportable surfaces and then placed in public, often chained or tied to some immovable object, such as a sign post.

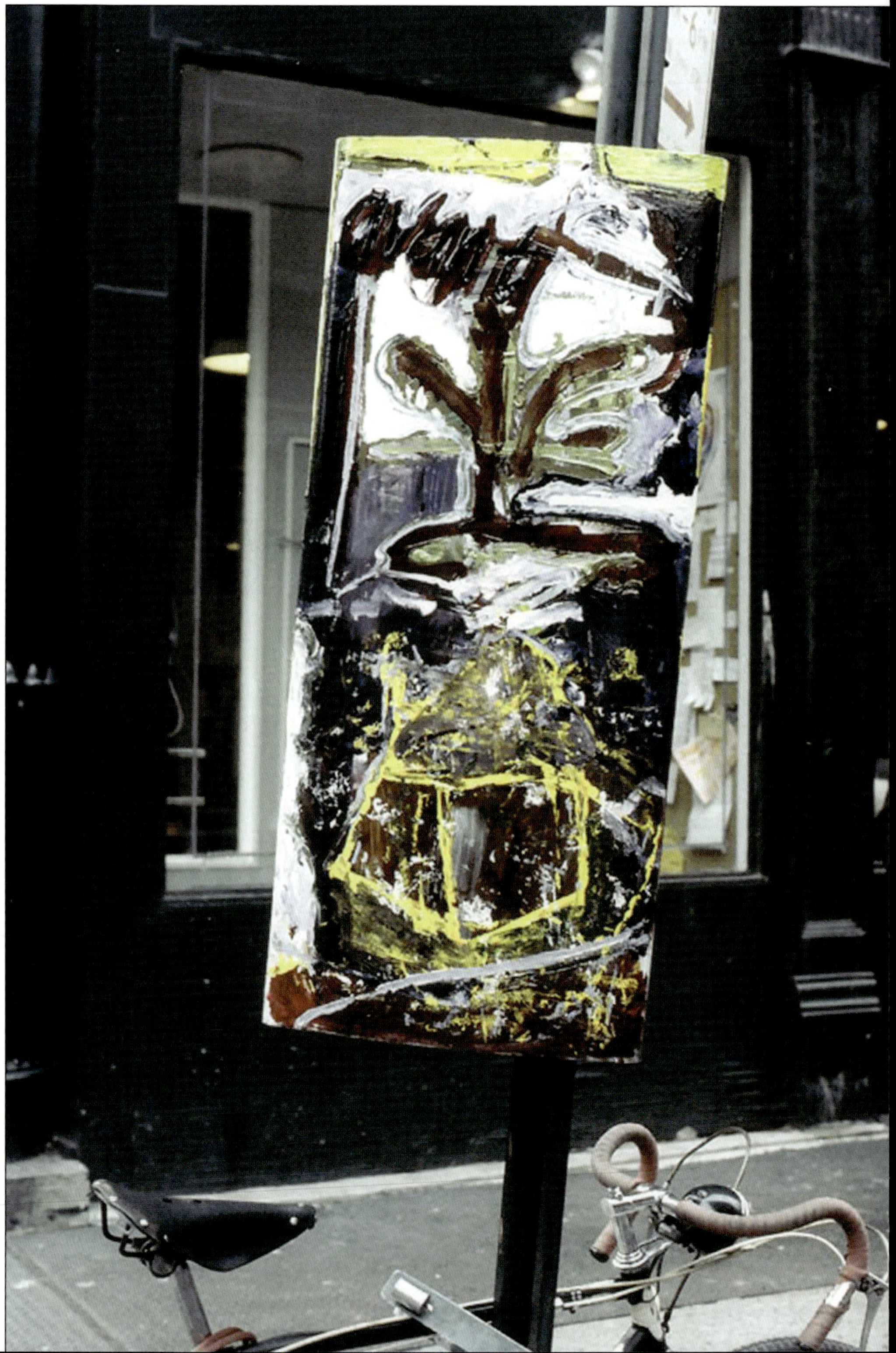

Love it or hate it, this type of graffiti » is movable and therefore can be taken away without destroying the artwork or the place it was put. It is also much easier to sell a piece that can be tucked under an arm and carried off.

GRAFFITI AS VANDALISM

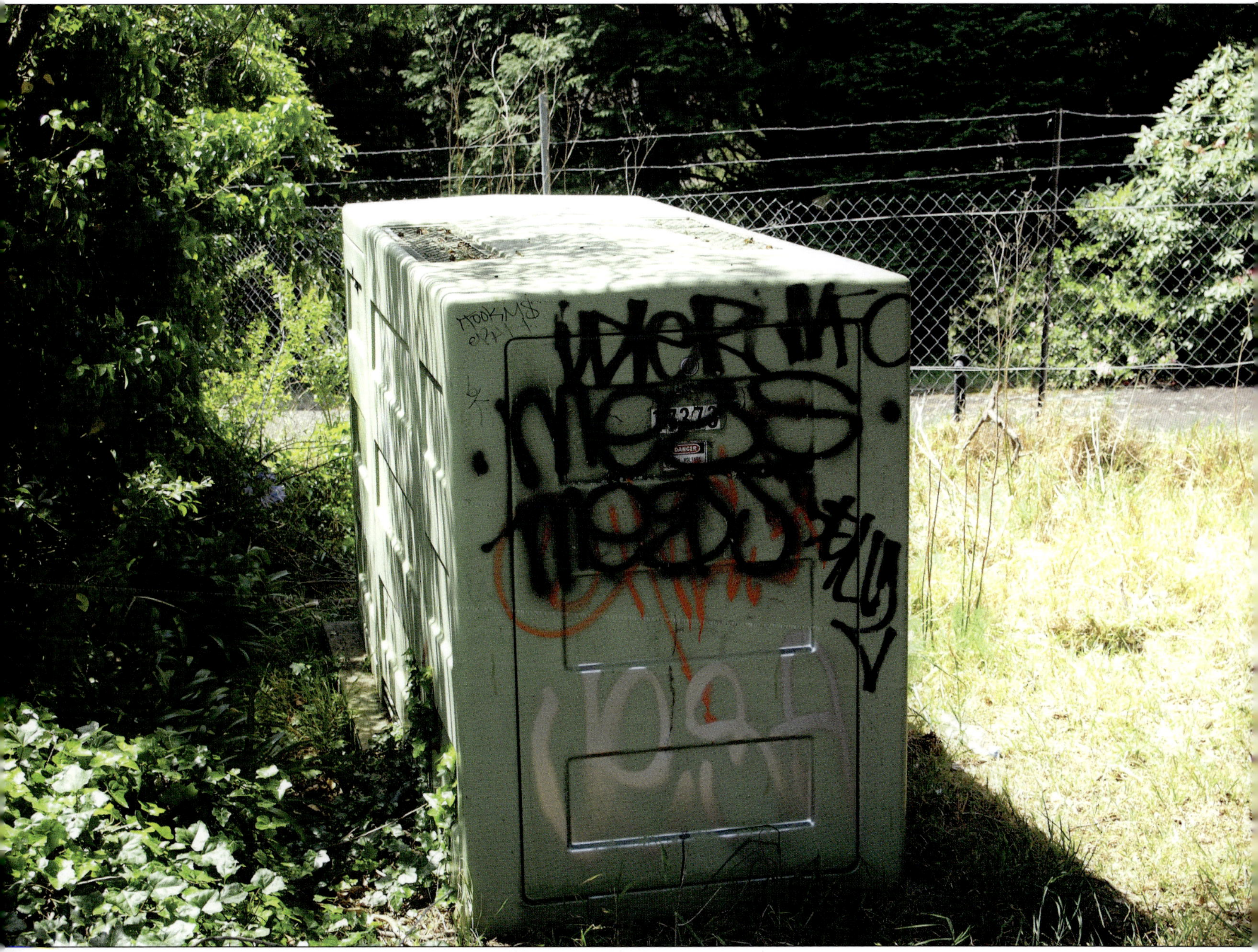

An electricity box covered in tags is seen by the general public as an act of mindless vandalism.
Photo courtesy of Homer Alvarez.

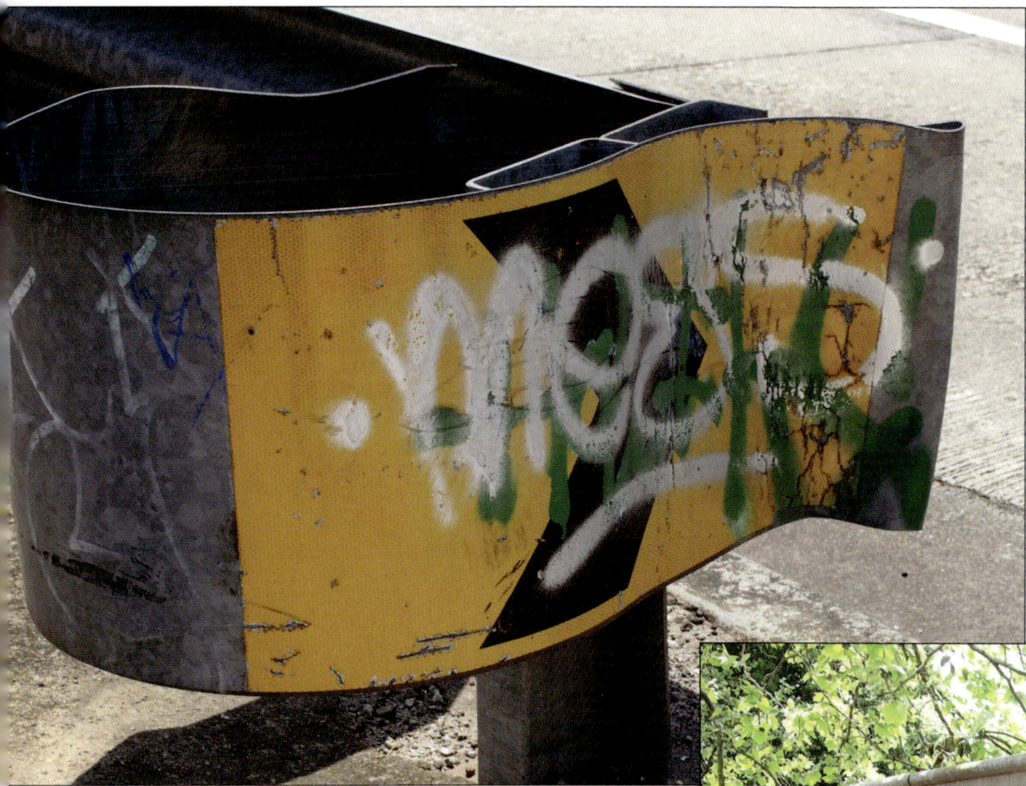

« A tag obscuring the markings of a road barrier.
Photo courtesy of Homer Alvarez.

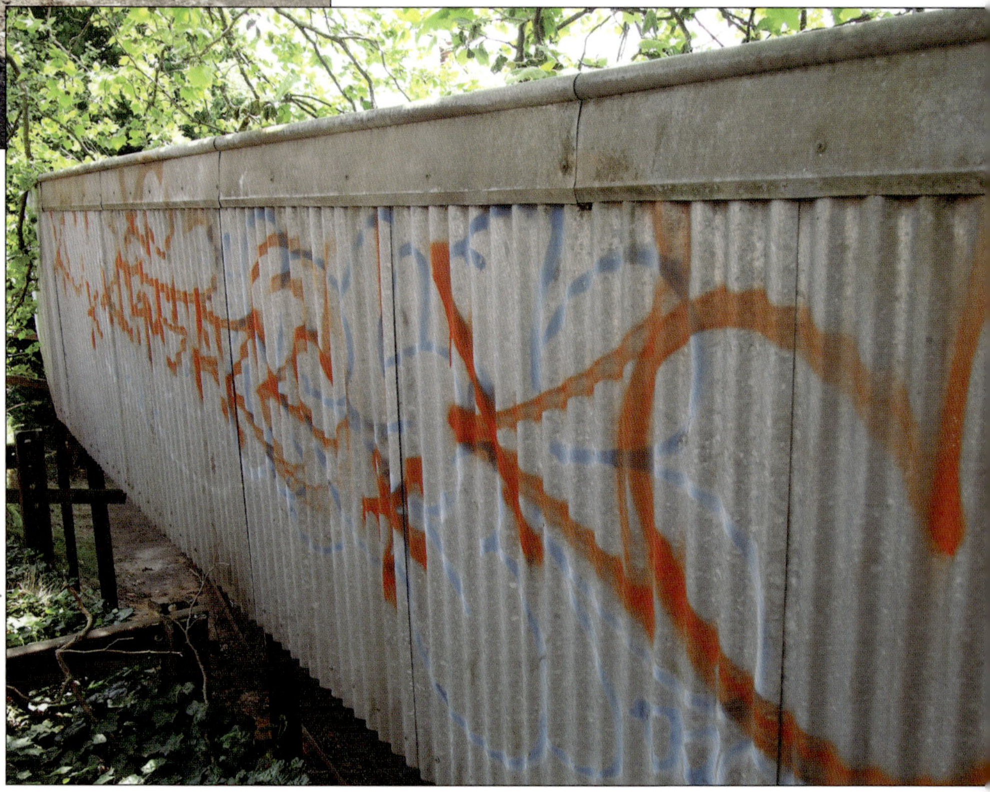

Graffiti sprayed onto a fence is especially » offensive if it is on private property. This kind of graffiti, painted onto someone's garden fence, has a threatening feeling about it as if the private space has been invaded.
Photo courtesy of Homer Alvarez.

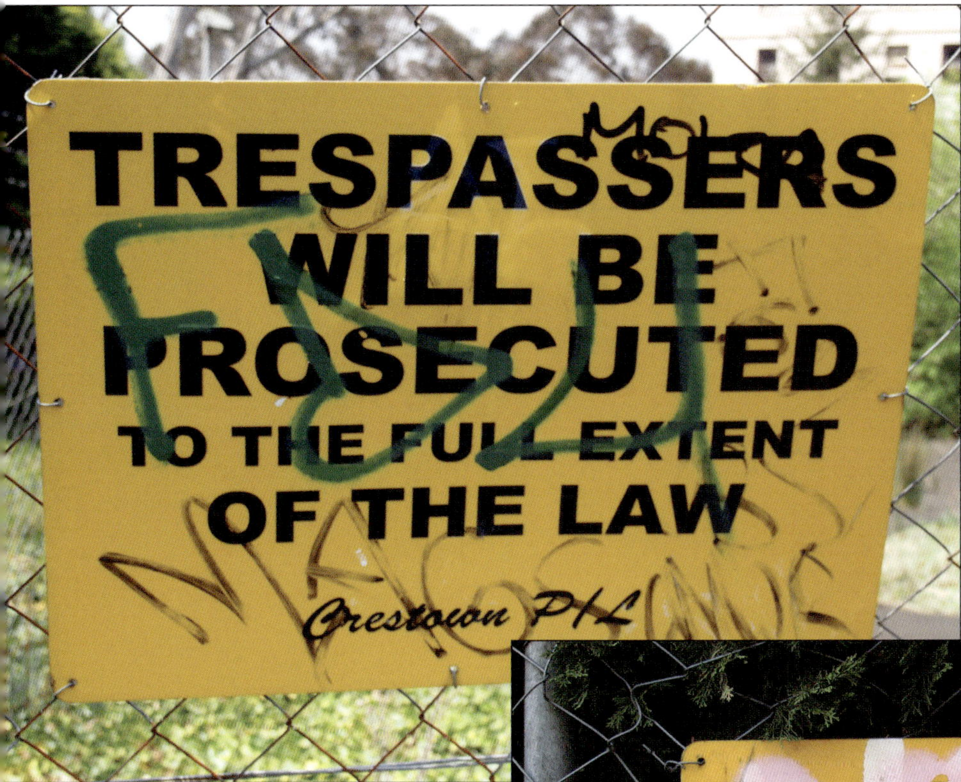

This sign warning trespassers they may be liable to prosecution is shown over a period of one week. The second picture of such defacing has almost obliterated the message and is an obvious act of contempt for authority.

Photos courtesy of Homer Alvarez.

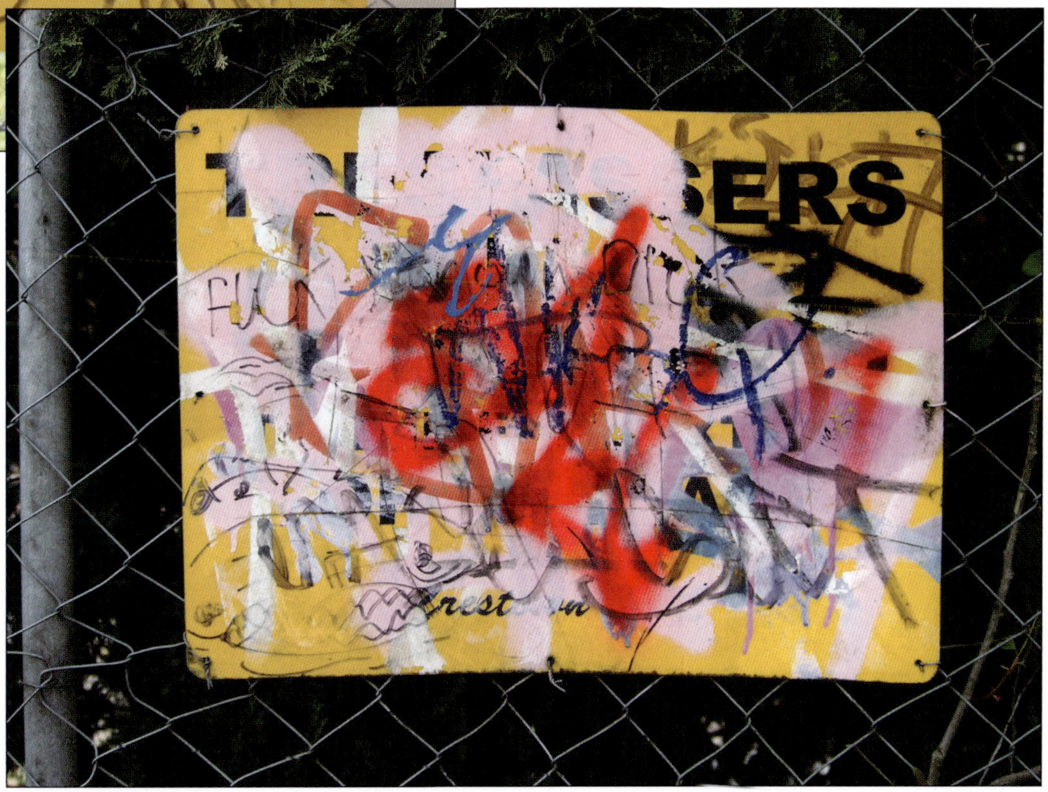

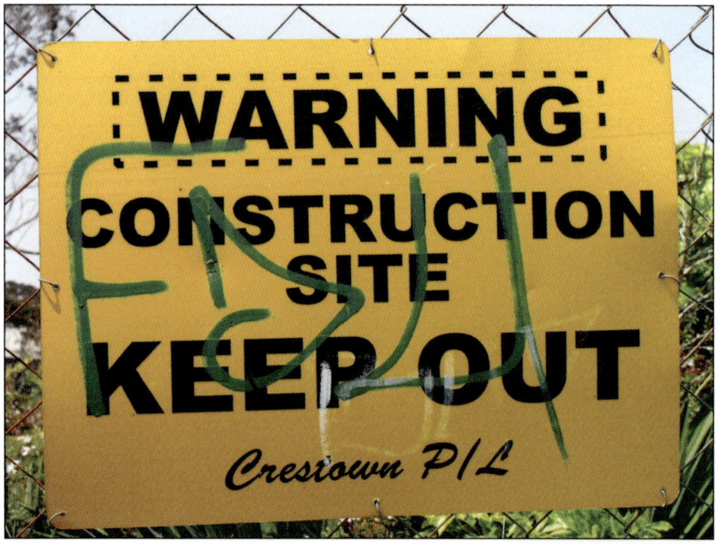

« A sign warning passersby of a construction site proves a more serious problem if defaced so that it can no longer be read.
Photo courtesy of Homer Alvarez.

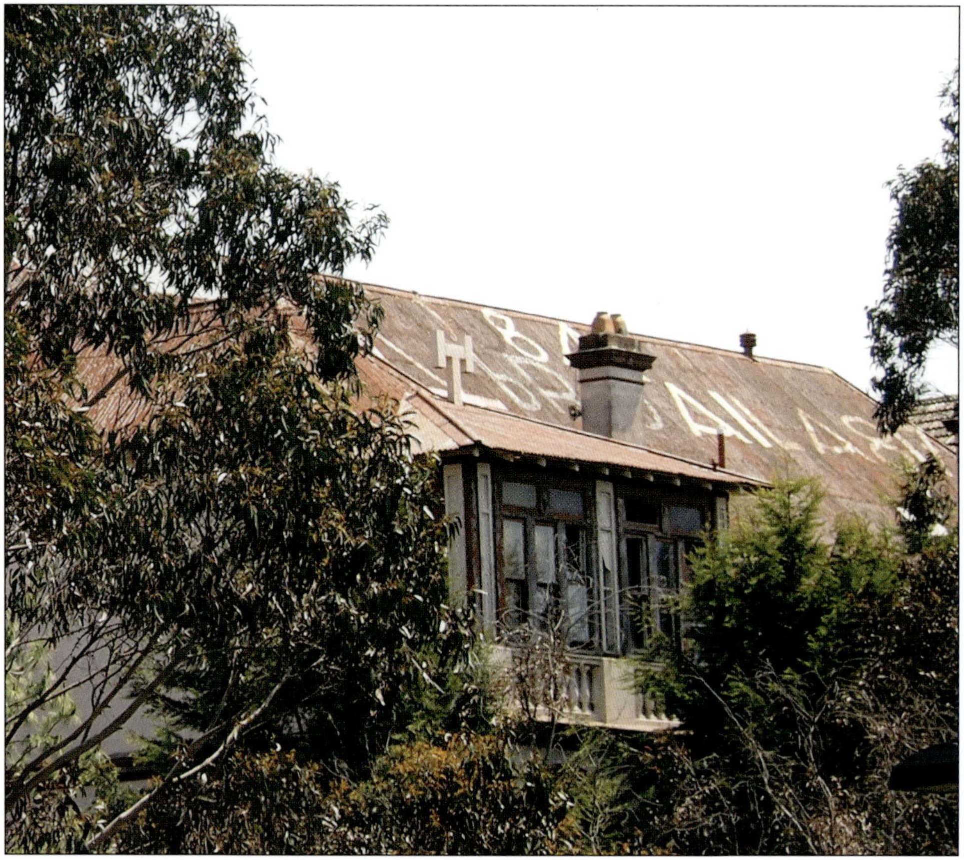

I first visited this lovely old building » in Katoomba in the late 1980s. It was called the Renaissance Centre and was full of boutique shops selling handmade goods, cafes, and restaurants. As soon as the last tenant left in the late 1990s, the whole place became a target for vandals of all kinds. Graffiti was probably the least of its worries.
Photo courtesy of Homer Alvarez.

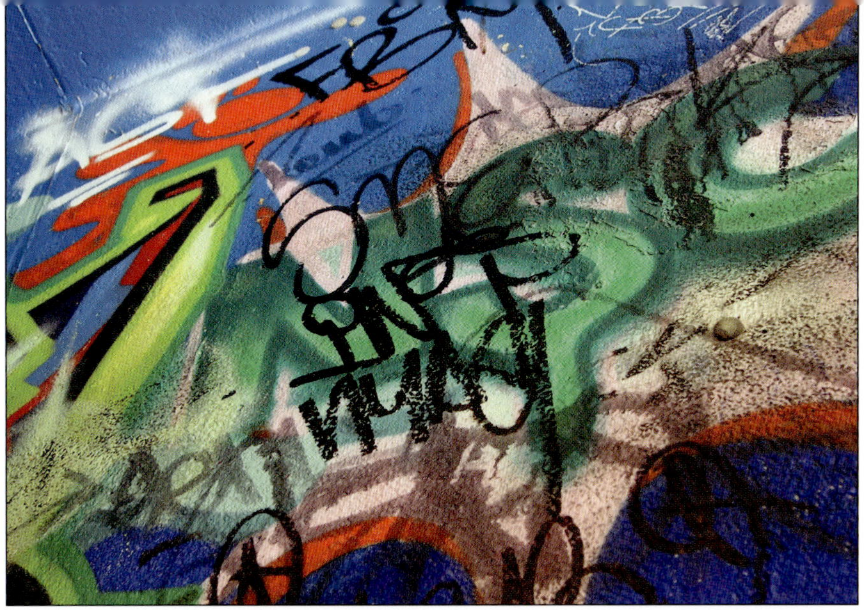

Tags have been painted over mural graffiti, ruining the piece underneath.
Photos courtesy of Homer Alvarez.

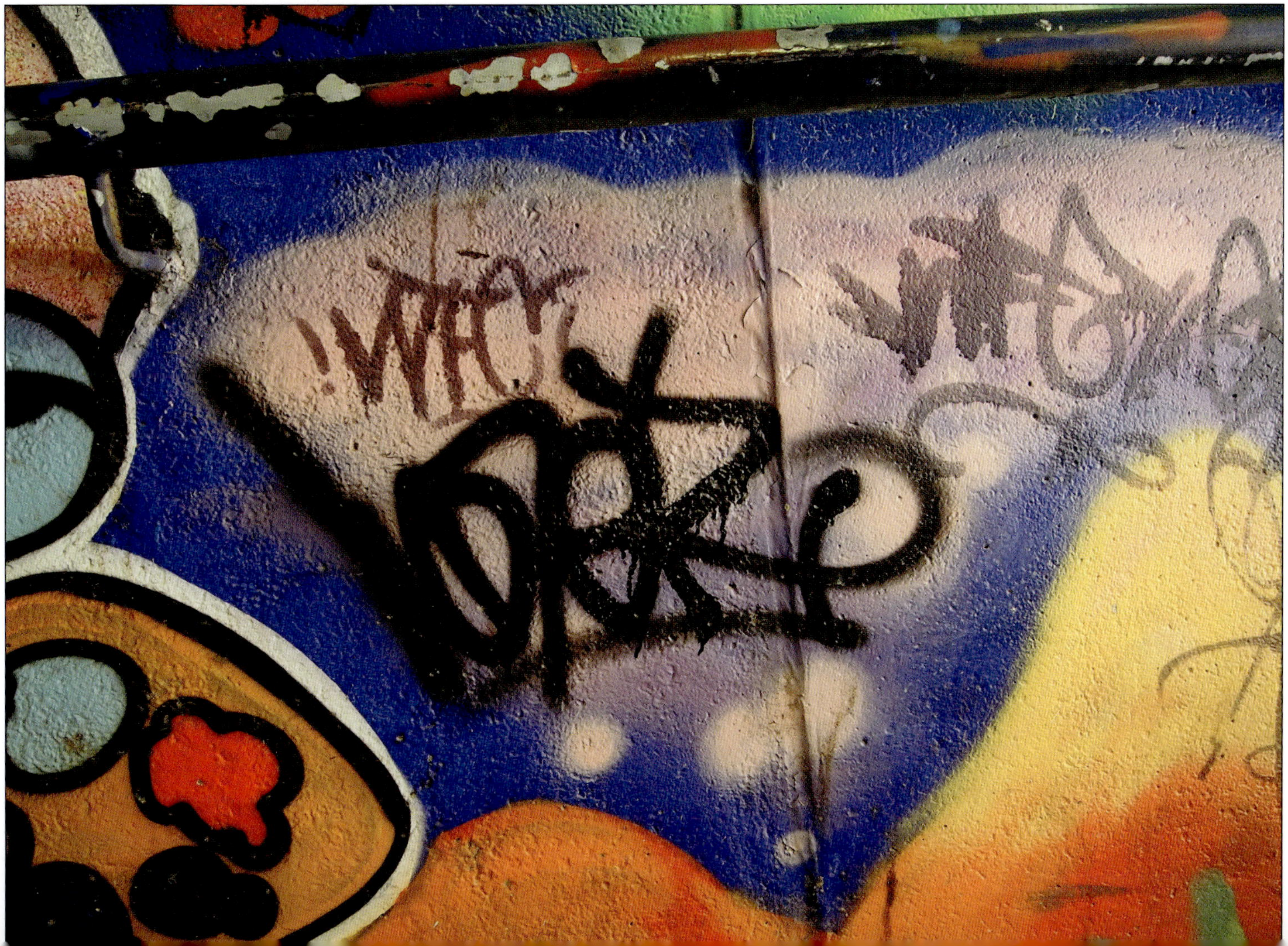

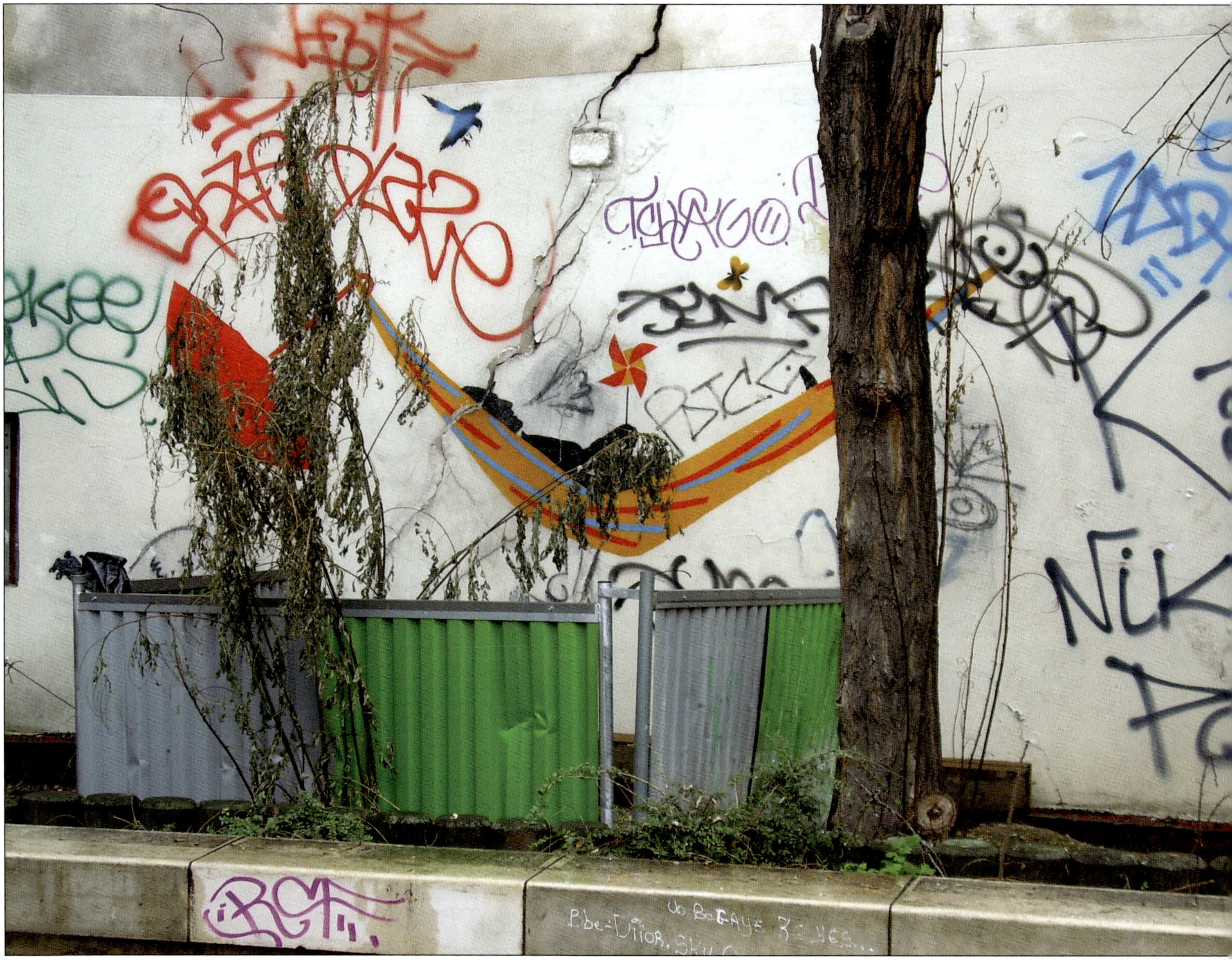

Even the great and respected Nemo of Paris has his whimsical pieces destroyed by tags that have been sprayed over with no regard to the piece underneath.

Photo courtesy of Sophie Masson.

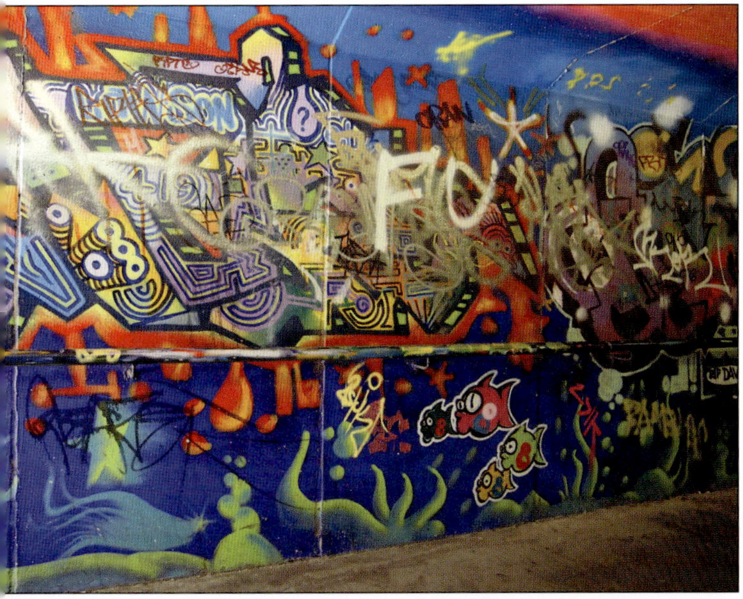

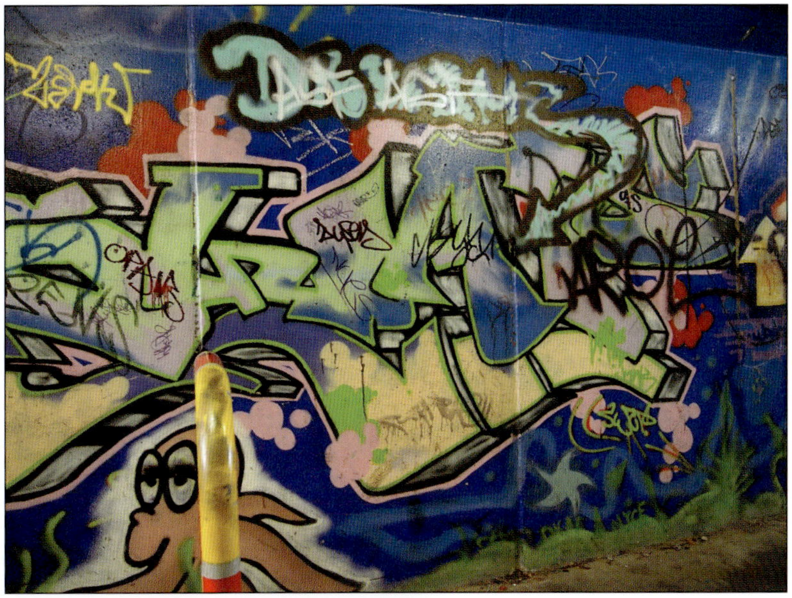

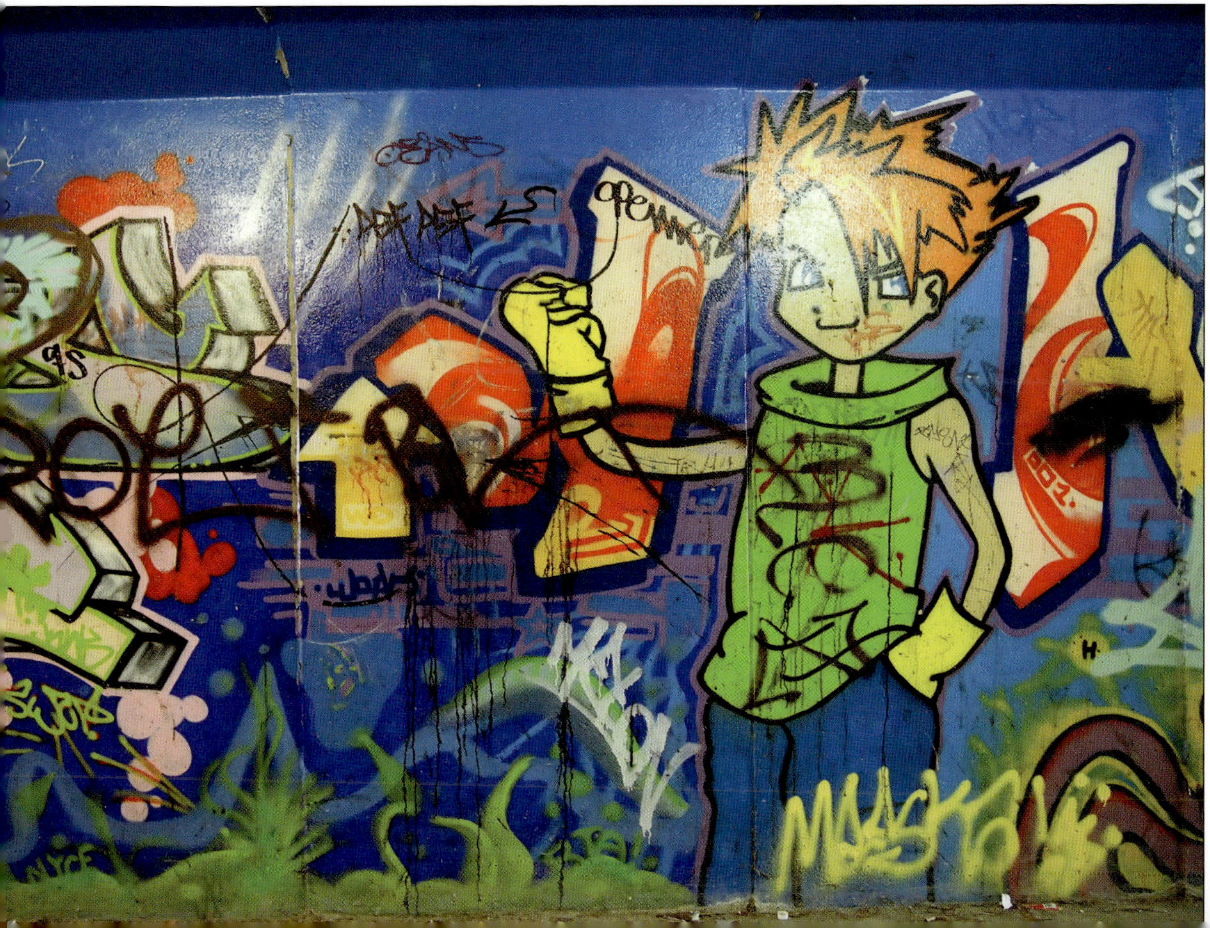

More tags that have been painted over major graffiti works. The murals in the underground garage were commissioned and may have attracted an element of disapproval from purist graffitists, but the works here were not authorized; instead, they make an interesting and pleasant atmosphere for the commuters who use the pedestrian tunnel where they were first made.

Photos courtesy of Homer Alvarez.

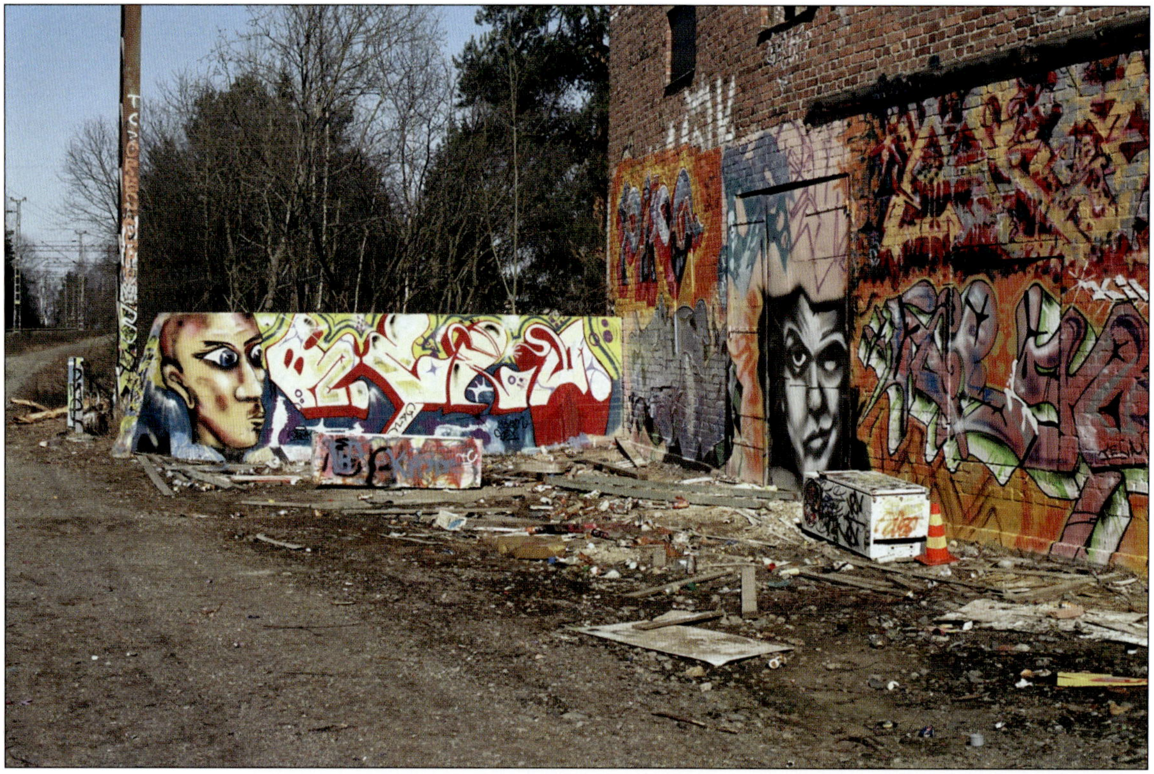

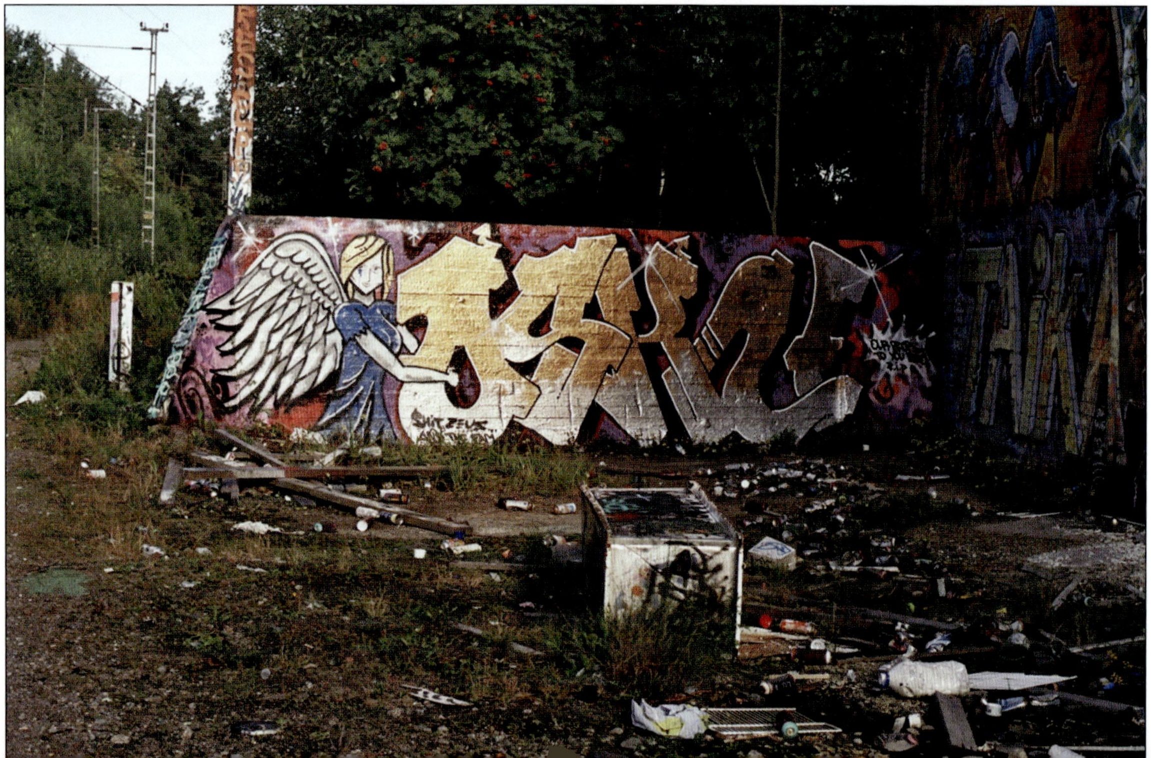

These photos were taken over a period of several years. The site is a disused factory and the photographer became intrigued at how the graffiti would change over time. The first picture was taken in April 2009, the next in August of the same year, and they both show different styles and character of work. The third photo, taken nearly two years later, shows a shift back to a lettering style. November 2011 seems to have been painted in homage to Halloween while the final work has again favored the lettering style. When the pieces that are painted over other pieces are of such high quality themselves, should it be considered vandalism or simply a change, like the window display of a shop?
Photos courtesy of Mikko Putkonen.

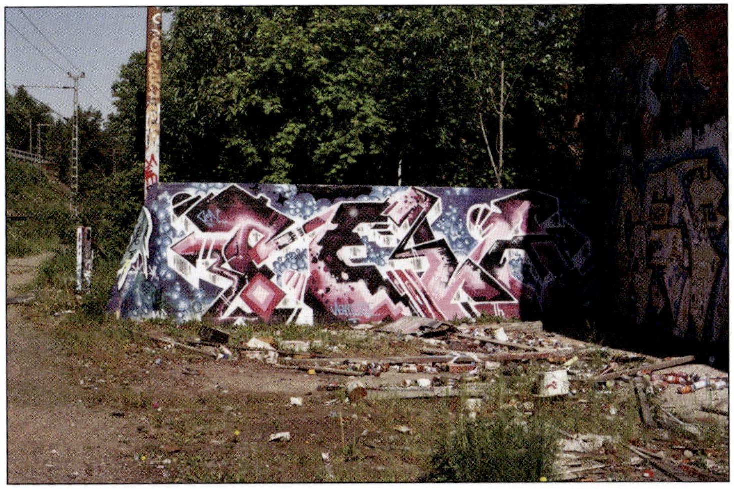

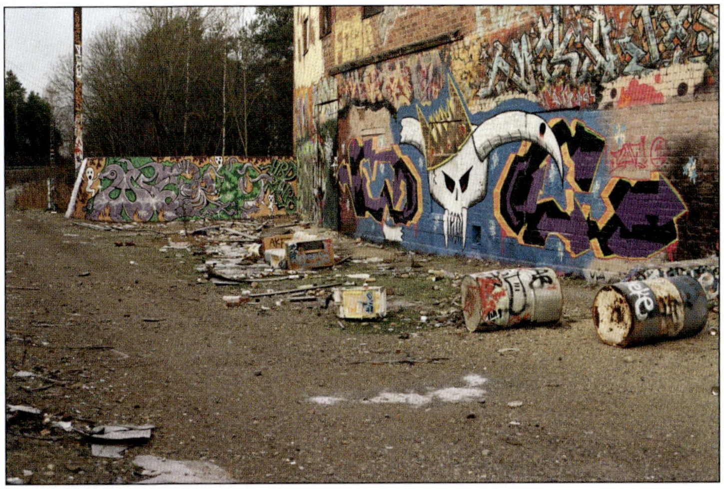

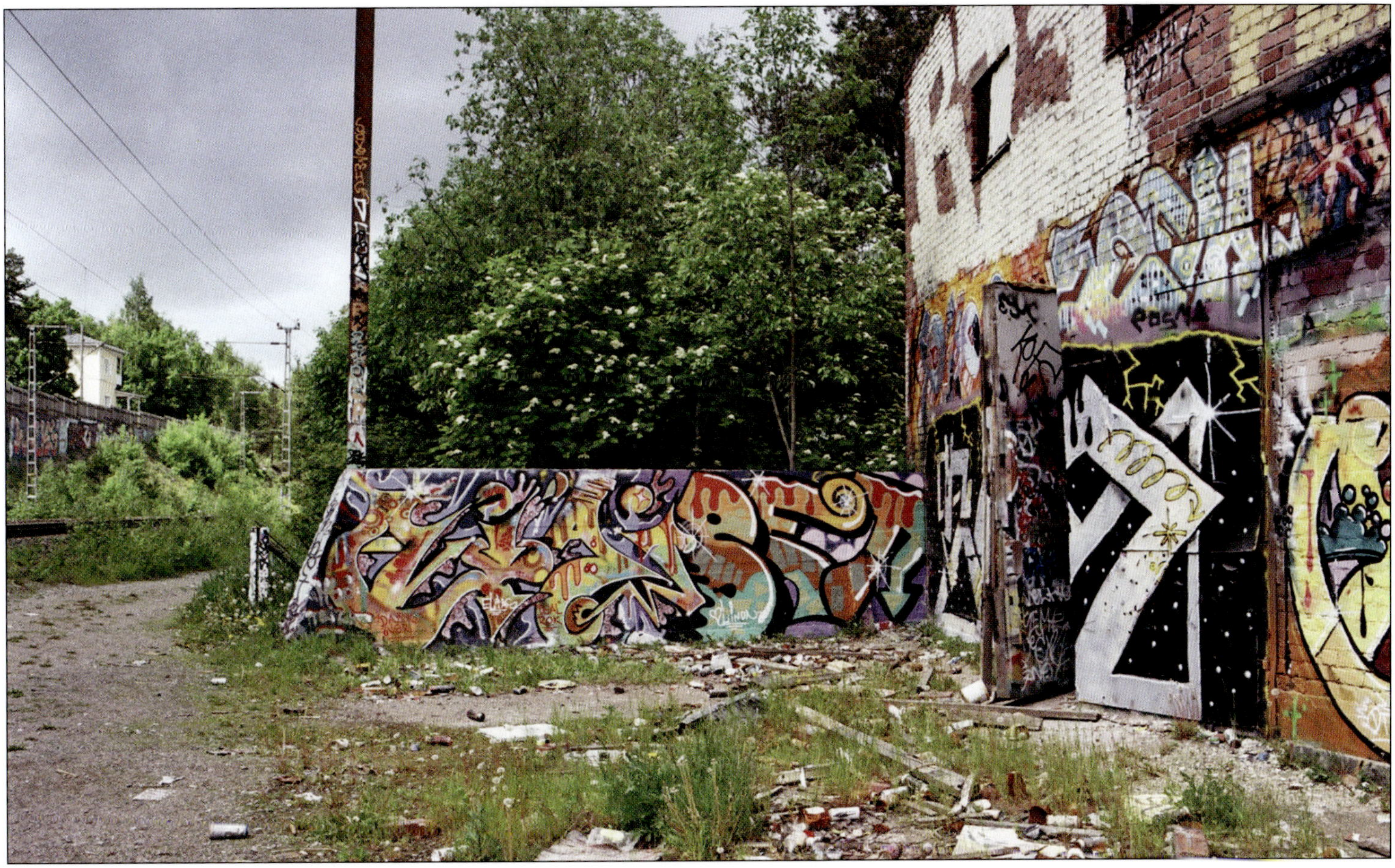

Tags, throw-ups, writing, and characters may be an integral part of one subculture, but for a large part of the general community, and particularly for city authorities, graffiti in general is an abomination. The marking of a piece of property not belonging to the graffitist without consent of the owner is considered an act of vandalism and carries various penalties if the perpetrator is caught.

Many cities across the world have brought in legislation to deal with graffitists caught in the act of defacing a building or other public or private structure. This is due in part to the costs associated with the removal of graffiti annually, which is phenomenal. For instance, Los Angeles pays more than $140 million in graffiti removal; the United Kingdom spends $1.5 billion, $200 million of which is in London alone. Germany rates much better, with an overall sum of less than $700 million.

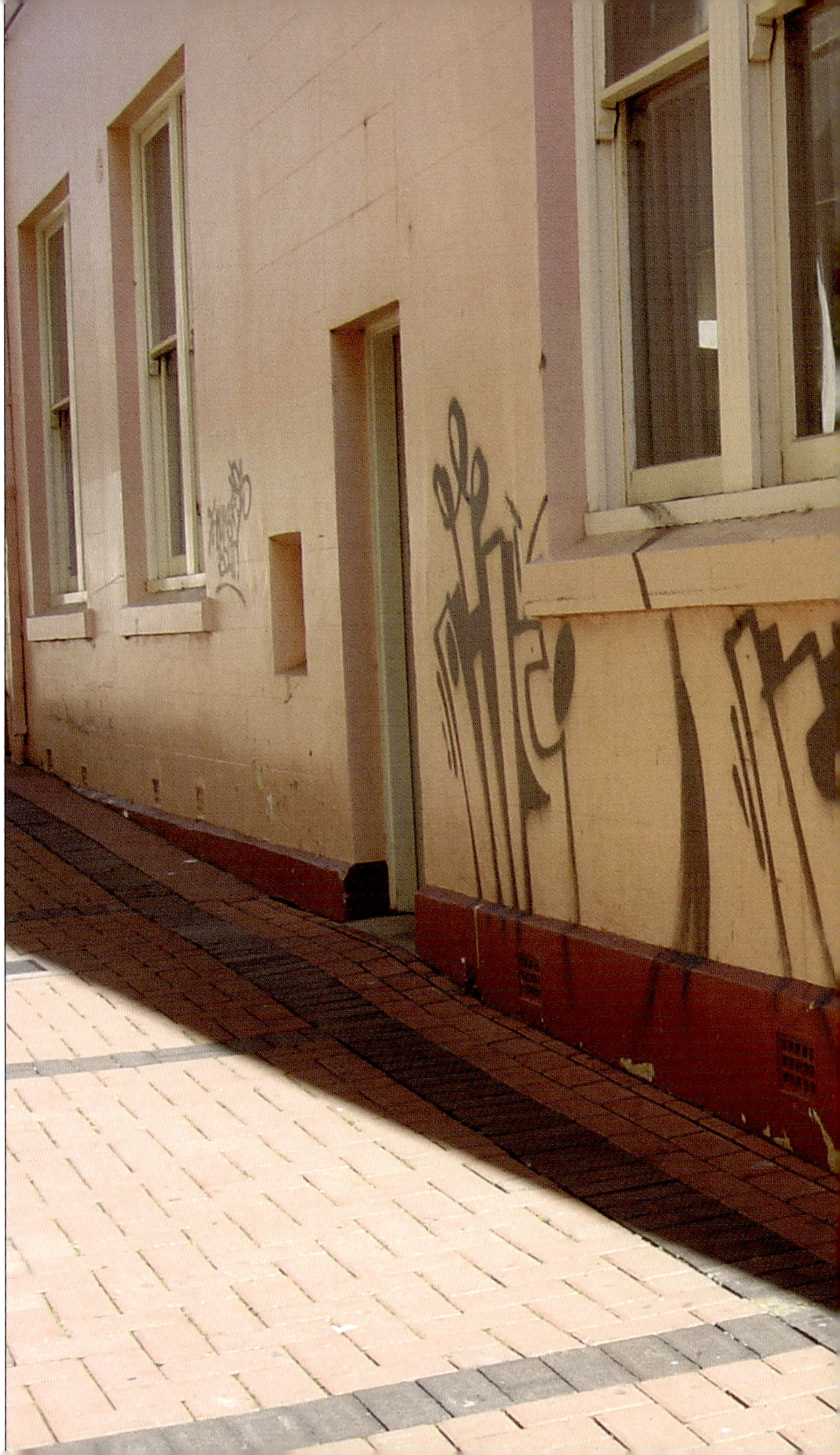

Tags are scrawled on the wall of a building » in a narrow alleyway. Someone, possibly a council worker, has attempted to paint over the offending work but in doing so did little more than make the situation worse. The graffiti shows through the paint and is called ghost graffiti.
Photo by the author.

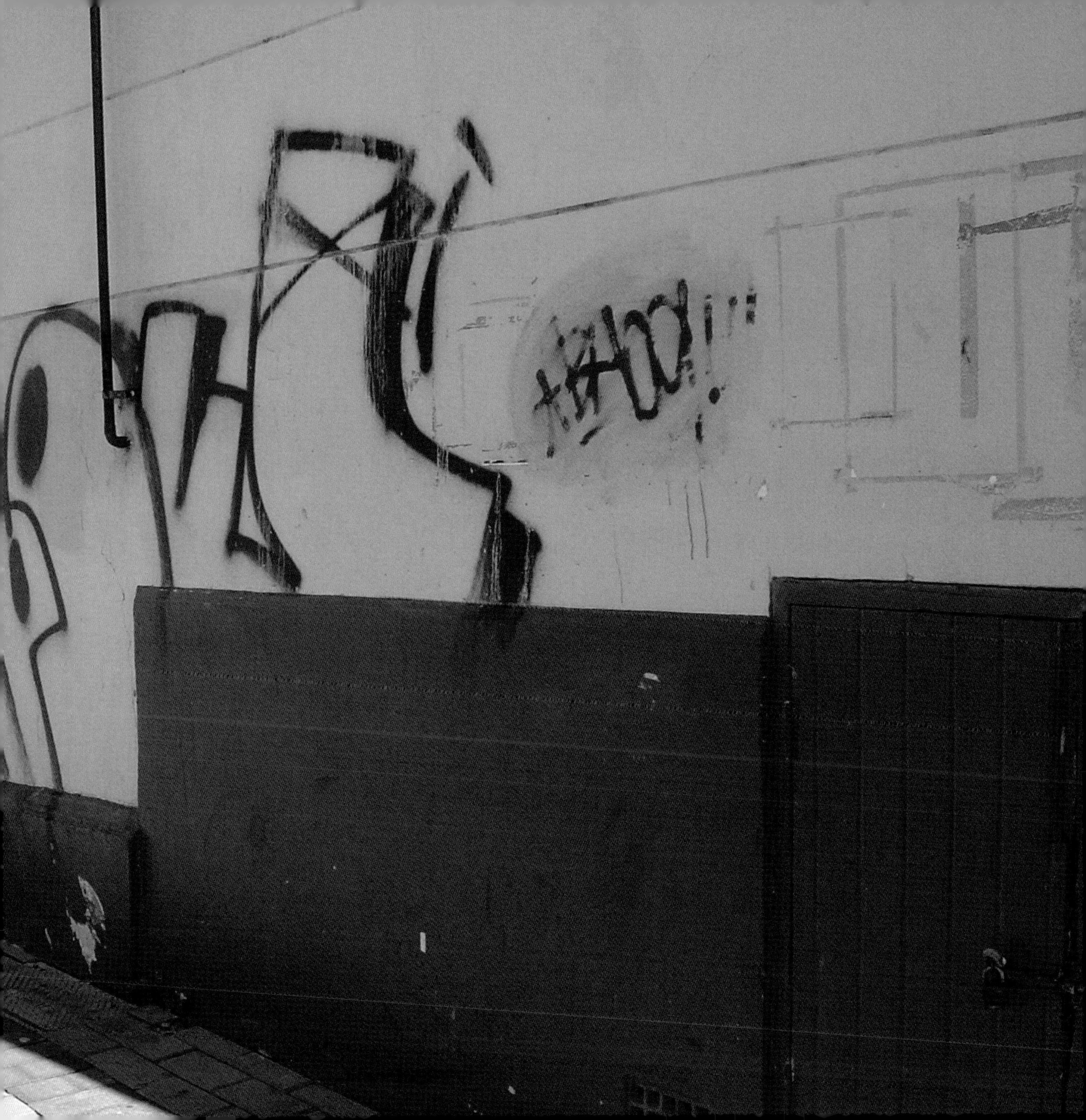

Different countries hold different rules and punishments for graffiti offenders. In New South Wales, Australia, government officials are trying to bring in new laws concerning graffiti. First, they want offenders to appear in court to be formerly tried. Second, they want to introduce a license sanction scheme as an extra penalty available to the courts as punishment for the offenders. Third, they want to make the community service orders to fit the crime by having graffitists sent to remove the graffiti they produced. Currently, there are also hotlines for the public to contact authorities about graffiti and volunteer community graffiti removal squads are being encouraged.

Graffiti vandalism is seen as a weightier problem in countries that are considered popular tourist destinations. Italy falls into this category, but has also had graffiti present for millennia. So many people want to leave a tiny part of themselves on the ancient monuments and tourist hotspots in Italy, but the Italians are fairly laid back about it as long as it is not too intrusive. However, once a Japanese teacher was on honeymoon in 2008 in Florence and he couldn't resist leaving a souvenir of his visit by writing both his and his wife's name on the wall of the Santa Maria Fiore cathedral. It is not known how he was caught, but when the man returned to Japan, he was given a heavy penalty for the graffiti: He was forced to resign his position as a teacher. The Italians, who learned about the punishment though it was ludicrously harsh, and at least one Italian official, noted that there was far more English and Italian graffiti on the walls of the cathedral than there was Japanese.

Meanwhile, in Singapore, a British graffitist was forced to flee the country for tags he wrote on a train in Singapore. If he did ever return, he would face a penalty of three to eight strokes with a cane. And in 1994, Michael Fay, an American boy, was held for tagging in Singapore and had his sentence reduced from six strokes of the cane to four after President Clinton interceded on his behalf. At the end of his punishment, his buttocks were bleeding but, it is reported, he was able to walk away from it.

In the United States, graffiti is considered a criminal offense in every state because it is automatically classified as vandalism. In Florida, however, various factors are taken into consideration in metering out punishment for offenders. If it is a first offense with $200 worth of damages to property, then it is considered a second-degree misdemeanor. If it is still a first offense with damage amounting to $1,000, then it becomes a first-degree misdemeanor. A first offense in which the damage to property is estimated at more than $1,000 is considered a third-degree felony. Any second offense, regardless of how little the damage, is always classed as a third-degree felony. Graffiti on a public place or to a religious site also attracts the third-degree felony charge.

For a felony charge, there may be a fine of $250 for a first conviction with the fine doubling for each conviction. On top of this, there may be imposed cleanup costs and community service as well for the offender. However, if it is a felonious conviction, prison sentences of up to five years can be handed down, plus fines of up to $5,000, payments for damage repair, and/or community service.

New York City has been one of the hardest hit by graffitists. The subway tunnels and trains seem to have special allure and, subsequently, there have been major problems with tags and scrawls all over subway cars. But tagging in subway tunnels and on cars can also have a tragic outcome, causing the deaths of many young taggers each year.

By the mid-1970s, graffiti-ing was endemic in New York City, with no solutions or removal systems capable of dealing with it. Whole trains were being covered with complex designs and the challenge of completing a piece of work as big as a whole train was too hard to resist. There was also an atmosphere of competition with individuals and crews all trying to become "All City," a term given to a graffitist who has covered a large area with graffiti or who has done many large and impressive pieces.

TAG THIS!

The problem of graffiti on public transport began in the early 1920s in New York City, when regular markings were made on box cars.

It has been noted that graffiti actually began to decline in New York City just as the fad was spreading across the rest of the world. Several factors were involved in the apparent reduction of unauthorized graffiti. Crime on the streets, fueled by a rise in the dealing and use of crack cocaine, meant that is was even more dangerous to venture out at night armed only with a spray can. At the same time, legislation was being formulated to bring about harsher penalties for offenders and paint sales were also limited. Added to this, the Metropolitan Transit Authority (MTA) put a lot of money and time into a large-scale removal campaign. One of the most successful strategies was to make new subway cars out of stainless steel, which in turn made paint more difficult to stick into place. It was this last initiative that eventually forced graffitists out of the tunnels and up onto the streets.

From the 1990s onward, New York City entered what was deemed the "Clean Train Movement" era. Although the trains soon became clean of graffiti, the streets were not, and graffiti spread like a rash across the city. The reaction was definitely mixed. Town authorities felt it was an abomination and a form of vandalism, while some of the citizens, even certainly store owners who had graffiti on their shops, thought it could make a building look bright and cheerful. At the time, graffiti was also becoming more sophisticated in its form and the time of tags was on the wane.

The mayor of New York City in 1995, Rudolph Giuliani, initiated the Anti Graffiti Task Force and it led to one of the biggest anti-graffiti programs in the United States. During this time, the sale of spray can paint was prohibited to people eighteen years or older, and all cans had to be kept in a locked cabinet in the store. Ten years later, another New York City councilor tried to bring in legislation making it illegal for anyone under the age of twenty-one to possess spray can paint or even permanent markers. This move was not successful, however, as many art students need this equipment for regular products. A lawsuit ensued and the legislation was not enforced. It is important to note that none of these laws or intervention programs in any city has successfully stamped out the practice of graffiti. Certainly they have minimized it, and the encouragement of making some walls and spaces legal to graffiti has helped to control it somewhat.

It seems that as graffiti moves from the street to the gallery as an art commodity, there is less graffiti actually found on the streets. Those that still make tags are usually kids, and the graffiti artists who still leave their pictures around are either die-hard protestors and social reformers or genuine artists wanting to bring color to drab city landscapes.

Recently the city of Philadelphia implemented several anti-graffiti programs. Spray cans were limited to the sale of people over eighteen and an amnesty for taggers was brought in so that anyone who signed a pledge saying they would no longer make their mark would not be penalized for existing graffiti. A clean-up campaign used graffiti offenders to remove the paint they had sprayed, and lastly the Philadelphia Anti-Graffiti Network (PAGN) program and its associate Mural Arts Project (MAP) was put into place. If an offender was found guilty, that person could opt to sign up for one or both of these projects. The latter was particularly successful in taking graffiti artists and helping them receive mentoring by professional artists who could help them advance into a solid career.

GRAFFITI REMOVAL

The removal of graffiti is a costly and time-consuming business. The proliferation of graffiti in and around urban areas has spread to such an extent that companies are producing all sorts of products to help reduce it. There are chemicals to paint over walls that are not conducive to paint sticking to them; there are varnishes that can be removed from a surface, taking the offending writing with it. Public restrooms are painted in hideous, riotous designs in the vain hope that it will deter people from scribbling their initials on the walls, as these marks will be lost in the turmoil of the design.

Fines and punishments are meted out on a regular basis, but there is no preventative measures or cure. One phenomenon has been noted—the reluctance of genuine graffitists to paint over commissioned murals. Although such artwork stands apart from the standard graffiti culture, it is recognized as a piece of artwork and it would be sacrilegious to deface it just as it is improper to scrawl a tag over another graffiti image.

Some governments around the world also offer cleaning suggestions on their websites. The South Australian Government has a full website devoted to various ways of removing unwanted graffiti. They advocate swift removal of a piece of graffiti, suggest-

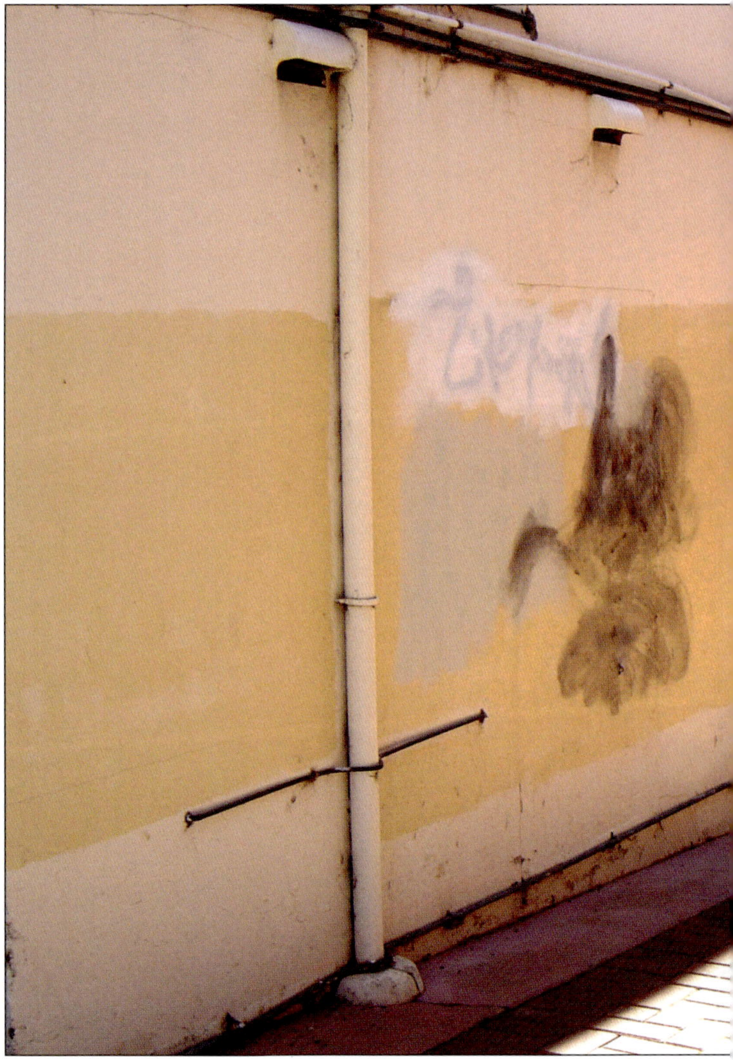

An attempt at removing graffiti » is not completely successful.

ing this is the best deterrent. They also advise contacting the police. A community group has been set up to help clean public spaces and they are also available for individuals to contact if necessary for advice on cleaning graffiti from private property.

The particular way to remove graffiti relies on what type of surface it has been painted onto. For porous surfaces such as brickwork, cement, and ceramic, it is suggested that any thick paint should be removed carefully with a scraper first. Then a biodegradable remover is applied with a cloth and is worked into the surface with a brush to get into the various nooks and crannies. The solution has to be left on for a minimum of ten minutes before wiping off with a clean dry cloth and leaving the area to dry. This procedure may have to be repeated several times before the graffiti is completely removed. When all is gone, the surface must be rinsed with water and then run over with a damp cloth. The process is similar for wood, only it must not be washed with water afterwards and it is suggested the wood might have to be sanded down and re-lacquered if necessary.

Many walls are now coated with an anti-graffiti preparation after their final coat of paint is applied. There are two main types of this solution, the first being a varnish-type finish that is applied over the wall. When graffiti is painted on top, the varnish is removed, taking its extra coat with it, but leaving anything underneath intact. The second kind actually resists graffiti being painted on it in the first place.

GRAFFITI AS ART

While the graffiti culture that grew out of hip hop mainly consists of tagging, and the use of characters and daubs is perhaps the most widely known type of graffiti, there has been another culture that has emerged alongside of it—graffiti as fine art.

Graffiti has been shown in galleries as fine art since the early 1980s and was viewed as offering something new and radical to the public. There was also a desire to shock as well as educate the public into thinking more about what graffiti actually was before they condemned it as mere vandalism.

It really wasn't until the early twenty-first century that graffiti was taken seriously as an art form. Graffiti artists befriended renowned gallery artists and collaborations abounded. The 2000s was also a time for something new to hit the art scene—from then on graffiti attracted large crowds and high prices for art done on canvases and made by graffiti artists in their signature styles.

It was also around this time that stencil graffiti art become increasingly sophisticated and showed a new draftsmanship that made the images universally appealing. Character, infamy, and eccentricity have always been sellers for artists and their galleries. Personas such as Banksy were instant marketable commodities. The concealment of Banksy's real identity did much to help sell his artwork, as well. Banksy's rise to fame also saw his art soar in value to the extent that enterprising people would remove it from the streets and sell it at auction.

Galleries such as the Brooklyn Museum have shown graffiti as fine art and attracted large crowds with their shows for years. The Grand Palais in Paris had a major showing of graffiti art in 2009 featuring 150 graffiti artists from around the world. Smaller galleries have also hopped on the bandwagon and offered shows for up-and-coming stencil and wheat paste artists. There is nearly always a degree of skill evident in these artists' works and common tags do not typically feature as high art.

The price of a Banksy has risen astronomically over the space of two or three years. For instance, in 2006 two prints of his sold for £25,000 (around $45,000). In early 2007 a new record was set for a Banksy when a piece was sold for £102,000 (around $200,000). Only a few months later one of Banksy's pieces sold for nearly one and a half times that.

Of course, most graffiti artists don't make that kind of money with their art. Prices range from a pittance to what constitutes a comfortable living, just as any other artist might expect.

STREET ART

How does street art differ from graffiti art? In many ways, it is indistinguishable, and many artists who make graffiti also make street art. It is generally thought of as being unsolicited art put into public places that is not meant to be offensive, vandalistic, or territorial.

One of the ways street art identifies itself would be in its use of multimedia to make artwork and an interest in new techniques and materials. The work usually makes social and political statements using a juxtaposition of images to environment plus choice words or phrases. John Fekner, who has long been involved in street art, says that it encompasses all art displayed in the public street that is not graffiti. Street art has also been called neo-graffiti and post-graffiti.

The basic tenet behind street art is to provoke thought and action on social and political change, as well as to help the down trodden and minority groups. It is an artist's voice trying to be heard among the tumult of commercialism to make a difference in the world. Street art, likes its close cousins graffiti and urban art, is found in every country of the world.

URBAN ART

While street art is closely affiliated with the art and culture of graffiti—and also rose out of the 1970s hip-hop movement—urban art goes a step further and embraces an array of artists and artistic styles as long as they relate to city living and are willing to embrace the diversity of multiculturalism. A true urban artist is also interested in socio-political issues pertaining to urban culture.

Many artists cross the boundaries of these closely-related genres and you will find names like Shepard Fairey and Banksy appearing in lists of urban artists as well as graffiti and street artists.

REVERSE GRAFFITI

Reverse graffiti is known to most of us in the form of a message fingered into the dust on the back window of our cars: "Clean me!" Reverse graffiti is not the application of paint, chalk, markers, or posters onto a surface, but the opposite. Words or a design are made by removing built-up grime or dirt. The effect can be visually stunning while the legal consequences are somewhat debatable.

> **TAG THIS!**
> In the Netherlands, any sort of advertisements selling products, as opposed to public campaigns, require a permit to put up in public—reverse graffiti is no exception.

It was the Moose, the pseudonym of the English artist Paul Curtis, who is credited with being the first street artist to recognize this technique of making graffiti. He said it was while he was washing dishes at a restaurant that the idea came to him. Also called green graffiti, grime writing, and dust tagging, reverse graffiti saw its first major application in São Paulo by Alexandre Orion.

It is difficult to prosecute someone for having made reverse graffiti, although there are authorities who have tried. First, nothing is added to the surface—no foreign substance is left to damage it or to leave a permanent mark. It is also usually temporary and easily removed by cleaning the offending area and so preventing a repeat performance. And because it is not strictly illegal and it is kind on the environment, reverse graffiti is now being used by advertising companies who want to offer their clients a cheap and eye-catching alternative to the usual billboard and media campaigns. Telfort was one of the first big businesses to use this form of advertising, which was then followed by Microsoft, the

Here is an extreme example of the simplest kind of reverse graffiti made on a dusty car.

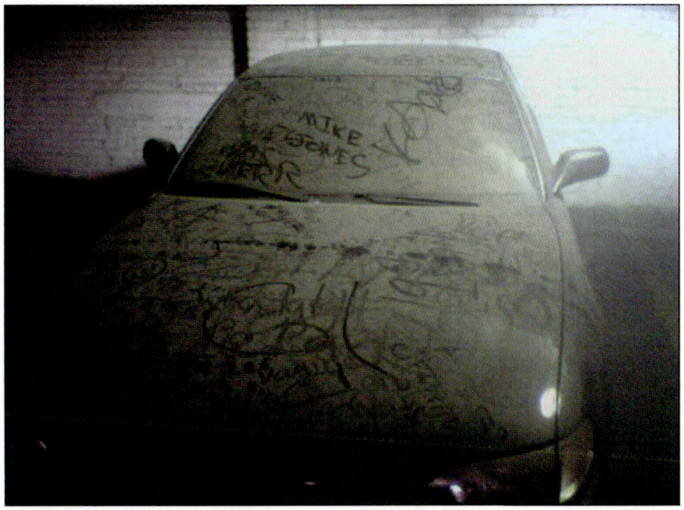

Another example of reverse graffiti.
Photo couresty of Dr. Kralle.

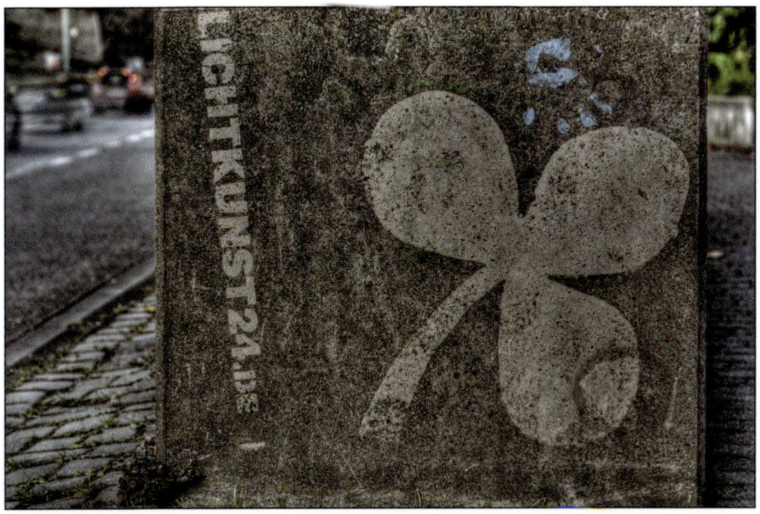

BBC, and Smirnoff. Not only do commercial businesses use the services of reverse graffiti advertising agencies, but local authorities and social services have also begun to use them as well.

STENCILING

This form of graffiti dates back to the time of the cave dwellers. The earliest stencils were hands placed on the crock surface over which paint was sprayed from the mouth; when the hand was removed, a negative space was left behind.

Since that long-ago time, not much has changed in terms of stencil use. Most graffiti artists make their stencils from cardboard or Perspex cut with a utility knife. The stencil is held or taped to the wall and then painted over with spray paint. Often the crude stencil will let paint drip from beneath it, but this is often a desired effect giving the piece

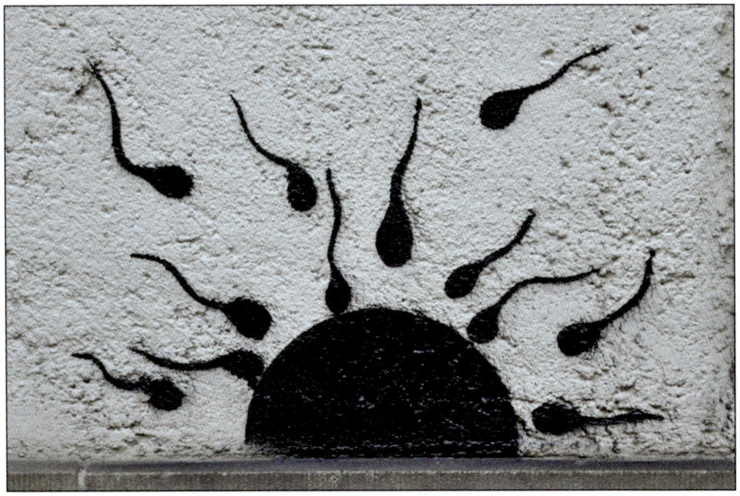

≈ Sperm stencil found on a wall.

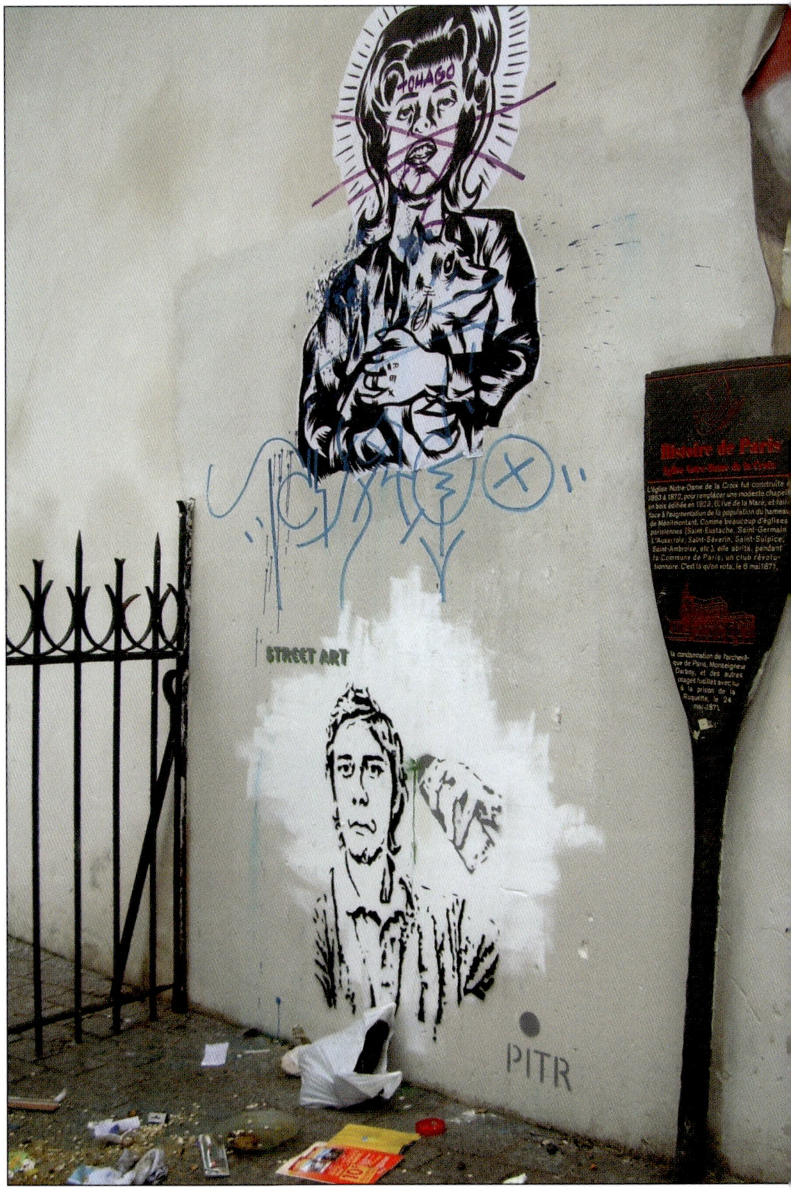

Stencil art found in Paris. »
Photo courtesy of Sophie Masson.

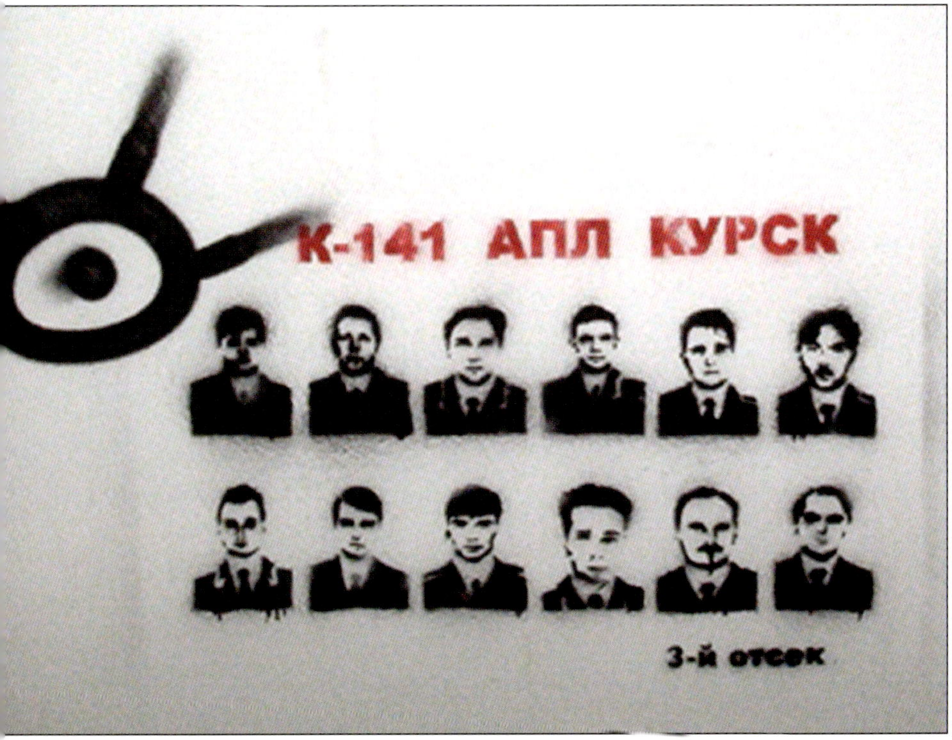

Stencil graffiti found on a Venetian wall.

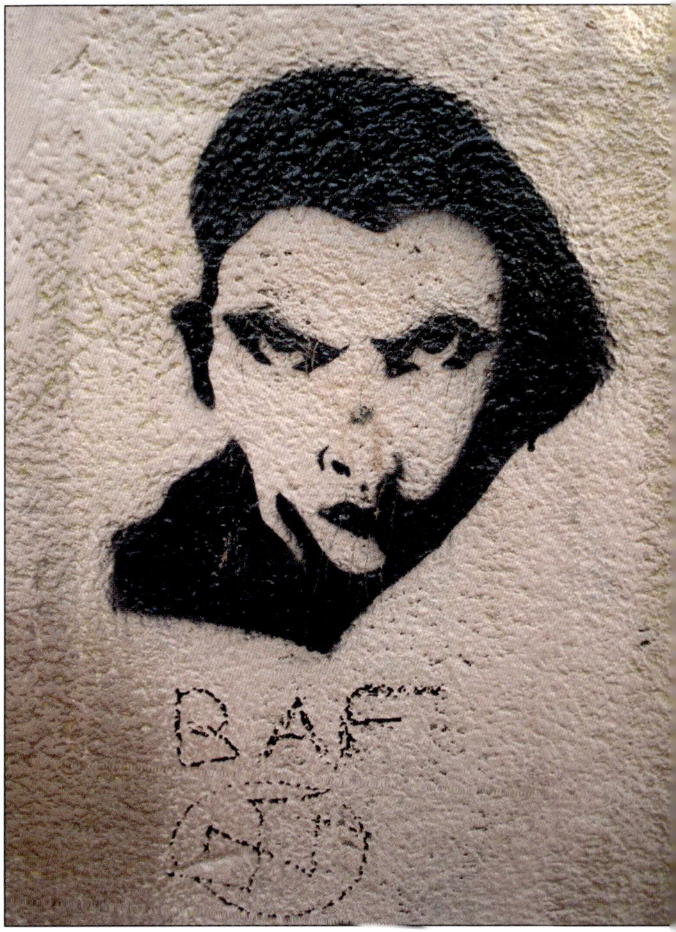

A stencil found on a wall in Lerida, Spain.

a time worn look and adding to the multiple layers over which they are often painted. Stencil graffiti does not have to be done with a spray can, however, as paint can be sponged, brushed, or rolled on as long as the stencil is held firmly to the surface of the wall.

Stenciling has become a major medium for graffitists, especially those who are using graffiti to make social comments. Stencil graffiti can also be photocopied and pasted up as posters. Lettering tends to be of the old-fashioned type used for labeling boxes; it also tends to have a functional and unromantic look about it, but one that is easily plastered over multiple surfaces in a short amount of time.

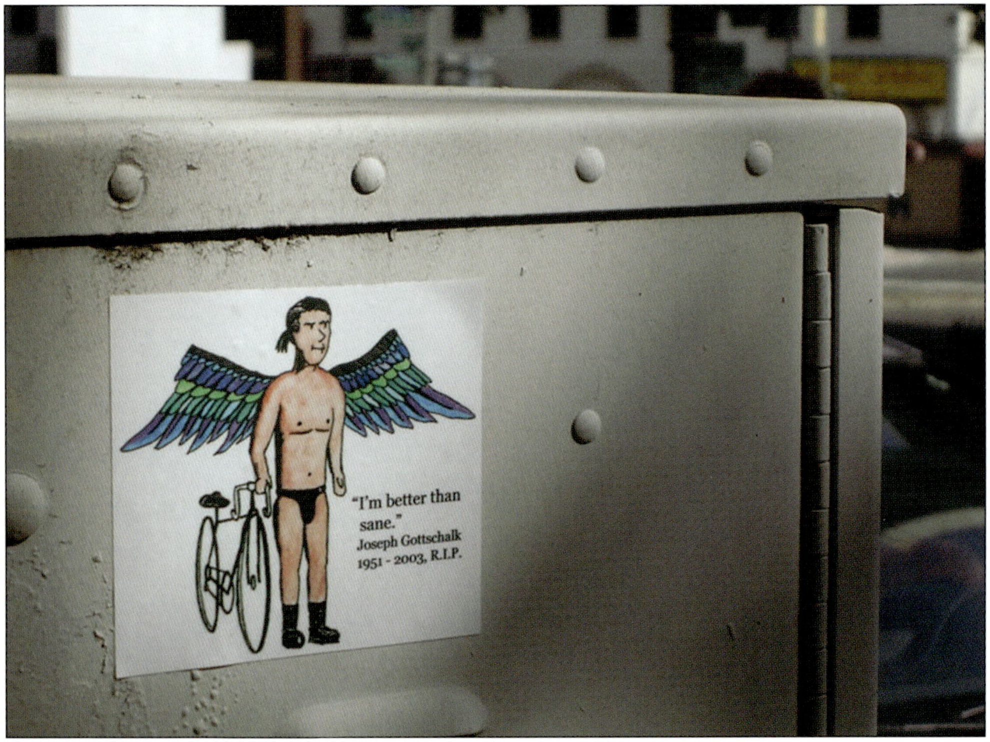

An example of sticker art. »
Photo courtesy of Unconstrictor.

STICKER ART

This is probably one of the quickest forms of graffiti to post on a wall. An image is printed onto a sticky paper so that it can be applied easily and subtly on a surface. Small stickers can be found anywhere and everywhere from street signs to windows, telegraph poles to subway seats. They are also easily removed and do not usually cause any lasting damage.

WHEAT PASTE

Wheat paste is the type of glue that many poster graffiti artists use to paste up their work. It is a type of homemade glue; however, today it can also be bought commercially. It is made of wheat flour and water cooked together to make a thick organic paste. It has been very popular for making paper mache and for use in children's craft projects. During the nineteenth century, it was the glue used by billposters—Toulouse Lautrec's famous posters were stuck around the city of Paris with it.

Wheat paste is not actually a graffiti art form in its own right, but many graffiti artists who use it to stick posters to walls are called wheat paste artists. In the United Kingdom, this practice is known as *flyposting*.

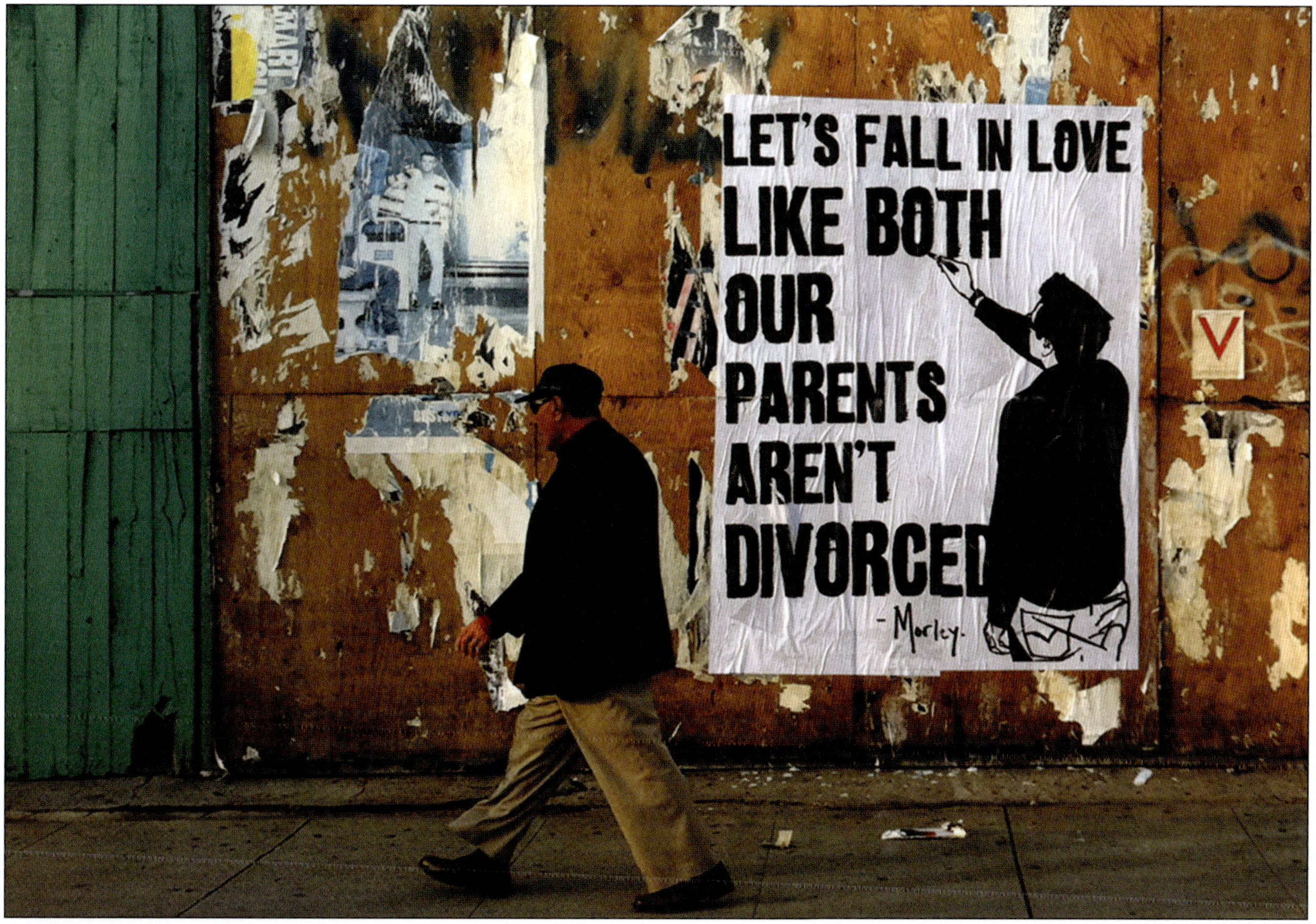

An example of wheatpaste graffiti.
Photo courtesy of Bedside.

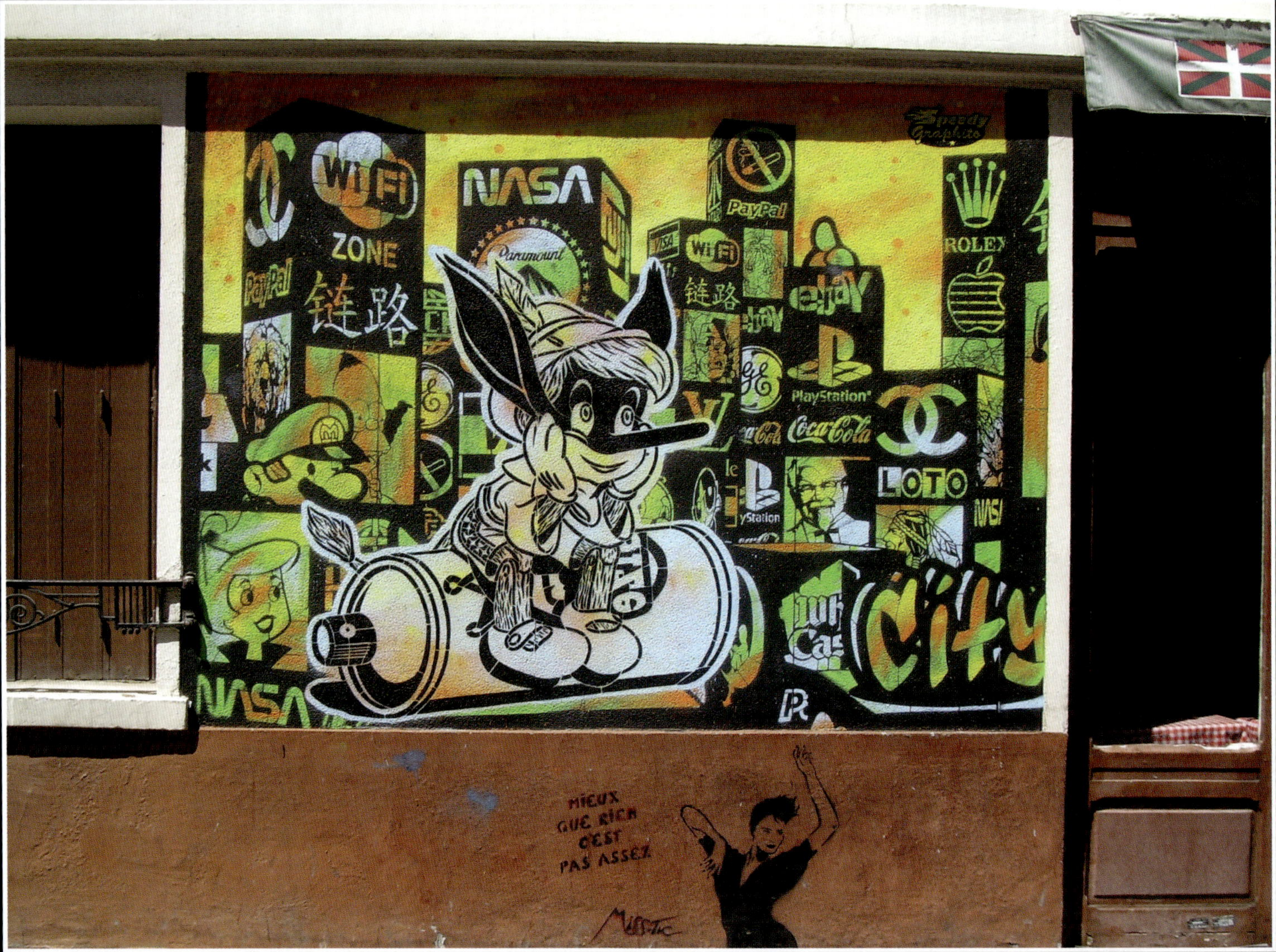

Note the work of Miss Tic under the main graffiti on this wall.

ABOVE

Above, like Banksy, has managed to keep his true name and identity a secret. Although his name is unknown, his birth date is recorded as 1981 and he was born in California. His graffiti art began when he was fifteen, when he started targeting freight trains and writing ABOVE on them. This changed over a period of three years, when he decided it was a more efficient way to get his message across by painting upward pointing arrows instead.

A three-year stint in Paris was an illuminating trip for Above, and he found that many artists were steering away from what had become the traditional type of graffiti: the act of lettering. Instead, artists were now exploring the use of logos or personal characters through which their work could be identified. Above's arrows fit in well with this new movement toward logos and characters.

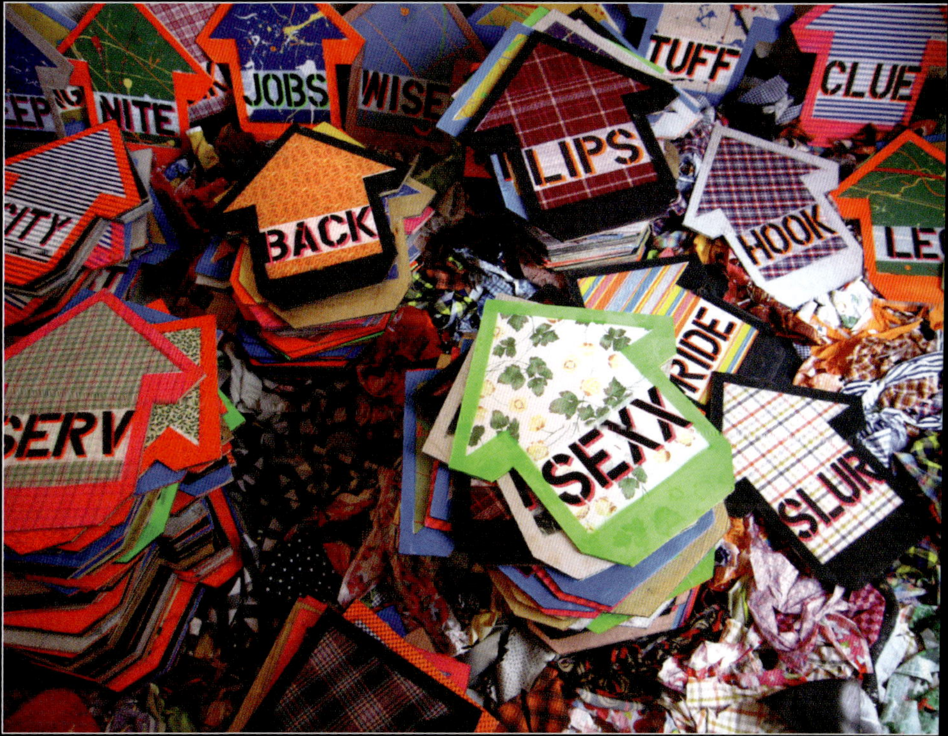

A pile of Above's signature arrows made in a variety of materials and colors.

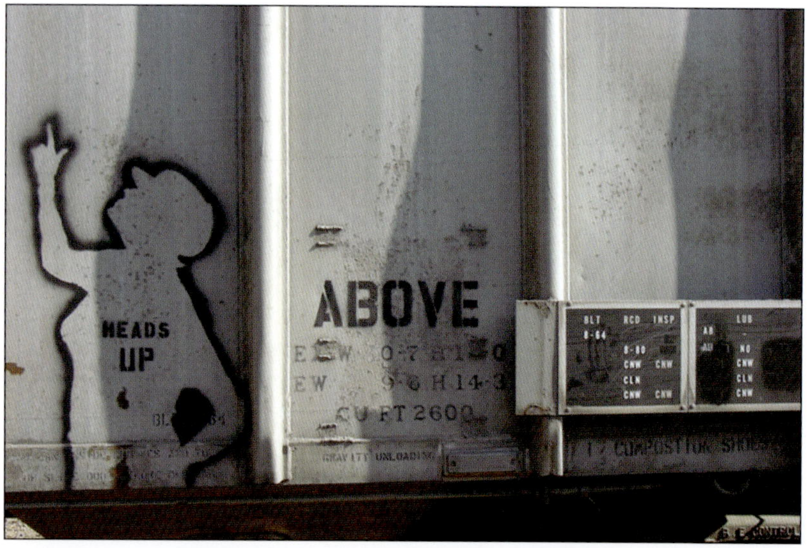

« A goods train car with a figure looking up and the word that gave Above his pseudonym.
Photo courtesy of Hedpot.

"The Shoe Tree." An installation of shoes hanging from a tree branch with Above's distinctive arrow reading "shoe" on one side and "tree" on the other. Work like this begins to defy the traditional notion of graffiti.

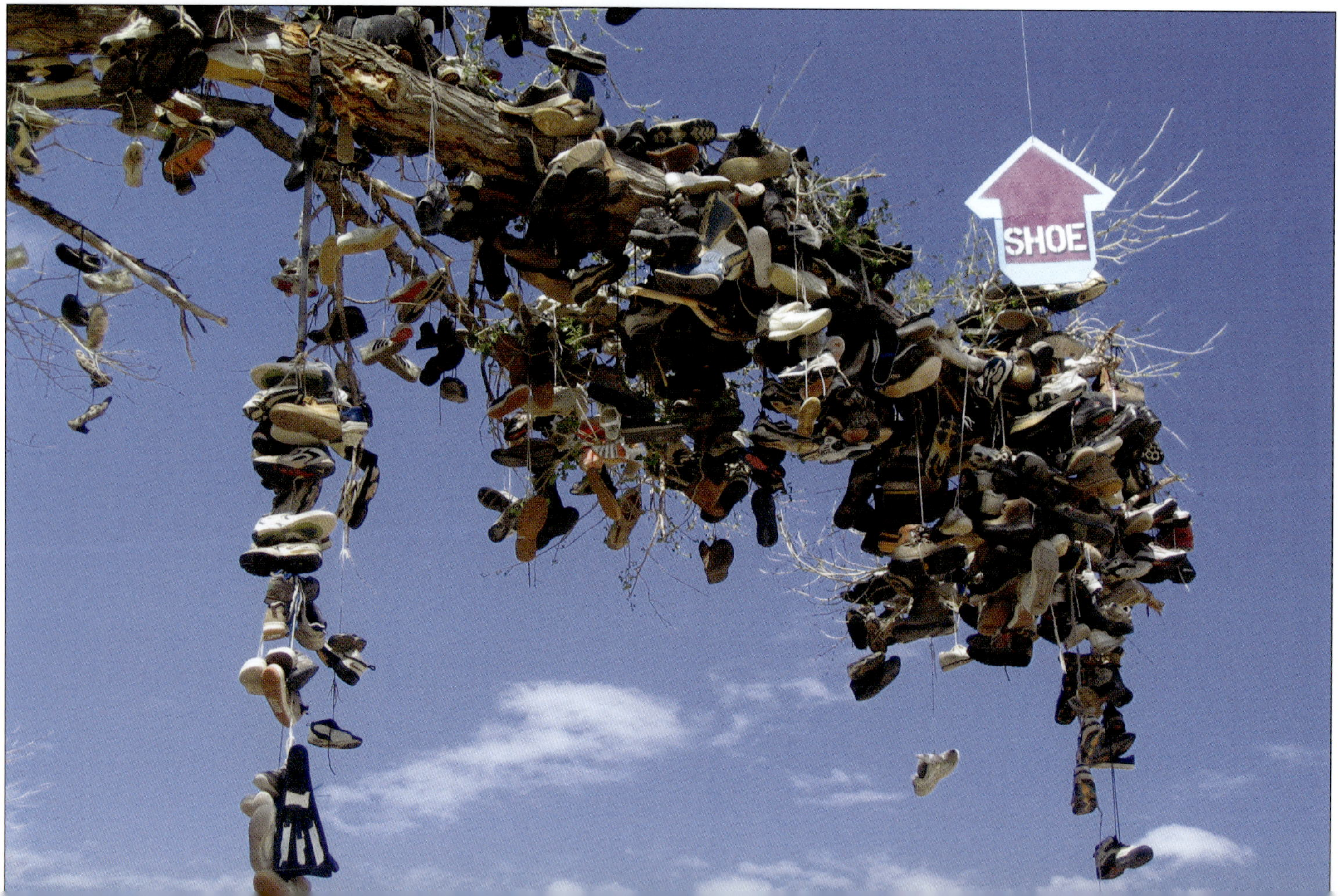

Upon his return to California, Above began a new period of innovative and highly energetic work. In 2004, he undertook what he called his USA Tour and traveled 5,000 miles across the states, installing his signature arrow mobiles in fourteen cities. During that trip, he also started writing words on both sides of his arrows; for example, on a complex mobile of old shoes that he suspended from a tree, the arrow perched at the end of the branch reads "shoe" on one side and "tree" on the other. People marveled at the heights he managed to hang some of his work, but when asked how he did it, he answered that knowing would spoil the imagination of the viewer.

Above's work might titillate the viewer with its whimsicality and feats of acrobatic daring, but he admits that he is limited by his knowledge of how systems in different countries work. One such case was his lack of knowledge about how overhead wires worked in Europe. Because he didn't know this, he avoided trying to use them for hanging mobiles. In 2005, Above made a tour of Europe and installed his old wooden arrows. While he traveled, he said he studied the electric wiring system of the various places he visited so that at a later stage he could use them if needed.

It was research he intended to use the following year for his sign language tour across Europe. He and a friend used forged Eurorail passes to allow them to make the journey and then proceeded to hang them as he went. He wrote on both sides of the arrows again, but this time in the language of the country being visited. The next grand plan involved a trip through Central and South America. For this one, he decided to return to his earlier work of writing, playing with words as he had been doing with his arrows but using more than just two words.

Above's work was constantly evolving and became increasingly encompassed by social issues that he discovered as he traveled: poverty and homelessness; the greed of a few at the expense of many. He made statements referring to the global financial crisis and the recent devastating earthquake in Haiti. As with many of his fellow street artists, Above would make posters and merchandise of his work and then donate the proceeds to charities.

Throughout the years, Above concentrated on his street art and urban graffiti, and he had little interest in gallery shows. However, Blek le Rat, a personal friend of the artist, talked him into a joint show at a gallery in San Francisco. The experience did nothing to endear that kind of work or lifestyle to Above, so he returned to his vocation as a street artist.

Perhaps as a result of his gallery showing and his heightened awareness of the irony of graffiti artists becoming hot sellers in galleries, Above made a piece showing a thief stealing a canvas that was unmistakably influenced by Banksy. Bansky's original words read, "Because I'm worthless." Above changed this to read, "Because now I'm worth it," making a statement about the monetary value of art.

Part of Above's antipathy toward gallery art may have stemmed from what he has termed his travel addiction. He only feels content when he is on the road and painting. In 2011, he headed for Australia, which had just been struck by disastrous floods. He came up with an image of Noah's Ark sinking under just the same magnitude of deluge as hit the city of Brisbane. While he was in South Australia, working by invitation of the Adelaide Council to paint a mural and mentor some artists, Above fell from a ladder and broke his shoulder blade. But instead of canning the project, the participating artists used the incident to form their work. The words "Sticks and stones can break my bones but words will always save me" were stuck on the wall.

Upon returning to the United States, Above settled down to work on something completely different—a book about his past travels and art exploits. It was published in 2011 and was titled, fittingly, *Passport*.

JEF AÉROSOL

Jef Aérosol is the pseudonym of artist Jean-François Perroy, who was born in Nantes, France, in 1957. He is one of the early instigators of urban art. He made his first piece of street art, a stencil, in 1982. It was a self-portrait taken from a passport-sized photo.

Photo courtesy of Sophie Masson.

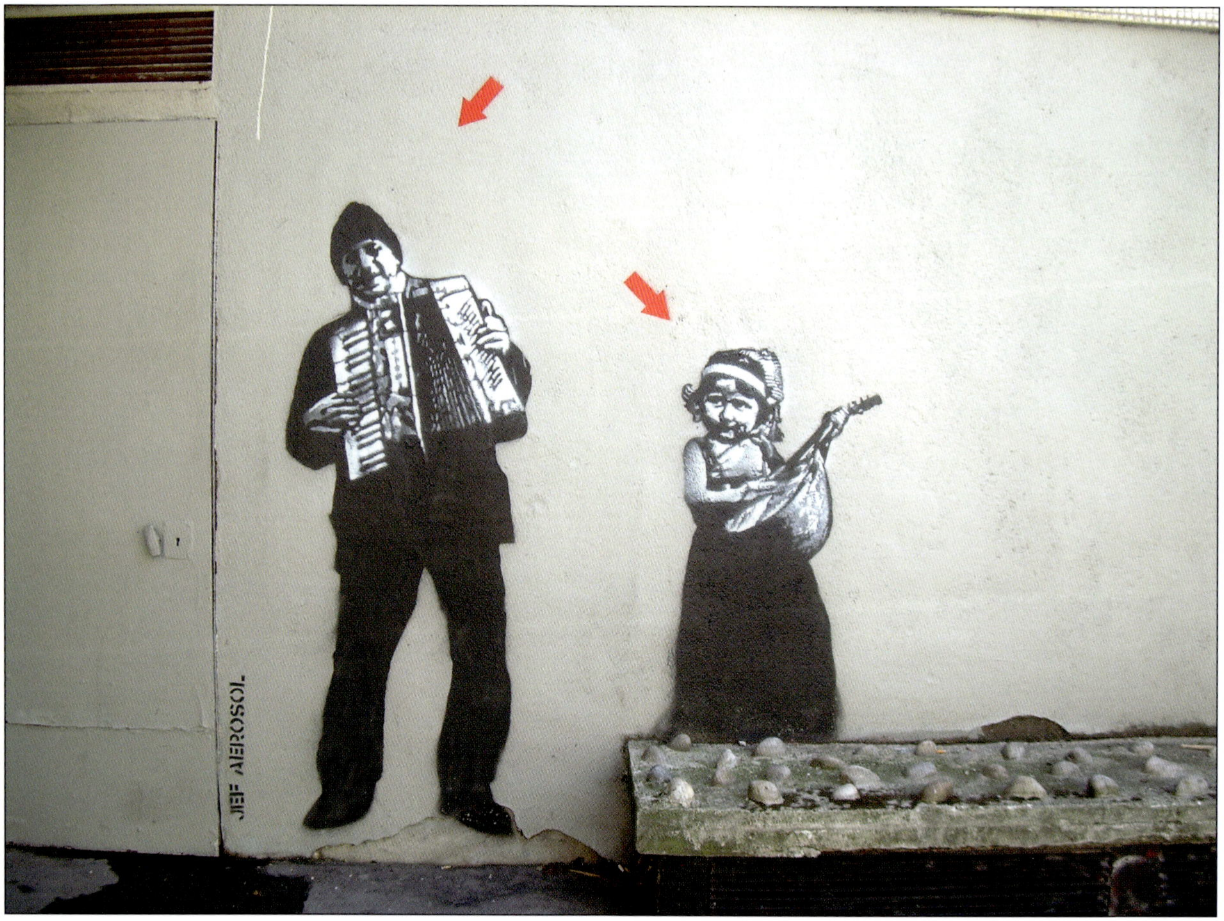

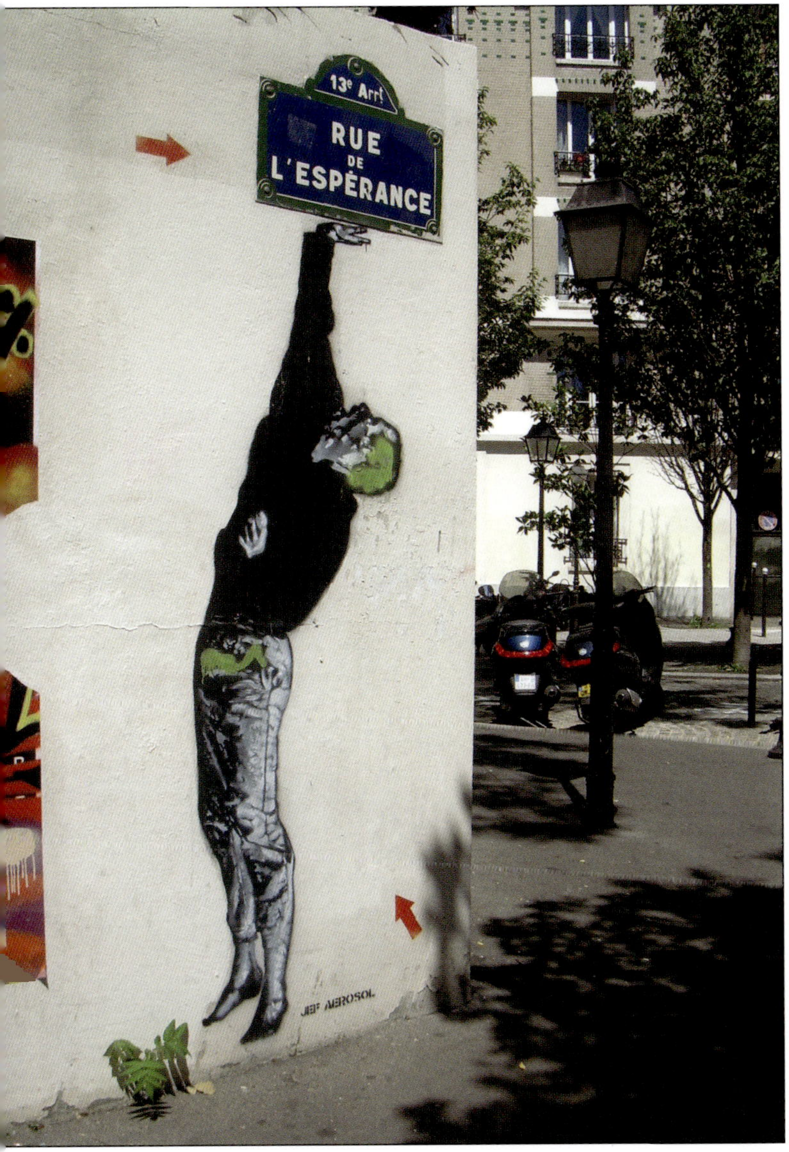

Photo courtesy of Sophie Masson.

Photo courtesy of Sophie Masson.

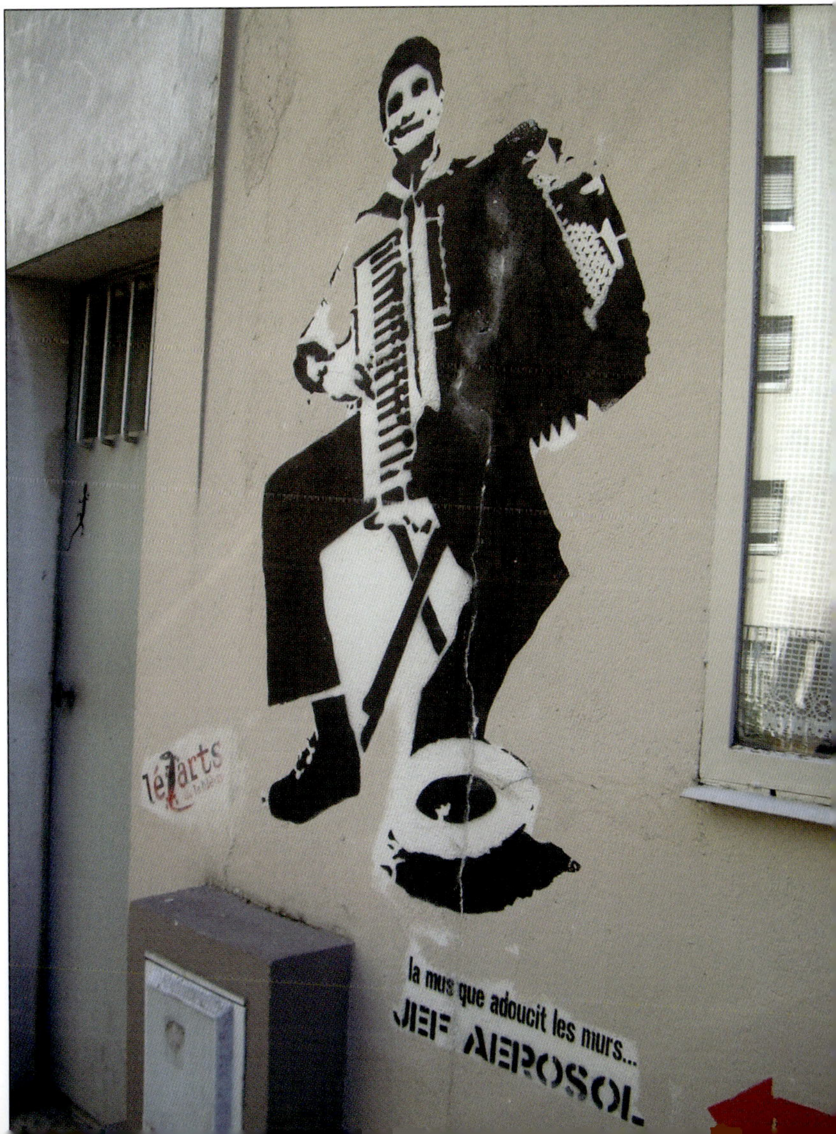

Aérosol made street art in a number of venues worldwide, including in Beijing and Tokyo as well as in many European and US cities. While Aérosol still makes street art, he is now represented by several galleries in France, Europe, and the United States.

BANKSY

Mention the word "graffiti" and many people's response will be, "As in Banksy?" Banksy is the pseudonym of the street artist who was born in Bristol, England, in 1974. He apprenticed as a butcher before joining the growing band of youth

A Banksy sighting.
Photo courtesy of Thekla.

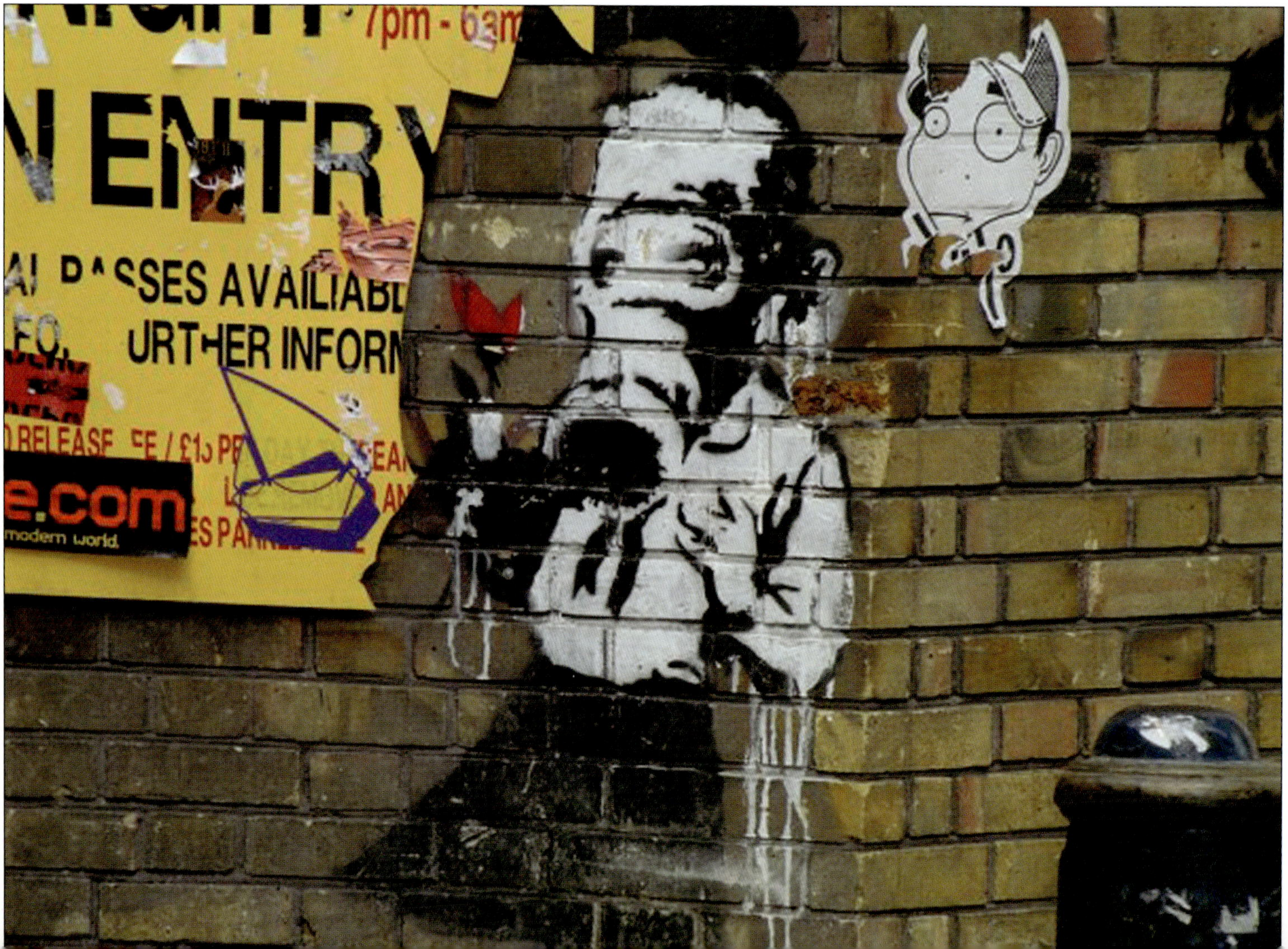

who had taken to painting with aerosol cans as if they were born to do nothing else. Banksy is well known for his stencil graffiti and it may be that he was initially influenced by artists such as Blek le Rat and Jef Aérosol in Paris. This, however, is something the artist denies, claiming instead that he was inspired by 3D from Massive Attack.

The person underneath the masked façade known as Banksy remains a mystery. Thierry, his filmmaker friend, describes him as being like Scarlet Pimpernel, elusive and hard to pin down. In his films, Banksy likes to be shown in silhouette, his face obscured and his voice subtly altered. He is quoted as having stated that this need for anonymity is in fact his way of being heard. He states that if you want someone to take notice, then you need to wear a mask, and if you want to be honest, you need to live a lie. If what he claims is how Banksy really lives, then it leaves plenty to the imagination.

Banksy on the » "Thekla Social entertainment boat," in Central Bristol, England.

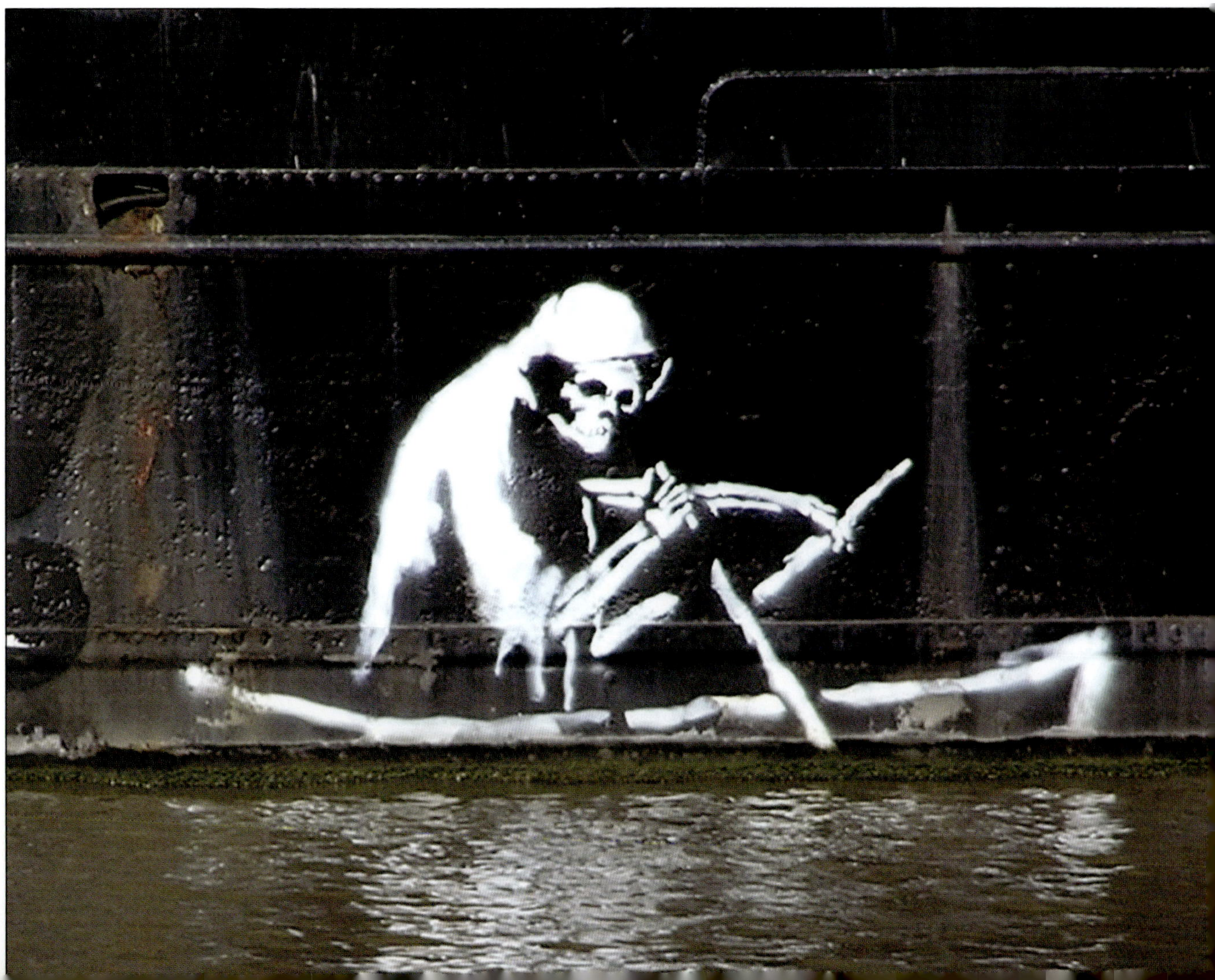

An article written in the *Independent* in the United Kingdom has suggested that the real man behind the persona of Banksy is Robin Cunningham and that he came from a privileged background. This has not been verified, but it would probably explain another reason for Banksy's decision to keep his real identity a secret.

Certainly Banksy's air of secrecy and mystery is part of his popularity and success. He is also a stickler for artists to learn basic art skills, like drawing. His own work shows an aptitude for draftsmanship and his stencils, although crudely made in terms of modern technology, do showcase a certain skill and craftsman's dexterity with his tools and materials. This aside, it is the humor, wistfulness, and melancholy of his art that resonates with the public, who are as little inclined to denigrate the work as vandalism as the art establishment now is. A few years ago, Banksy graffiti would have been happily eradicated by town authorities along with the other tags and scrawls. But now that he is recognized as an artist, his street art is often covered over with Perspex panels to keep it from being defaced or from simply wearing away.

The common themes in Banksy's art include comments on the nature of society and capitalism, commercialism, anti-war messages, and the disillusionment felt by youth of his country.

JEAN-MICHEL BASQUIAT

Basquiat was a highly intelligent artist with a tragic family background. He was born in 1960 in Brooklyn, New York. His eldest brother had died before his birth, but he had two younger sisters. Basquiat showed great promise as a child, learning to read by the age of four and speaking, reading, and writing fluently in Spanish, French, and English by the time he was eleven. The first major catastrophe happened to Basquiat when he was only eight: He was run over by a car. His injuries were serious and resulted in a splenectomy. The next family misfor-

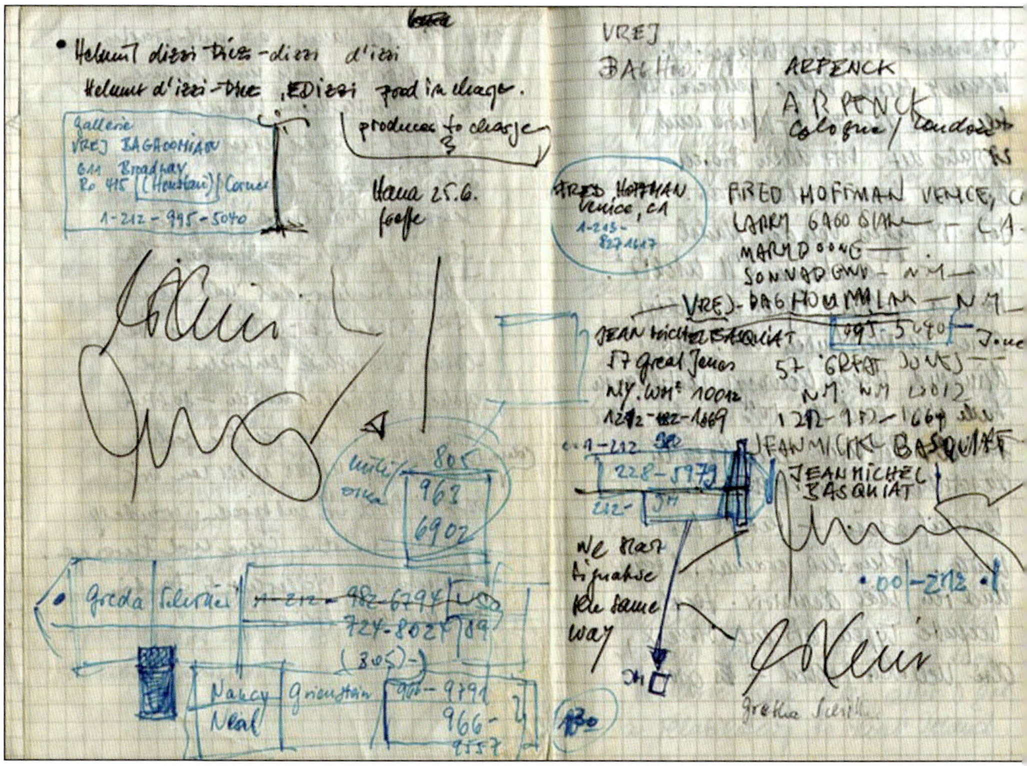

"Contract of Fiction » between Basquiat and Diaz"

tune was the break up of Basquiat's family, possibly because his mother was suffering from a mental illness. He and his sisters lived with their father after the breakup, moving around Puerto Rico for a couple of years. Not long after their return to New York, Basquiat's mother was admitted to an institution for mental illness; she would return intermittently to the hospital for the rest of her life.

By the time he was fifteen, Basquiat had run away from home and was living on the streets along with many other homeless youth. Although the police soon found him and took him home, he wasn't able to settle. Once he dropped out of high school, his father refused to continue to look after him. The teenager moved in with friends and began trying to make a living through his art, which at the time consisted of hand-painted T-shirts and postcards.

Basquiat's first graffiti art was done with a friend, Al Diaz, with whom he worked under the name SAMO. The letters came from "same old shit" when the two were smoking marijuana while in high school. The saying was abbreviated to "same old" and then just "samo." SAMO became a character in a cartoon devised by the youths and another friend, Shannon Dawson. The enterprise became popular while they were attending the City as School high school, where they distributed photocopies of their little booklet. In 1977, they began using it in their graffiti, often accompanied by a copyright symbol at the end.

Basquiat and Diaz would often paint and include text. Their work featured messages such as:

"Plush safe he think. SAMO"
"SAMO as an escape clause"
"SAMO saves idiots and gonzoids"

The prevalence of the messages became so widespread (they could easily do thirty per day) across the city that it was hard to miss and became well known; it even verged on being quite popular. Looking back on that time, both Diaz and Basquiat said it was the stuff of their teenage years and nothing serious. Diaz did suggest, though, that there was a lot more intelligence behind their work and he complained that the new graffiti emerging in the city was nothing but inane rubbish.

Within two years of their first collaboration, the pair was already attracting media attention. According to Diaz, he had wanted the graffiti to remain mysteriously anonymous, but Basquiat seemed bent on trying to be recognized by the real art world. Basquiat would target galleries and it has been suggested that this was a display of his desire to become noticed, although he denied this when interviewed about his graffiti activities.

The partnership between Basquiat and Diaz lasted approximately three years, and when it ended, along with their friendship, Basquiat wrote "SAMO is dead" often over existing SAMO graffiti. It was the end of one chapter as an artist; for Basquiat, though, another had just begun. The joint venture had proved useful to Basquiat, putting him well on the way to becoming a successful artist who no longer made just graffiti.

From 1980 on, it looked as though Basquiat was set to make a stunning career as an artist. He appeared on television shows and got to know influential people along the way. It was also about this time that he formed his band Test Pattern. In 1980, Basquiat had a chance meeting with Andy Warhol in a restaurant, which would eventually lead to them collaborating on projects.

Basquiat's first legitimate gallery exhibition was as part of a group show, *The Times Square Show,* hosted by Collaborative Projects Incorporated (Colab) and Fashion Moda. Colab was a collective formed in 1971 and made up of artists across several media, including music and performance as well as visual arts. Fashion Moda was another artist-run and multimedia experimentation space where John Fekner often showed work.

Basquiat's participation in the show led to a review and article about him in *Artforum* magazine, securing him a name in the art world. He worked in a regular studio, producing a body of work for exhibitions at Gasgosian Gallery in West Hollywood. It was here that he began a friendship with Robert Raushenberg, whose work was a great inspiration to the young artist. As his work became valuable, old pieces of SAMO graffiti were carefully removed from city walls and put up for auction.

From 1983 to 1985, Basquiat worked with Warhol on a series of paintings at the suggestion of Bruno Bishofberger, a Swiss collector and dealer. Basquiat treasured his friendship with Warhol and, when the older artist died in 1987, the effect on Basquiat was devastating.

Although by the mid-1980s, Basquiat was well established in the US art scene as a rising star, his personal life was riddled with problems, the primary one being that he was a heroin addict suffering from depression. He found it hard to maintain any strong relationships and, in 1988, he was found dead of a heroin overdose. He was only twenty-seven years old.

BLEK LE RAT

Xavier Prou is the real name behind the graffitist Blek le Rat, and he is considered the godfather and grandfather of street art. Born in Paris in 1952, Blek took on the image of the rat as his personal art symbol because he saw this creature as the only free animal in the city, the spreader of the plague, and therefore the perfect representa-

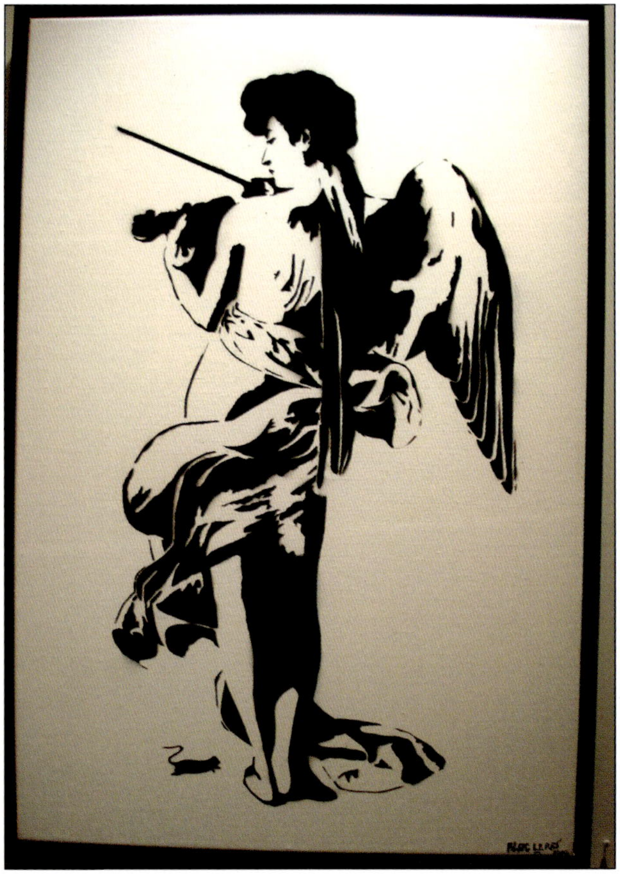

Blek le Rat Subliminal Projects. »
Photo courtesy of Stefan Klou.

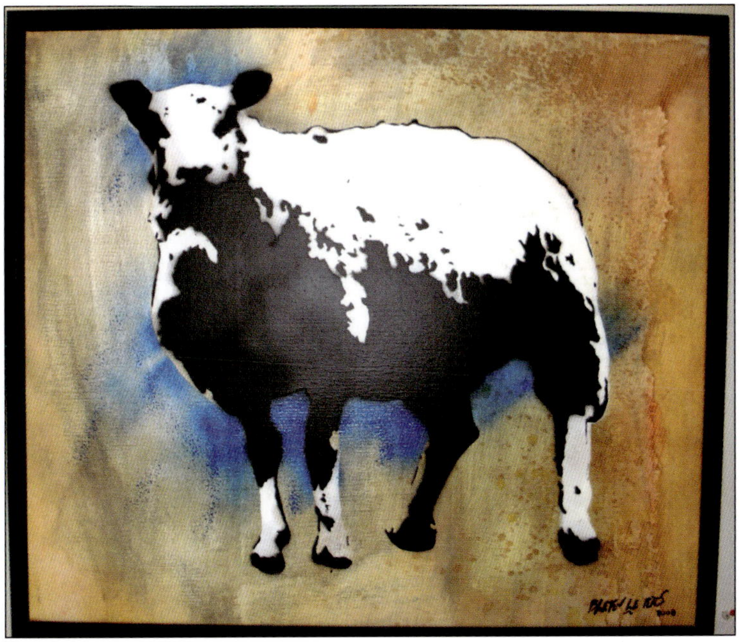

≈ Blek le Rat Subliminal Projects, painting on canvas.
Photo courtesy of Stefan Klou.

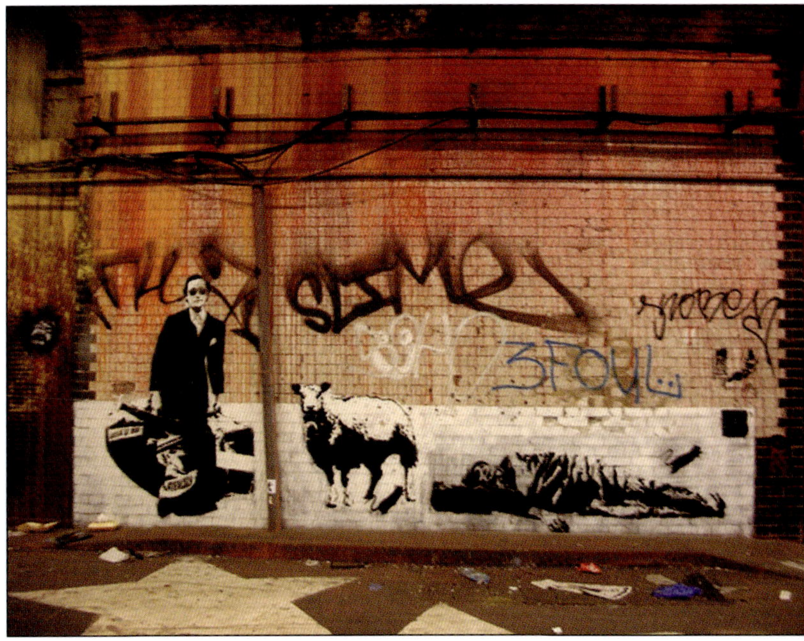

≈ Blek le Rat stencil graffiti.

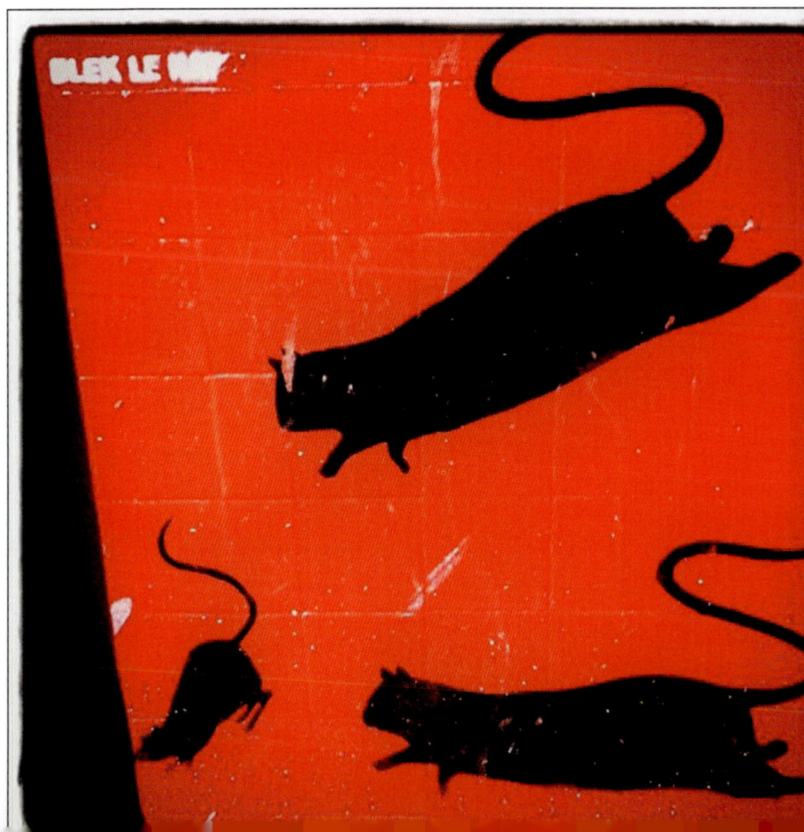

Blek le Rat. »
Photo courtesy of Eric Stauer.

tive of street art. Although his career didn't truly begin until the early 1980s, Blek was influenced by New York graffiti he'd seen ten years before on a trip to the United States.

When he first attempted the spray can US hip-hop style graffiti, he said that the result was terrible. Also, he didn't think that the New York style suited Paris and began to form his own work with the architecture and history of his city in mind. As an art school graduate, Blek also had extensive training and experience in various printmaking methods—all an excellent background for a would-be stencil graffiti artist.

Another strong influence on Blek's work was the Canadian artist Richard Hambleton, who was at that time painting life-size figures. Blek emulated the life-size theme and is credited with being the first street artist to apply this to stencils. It is also thought that he was the first graffiti artist to make pictures with stencils and not just lettering.

Blek was arrested in 1991 when police made the connection between the artist and his work. At that time, he was stenciling an image of Caravaggio's "Mother and Child." His experience with the authorities and the punishment he underwent for his crime made him far more cautious with his work afterward. He only put up pre-stenciled works from that time on, as they were both quicker to do and the punishment was less severe.

Like many other older graffiti artists, Blek has matured and his work makes considerable social comment on isolation and homelessness. Blek's work has been compared with Banksy's both in positive and negative ways—both by the public viewer and by Banksy himself. The relationship between the two artists is delicate. Blek has felt both flattered and irritated by the parallels drawn between his work and the Englishman's. Banksy has complained to Blek that he doesn't like Blek's constant criticism and accusations of theft, while Blek is disdainful of Banksy's apparent sell-out to commercialism. On the other hand, Blek admits that without Banksy's success, he probably would not have enjoyed an increased interest in his own work and the financial rewards it has brought.

Blek has gone on to successfully exhibit at galleries in London and Los Angeles, although he claims he prefers to work on the streets. However, Blek now concedes he will only paint on walls that he has permission to work on, as he feels too old to be breaking the law and paying the fines anymore.

BLU

Blu is an Italian artist who, like Above and Banksy, has kept his true identity under wraps. His earliest work, dating back to 1999, was fairly typical spray can graffiti art, but within two or three years he had started to use house paint, which he applied with paint rollers. The rollers were set atop elevated poles so that he could extend his reach. Using this relatively simple equipment, Blu began to paint large cartoon-type figures in various places.

OK NO was a multimedia art collective that Blu belonged to. To accompany their performances, he began to make video clips using digital animation. Forming another collaborative team, not dissimilar to Nemo and Jérôme Mesnager, Blu teamed up with Ericailcane, another street artist, who specialized in

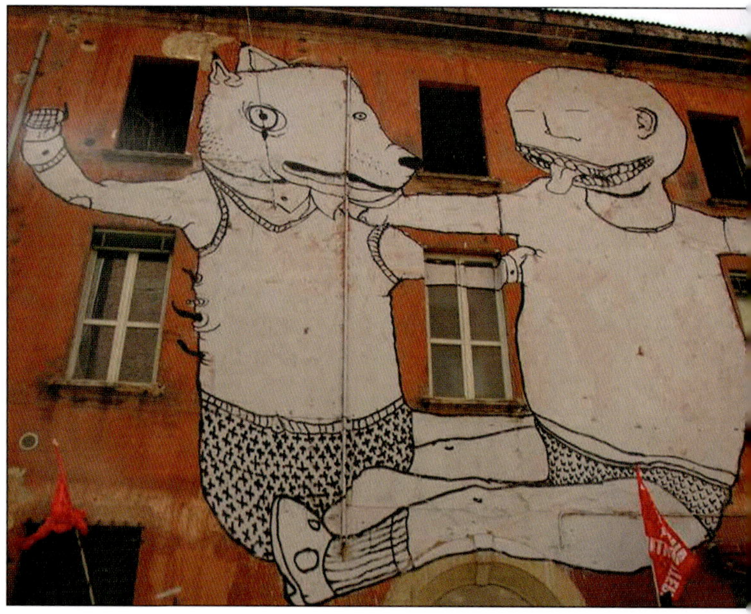

Blu found in Avesella. »

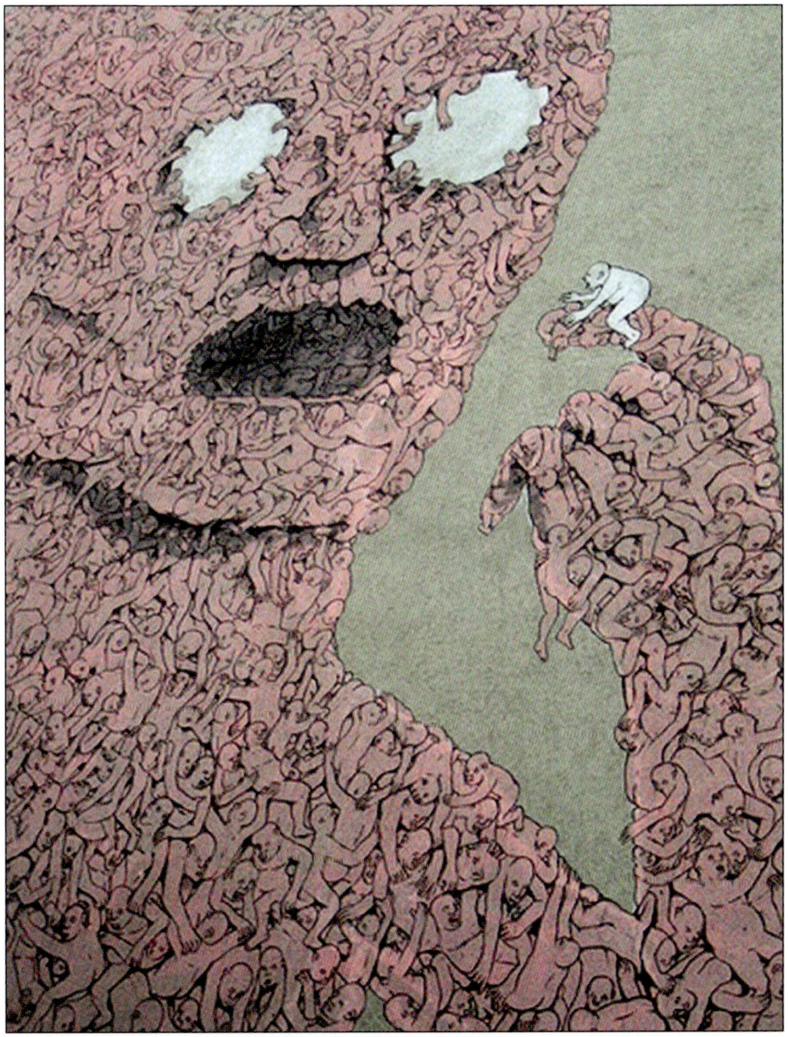

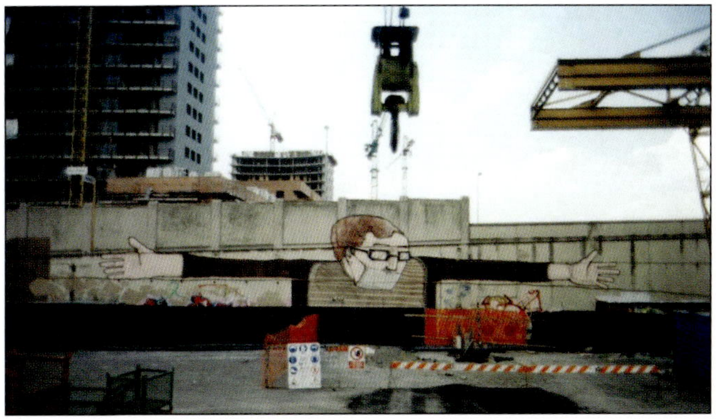

Photo courtesy of Questiano Stefaroli.

« Blu found in Berlin.

animals. The result was a whimsical interplay between human and animal figure in two distinctive styles.

Some of Blu's major pieces have been executed outside of his native Italy. In 2005, he was invited to paint a wall in South America, on Avenida Bolivar, where a quarter of a century before Victor Canifrù celebrated the Sandinista revolution. The work features a lion made up of bananas and is called The Banana Man by the locals. It was Blu's response to the circumstances that led to plantation workers protesting. Blu continued his travels across South and Central America, painting murals along the way. Another major work was undertaken in Brazil, in São Paulo, taking on a religious subject this time. Blu borrowed the image of the "Christ of Corcovado" in Rio De Janeiro and presented the Christ figure as being up to his armpits in weapons.

From South America, Blu went to the West Bank at the invitation of a London-based collective called Santa's Ghetto to attend an international festival of street artists. His contribution was to paint a large figure trying to prize a crack wide open in one of the wall's towers. Shortly after, Blu traveled to London and left several of his pictures on public walls as well as exhibited at the Lazarides Gallery. This was followed up the next year by the Tate Modern gallery inviting him back to take part in an exhibition of street art.

Blu has also painted murals in Spain, Germany, and Eastern Europe.

CES53

Ces53 is an artist from the Netherlands and his real name is Tonny Van Hoenderloo. He has used his moniker Ces53 since 1985, which was around the time he began to work as a graffiti artist. His first work was on trains in Holland, Belgium, and Germany. His work was very much in the traditional graffiti style in the beginning, although it was of exceptional quality. Throughout the years, he has branched out into sculpture and painting on canvas.

Extra colorful graffiti on the side of a train is so beautifully executed it looks as though it were a commissioned artwork.

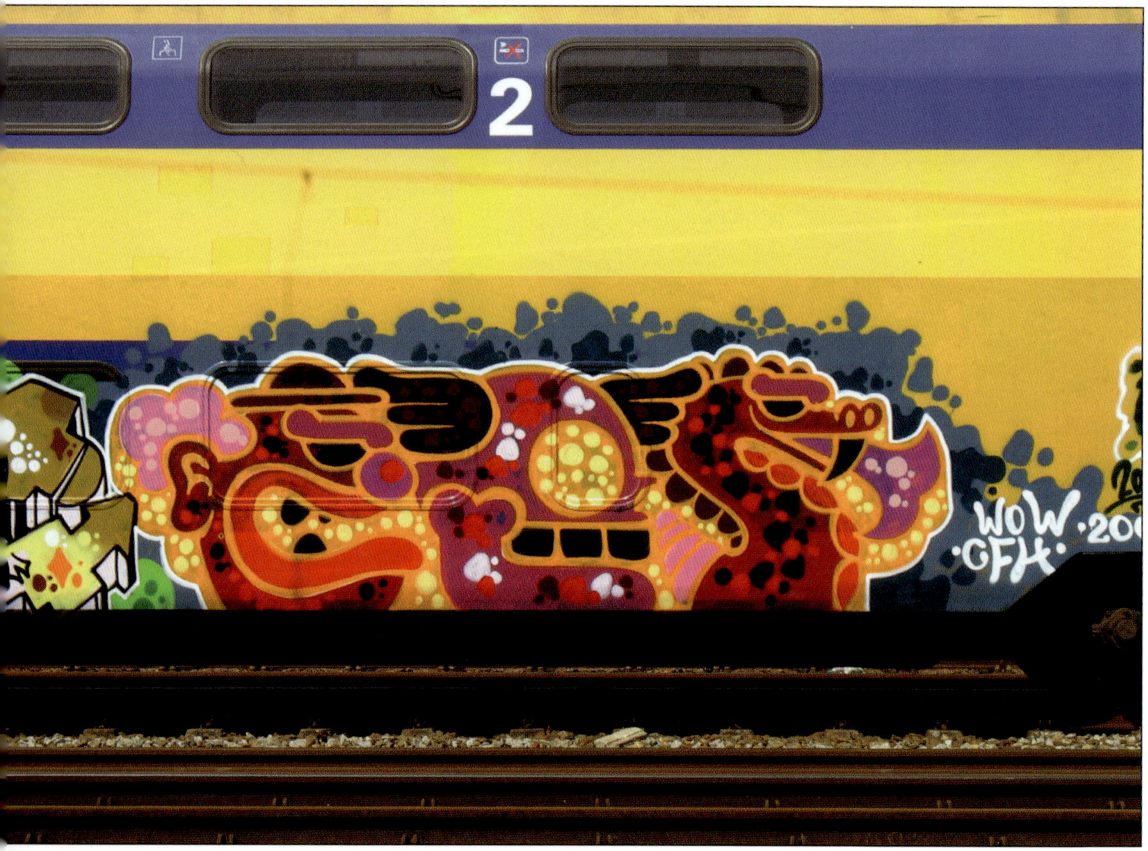

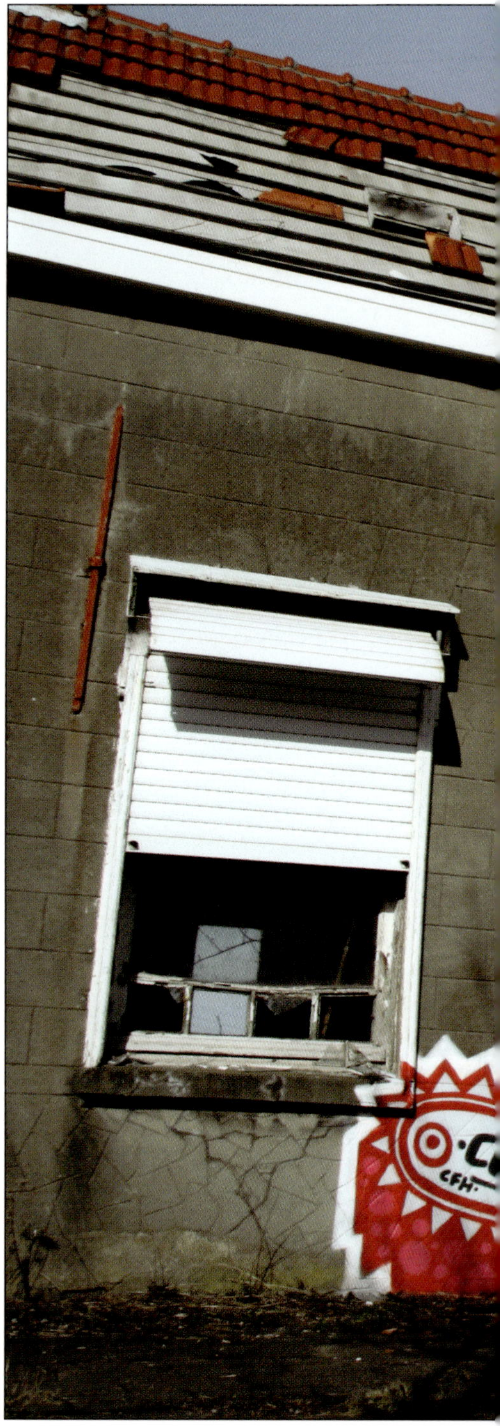

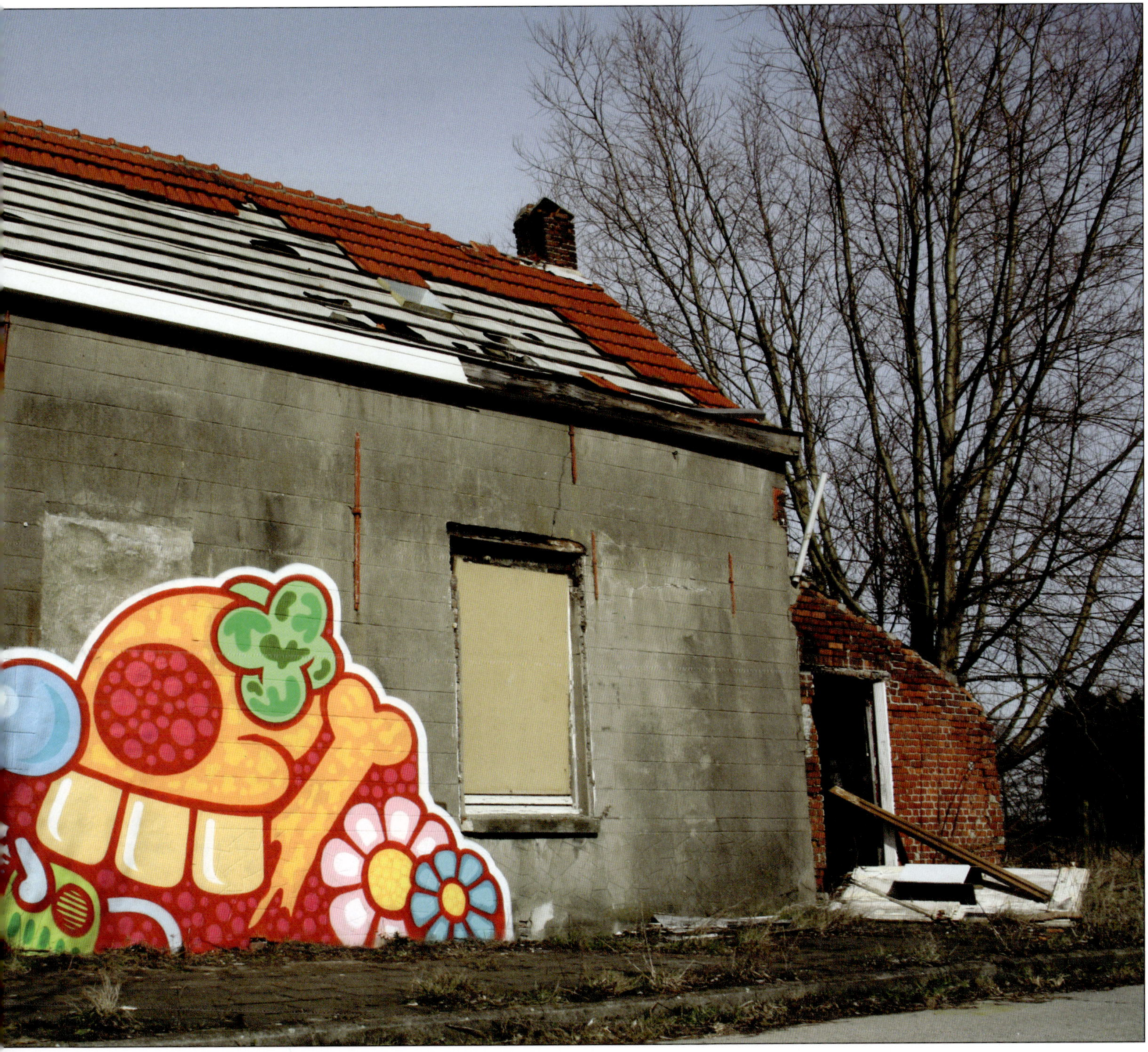

D*FACE

D*Face is the pseudonym of Dean Stockton, a London born and based graffiti artist. Stockton claims that he became interested in graffiti from a very young age after seeing *Spraycan Art* and *Subway Art* by Henry Chalfant. Always an avid skateboarder, Stockton was inspired by a skateboard magazine, *Thrasher*, to create stickers to put on his board as well as places significant to a skateboard rider. Unlike many of his street savvy skateboarding contemporaries, Stockton attended design school. His street art influences were Shepard Fairey and Jim Philips, as well as those on the hip-hop scene.

Stockton opened his own gallery, one of the first to concentrate on promoting street art. The Outside Institute was later renamed the Stolenspace Gallery, where he showed his own work in several highly successful exhibitions.

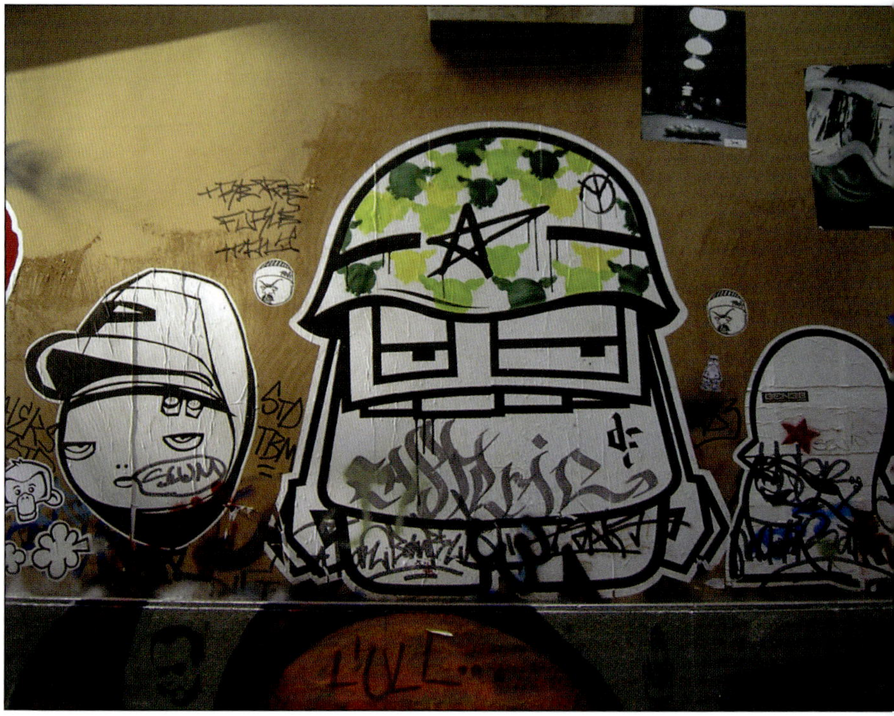

D*Face in Barcelona.
Photo courtesy of Duncan Cumming.

SHEPARD FAIREY

Shepard Fairey grew up in a comfortable middle-class family in South Carolina. He was born in 1970 and attended the Idyllwild Arts Academy, then graduated from the Rhode Island School of Design in 1992. He began his art career at the tender age of twelve in 1984, when he began producing T-shirts bearing his designs.

It was Andre the Giant's graffiti sticker campaign that shot Fairey to fame. The image was created while he was at RISD to amuse and impress his friends. It took him by surprise when people beyond his social circle began to notice and comment on the stickers. So after graduating, Fairey started up a small printing business in Rhode Island called Alternate Graphics. The business printed T-shirts and stickers that were a natural extension of his illicit graffiti activities, which increased at this time. From the sticker campaign, Fariey moved on to guerilla marketing along

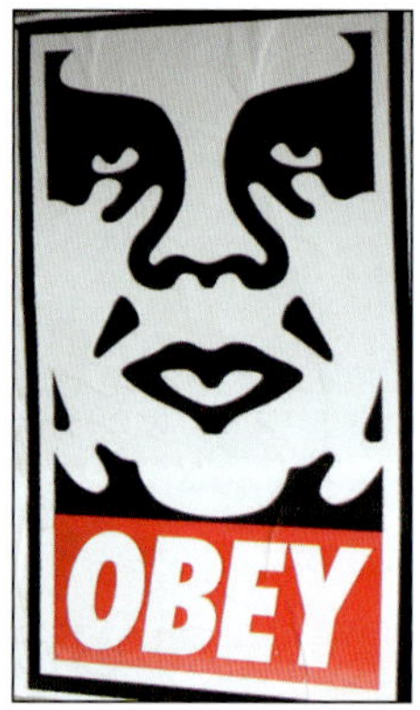

This is the image that made Shepard Fairey famous in the art world—the stenciled face of the actor known as Andre the Giant.

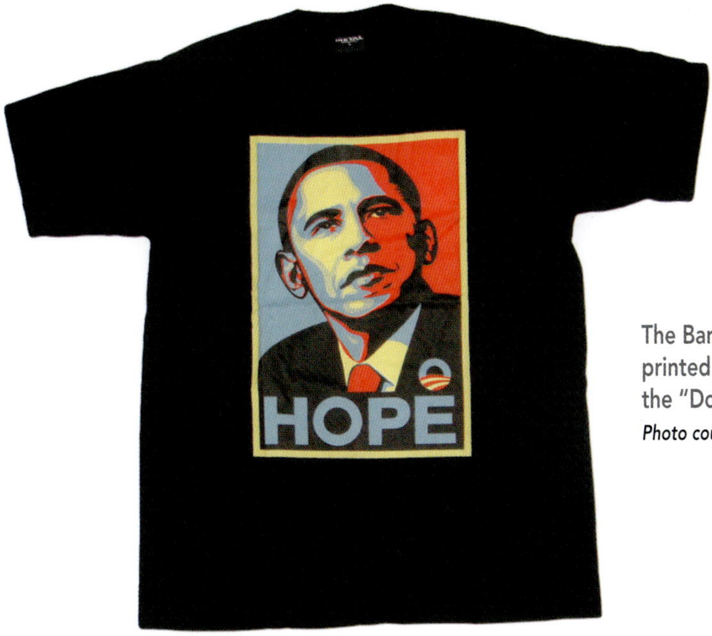

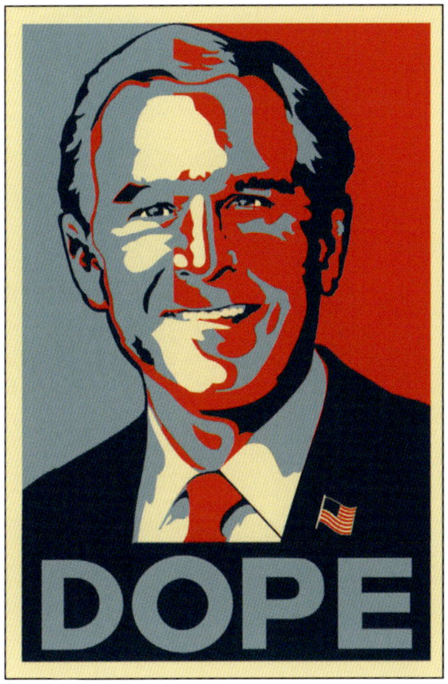

The Barrack Obama "Hope" poster printed on a T-shirt and its parody, the "Dope" poster.
Photo courtesy of J. Rankin.

with two friends, David Kinsey and Phillip De Wolff, putting together ads for huge companies such as Pepsi and Hasbro.

Fariey's career has been an interesting mix of the legitimate and the illegal. He produced album covers for top name bands in the early to mid-2000s while at the same time participating in an anti-war/anti-Bush street campaign by designing posters. Having previously avoided major prosecution for his graffiti, Fairey was finally arrested in 2009 on his way to the opening of his one-man show at the Institute of Contemporary Art in Boston, Massachusetts, on two outstanding warrants for graffiti offences for damage to Boston property through the application of graffiti.

Apart from his initial Andre the Giant sticker success, Fairey is also known for his posters supporting Barack Obama's campaign for presidency in 2008. The poster used an altered version of a photo of the US senator that had been taken from an article published by the *Associated Press*. The poster, which first featured the word "Progress," finally utilized the single word "Hope" underneath the image of Obama. Fairey claims that the poster was then happily endorsed by the official Obama campaign. Fairey even received a letter from the newly-elected president thanking him for his contribution to the election and saying he was proud to be part of Fairey's artwork.

However, this did not stop *Associated Press* from taking legal action against the artist for appropriating an image that he had no legal right to. Fairey was adamant that he had used a different photo than the one the AP claimed he had lifted, but in 2009 he admitted to the copyright violation. His lawyers refused to continue to represent him, and he was given three hundred hours of community service, was placed on two years' probation, and was fined $25,000 for contempt of court.

Ironically, Fairey has earned himself a reputation for not allowing use of his own images by other artists, fiercely guarding all copyright. He has defended his borrowings by mentioning his many donations to charitable causes. Other accusations of selling out to commercialism have also been made at the artist, but he justifies his acceptance of commissions from big companies by saying that they help keep his studio running and therefore give him time and money to work on his private and charitable projects.

JOHN FEKNER

"Itchycoo Park" were the words John Fekner used in his first piece of graffiti on the roof of the park house in Gorman Park, at 85th Street, in the Queens neighborhood of Jackson Heights. The words were from the title of a pop song by Steve Marriott and Ronnie Lane of the Small Faces, which was released in 1967. It was a name that caught the fancy of

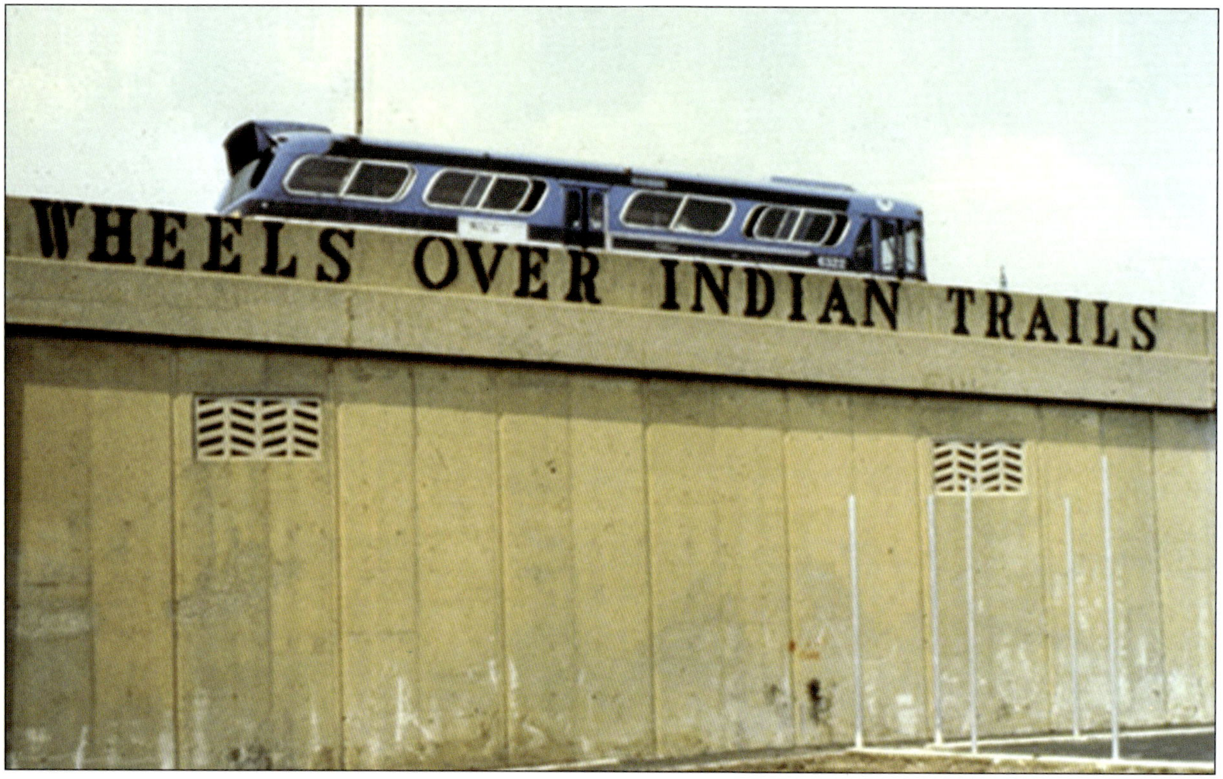

« Wheels over Indian Trails.

the Jackson Heights football team, who appropriated it for themselves when they became the Itchycoo Chiefs. The same park would eventually form a base for Fekner's artwork in years to come.

During the 1970s, Fekner started a project called Warning Signs throughout New York City. The signs were stenciled on cardboard with hand-cut lettering. The messages were meant to warn citizens of the environmental and social dangers that beset them. High on the list of dangers were abandoned buildings, new building sites, and rundown areas that had neither charm nor purpose. The idea was to draw attention to the growing eyesores in the city. The graffiti was also a means to an end, but not an end in itself. When a building was finished or demolished or refurbished, then the signs would naturally vanish with no need to replace them. The stencils usually contained words like: *Industrial fossil*, *Instant This Instant That*, *Growth Decay*, *Urban Decay*, *Abandoned*, and *The Remains of Industry*.

In the early 1980s, Fekner began working around a new site, Fashion Moda, in the South Bronx. It was a storefront that had become a hub for experimental art where graffiti was welcomed and its potentials explored. Stencils he exhibited in the area were: *Decay*, *Broken Promises*, *Save Our School*, *Last Hope*, *Broken Treaties*, and *Falsas Promesas*.

Fekner went on to explore other media, including video, computer graphics, and music. He combined these with painting to build multilayered pieces whose energy is best summed up in the artist's own words in the song "Rapicasso": "Watch the street, see the modern art, it's the present and future tied to his art."

These days, apart from his temporary paintings, much of Fekner's art is made using the internet. He says, "The content of the work centers on issues of humanistic concern, environmental problems, media control, and a society driven by greed, consumption, and instant gratification."

CRISTIAN GHEORGHIU (SMEAR)

Cristian Gheorghiu is the real name of a notorious graffiti artist called Smear. He used a simple tag with which to mark a large section of Los Angeles. Because he was so prolific, he has gained an almost heroic reputation. One of his trademark images is known as Liquor Face. He has also produced a self portrait, indistinct but with the word "Smear" written beneath it.

From graffiti tagging, Cristian Gheorghiu began to make mixed media art, combining his love of popular culture and cartoon characters with an expressive painterly style. He began to exhibit these in galleries starting in 2006; this has given him an opportunity to break away from the old graffiti tagging tradition that would haunt him for the next six years in the form of court cases and impending fines. He steadily built a name for himself as a reputable artist, which later made a judge urge him to use his experiences to inspire others to follow his example.

Smear was arrested in 2007 for having graffitied Los Angeles city buses. The penalty was a hefty $28,000 and a forty-month suspended sentence. This was followed two years later by an arrest during an anti-tagging campaign on a crew

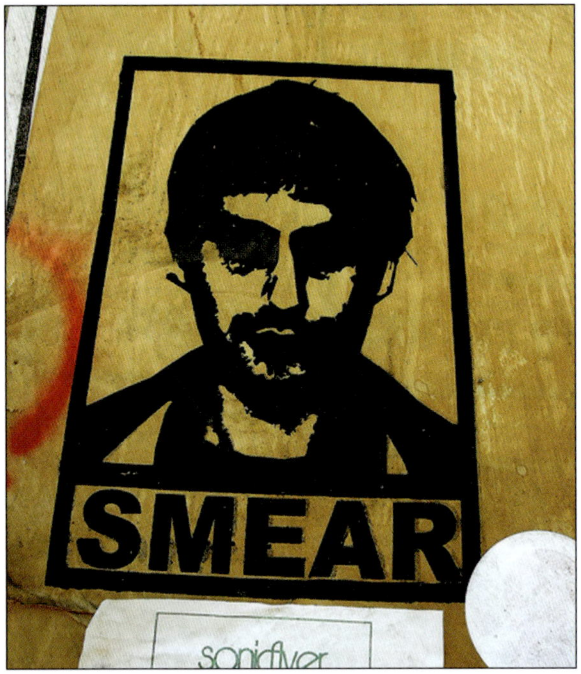

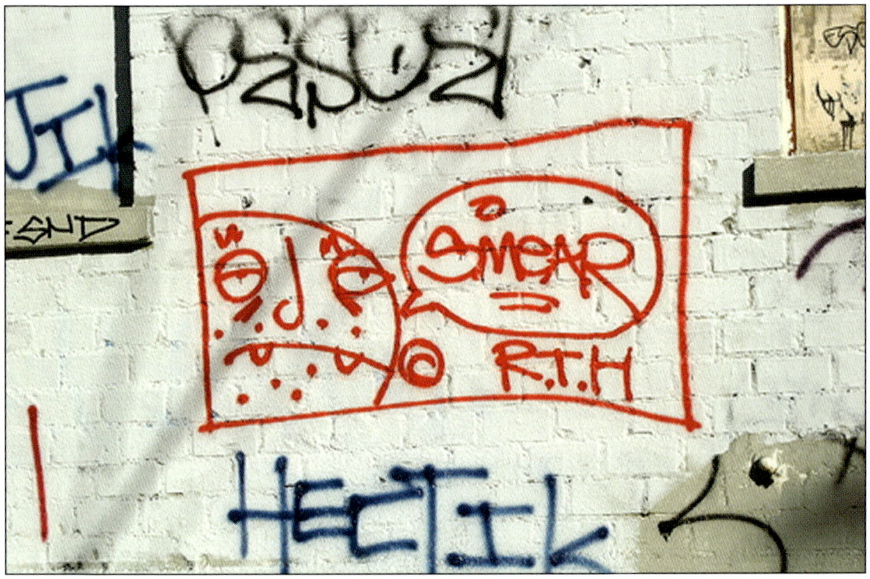

Photos by Cristian Gheorghiu.

calling themselves the Metro Transit Assassins. It is thought that Smear may once have been a member of the crew but there was no evidence to charge him with and he was released after a week in jail.

In 2010, Smear was in trouble again with the city authorities when he was named as a member of the MTA crew. A lawsuit was filed against eleven members of the crew and the city was calling for $5 million in recompense for damage done by tagging. Not only was there an impossible sum of money to be paid, but there was also an attempt to stop the artist from using the word "smear" on any of his artwork. The lawsuit was the first of its kind to be aimed at graffiti artists and was modeled on those used for the worst kinds of street gangs.

Gheorghiu's troubles escalated when he violated a probation order. He had been away from his home and authorities mounted a search with the intention of finding incriminating evidence (in the form of graffiti paint). Not long afterward, Gheorghiu served a thirteen-day prison sentence followed by forty-five days of community service. When the judge handed down the terms of his punishment, he mentioned that because Gheorghiu had been a graffitist who had become a proper artist, he could inspire others to do so too.

The original terms of the injunction were agreed to be dropped if the offenders performed their community service and paid their fines, which Georghiu did. His case was dismissed in June 2012.

RICHARD HAMBLETON

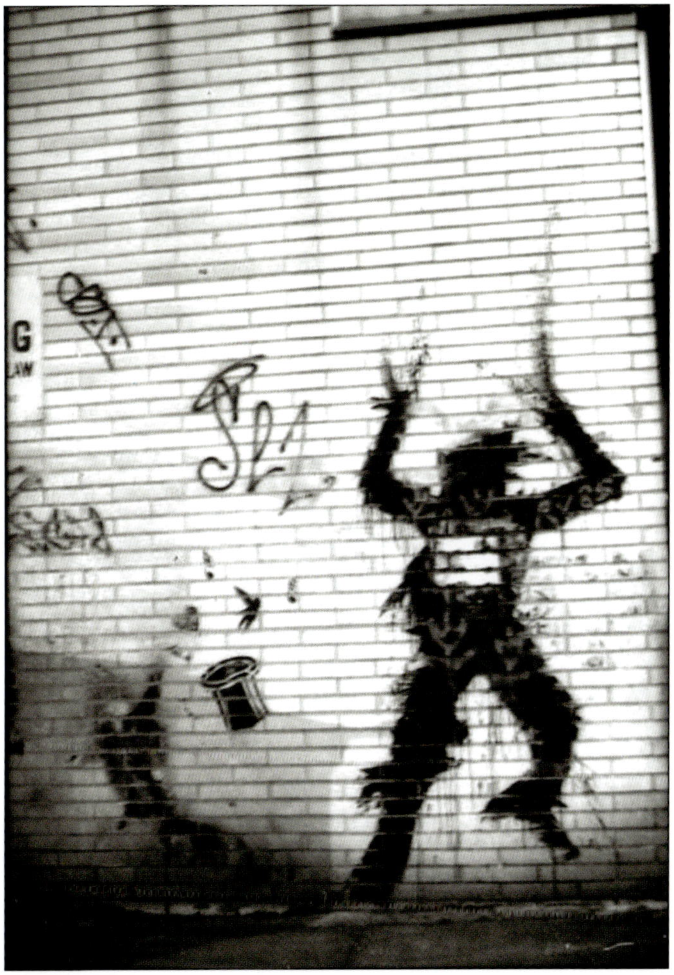

Shadowman

Born in 1954, Richard Hambleton is yet another early graffiti artist who has been dubbed the godfather of graffiti. A Canadian by birth, Hambleton managed the amazing feat of creating his distinctive crime scene body outlines in fifteen cities across the United States and Canada. This confrontational image, often taken for the real thing by the general public, stood as the precursor to his later "Shadowman" work.

Always defending his work as public art and never graffiti, Hambleton developed his style during the early 1980s. Unlike the crime scene outlines, his Shadowman figures were painted vertically on walls, particularly in dark alleyways where their loose, life-sized forms could scare away unwitting passersby. The Shadowman was first seen in New York City where Hambleton had made his home, but it didn't take long for him to make his way across the globe, where he lurked on the sides of buildings in London, Paris, and Rome before making the move to the Berlin Wall. In 1984, Hambelton painted seventeen Shadowmen on the east side of the wall; the following year, they appeared also on the west side.

As many of his contemporaries were doing, Hambleton also decided to move away from street art and start producing work on canvas. One of the first images he used for his new style of painting was the Marlboro Man, a well-known, stereotypical masculine figure. Hambleton sometimes added a bucking horse to increase the macho appearance of his Marlboro-type man. Lettering was sometimes applied that echoed the typeface used in the authentic advertisements. And in direct contrast to his previous work, Hambleton began to play around with color, texture, and light-play in a series of non-figurative, abstract pieces. He states that this was a deliberate choice in response to an overwhelming fashion at the time for figurative pieces; they were also experiments in mood and atmosphere.

Hambleton never returned to graffiti art, preferring to enjoy his status as an artist exhibiting in galleries. But that does not stop many later street artists naming him, along with Blek la Rat and Banksy, as a major influence in the graffiti art world.

KEITH HARING

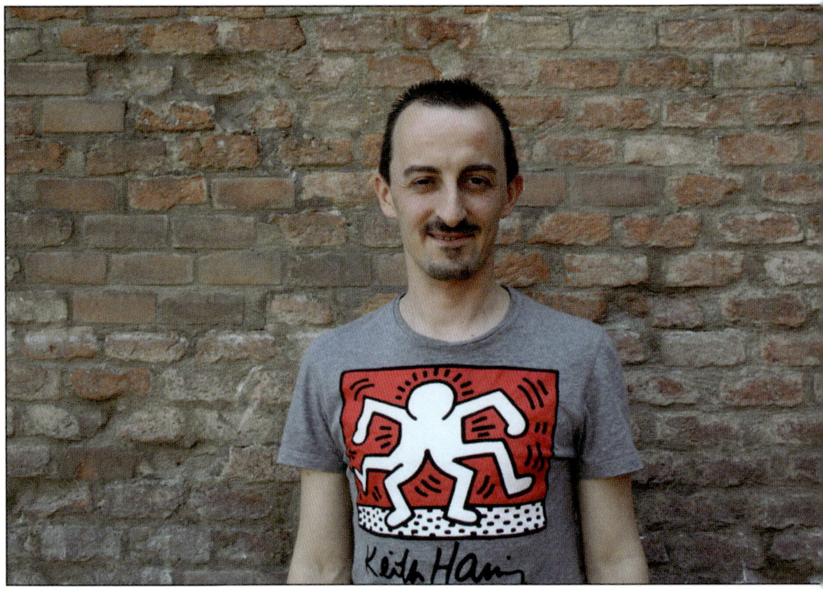

≈ A T-shirt featuring a distinctive Keith Haring design.
Photo courtesy of Ufficio stampa Arcigay.

Haring may well have got his talent from his father, Allen Haring, who was a cartoonist. Haring was born in Pennsylvania in 1958 and from 1976 to 1978 he studied commercial art at the Ivy School of Professional Art in Pittsburgh. Before finishing his degree, he had changed over to fine arts. In New York, where Haring moved to study at the School of Visual Arts, he discovered the world of graffiti and was instantly mesmerized by it.

Throughout the 1980s, Haring was heavily involved in the graffiti art scene. He took the image of the radiant baby, a simple outline cartoon of a crawling figure with lines radiating out from it, as his insignia. He participated in group shows and made friends with other well-known graffitists, including Jean-Michel Basquiat. Haring also became a good friend of Andy Warhol's.

Over a seven-year period, Haring produced fifty public works around the world, but during that time he also started to paint on canvas. By the mid '80s Haring had opened a store, selling reproductions of his graffiti style work on T-shirts and posters. Unfortunately Haring, who seemed so full of life and energy, who was creating all the time, contracted HIV and died of complications associated with it.

INVADER

Invader is the pseudonym used by a cousin of Thierry Guetta, and it was through Invader that Guetta became involved in graffiti art himself. Invader took his name from the popular video game *Space Invaders*, and his small mosaics are images based on the pixilated characters. Not only does his name reflect the inspiration behind his art, but Invader also photographs his work in the many cities he has pasted it, later calling it "an invasion."

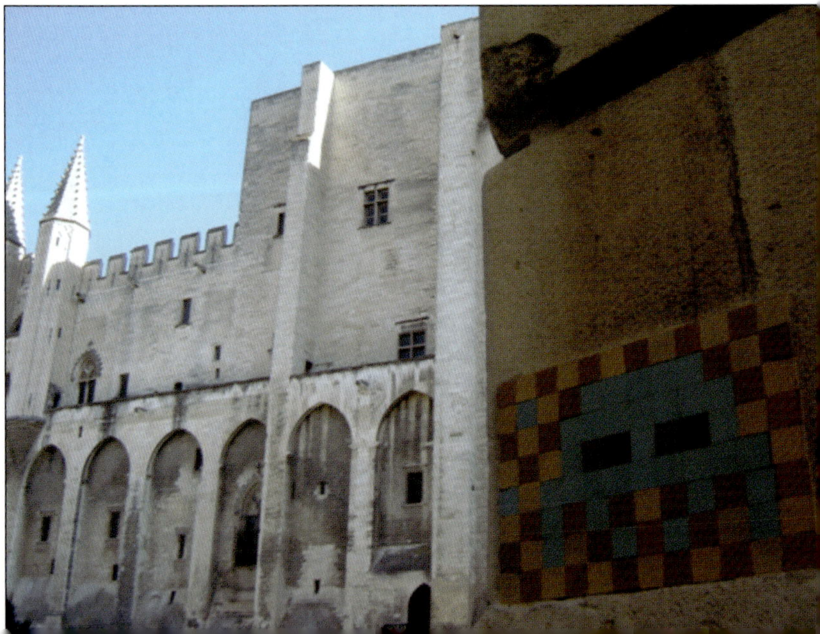

Mosaic by Invader in Avignon. »

In 1990, Paris, Invader's hometown, was the first city in France to experience the "invasion," although the full-scale operation didn't truly begin until eight years later. From the end of the decade onward, the invasion spread across the country and then jumped continents. The invasion continued until it became a worldwide phenomenon.

Although best known for his space invader mosaics, Invader has also worked on a series inspired by the Rubik's Cube, which he deemed Rubikcubism. The works are made from the cubes themselves. Invader has also participated in group shows in major galleries across the globe.

JANA & JS

Jana & JS are graffiti artists—one is German and the other French—who work together making street art. Many of their works show people taking photographs, often

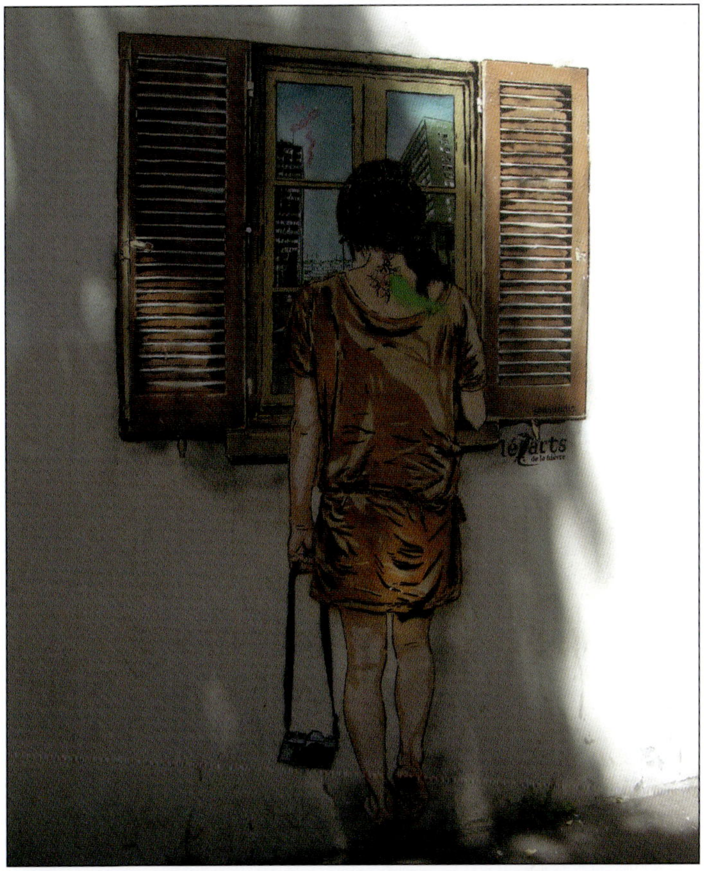

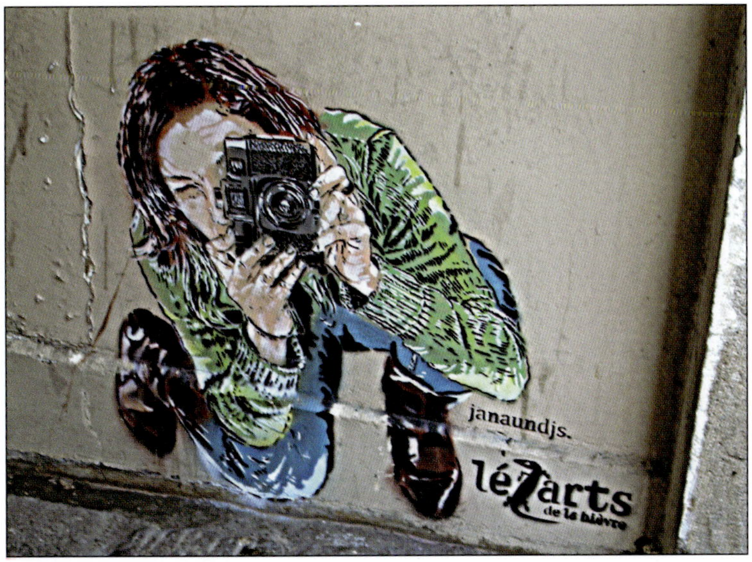

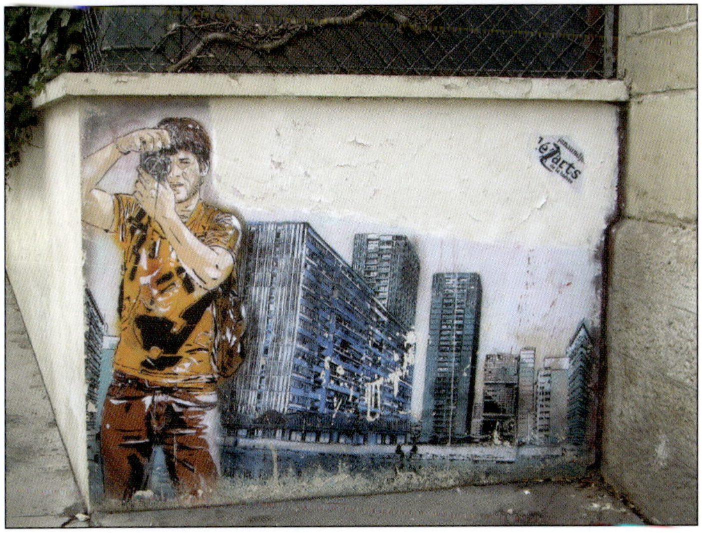

Jana & JS sightings.
Photos courtesy of Sophie Masson.

self-portraits, which makes the image look as though the photographer is looking in a mirror. They are quite new to the street art scene.

JR

JR is an artist who has kept his real name and identity a secret. He began his artistic career as a teenage graffiti artist who loved the danger and daring associated with marking hard to reach places. When he was about seventeen, JR found a camera left on a train and he started photographing his graffiti. He then made large prints of his photos and pasted them around Paris. As he grew older, JR became more interested in the social aspects of street art and graffiti. He would take photos of people he met on his travels around Europe and paste them up.

Over a two year period, JR began a series of works titled *Portraits of a Generation.* It involved taking photos of youths from local Parisian housing estates and pasting them around the city. What began as his own illegal project was quickly legitimized by the City of Paris authorities who thought it was a highly appropriate and artistic idea.

More portraits followed: In 2007, JR took photos of both Palestinian people and Israelis. He showed them face-to-face, putting them up in cities on both sides of the Separation Barrier before exhibiting them in Paris. JR continued his work of documenting and showing photos of isolated and often disempowered members of various communities. In 2008, his major project *Women are Heroes* looked at the way women have to stand firm under difficult circumstance, often in war.

One of the important aspects of JR's work is the way he involves the local communities in his projects, making not only street art but true community art projects.

MARK JENKINS

In some ways, it is not possible to call Jenkins's work "graffiti" and yet in other ways, it fits the bill exactly. Jenkins doesn't scratch or paint a surface, but makes sculptures that have similar qualities to graffiti and that make the same kinds of statements about life that street and urban art do. The medium he works in is clear box sealing tape (rather like overlarge Scotch tape). His first works (done in 2003) were made using his own body as a cast. These were

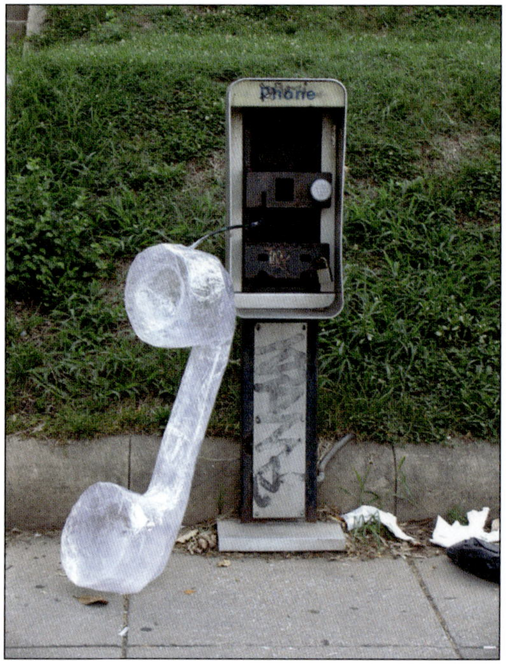

Call waiting. »
Photo courtesy of Storker.

then displayed around the streets of Rio de Janeiro. Two years later, he was dressing the life-sized figures in clothes to make them look more realistic. They became the basis of his Embed series.

Jenkins has built a reputation and is now invited to give workshops in his sculptural technique; he also exhibits in galleries, although he still enjoys making street art.

KING ROBBO

King Robbo is considered Banksy's archenemy. The two of them are at war with each other, one source stating that it began in the 1990s when Robbo said he gave Banksy a slap. Banksy, on the other hand, denies this. The ongoing and escalating feud certainly helped give Robbo a lift to fame, riding on the back of his rival's reputation.

Robbo began work as a graffiti artist in 1985, possibly even earlier. It was that year, though, that saw him paint a train and also a large mural alongside Regent's Canal in Camden, London. Surprisingly, the mural stayed put with little desecration apart from the odd tag or two for many years. Trouble started, however, in 2009, when another graffitist,

King Robbo.
Photo courtesy of Sophie Masson.

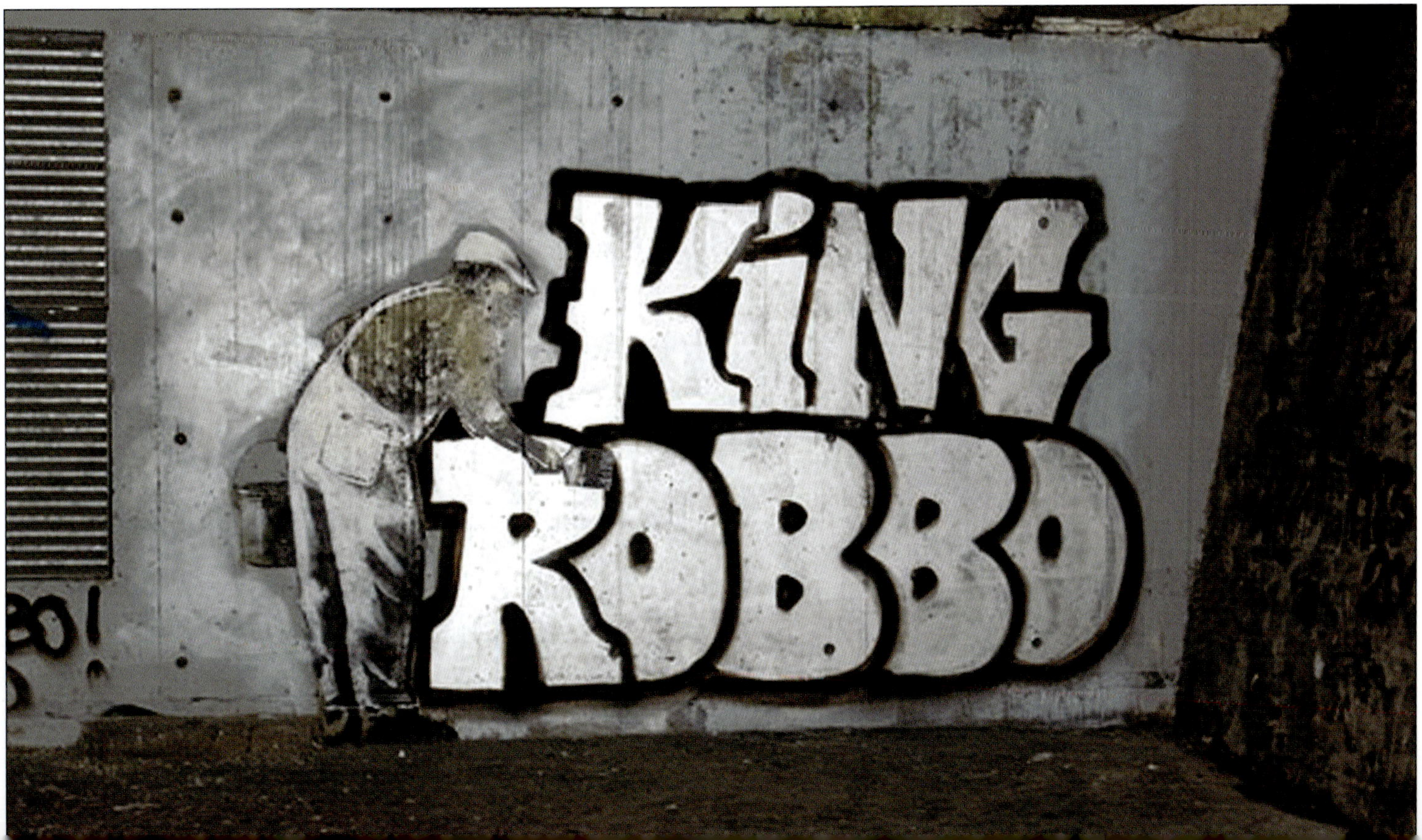

thought to have been Banksy, posted a work over the top of it, covering it almost completely, with a poster of a man putting up wallpaper. Then on Christmas Day of the same year, Robbo, apparently wearing a wet suit, retaliated by painting the words "King Robbo" in silver over the top of the wallpaper man so that it looked as though he, the character, was painting the words. This was followed by the word "Fuc" being put before the word "King." One of the highlights of the ongoing battle was Robbo's picture of the cartoon character Top Cat leaning on a grave stone that had "RIP Bansksy's career" written on it. Other works by Banksy were targets of defacement by Team Robbo, as well.

The war between the graffiti giants became the subject of a documentary called *Graffiti Wars*. Like other films by Banksy, it is possible that the war with King Robbo was nothing more than a piece of theater, another part of Banksy's living a lie.

King Robbo grew up in London's east end, an economically depressed area with all its attendant problems, in the 1970s. He admits to hanging out with a rough crowd and watching them spray tags on walls. It wasn't long before he joined them. Everyone added the letter "o" to their names, Robbo said, and that's how he ended up with Robbo.

Robbo was expelled from high school and ended up working in his uncle's building business. Night became his free time when he could go about spraying graffiti under cover of dark. Robbo's parents were perplexed by their son's activities. They couldn't understand undertaking such a demanding activity if there was no money to be made. Robbo says he was just addicted to doing art. Robbo eventually became the main instigator of many daring graffiti writing sprees and he gathered many acolytes. Part of the fix for him was the element of danger and his ability to avoid capture.

Robbo explains that Banksy started their rivalry at their very first meeting. They were introduced at a party. Robbo pretended to have heard of Banksy as he thought this was the polite thing to do, but was flabbergasted when the courtesy was not returned and Banksy baldly came out with the fact that he had never heard of Robbo. Robbo took this as a deliberate insult and slapped Banksy in the face, knocking his glasses off. The two went their separate ways and pretended nothing had happened. Robbo believes it was his mentioning the incident in a newspaper article that set off the feud.

The story of King Robbo and Bansky, whether fact or fiction, has a happy ending, although Robbo had to suffer a life-threatening injury for it to come about. In April 2011, the artist, getting ready for an exhibition, had a fall and sustained head injuries. His condition was so bad that he was put into an induced coma where he remained for months. Banksy, feeling that it was time old wounds were healed, painted over the Regent's canal mural in a black and white version of the original work. Later, Team Robbo tried to recreate the colored version but it has peeled away and leaves Bansky's painting to his onetime adversary.

LE BATELEUR

In English, Le Bateleur means "the street magician." This artist's work is highly political and the name he has chosen to represent his street art refers to a character from the street theater performed at the time of the French Revolution to help

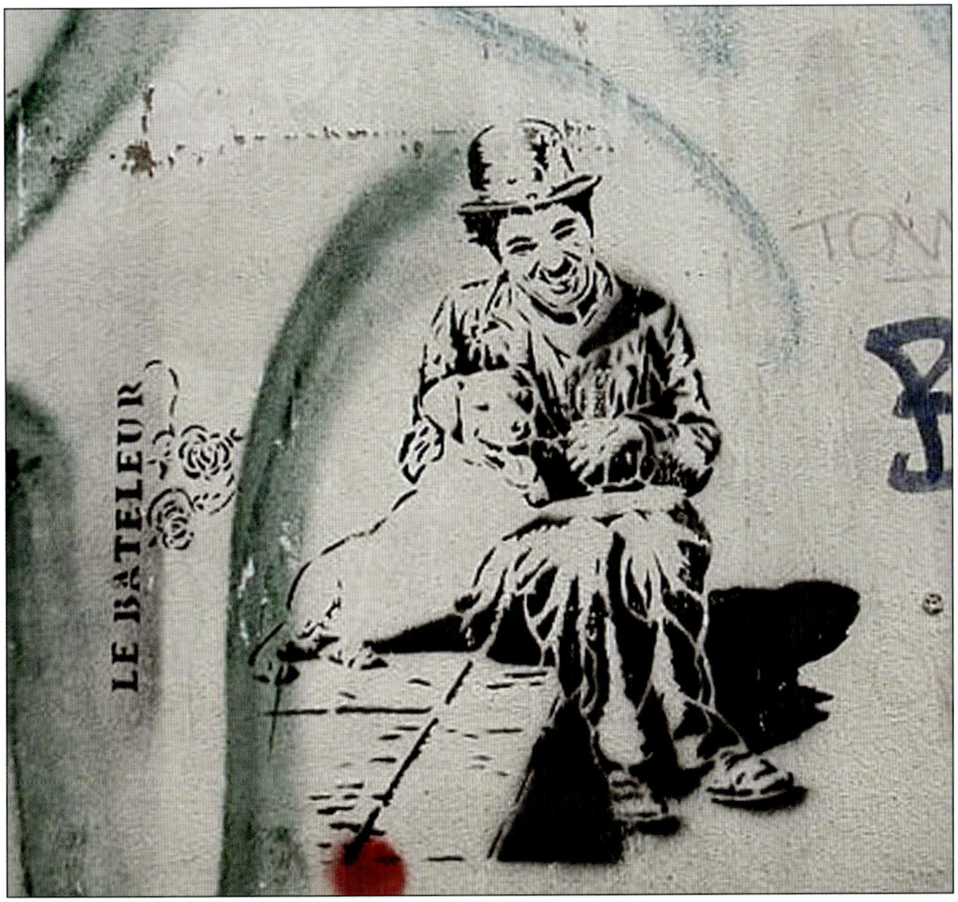

Photo courtesy of Sophie Masson.

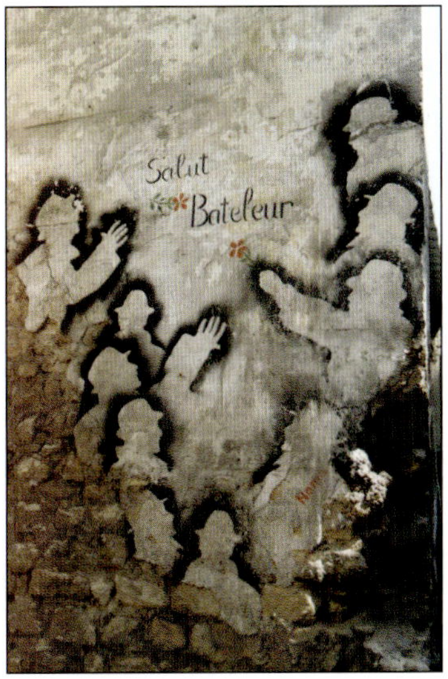

The great Nemo graffiti artist pays a touching homage to his compatriot, Le Bateleur.
Photo courtesy of Sophie Masson.

Photo courtesy of Sophie Masson.

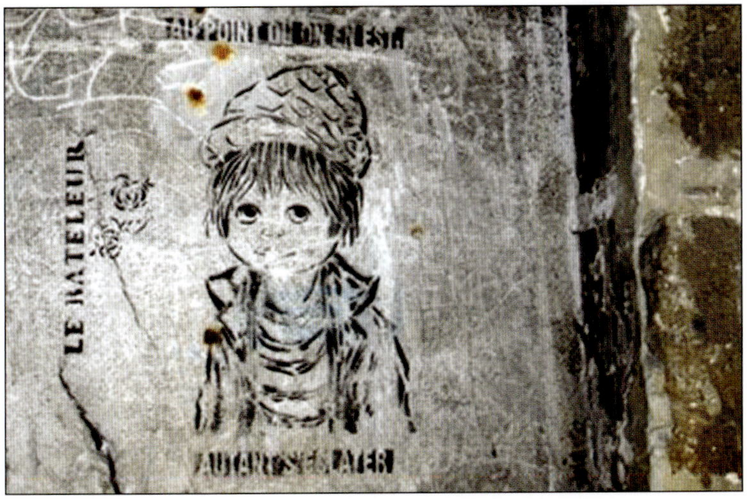

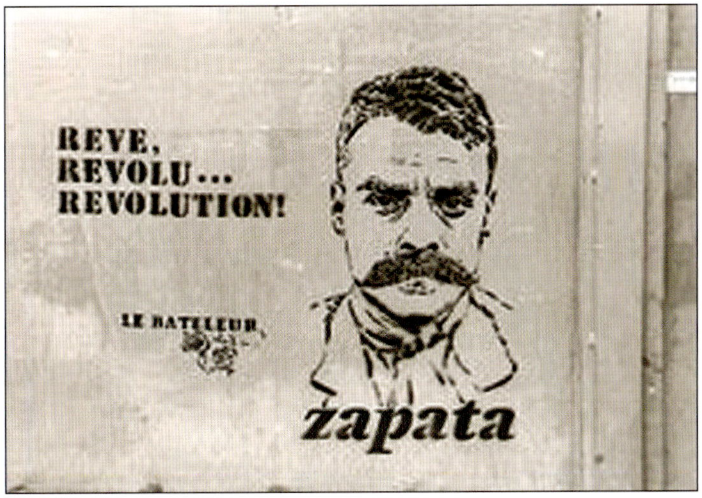

bring down the aristocrats. It is also one of the Tarot cards. It has been said that when this card kept turning up in readings the artist had done, he decided it was meant to be his street name.

Le Bateleur was born into a poor family in Menilmontant in Paris. His mother died when he was three and his father seemed incapable of bringing up him and his siblings on his own. A grandmother stepped in to help out, but when she died, the father did not cope at all and the authorities took the children into care. Le Bateleur was ten at the time and stayed in a children's home until he was eighteen. He loved drawing, but the activity was not encouraged at the home, where they were trained to be cooks instead.

When he was old enough to leave, Le Bateleur went straight to the streets and began to live a hard life of drugs and crime. The result was a three-year stint in jail. After his release, Le Bateleur began a serious relationship resulting in the birth of a child. This new incentive gave him the strength to make a new life for himself. The little family traveled around but finally went back to Paris. It was from this time on that Le Bateleur made street art.

Using a combination of image and text, Le Bateleur's work highlights issues of social injustice, hypocrisy (particularly of ruling bodies), and police brutality. Having been a homeless person himself, he was also a strong defender of their rights.

One of his parodies was on the French sign "DEFENSE DE AFFICHER," which means "do not post bills (posters)." Le Batleur made a pun on the word *afficher* and wrote "Defense de Ficher," which refers to the keeping of police files. Le Batleur did not burn midnight oil putting up his subversive messages, but rather hid within the crowd and posted them at lunchtime when lots of people were milling about on the streets.

Le Batleur was a true revolutionary, seeing his art as a means to an end, and he always refused to show his work in galleries. Because of his harsh living conditions, Le Batleur died at the age of thirty in 1996.

DON LEICHT

Leicht is both a painter and sculptor who has been a close collaborator of Fenken's for many years. In fact, they shared a studio at P.S. 1 in Queens until 1976. In 1980 they set about making a suite of works for an area in the South Bronx that had been designated for the People's Convention. It was an area that housed high Latin American, Native

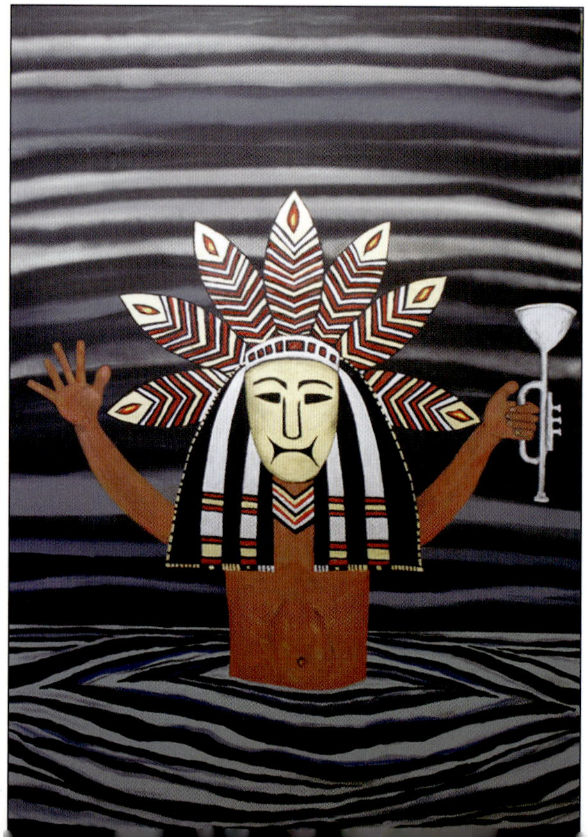

This naïve style artwork looks to be a work on canvas » or some other portable surface rather than street graffiti. *Photo courtesy of Don Leicht.*

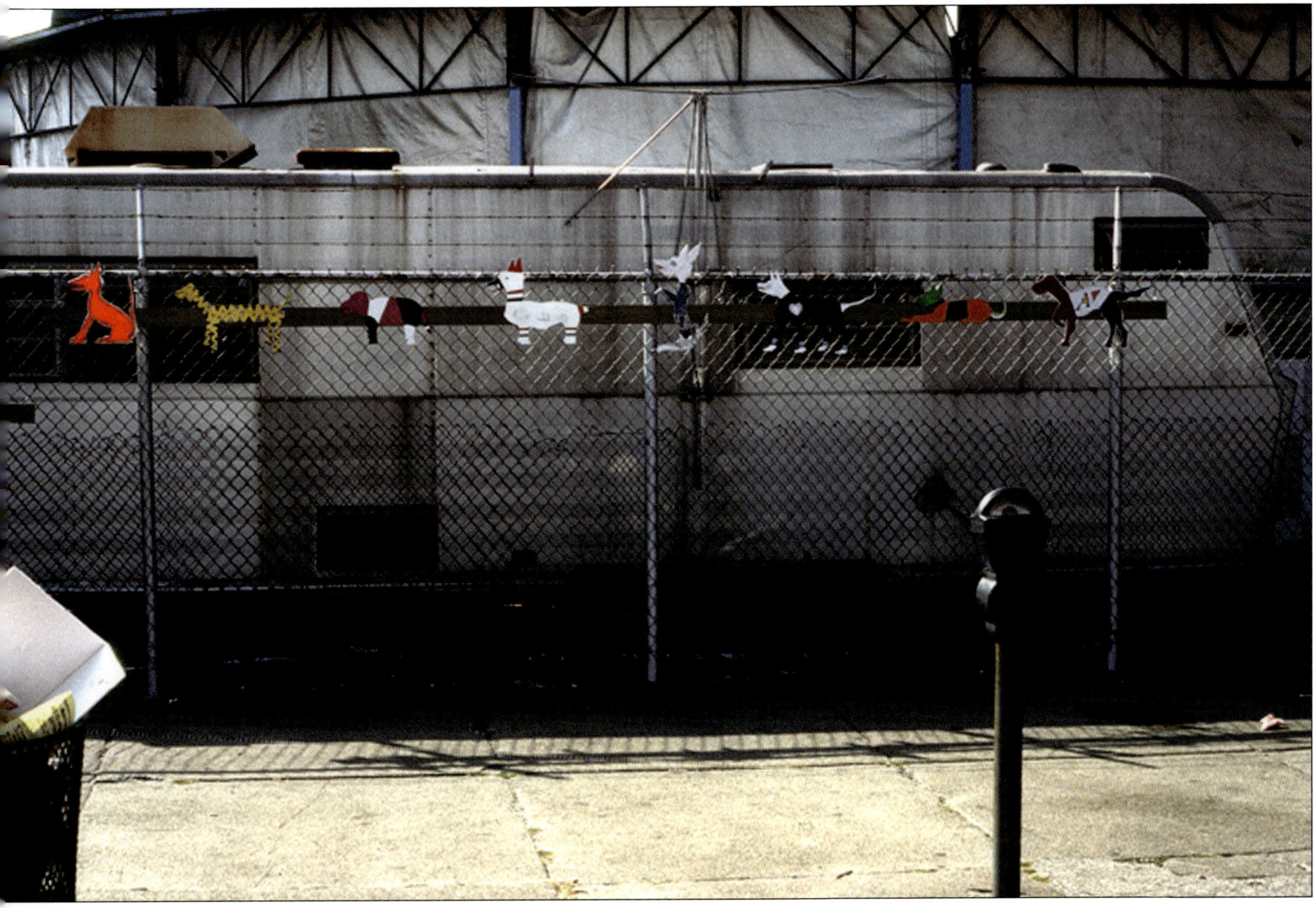

Whimsical painted dogs cut out and placed on a fence bring a touch of color and life to a rather drab neighborhood.
Photo courtesy of Don Leicht.

American, Indian, and African American populations. As groups, they were socially and economically disadvantaged and the governments of the time were doing nothing to alleviate the problems, hence Fekner's *Broken Promises* signs. Leicht's contribution to the project was a number of small painted sculptures, which he called Birdfeeders, designed with the children of the area in mind.

JÉRÔME MESNAGER

Mesnager's work is as famous as his friend Némo's, but unlike many graffiti artists, he works under his real name. Mesnager was born in 1961 in France and went to the Ecole boulle in 1974 to learn to be a cabinet maker. In 1979, he

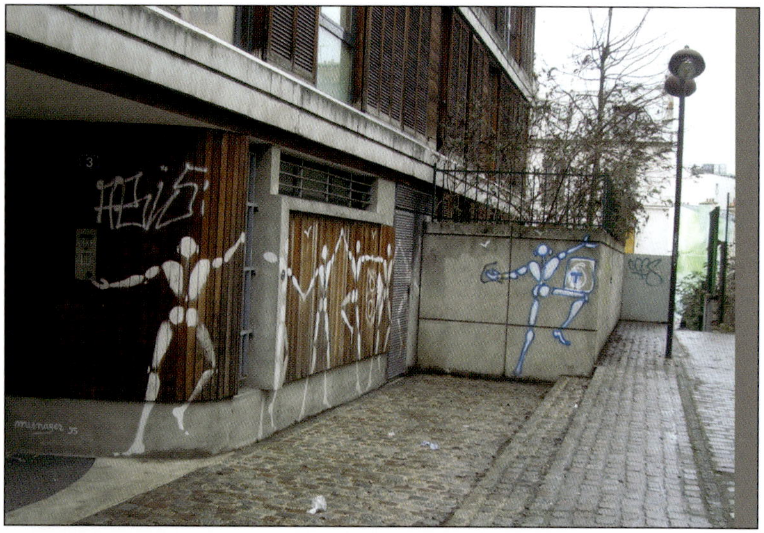

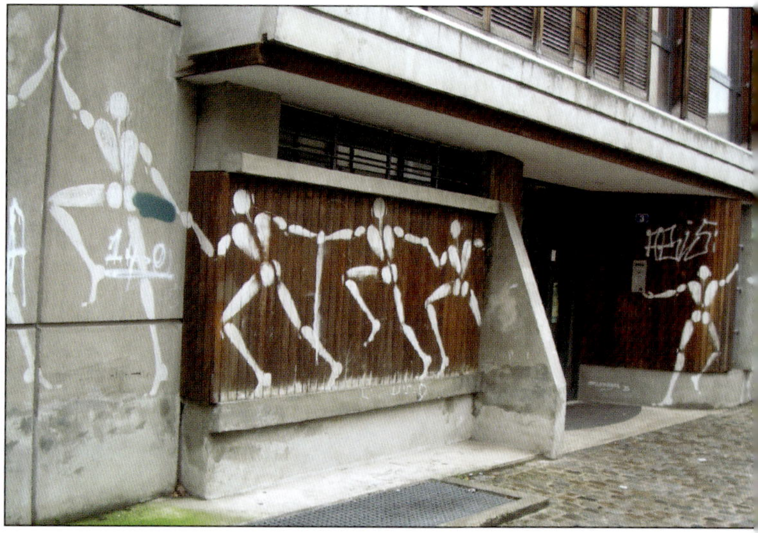

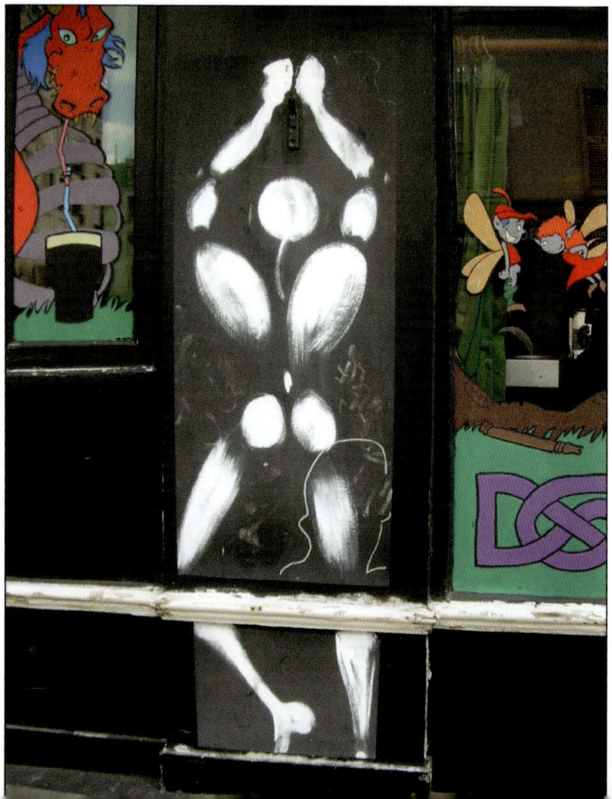

Mesnager always uses the same style of figure painted in white. Sometimes he collaborates with Nemo and the stylized white figure will be seen cavorting with his black clad friend in the raincoat and hat.

Photos courtesy of Sophie Masson.

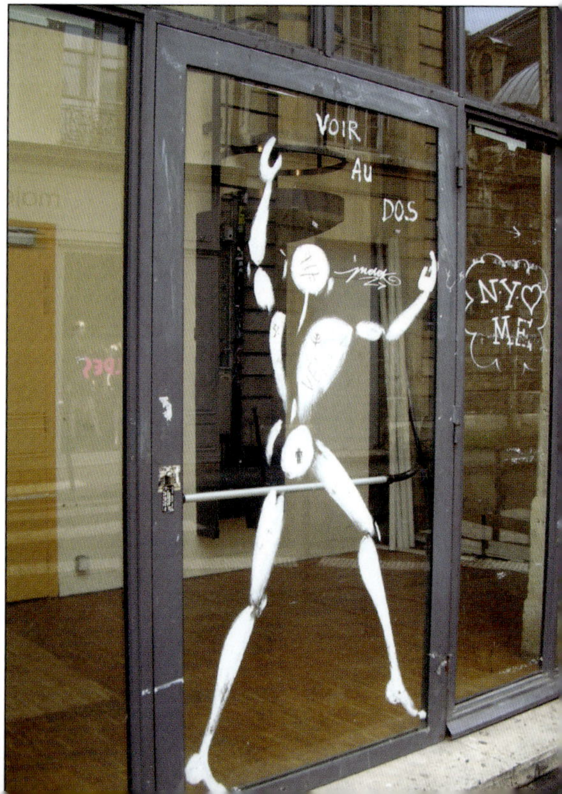

studied cartooning at the School of Applied Arts in Duperre. Street art became a reality for Mesnager in 1982 after he helped set up a group known as Zig-Zag. The group aimed to paint graffiti and tags all over Paris in a haphazard fashion.

Mesnager's best known character is the "Bonhomme Blanc," or "Corps Blanc." The literal translation of the name into "White Body" does not accurately reflect the subtleties of the French and it has been suggested that "White Ghost" is closer to the intended feel. This interesting stylized figure, who looks like the wooden mannequins artists use for drawing poses, has appeared in many places the world over: New York, Cuba, China, and Columbia, to name a few.

The Bonhomme Blanc is painted freehand, without using stencils or posters. They are painted in white very quickly; the artist claims he can do one in as little as 26 seconds straight onto the wall. Mesnager took the idea from leaning against a wall and imagining it leaving a mark only where his actual body rested.

His ghosts interact very happily with other people's graffiti, never dominating or putting the other down, but instead joining it in a joyful caper.

MR. BRAINWASH

Exit Through the Gift Shop is an intriguing documentary made by Banksy mainly documenting the work of filmmaker and artist Thierry Guetta, AKA Mr. Brainwash. Banksy introduces the subject of the film, a French-born American who became obsessed with filming everything around him. When Guetta's graffiti-making cousin, only identified as Space Invader, visits his cousin in Los Angeles, Guetta finds a whole new subject matter for his video camera: graffiti artists at work. He filmed hundreds of hours worth of artists putting up their posters, stickers, stencils, and spray can art all over the city and then all over cities outside of the United States. He struck up a friendship with Shepard Fairey, Swoon, and others of their caliber. Guetta had filmed almost every major graffiti artist but had found that one in particular eluded him: Banksy.

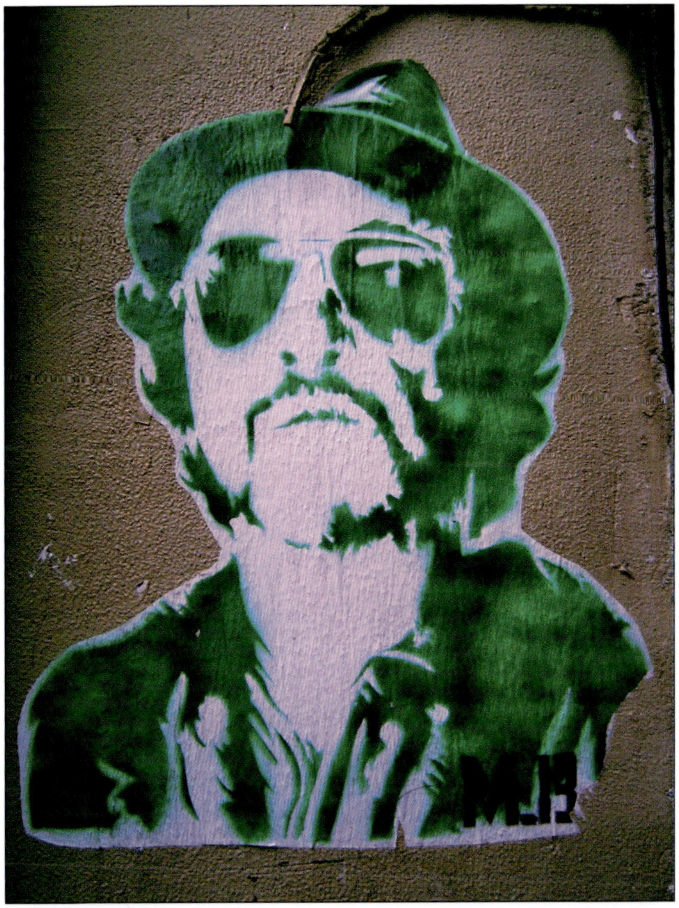

Mr. Brainwash uses his own image » to promote his work as an artist. His style borrows a lot from his artist friends, such as Banksy.
Photo courtesy of Sebastian Horndasch.

By a chance encounter with Space Invader, Banksy, on a trip to Los Angeles, was introduced to Guetta and the two became friends. Guetta documented all of Banksy's graffiti activities in LA and then followed him back to London. When Banksy put on his big LA exhibition in an old warehouse, complete with camouflaged elephant, Guetta was so impressed that he used the idea as the base of his own blockbuster exhibition a few years later. With the help of an event manager recommended by Banksy, plus the artist's official stamp of approval, along with Fairey's, Guetta pulled the exhibition off with 4,000 people attending the opening night. The event made Guetta an instant success and resulted in both Banksy and Fairey doubting the nature of what they themselves were doing and questioning the whole notion of art.

It has been suggested that the film, *Exit Through the Gift Shop*, is actually a hoax, or if not exactly a fraud, then a work of fiction and that Thierry's story is a total fabrication. Whether the story behind the man is a myth or not, the fact is that he did put on a gargantuan exhibition and spectacle called "Life is Beautiful." Within the exhibition, Thierry purportedly used the work of another artist, Glen Friedman, a photographer. Friedman found that Thierry had taken his photo of the rap group Run DMC and used it as the basis for one of his own works. Mr. Brainwash has since gone on to produce other blockbuster shows.

MOSKO ET ASSOCIÉS

Mosko et associés is another pair of artists—Gerard Laux and Michel Allemand—who work together under one name. The name "Mosko" is a tribute to the area of Paris in which Gerard grew up, Moskowa, and that is also where the two artists met in the 1980s and began working together. Gerard was already making graffiti when he met Michel, who was a photographer and working on a series of pictures on street art. Gerard persuaded Michel to start painting instead and the rest is history.

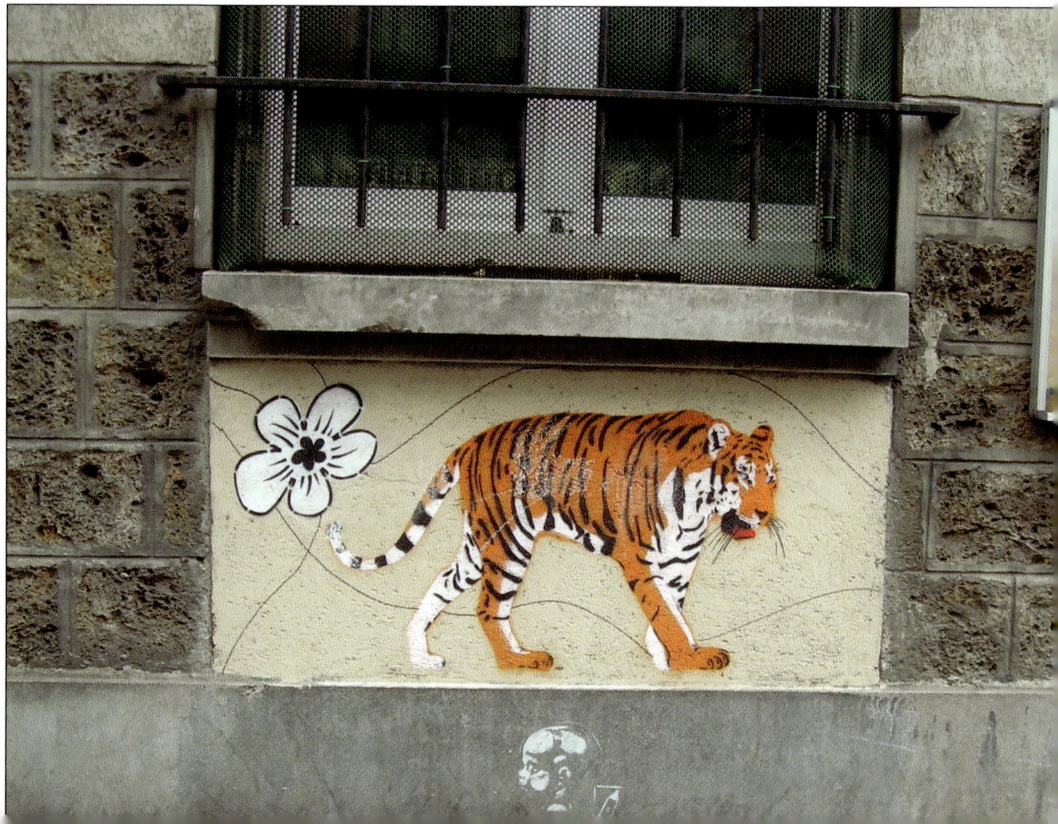

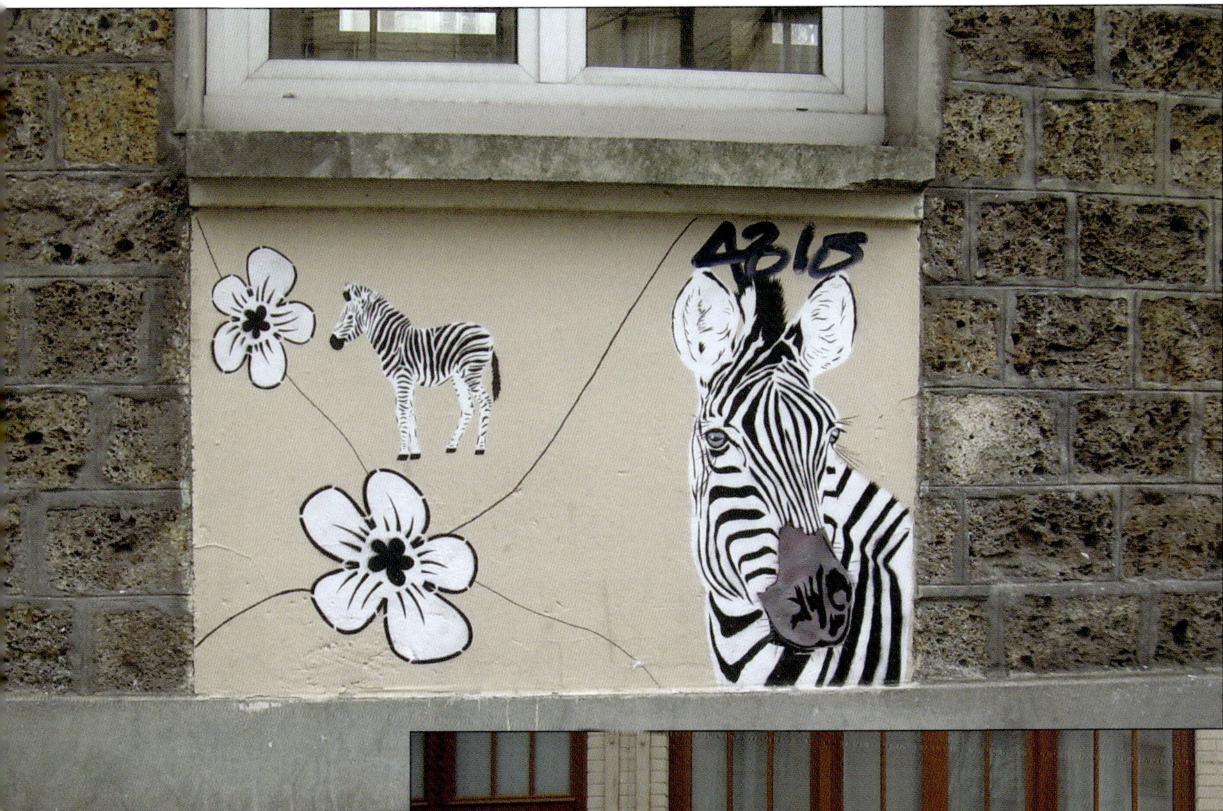

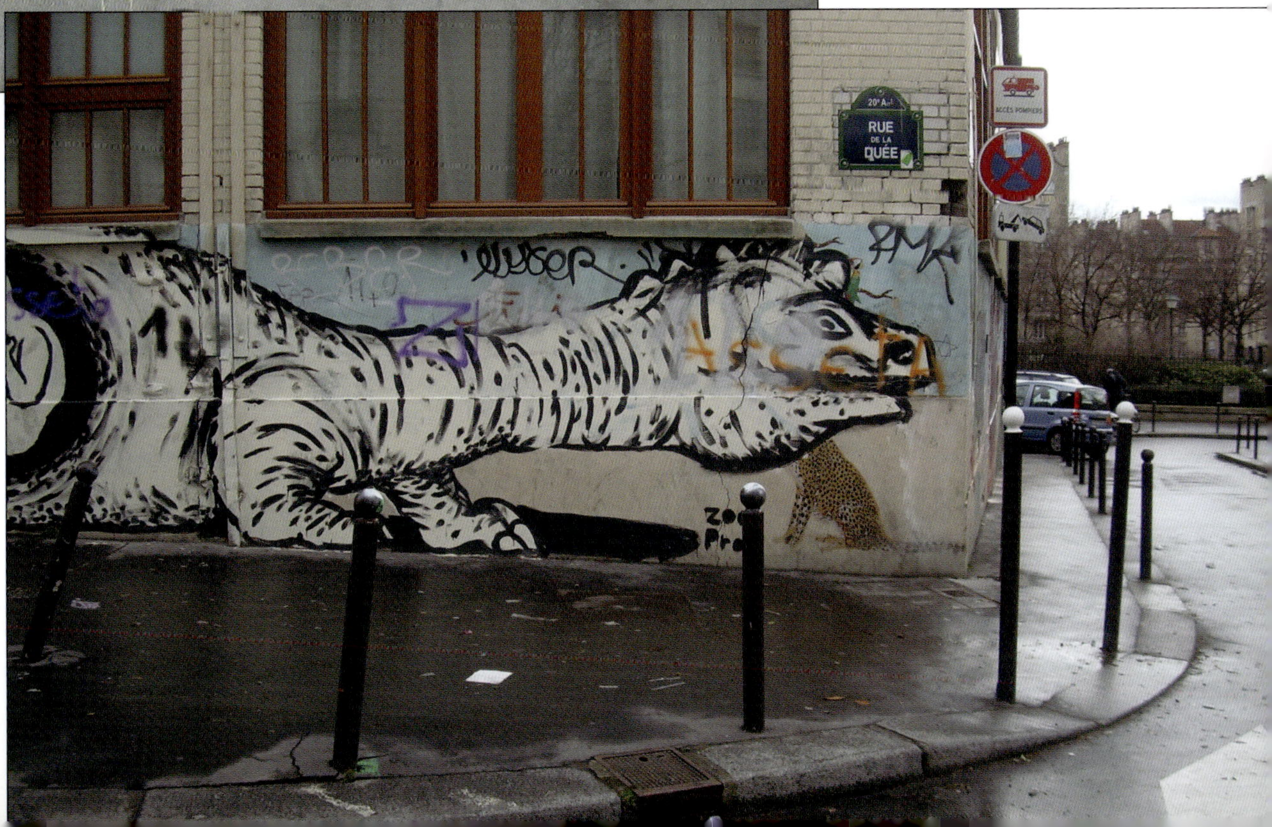

Mosko et associés graffiti found around Paris.
Photos courtesy of Sophie Masson.

NEMO

Nemo takes his name from a children's book character from the early twentieth century. When Nemo's son started school, the artist stenciled the route from home to school with the character of Little Nemo by Winsor McCay so that his son would feel more comfortable about walking there and back on his own.

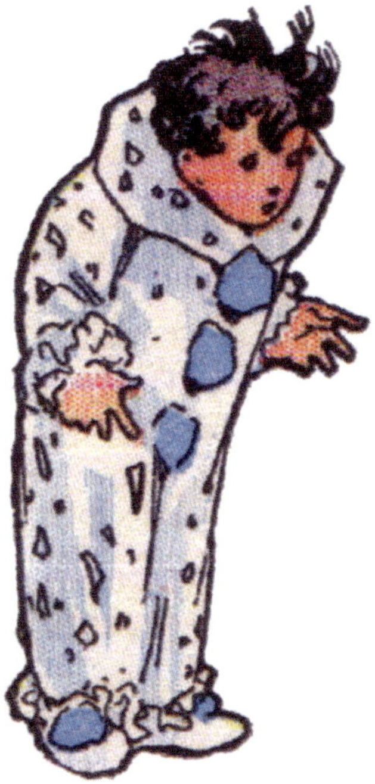

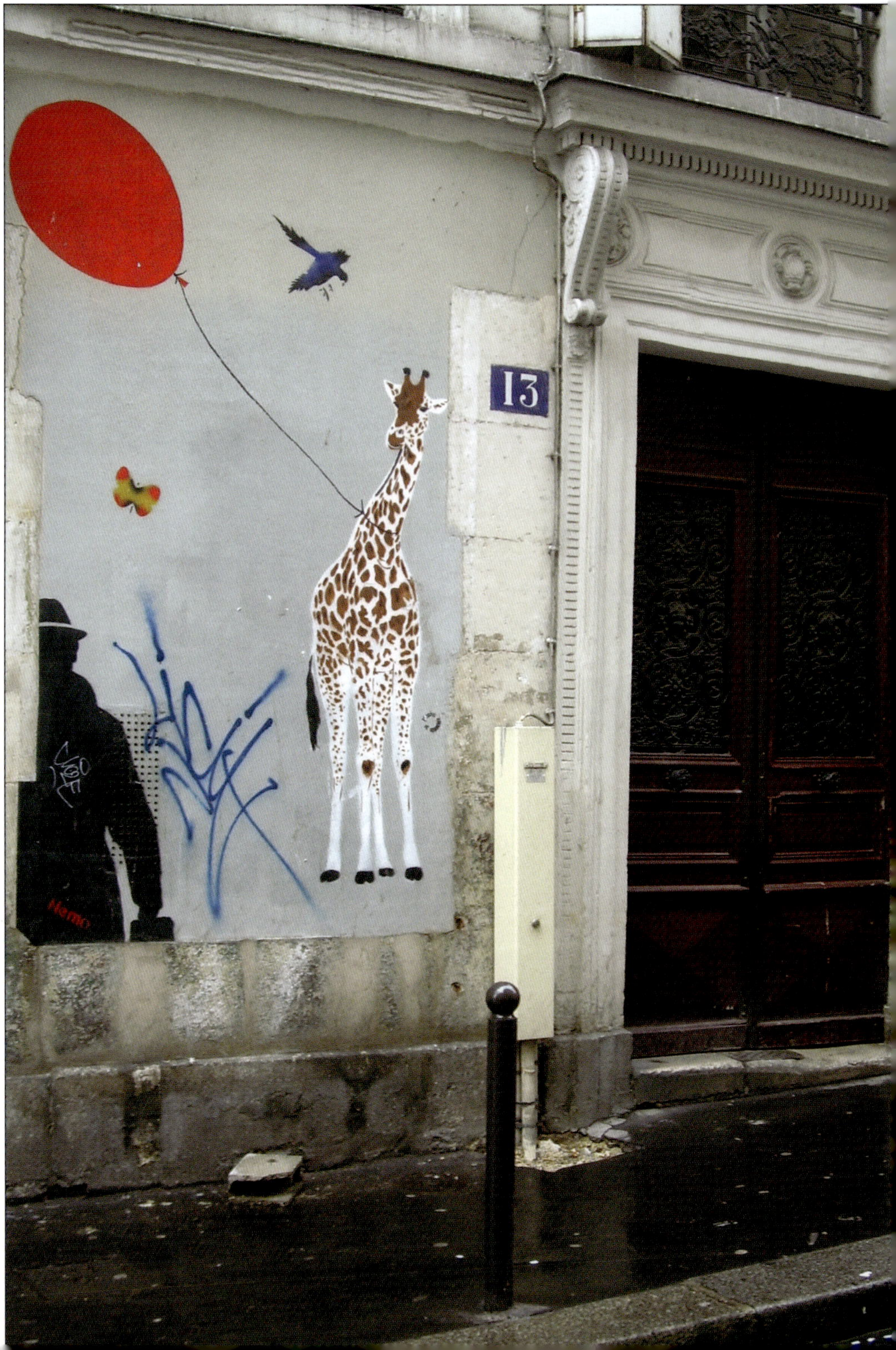

In the early days, Nemo used the little boy from a comic strip as the main character for his quirky narrative pictures, but as the artist's own little boy grew up, Nemo took on another protagonist—the man in the black rain coat. The figure is never sinister because he is always presented as a humorous fellow, often surrounded by whimsical animals, balloons, and flying boats.

Photos courtesy of Sophie Masson.

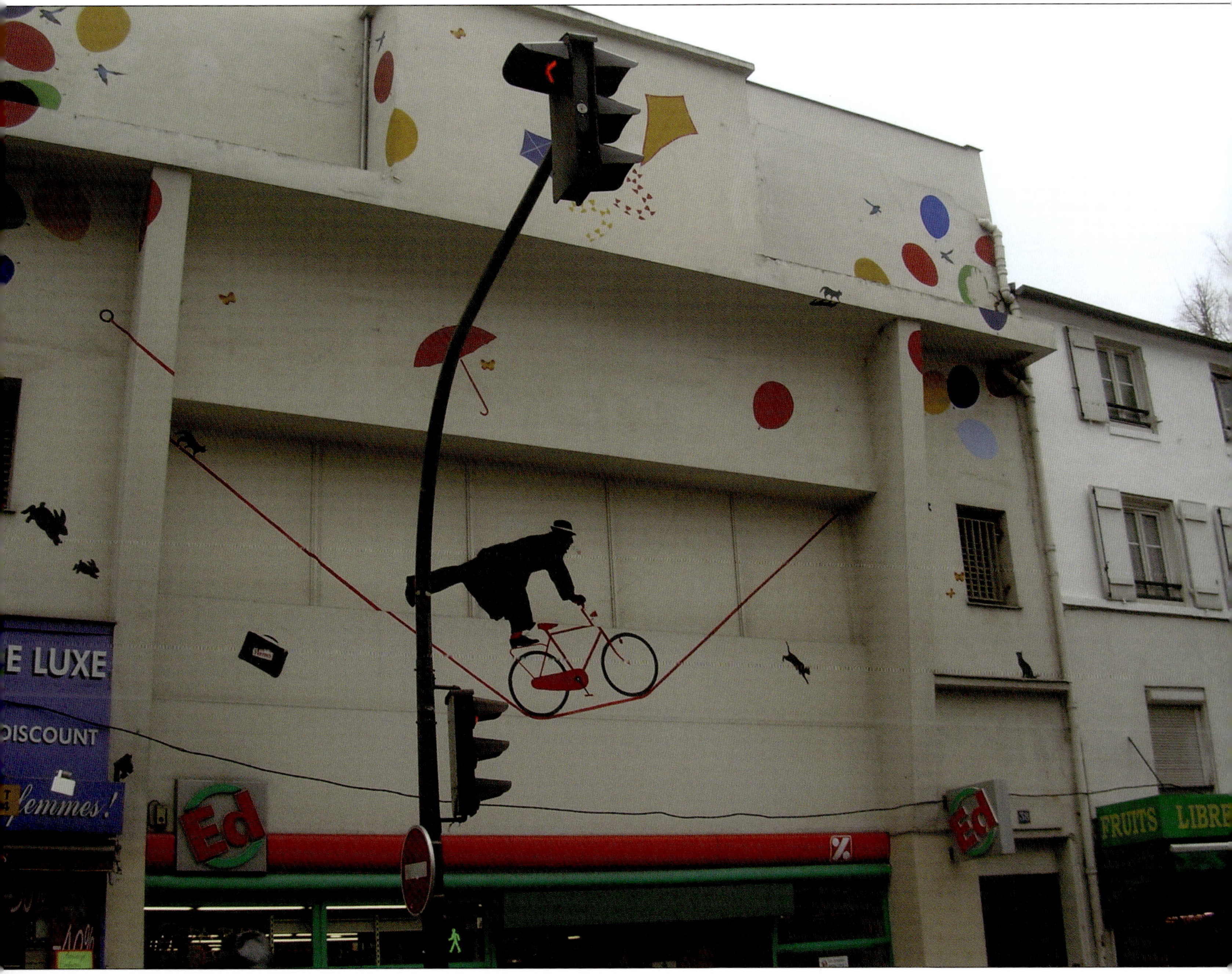
E LUXE
ISCOUNT
femmes!
Ed
Ed
FRUITS LIBRE

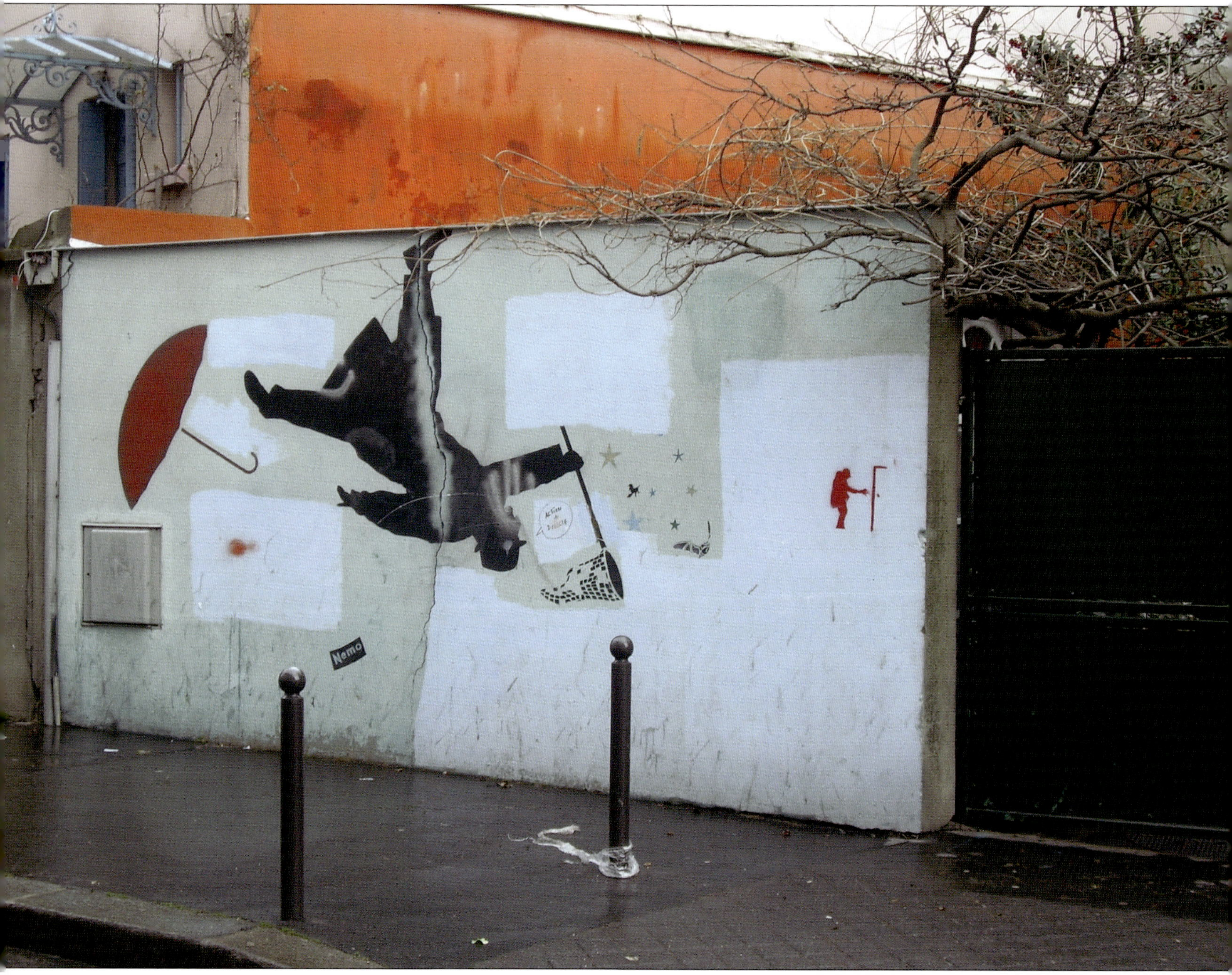

Photos on pages 166 and 167 courtesy of Sophie Masson.

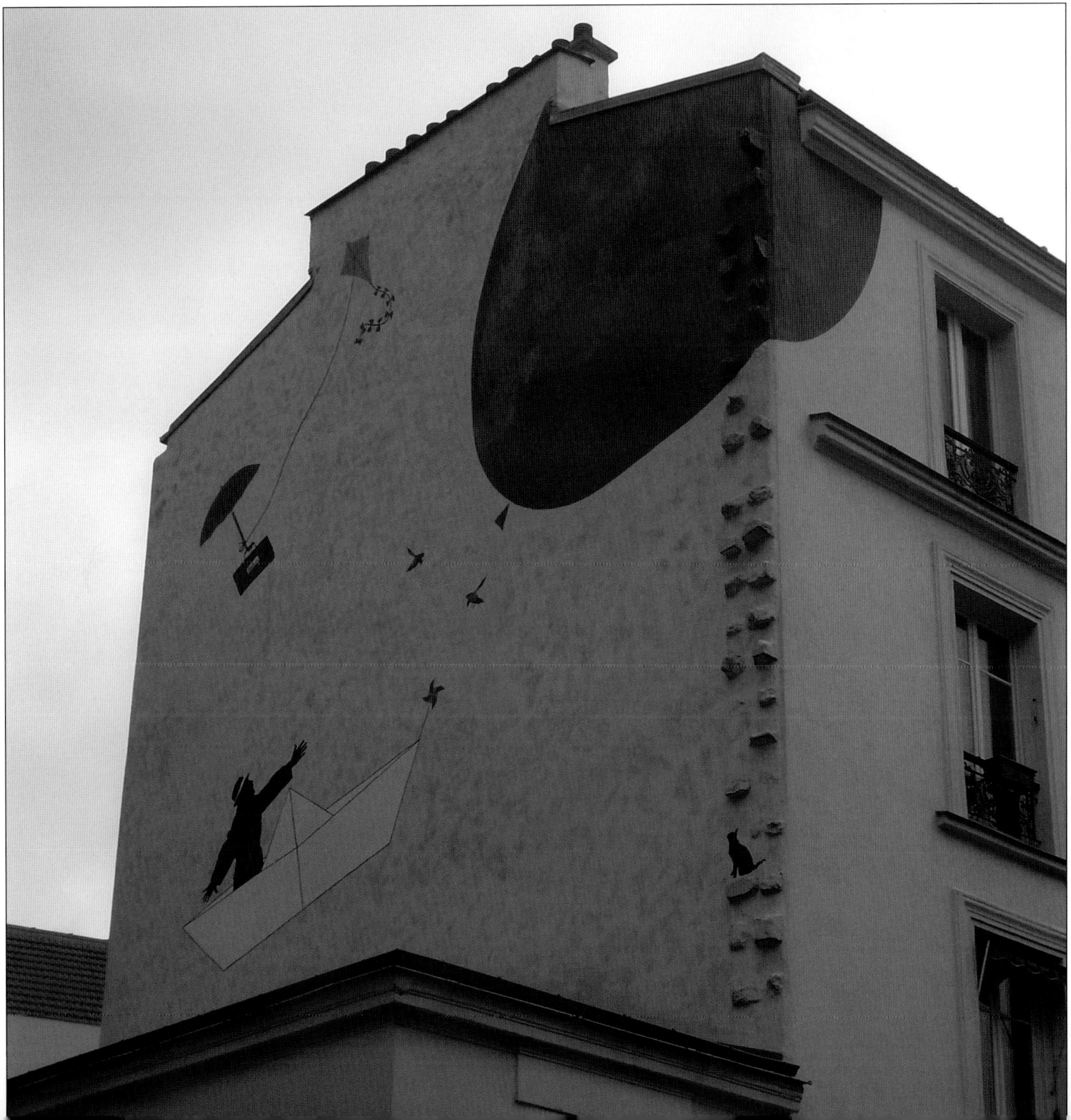

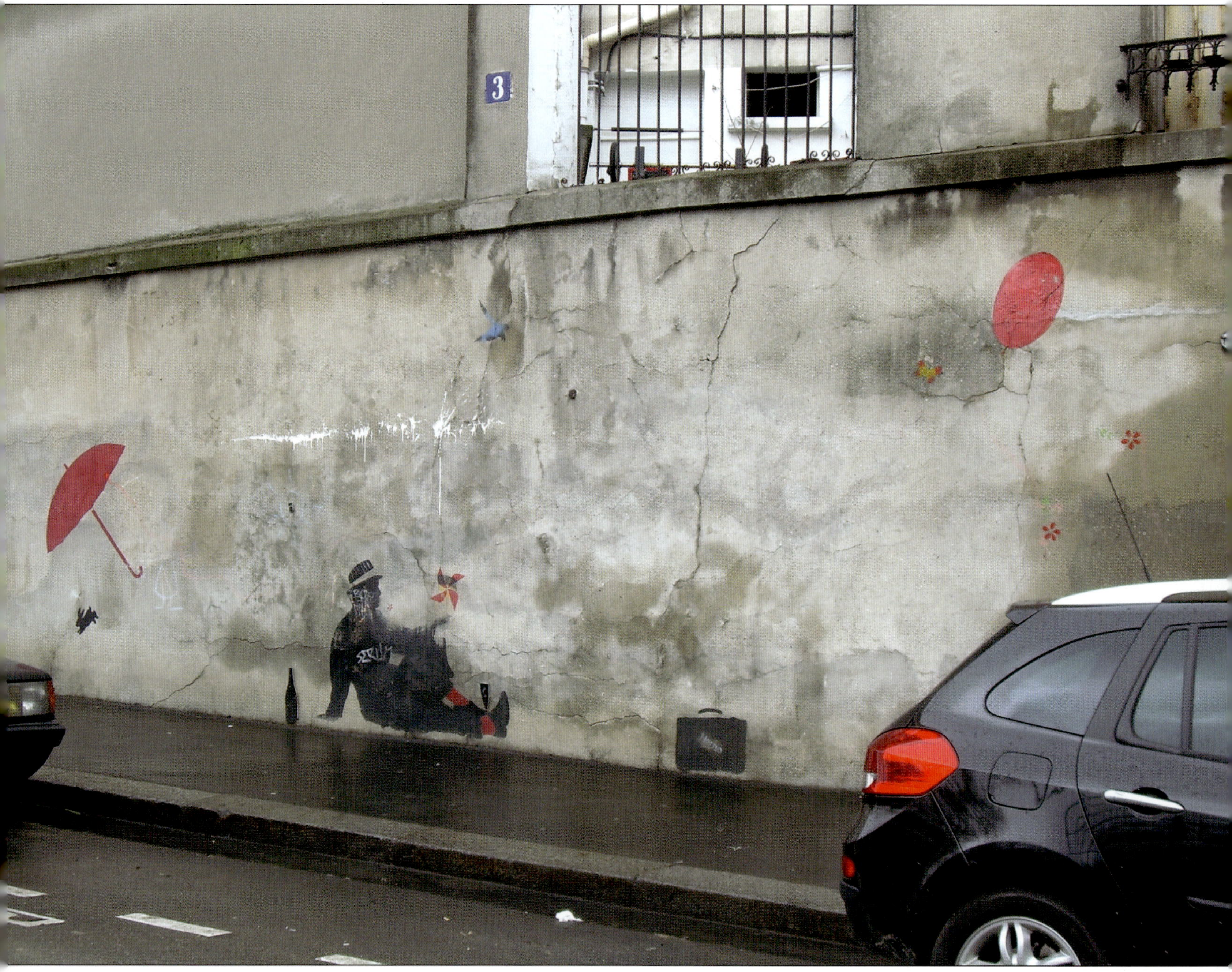

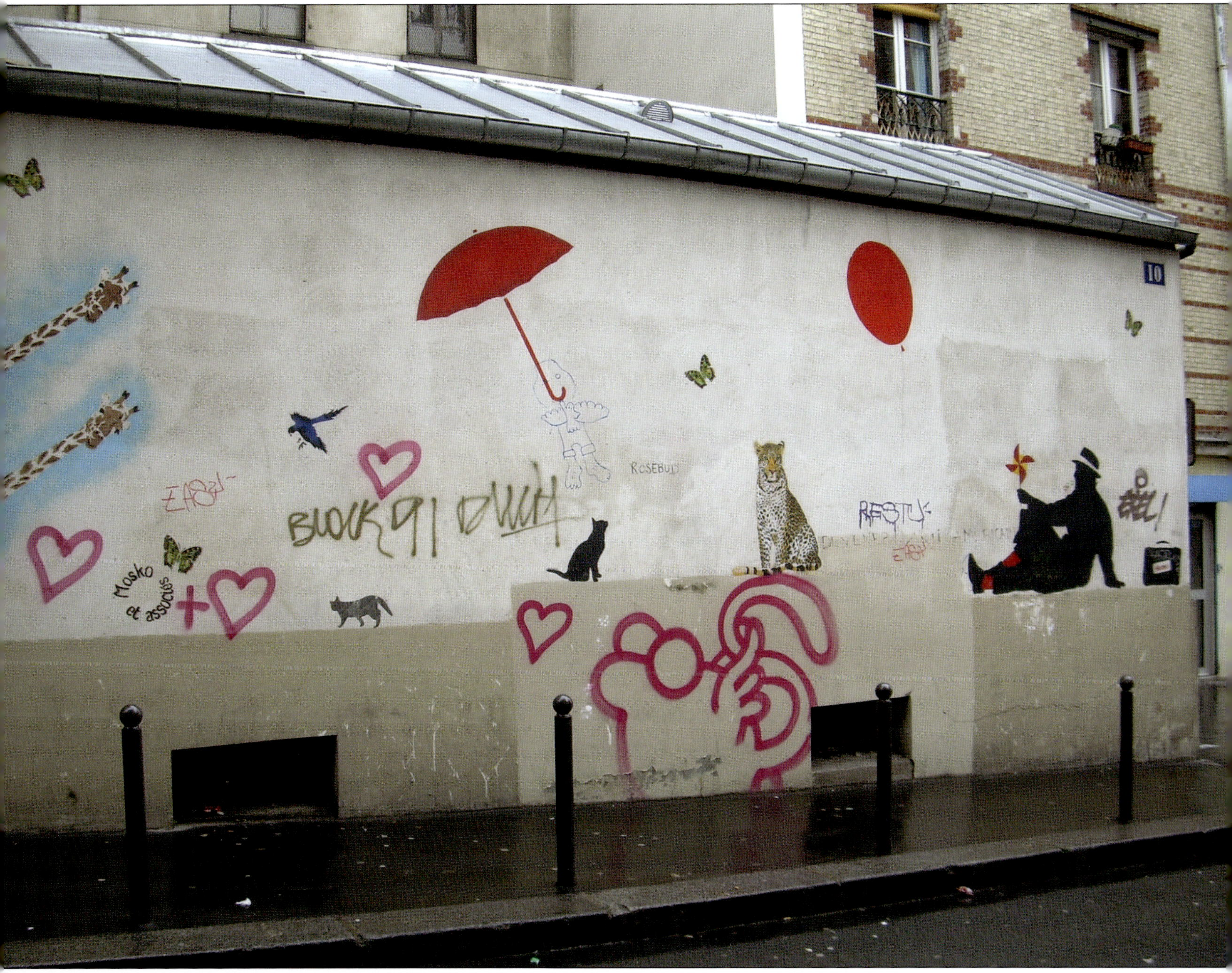

Photos on pages 168 and 169 courtesy of Sophie Masson.

After the Little Nemo pictures, which ceased as the artist's son got older, he began making other *pochoirs* (French for "stencils") to brighten the environs for the children of Belleville in Paris, a low socio-economic area with a high immigrant population.

Nemo's later character is a man in silhouette wearing a hat who is accompanied by little birds, butterflies, and an odd hippo. Instead of presented as sinister, he dances across walls, topples down staircases, and sits playing with merry-go-rounds. His long coat and hat give him the appearance of an old-time detective.

Sometimes the man in black teams up with a stylized figure in white by fellow artist and personal friend Jérôme Mesnager. The two styles are completely different but harmonize well through their bold designs in black and white.

Nemo only paints in less affluent areas of Paris, enjoying the spark he brings to the people who live there. In return, they can't wait to see a new *pochoir* after the old has been obliterated by the graffiti police.

ALEXANDRE ORION

Orion was born in the late 1970s in Brazil and is both a graffiti artist and a photographer. His work differs from many artists in that he not only makes black and white graffiti pieces, but also photographs people interacting with them, which forms part of his exhibition. Orion's early work consisted of hand painting T-shirts as a teenager before he

Photo courtesy of Trans Art.

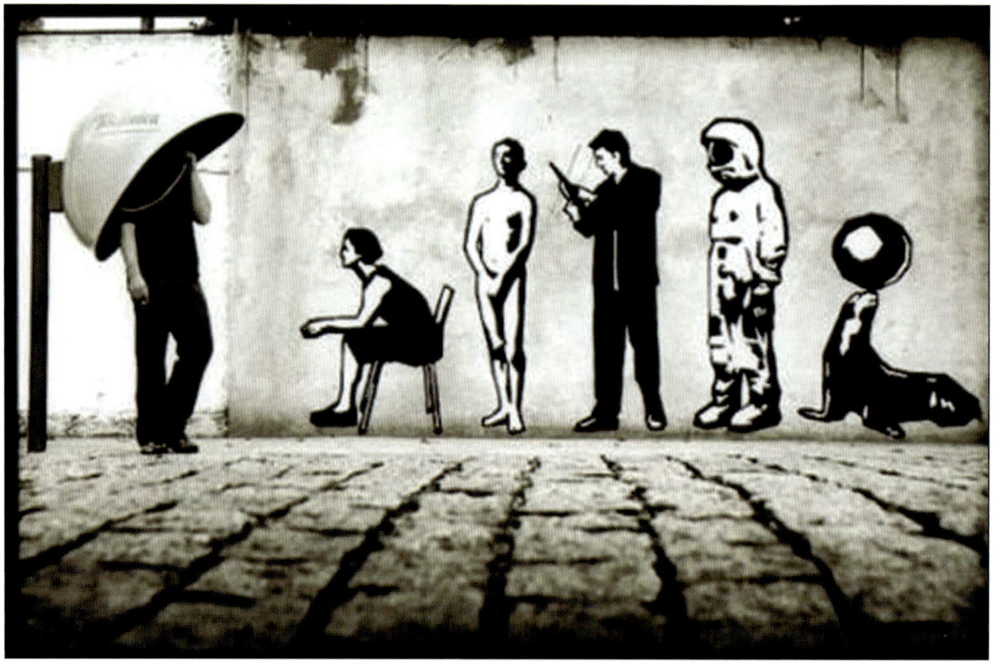

Photo courtesy of Trans Art.

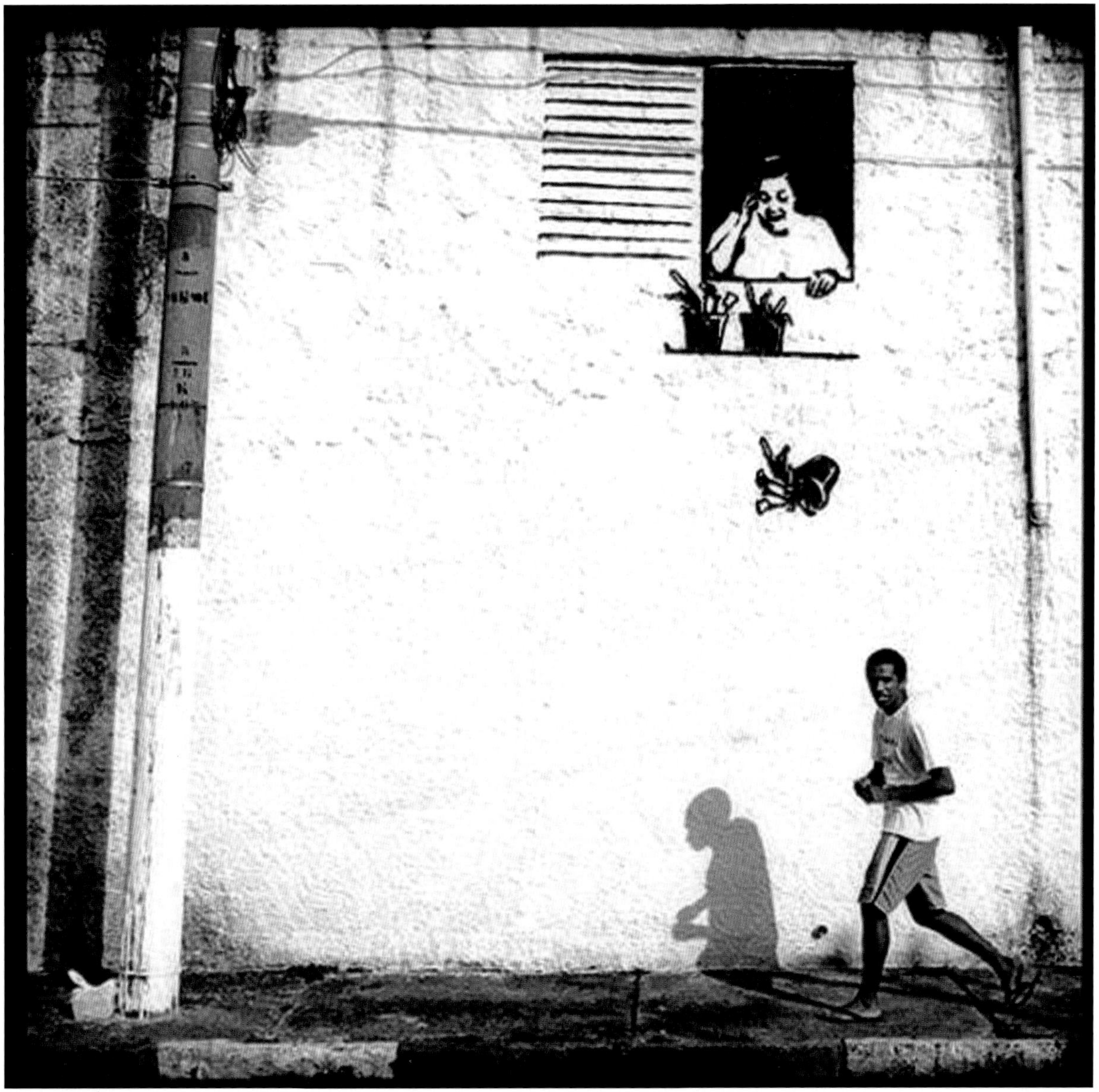

discovered graffiti. As he matured, Orion questioned the role of graffiti in society and became fascinated with the way people reacted to it, particularly to his own pieces.

Apart from his painted and photographed works, Orion has also experimented with reverse graffiti. One of his pieces involved drawing a series of skulls in the grime of the Max Feffer Tunnel in São Paulo. The impermanence of graffiti and reverse graffiti in particular meant that the tunnel mural did not last and was removed when the whole of the wall was cleaned. By graffiti-ing in this way, it is possible to draw attention to parts of a city that are in desperate need of an overhaul. His work has been exhibited in Paris, New York, and San Francisco.

CHRIS PAPE (FREEDOM)

Pape began spraying graffiti tags in 1974. He targeted the usual subway cars and tunnels. His first pseudonym was Gen II, but he later took on the name Freedom. It was with that moniker that Pape took to regularly graffiti-ing a tunnel that runs underneath Riverside Park in Manhattan. Consequently, the tunnel is now unofficially known as the Freedom Tunnel. Within this personal gallery, Pape has done a so-called self portrait in which he sports a spray can for a head. Having started as a simple tagger, Pape has certainly developed as an artist over the years, adding to his more recent repertoire images of classical art in black and silver paint.

LEE QUIÑONES

Quiñones is a Puerto Rican artist who was born on the island in 1960 but who grew up in New York City. At the age of fourteen, Quiñones began his career as a graffitist. A mere two years later he had managed to make an enormous amount of graffiti—many pieces being quite large in scale.

Quiñones's specialty was in painting entire subway cars. In 1976, he had painted ten cars without any additional help. Since then, he has managed to cover at least 125 of them. Among them were cars that were given titles like Hell Express, Earth is Hell, and Heaven is Life. Quiñones's reputation was so respected that other graffiti artists didn't dream of interfering with his work or even touching a car he was working on. And the fact that the authorities allowed cars with Quiñones's work to keep running in the public system without removing it for several years is testament to the quality of his work.

In 1978, Quiñones began to paint handball courts in his neighborhood. Again, he wanted to paint big in order to cover complete areas. Yet, only a year later, he started painting on canvas as well, and these were scaled much smaller to fit in a standard indoor space. The first of Quiñones's gallery exhibitions was held at Galleria Medusa, Rome, in 1979. It was a success and he has not looked back since.

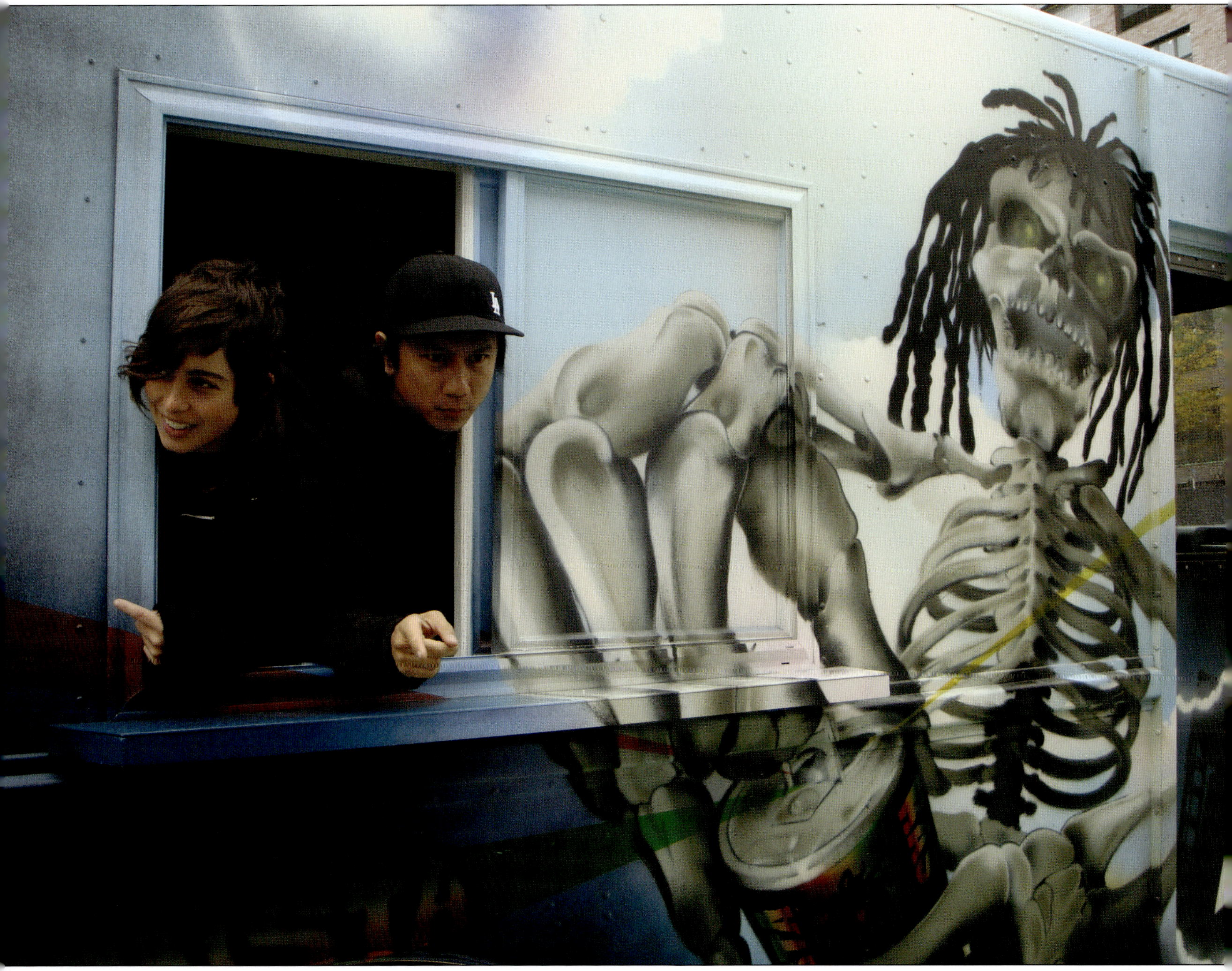

Photo courtesy of Po'Jay.

WAYNE ROBERTS (STAY HIGH 149)

Roberts was another of the older generation of graffiti artists. He was born in 1950 in Virginia, moved to Harlem with his family in 1957, and later lived in the Bronx. It was while he was living in there, in about 1969, that a friend gave him his nickname because of his propensity to smoke an ounce of marijuana each week. While Roberts was working as a messenger on Wall Street, he noticed names and tags written on the subway on both trains and the stations and this inspired him to write Stay High, which he later added the number 149 too as that was his street number. A year or so later, Roberts added his distinctive haloed, smoking stick figure that he'd borrowed from the television show *The Saint*. Roberts reversed the figure and added the cigarette, which was, of course, a joint.

The tag went up everywhere. Roberts traveled a lot on the subway because of his work and could target a hundred trains a day during the work day. To this, he would add another two hundred tags at night. The proliferation of smoking tags made Roberts the focus of an essay on graffiti and showed not only the tag, but also a photo of the perpetrator himself. The outcome was that the police were able to easily pick him up and arrest him. He had to pay a $20 fine and give up his tag. This did nothing to prevent him from hitting the streets with a new tag, though: Overdose. He didn't like his new graffiti identity and ditched it a month later to take on a new moniker he discovered while reading the paper: Voice of the Ghetto.

The new tag was written in three-color uni-wide magic markers and he attempted to keep his true identity a secret, but he was soon discovered by association with the use of the markers by his old graffiti pals Deadleg 167 and LSD OM.

Robert's career as a graffitist seem to come to its highest point in 1974 when he was written about in a book called *The Faith of Graffiti*. A year later, Roberts ceased production—that is until the year 2000, when he was recognized at a gallery show he was attending. He was swamped by fans who wanted his autograph. It sparked a new interest within him in terms of graffiti and, as a man in his fifties, he returned to his old tag complete with smoking Saint.

Although Roberts was famous, he did not make money out of his canvases, which he hawked around the streets selling to anyone for as little as $25. He died in 2012 from complications of liver disease. On his website, Roberts stated that he did graffiti because he found it beautiful. He felt the new generation should do more permission walls to beautify the city while getting the citizens on their side rather than doing it as an act of anti-authoritarianism.

SANE SMITH

This graffiti moniker belongs to a couple of New York brothers: David, who wrote as Sane, and Roger, who was Smith. They were taggers and set for themselves the objective of leaving their tag every twenty feet in the 60th Street Tunnel. Another of their infamous works was done on the top level of the Brooklyn Bridge. For this act, the pair was sued for $3 million by the city of New York, which is the largest amount ever brought against a graffitist. Sane Smith was one of the top twenty graffiti painters wanted by the New York Transit Police and evaded capture for three years or more.

In February 1990, Sane was arrested and became the first graffitist to be charged with third-degree criminal mischief. By October of the same year, he was dead. How he drowned in Flushing Bay has never been solved. After his death, the charges against Smith for the Brooklyn Bridge issue were dropped. Although Smith has a degree in computer science, he continues to paint graffiti and is known to collaborate with the painter Chris Pape, who uses the pseudonym Freedom.

ARTHUR STACE (MR. ETERNITY)

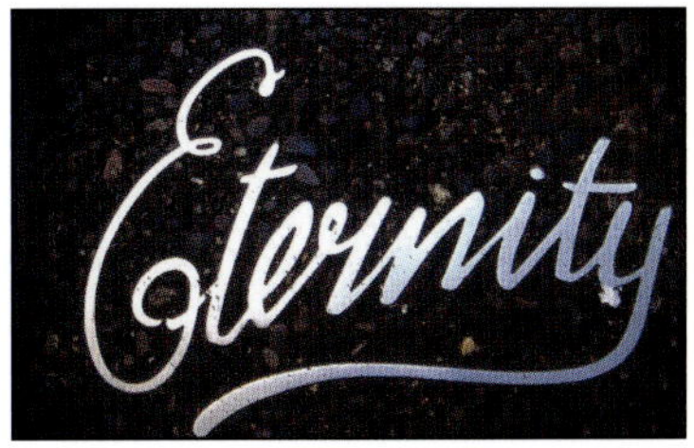

A replica of *Eternity*, as written by Arthur Stace, has been placed on the Sydeny Town Hall.

Arthur Stace would never have called himself a graffiti artist, yet he wrote his elegant word "Eternity" all over Sydney. Stace was born in Balmain, Sydney, in 1884. Both of his parents were alcoholics and his family was very poor. Almost always neglected, the young Stace had to find food for himself and often resorted to stealing it. When he was twelve years old, he became a ward of the state. Barely three years later, he was in jail, having fallen into the same trap as his parents by becoming an alcoholic. Upon his release, he worked for his sisters who both owned brothels—he would go out drumming up customers for them.

In 1916, Stace enlisted for World War I. His health, probably never very good his whole life, failed him, and he was discharged from service in 1919. A major change came for Stace in 1930, when he overheard a sermon at St. Barnabas Church in Broadway, Sydney. It was at this time that he heard the word "eternity" mentioned in a religious context. Later he heard the following exclaimed by the evangelist John G. Ridley: "Eternity, eternity, I wish I could sound or shout that word to everyone in the streets of Sydney. You've got to meet it, where will you spend Eternity?" Stace broke down crying and felt an overwhelming urge to write down the word "eternity." Stace claimed to be almost entirely illiterate, and although he could write his name, it was in clumsy, ugly script. He was astonished when he managed to produce the beautiful script lettering he became famous for.

For nearly a decade, Stace would go out and write "Eternity" on walls all over the city. He managed to avoid arrest, although the police were constantly sent after him. For thirty-five years, Stace would go out each day and chalk his word. Although commuters would see "Eternity" freshly written every morning on their way to work, the identity of the writer was a mystery to the general public. It wasn't until the Reverend Lisle Thompson, in whose church Stace worked as a cleaner, saw him pick up a piece of chalk and write the word that his connection with the graffiti became well-known. Thompson wrote about Stace and an interview was conducted with the *Sydney Morning Herald* in 1956.

In 1967, Stace died of a stroke. He bequeathed his body to science, presumably having no need of it for eternity. To celebrate the gentle man and his important message, the year 2000 celebrations featured a tribute to Mr. Eternity by lighting up the Sydney Harbor Bridge with the word "Eternity."

MICHAEL JEROME STEWART

Stewart's rise to fame came as a result of his death, which happened immediately after he was arrested in 1983 for writing graffiti on a subway wall. Stewart had been writing on the wall of the First Avenue station in Manhattan one early morning. The police arrived and took hold of him, but he fought and got away. He was then caught again on the street and fell unconscious soon after. While he was still in this condition, he was taken to the police station and charged with resisting arrest and possession of marijuana before being taken to the hospital. He arrived there bound and cuffed and still unconscious, but with a very high blood alcohol reading. He passed away; his autopsy later revealed that he had died of heart attack. However, this was challenged by the doctor who had been at the autopsy. He was certain that strangulation had been the true cause of death. The case was open to investigation to see if there was anything to back up such assertions.

In the final report as to the cause of Stewart's death, the medical examiner changed his original findings. Instead of dying of a heart attack, the doctor vaguely suggested that the victim had died of an unspecified injury to his upper spinal cord. He would not state further the nature of the injuries or say explicitly how Stewart sustained them. Witnesses were called to identify police in question, but could not give statements that correlated in any way to make a case against any of the officers supposedly involved. When a jury member hired a private investigator to look into the matter, the case was dismissed.

The following year saw three police officers accused of the assault on Stewart and another three charged with perjury. All six were acquitted of the charges, amid questions over possible racial prejudice having been a factor among the all white jury. And while the MTA believed that at least one of their officers was at least guilty of perjury—which sparked a new training scheme for their offices—there was still no justice for Stewart's family. After a civil suit was filed, the case was settled out of court for $1.7 million.

The transit police remain adamant they did not cause the young man's death while artists have transformed Stewart into a martyr who died at the hands of police brutality because he was black. In fact, many artists found inspiration in the case to create works as homage to Stewart—Jean-Micahel Basquiat and Keith Haring being two of them. And while Stewart's death made him a household name, there is actually little said about his graffiti and much of it has been lost.

TEJN

An innovative and influential graffiti artist is Danish born Tejn. In 2008, when he was thirty-two (and therefore much older than many graffitists when they first start), Tejn began to make street art. What makes his work so different from

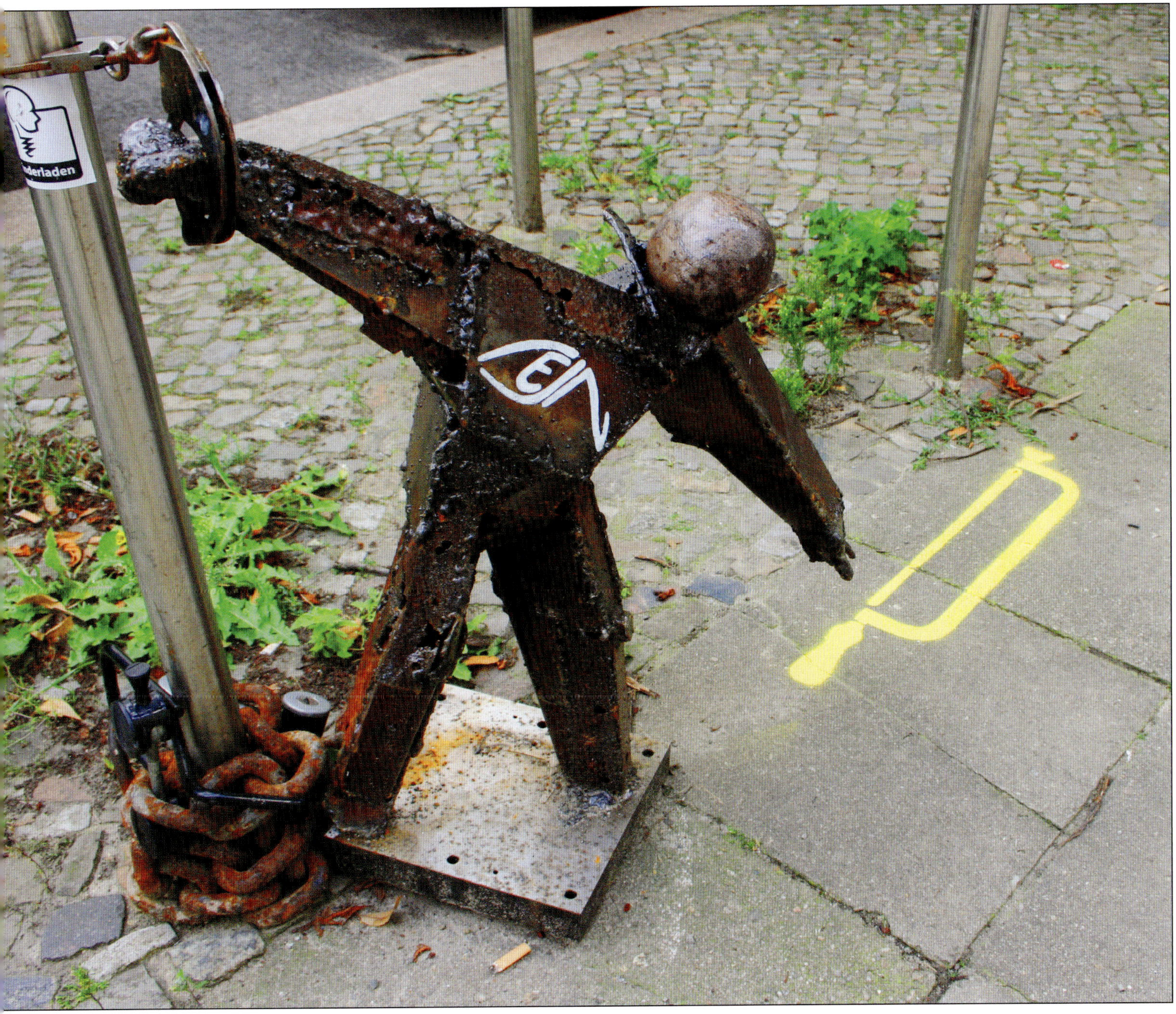

Example of Tejn's street art.
Photo courtesy of Ou812.

many other street artists is that he works largely in a three-dimensional medium: sculpture. His witty, politically, and philosophically motivated works are chained to immovable objects in the public. These have become known as lock-ons. Apart from these welded pieces Tejn also makes two-dimensional works on paper—drawings, paintings and prints—that he puts up with wheat paste on walls and other facades.

ZEVS

This French artist, named after the train that nearly ran him over—Zeus—is best known for his invention of the concept of visual kidnapping. In 2002, while in Berlin, Zevs cut out a figure from a Lavazza poster and wrote above the vacant space "Visual Kidnapping." The idea was that advertising kidnaps the attention of the viewer and, by way of playing to their sense of consumerism, makes them pay a ransom in the form of buying the goods advertised. Zevs decided he would reverse the process and kidnap the article in the poster that was kidnapping the attention of the viewer. Zevs says he holds the cut-out figure for a ransom sum of 500,000 Euros: the price of a typical advertising campaign.

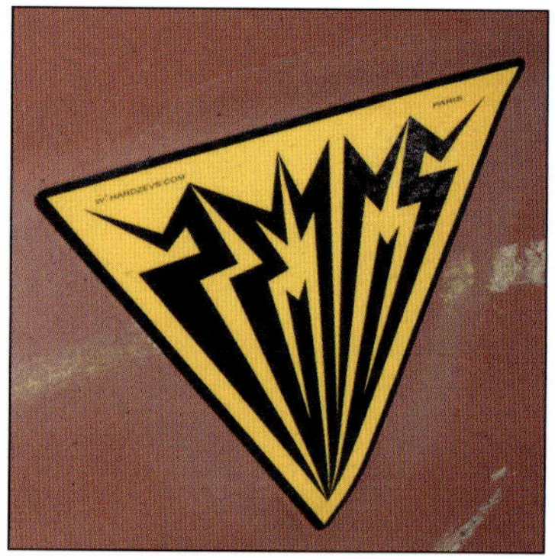

The logo for Zevs.

Zevs is also famous for his reverse graffiti and his dripping logos. The latter are painted versions of real brand-name logos, but they are painted with large amounts of runny paint that creates the illusion of the logo dissolving into itself.

WOMEN AND GRAFFITI

Though most graffitists mentioned throughout are men, there are most certainly women street artists abounding—some well-known and others anonymous. However, even in the anti-authoritarian tradition of graffiti art there is still a large bias toward male involvement and the media's representation of the art form. For example, in 1971, during the graffiti movement's formative years, there was hardly ever mention of women artists while males were repeatedly profiled. That is, with the exception of one prominent woman: Barbara 62.

Today, women are gaining a reputation for their street art, but as most of them will tell you, there is a prevalent attitude that in order for a woman to participate successfully in the graffiti art world, she has to act tough. Lady Pink, from Ecuador, says that she had to openly display her tomboyish-ness and shun the whole female stereotype in order to be taken as a serious artist. On the other hand, Akit states that her distinctly feminine presence among a group of male colleagues has worked well in getting them all off the hook with police. So while the stories and situations vary, it is still somewhat of a male-biased profession.

Although there are plenty of women now who work in regular graffiti media (paint, stencil, stickers, etc.) there is a growing band of women who are using media that has been traditionally considered "woman's domain." Yarn bombing—the act of wrapping bits of city in knitting or crochet—is one style of street art that is growing fast in popularity, and there is even one female artist who paints entirely in icing.

It has been noted that in recent years that women urban artists are more likely to take on new ideas and embrace new trends, collaborations, and innovations than their male counterparts. Perhaps in the decades to come, women will more prominently join the ranks of the more famous male graffitists in recognition and popularity.

Claw Money

Claw Money's real name is Claudia. She's invented an insignia to go along with her graffiti name—a cartoon paw with three extended claws. She studied at the Fashion Institute of Technology in New York City in the early 1980s, but had quit in 1986 and took to painting graffiti with a couple of crews instead: TC5 and FC. Throughout the late 1980s and early 1990s, Claw bet and worked with a whole range of graffiti artists, many of whom were notorious and wanted by the transit police.

Far from hurting her chances at getting a reputable job, it was directly because of her contacts in the graffiti world that Claw landed a job as editor and director of *Swindle Magazine*. From this point on, she has turned away from directly making street art, but it is undoubtedly that kind of popular culture that influences her fashion designs to this day.

Miss.Tic

Miss.Tic is one of the older generations of street artists and was born in Montmartre in 1956. When she was ten years old, her grandmother, mother, and brother were all killed in a car accident; this tragedy was followed six years later by the death of her father. Although Miss.Tic did not attend art school, she did train in theater set design and

Photo courtesy of Sophie Masson.

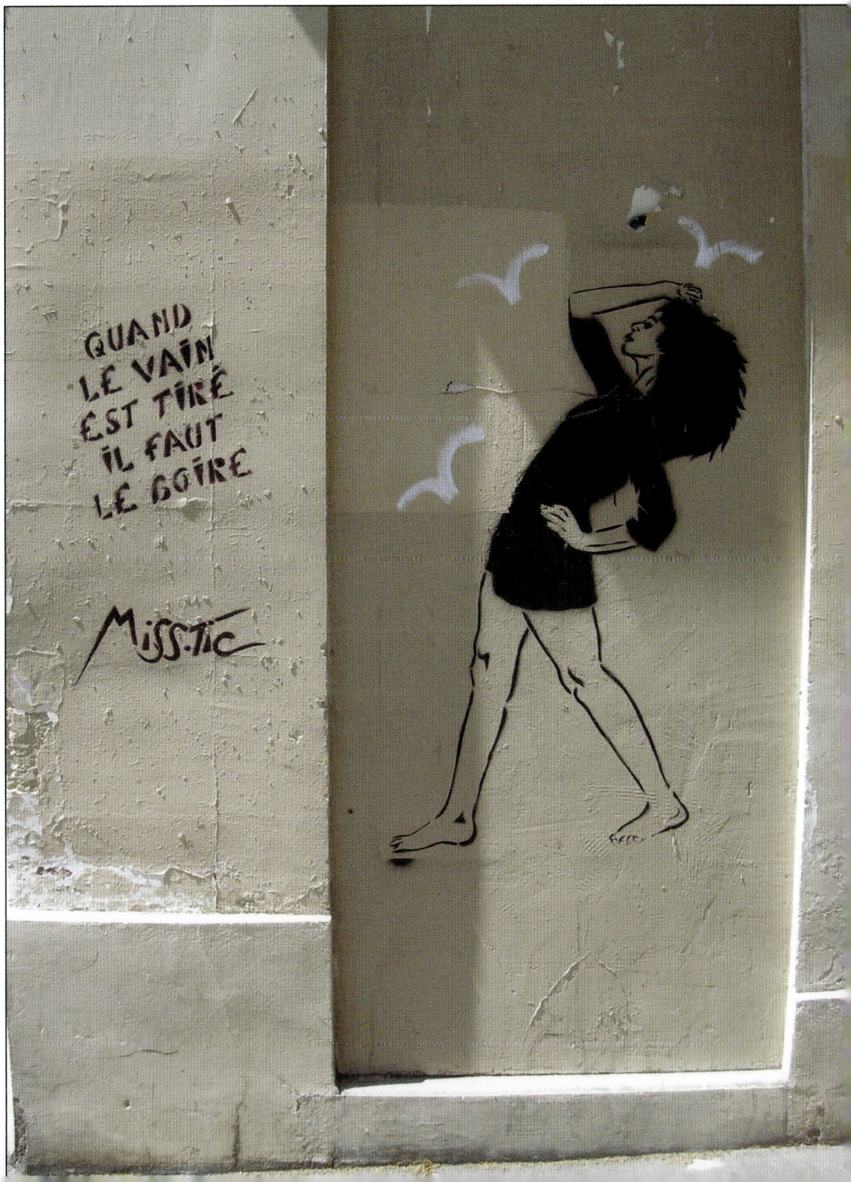

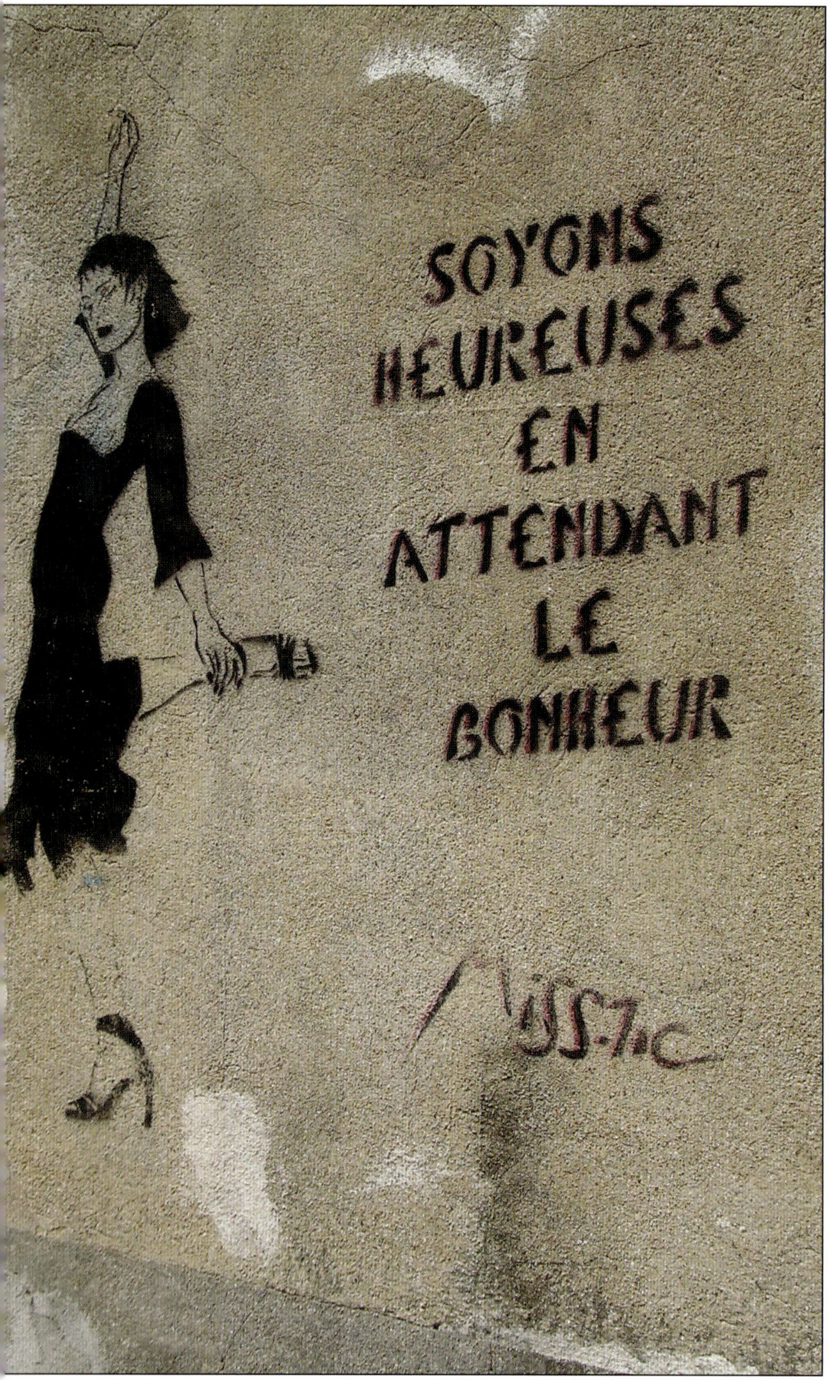
SOYONS
HEUREUSES
EN
ATTENDANT
LE
BONHEUR
MISS.TIC

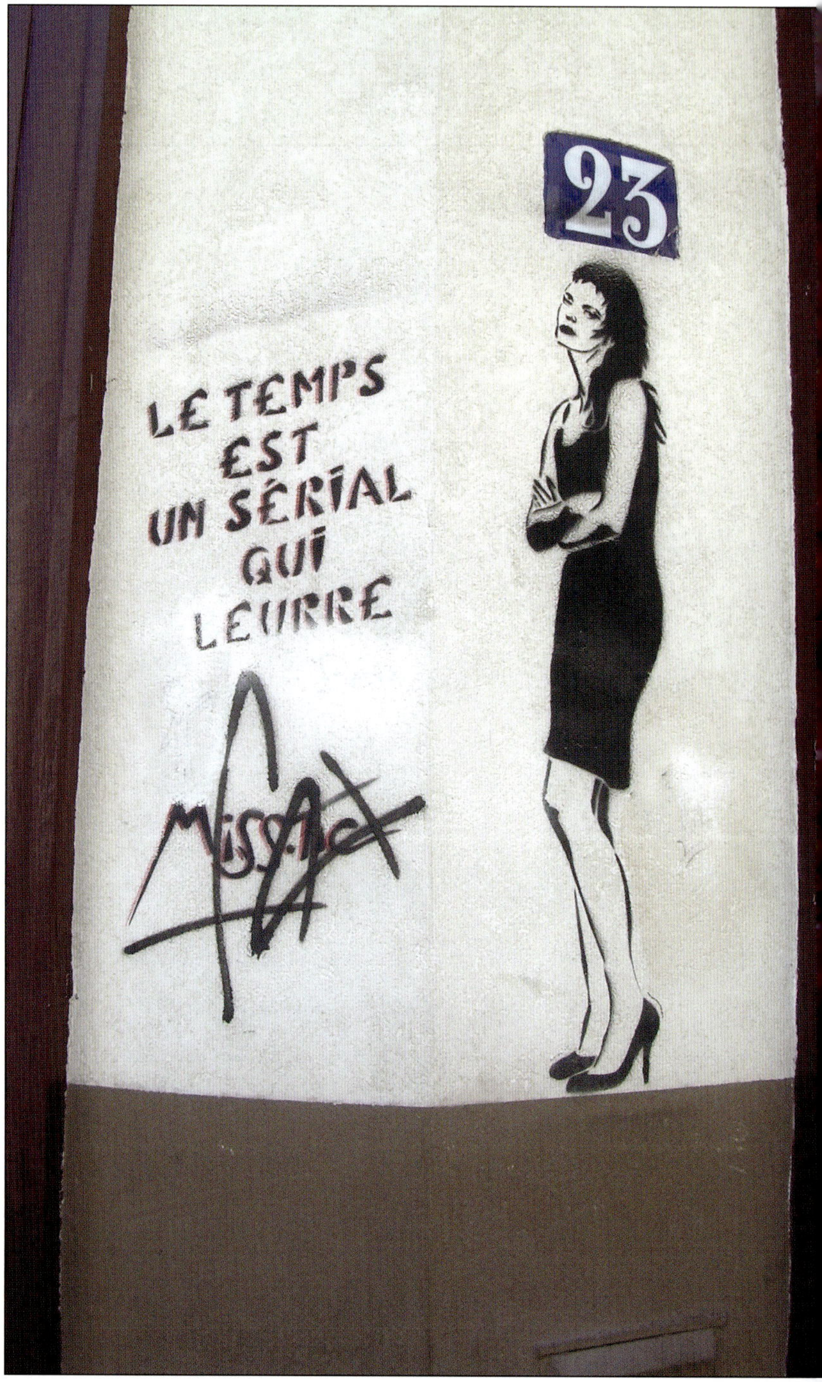
23
LE TEMPS
EST
UN SÉRIAL
QUI
LEURRE
MISS.TIC

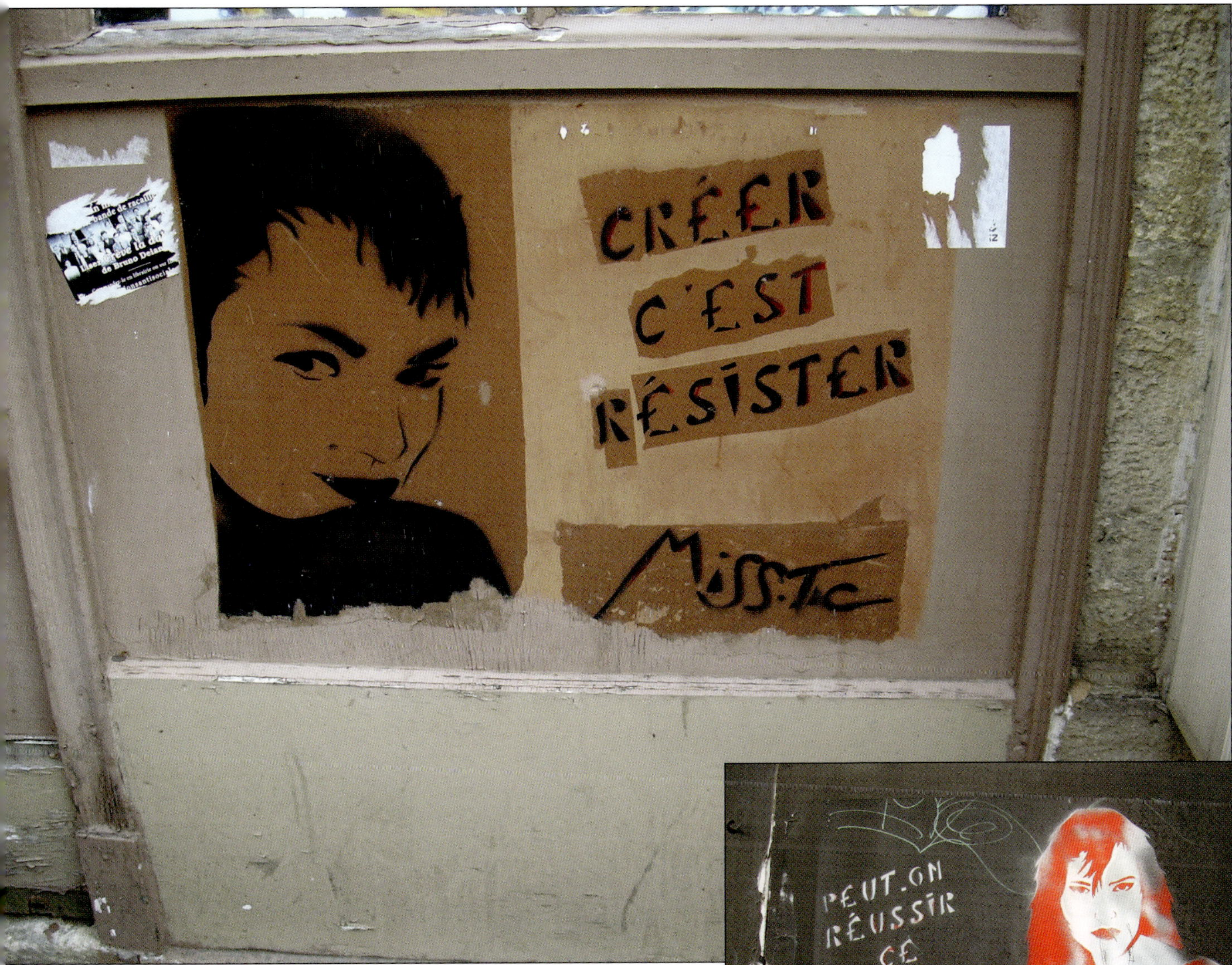

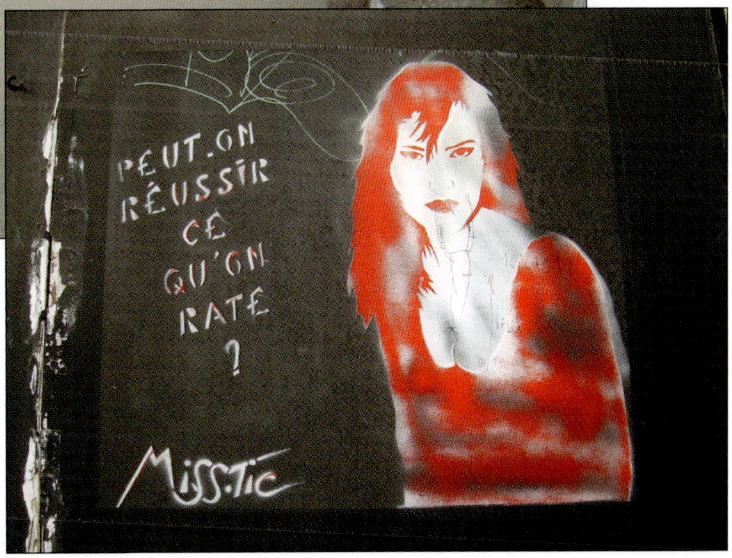

Miss. Tic's distinctive stencil graffiti features stylish women that are possibly self portraits.
Photos on pages 180 to 183 courtesy of Sophie Masson.

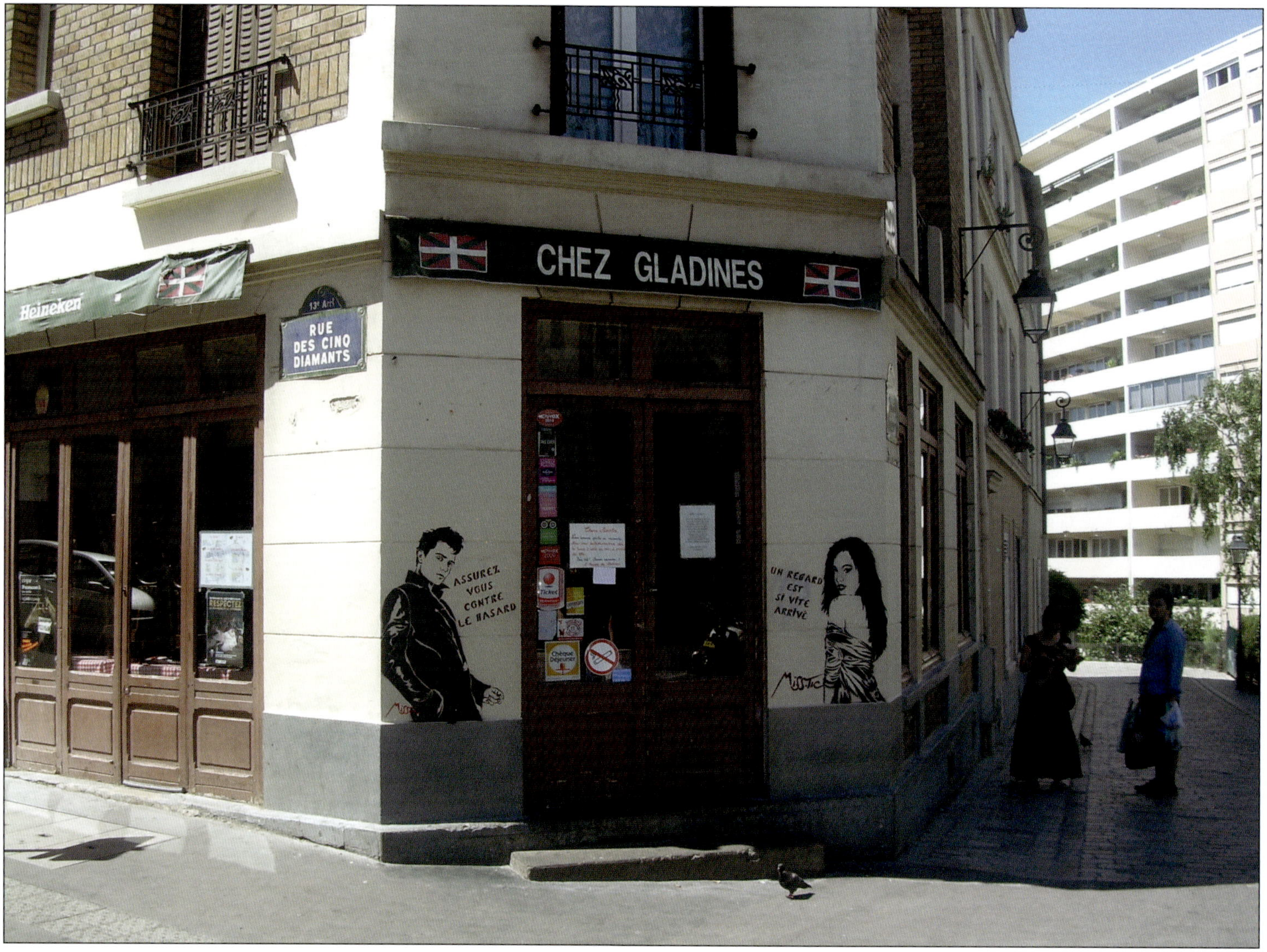

photoengraving. In the early 1980s, she moved to California and lived there for a number of years. Upon her return to Paris, Miss.Tic started her career as a graffiti stencil artist. She returned because of a broken heart, she claims, the errant lover being none other than Blek le Rat.

In contrast to Miss Van's work, Miss.Tic's female figures are stencils of modern, urban women, French chic in their tight-fitting black dresses; these are possibly self-portraits, as some believe. They are sometimes balletic, business-like,

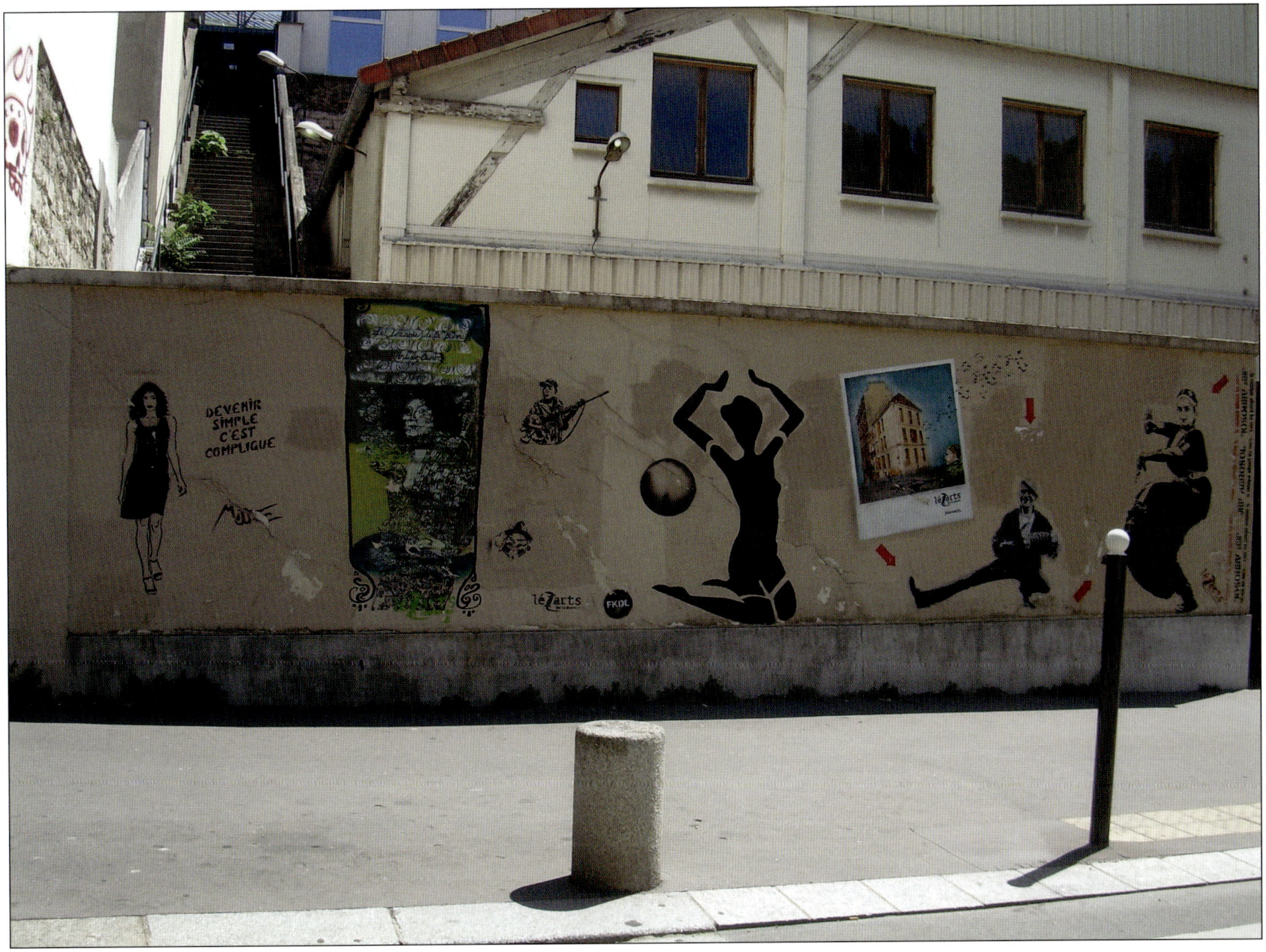

sexy, secretive, or pensive. They are often accompanied by cats and usually have a stenciled slogan or saying next to them such as, “Idealiste devenez ideal” or “Greer, c’est resister.”

For the past ten years Miss.Tic has also made stencils inspired by paintings by French masters. One of these is a version of Courbet’s *Sleep*, showing two naked women lying among rumpled sheets in a suggestive, intertwined pose, oblivious to the viewer. Many of Miss.Tic’s later works have been done on canvas.

Miss Van

Miss Van—Vanessa Alice Bensimon—is one of the foremost female graffiti artists and is based in Toulouse, France. Her figures are often of cartoon-style girl-women, often in provocatively sexual poses, with pouty mouths and dark eyes. Miss Van has gone on to exhibit her work in galleries around France.

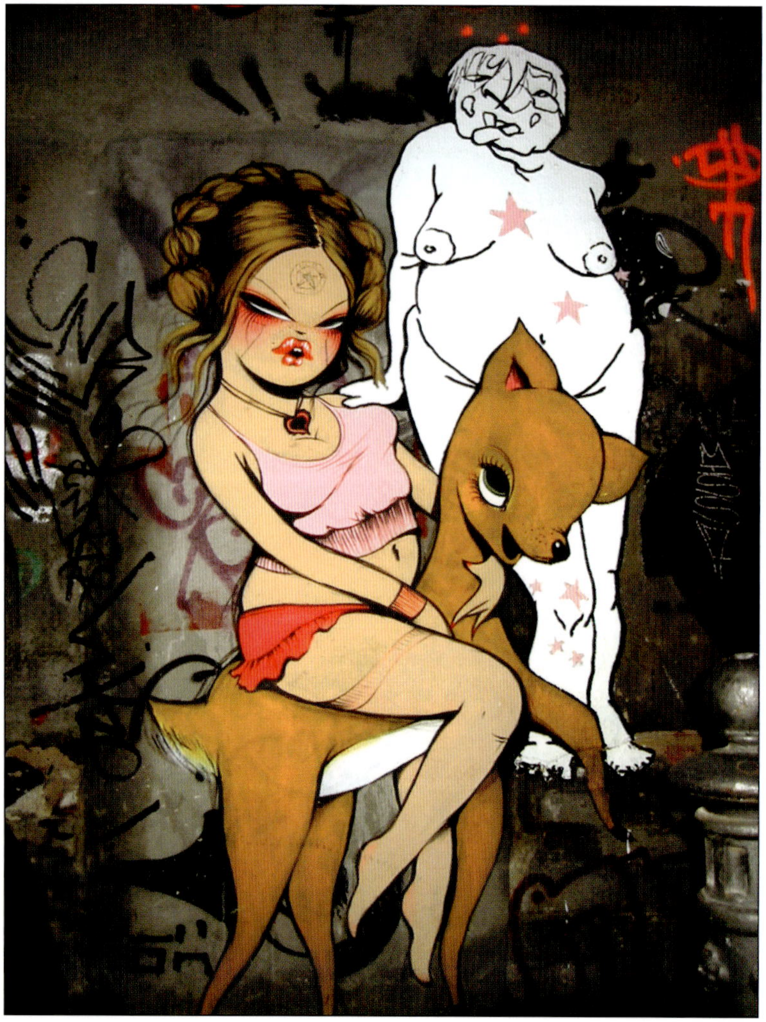

Miss Van.
Photo courtesy of Ricardo Chico.

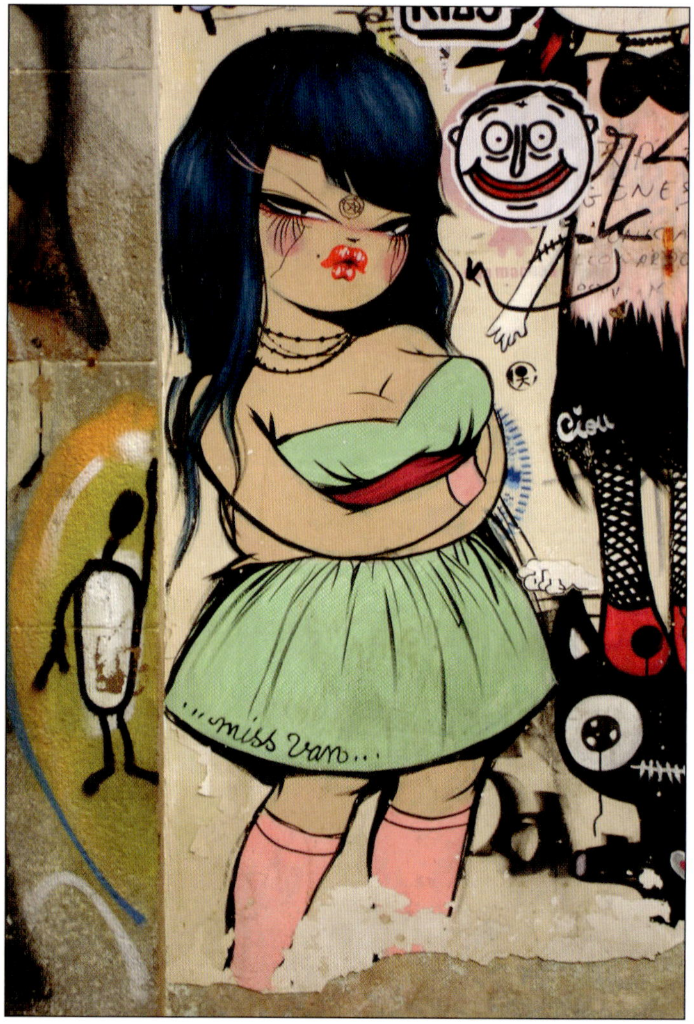

Miss Van.
Photo courtesy of Aikijuanma.

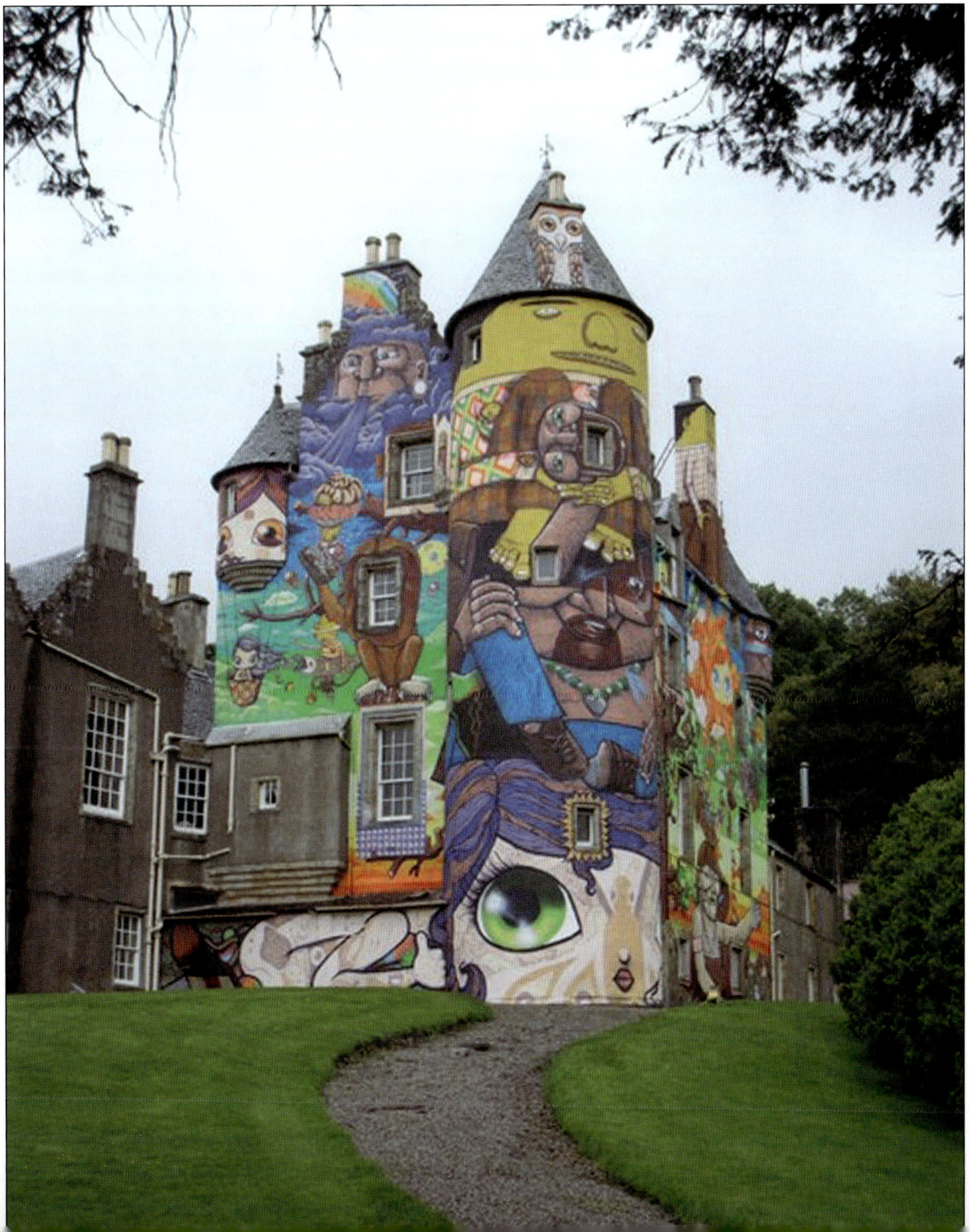

« A very unusual project was put together for the Castle of Kelburn in Scotland. Four Brazilian graffiti artists, of which Nina was one, were invited to live in the castle for a month and work with local artists to cover the ancient building with graffiti. The castle had been rendered in concrete some years ago and it badly needed to be replaced. The daring scheme came into being when Lord Glasgow gave into a request by his children to let the artists paint the façade. The graffiti was never meant to be a permanent fixture, but the work has proved so popular that Historic Scotland, the national heritage committee, voted for an extension of the work's life span.

Photo courtesy of Lairish Rig, Geography Org, United Kingdom.

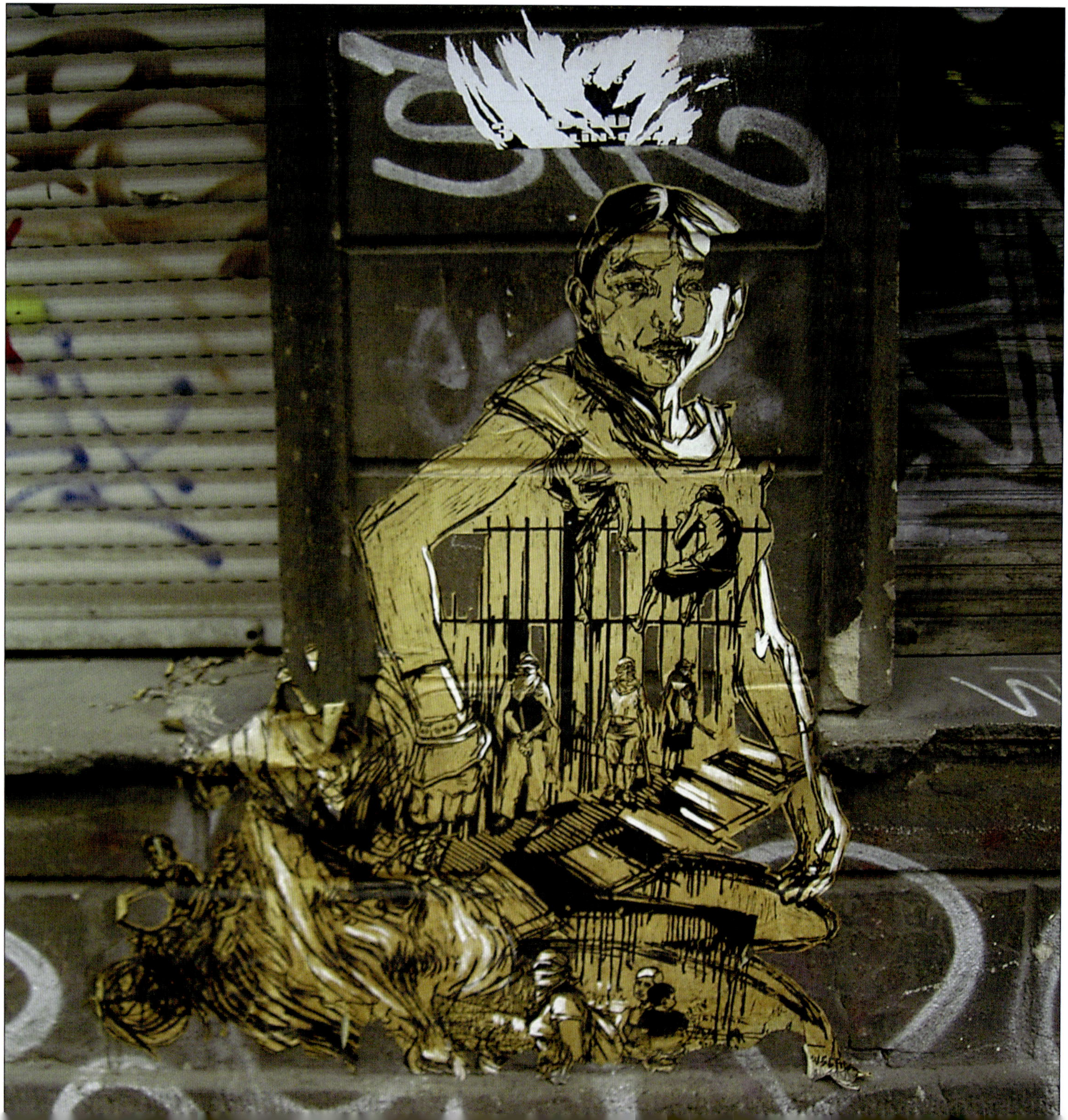

Nina Pandolfo

Nina Pandolfo was born in Brazil in 1977. She loved drawing and painting as a child and it was her mother who taught her the various techniques of the craft. As a teenager, she began to paint on canvas and was also involved in street theater. At about the same time, she claims that she started noticing murals springing up on the walls around her neighborhood. With no knowledge that painting on walls was typically considered against the law, Nina viewed this type of art as something similar to street theater. Intrigued by the concept, fourteen-year-old Nina attended a workshop on graffiti, but her teacher was discouraging, stating that the young girl was not doing it right and would never make a proper graffiti artist. So Nina stopped attending these workshops but learned more about graffiti when she went to high school the following year. With the encouragement of graffitists at her school, Nina produced her own pieces.

It has never fazed Nina whether her art is truly considered graffiti. She believes she is incredibly lucky to be able to make a living out of her passion to paint pictures. Her artwork is more illustrative than confrontational; her figures are childlike and evoke innocence, even naivety. The girls in her pieces have enormous doll-like eyes and the colors are bright pinks, reds, greens, and blues. Although human figures are dominant, the works are peppered with little insects, plants, balloons, and paper cranes, as well. Nina moves from canvas to wall and back again without blinking an eye, not worried about the way other artists see her or judge her work.

Swoon

Swoon, whose birth name is Caledonia Dance Curry, was born in 1978 in New London, Connecticut, and is one of the few well-known women graffiti artists. Her specialty, which she began in 1999, is life-size prints of cut-out figures, usually of women and often family members, on paper that she applies to walls, bridges, fire escapes, and street signs with wheat paste. Some of the major influences on her style are Indonesian Wayang puppets and German Expressionist Woodblocks, which is clearly shown through her wheat paste posters.

Swoon studied art at The Pratt Institute in Brooklyn, New York, and her work shows the aptitude of a trained drafts-person. From pasting drawings and prints all over the city, Swoon has gone on to initiate a number of fairly outrageous and extravagant art events. One of the most spectacular was to build a series of rafts made from refuse found in New York City. The crew, many of whom were artists and performers, sailed their fleet to Venice, docking in time for the Venice Biennale of 2009.

« Swoon is well known for making intricate wheat paste and stencil graffiti posters.
Photo courtesy of Duncan Cumming.

TAG THIS!

Who Put Bella in the Witch Elm?

Bella (her real name remains a mystery) was not a graffiti artist. She was a young woman whose remains have never been identified—the victim of a brutal murder. In 1943, four young boys were in Hagley Wood near Wychbury Hill in Worcestershire, England. It appears they were poaching, hungry from harsh rationing; they probably thought they'd get a fat rabbit for dinner. Upon seeing the old Wych Hazel tree in the wood, they thought it might house a bird's nest and eggs were not a bad treat either. One of the boys, Bob Farmer, climbed the tree and on looking down into its hollow center, he saw a skull. At first he thought it was only the skull of an animal and plucked it out to examine it. With a shock, he realized it was human and shoved it back in place. He scrambled down the tree and he and his three companions fled home. No one said anything about the adventure for some time.

Finally, Tommy Willetts, the youngest boy, found the pressure too much for him and he told his parents about their discovery. The police were called, the trunk was inspected, and a human skeleton was found wedged within. There was also a woman's shoe, a wedding ring, and vestiges of clothing. One severed hand was found buried close by under the tree. At the autopsy, it was determined that the victim was a woman and that she had been in situ about eighteen months, which meant she had been murdered sometime in 1941. Taffeta was found lodged in her mouth, suggesting she

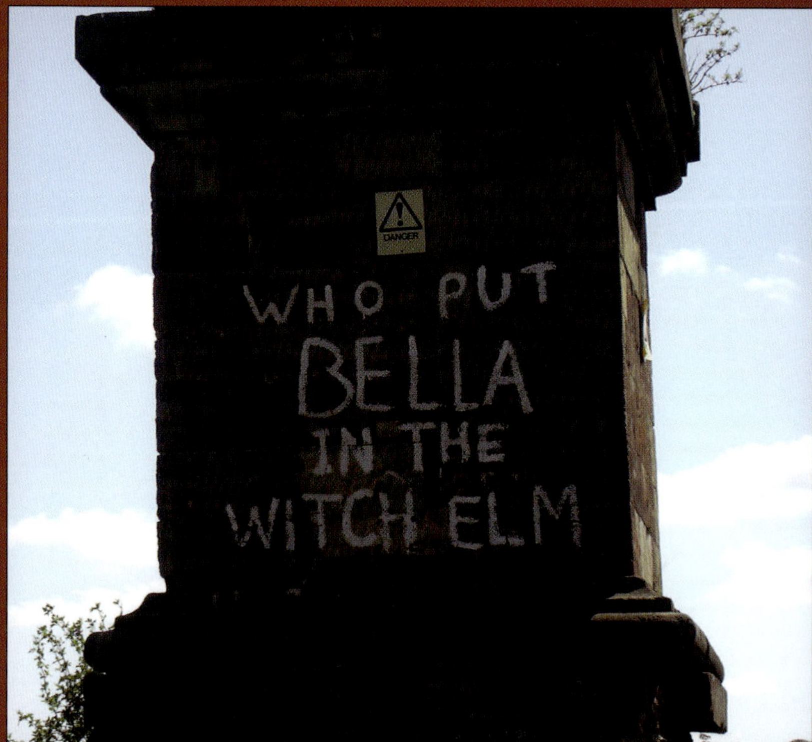

Graffiti written in white paint on a monument » references a mysterious war-time murder.

had been asphyxiated. It was also thought that the body must have been placed in the tree at the time of death or shortly after because it would have needed to be pliable to get into the space.

There were other items found with the body, such as a photo, but as WWII was raging, the case was postponed due to lack of manpower and the abundance of missing persons cases at the time. Unfortunately, questions into the murder and who did it were left unanswered.

In 1944, though, a message was found written on a wall in Upper Dean Street, Birmingham, that read: "Who put Bella down the Whych Elm–Hagley Wood." The graffiti appeared often after that, although the last known example was written in 1999 on the Wychbury Obelisk. It was sprayed on in white paint.

Graffiti has expanded extensively to cover all sorts of artwork created in many different kinds of media. It is still pretty well confined to the streets—or at least, the artists who made names for themselves seemed to have begun their art careers that way. Many have been lured by the siren call of money and recognition in the mainstream artworld, and who can blame them? Living for your art and starving in a garret are not comfortable life choices to make. Even though some the these artists now make large sums of money, and others more modest amounts, many of them feel the need to give back to the people who supported them in the first place: the people in poor neighborhoods, disaffected youth, and minority groups. Many famous graffitists give money to charities and to projects that will help these people change their lives, or at least the environments in which they live.

The changes to street art that have occurred in the last ten to twenty years have really pushed the boundaries of graffiti to a point that it is difficult to succinctly define. Perhaps this is not a bad thing, but an enrichment and acceptance of what only a few years earlier was thought to be pure vandalism.

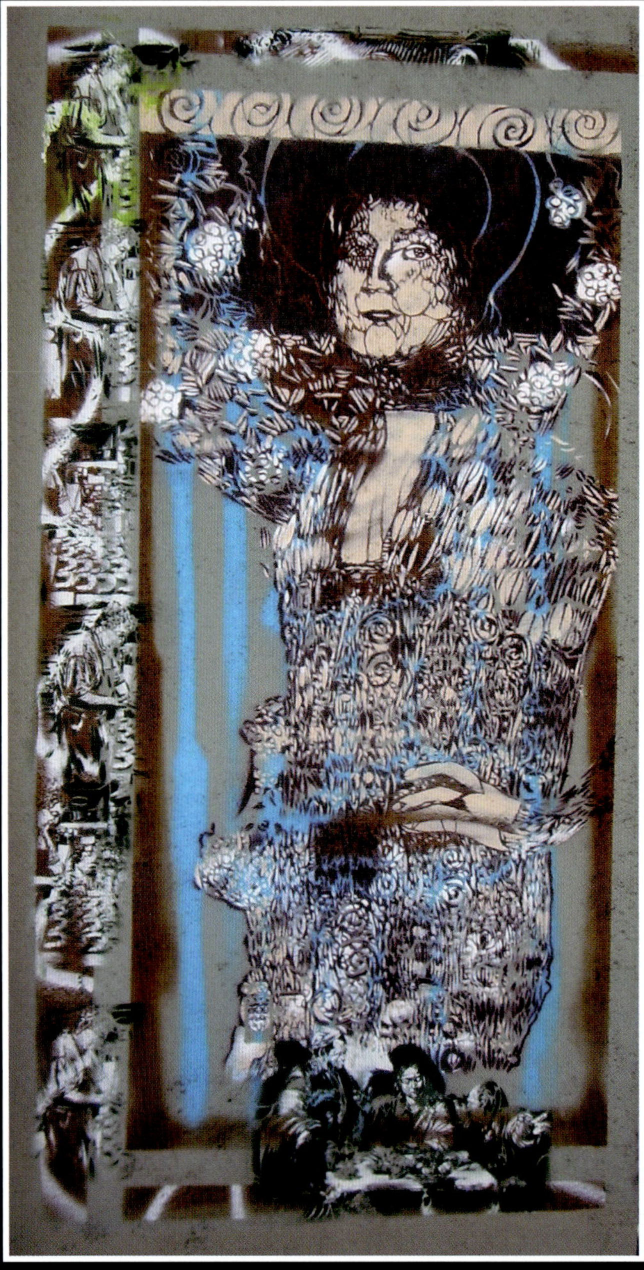

Photo courtesy of Sophie Masson.

CHAPTER SEVEN

BEYOND TRADITIONAL GRAFFITI

If we limited our definition of graffiti to that provided by the dictionary, this book would be very short of material. Graffiti, as many of us know it, was never scratched onto a surface as the word suggests, but was instead painted with spray cans, a completely different method altogether. We have also learned that it isn't possible to only look at unauthorized painting and scratching as graffiti, as many now publicly-acknowledged graffiti artists show their work in galleries and sell their art for money.

Graffiti as a phenomenon did not begin only in the 1970s in New York, but has been practiced for millennia. Graffiti is seen as an art form, as a type of vandalism, as well as a means to documenting historical evidence.

Taking all of this into consideration, it is possible to broaden the subject even further and to thus include media such as Sidewalk Art, Reverse Graffiti, installations, and even performance and mixed media art in the category of graffiti. These are practices that are already in place, but surely there will be further developments in the area of graffiti in the decades to come.

SIDEWALK ART OR STREET PAINTING AND PAVEMENT ART

Have you ever watched an artist render a colored chalk drawing on the sidewalk? Well, this is essentially a form of graffiti that has been unsolicited and very temporary. It is also a form of busking, as many artists put out a hat to collect coins in appreciation of their efforts. A popular subject of sidewalk art is copies of famous paintings: the Mona Lisa, the Sistine Chapel, works by Rembrandt and Renoir, to name a few.

In Italy, the tradition of drawing famous artworks on the pavement goes back centuries, and these artists are called Madonnari because they usually paint different famous versions of the Madonna. Back in the sixteenth century, itinerant artists were hired to work on the magnificent ceilings and walls of churches and cathedrals throughout Italy. When the

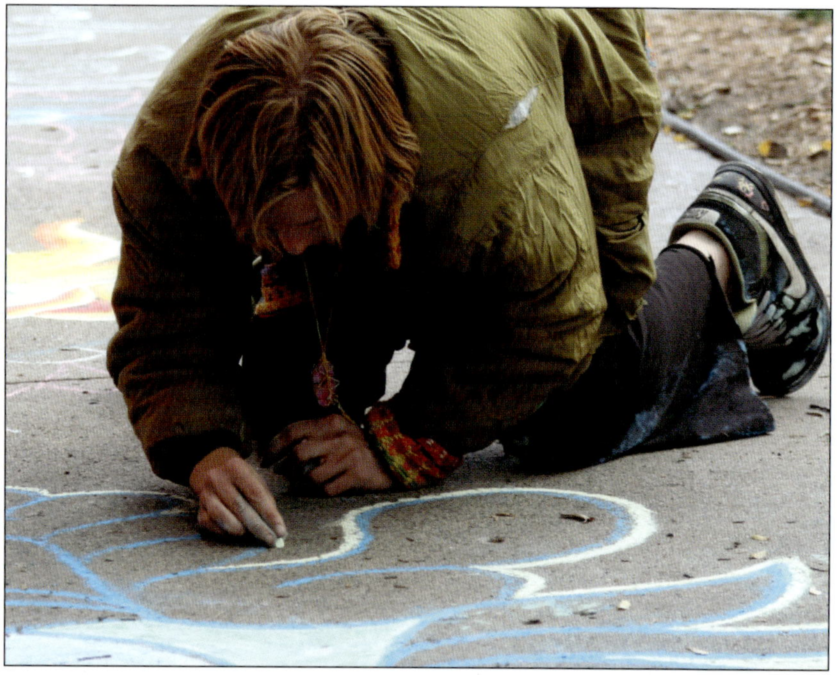

This art form has not been traditionally thought of as graffiti but has been counted as a style of performance art. The artist puts out a hat in the manner of a busker to receive donations from the passing public.

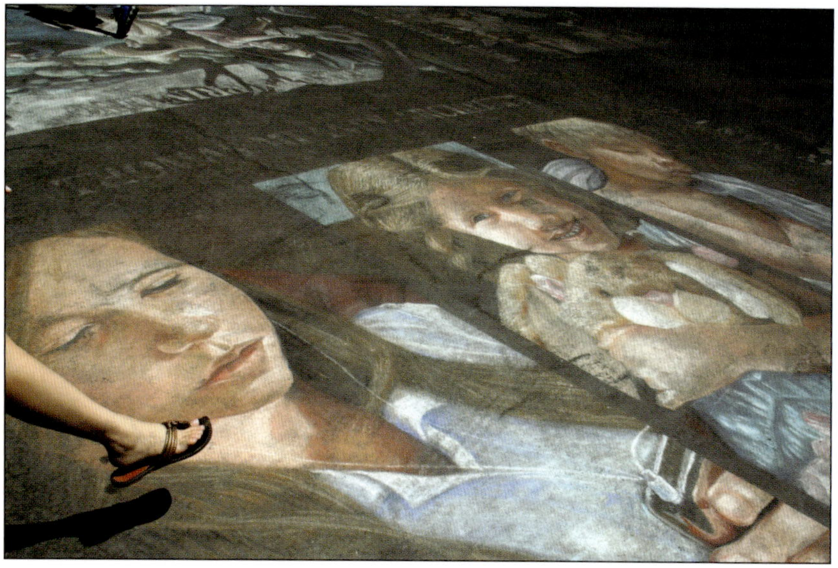

This beautifully rendered drawing wouldn't look out of place in a gallery. Chalk artists, even when self-taught, tend to lean towards realism not found in wall graffiti. Many like to copy famous paintings.

work finished, the artists were left jobless and they had to rely on their skill to get money until their next commissioned job. They would often draw the figures from the paintings they had just finished on the sidewalks and the people walking past would pay them. After a while, they would travel to another town and show their images there until another legitimate job came up.

In Britain, traditional sidewalk artists were known as screevers, which is derived from a writing style, a type of copperplate. Drawings were made on sidewalks but they were usually accompanied by text, often moral or biblical. The idea was to produce a brilliant text in beautiful writing that would catch the eye of a wealthy passer-by, who would then pay a few pennies as a reward for the public sentiment and the benefit of all

TAG THIS!

Apparently the famous El Greco started his career as a pavement artist.

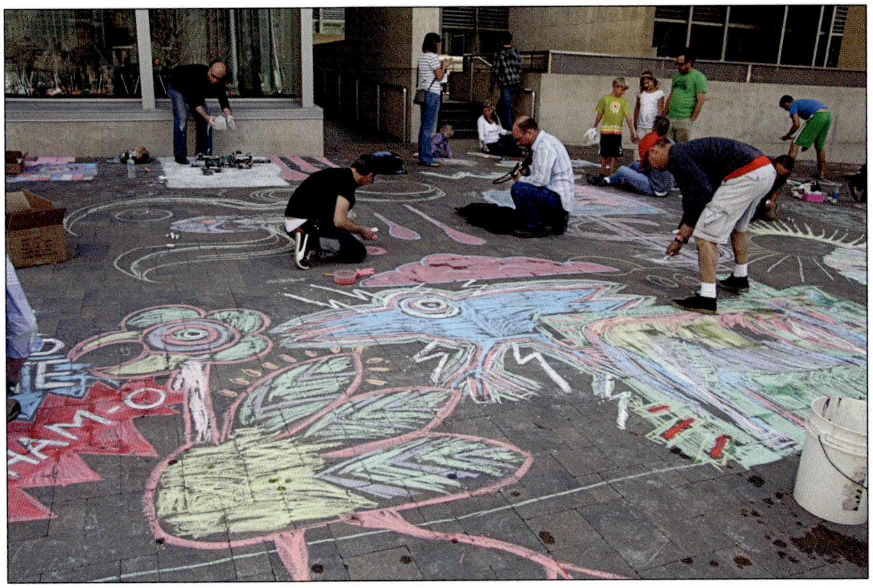

»
Making drawings on the sidewalk in chalk has became a popular pastime and festivals have sprung up in which professionals and amateurs draw side by side.
Photo courtesy of Steven Depolo.

society. In the 1890s, it was documented that approximately five hundred street artists were working full time as screevers.

Sidewalk art is still popular today. It does not elicit the negative response that regular graffiti does because it is seen to have more artistic merit (very rarely is it abstract or crude) and it is temporary, easily washed away by the rain or a street cleaner. Festivals have sprung up all over the world for chalk sidewalk artists to show their talent.

While the tradition remains of painting copies of famous works, a new type of super slick and clever drawing is emerging. Artists prepare their work in the studio using digital software to help them work out a perspective that will make the viewer think they are seeing something three dimensional on the sidewalk. The effect can be brilliantly startling—a great crevasse will appear in the middle of a street with cars falling into it or the uncovered tomb of an army of terracotta warriors that turn out to be LEGO men. This kind of work is called 3-D pavement art, one-point perspective (because you have to stand in one point of the street for the perspective to work), or anamorphic art.

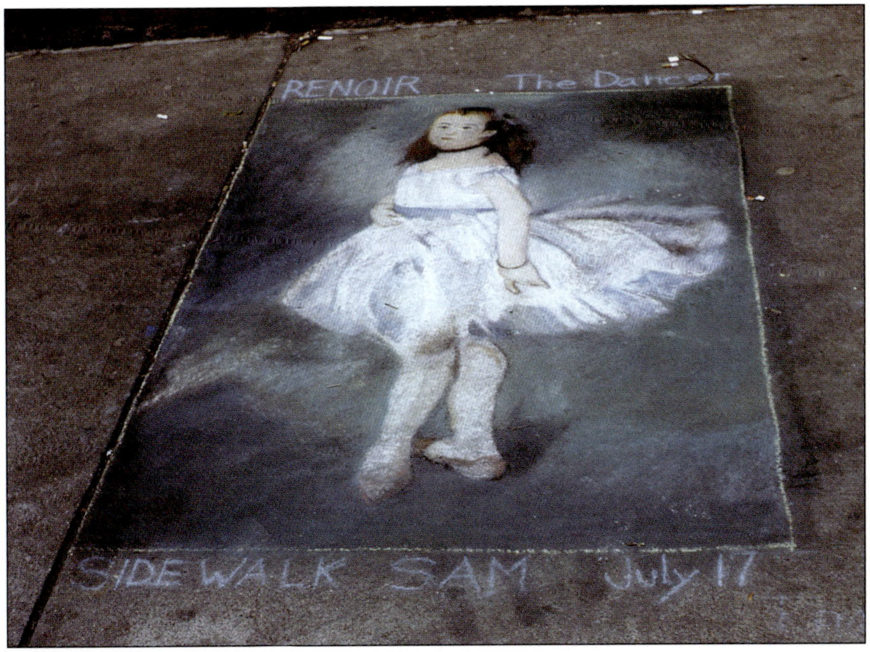

A copy of a Renoir dancer poises gracefully and stares up at the passerby.

Tracy Lee Stum

Stum holds the record for making the largest sidewalk chalk drawing in the world. Her subject was Leonardo da Vinci's *Last Supper* and it was commissioned by Sony Entertainment. Stum trained at the Tyler School of Art at Temple University in Philadelphia before continuing her studies in Rome and then Florence.

Stum also paints large three-dimensional-looking works on the streets, but she does not rely on computer generated graphics to help her achieve the correct perspective. Much of her work is sponsored by corporations, educational institutions, and government agencies the world over. She also donates time and work to charities.

The artist at work.
Photo courtesy of Olivia Weinstein.

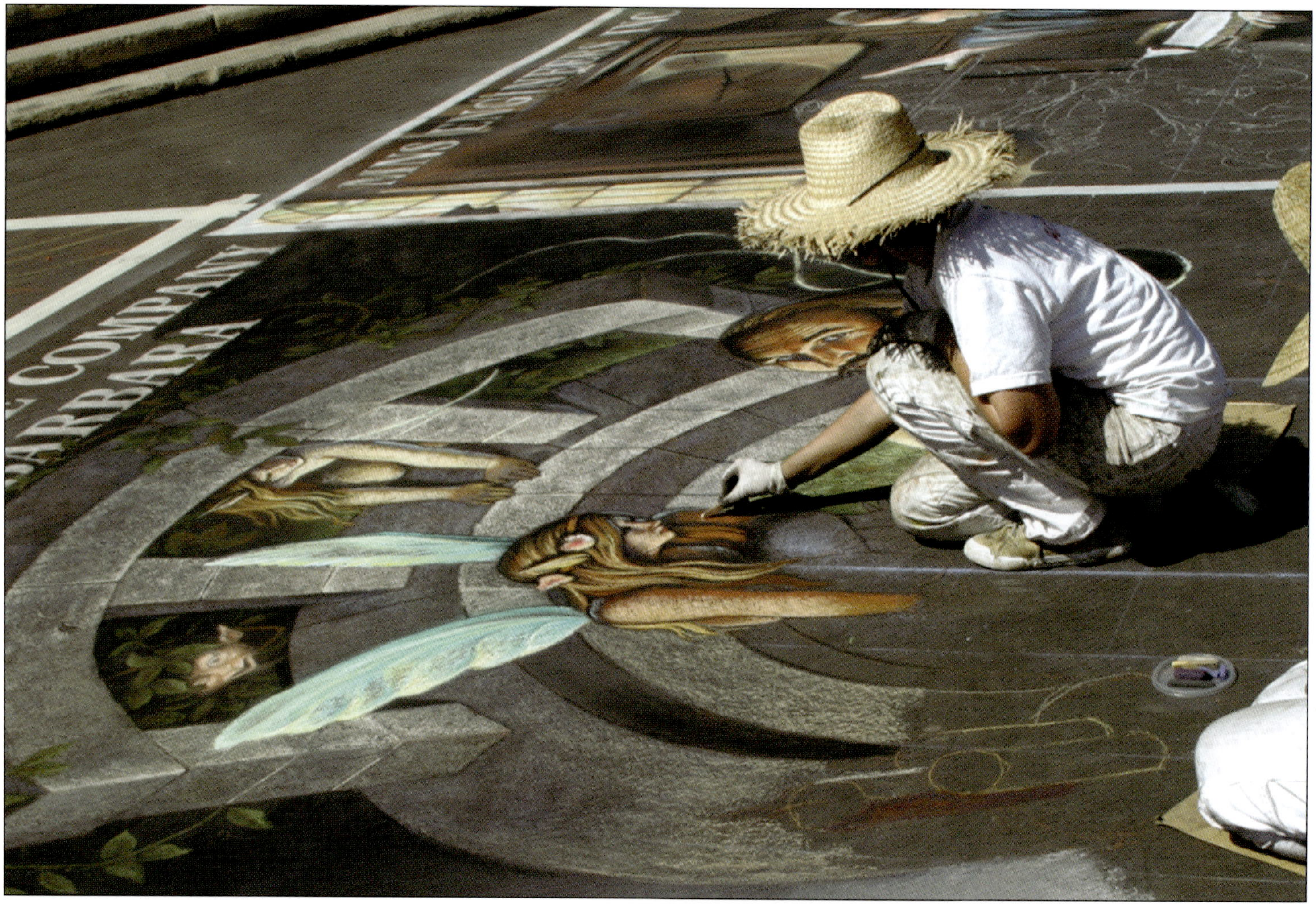

Kurt Wenner

Kurt Wenner, like Stum, has had rigorous art training. After graduating from the Rhode Island School of Design and the Art Center College of Design, he worked as a scientific illustrator for NASA, visualizing the concepts and projects NASA was contemplating undertaking. However, in 1982, Wenner quit his job and went to Italy to study art in the form of the old masters. Within nine years, he had built a reputation as a fine artist in Italy and was commissioned to paint a special work to celebrate the visit of Pope John Paul II when he visited Mantua.

After that, Wenner turned his hand to making 3-D works on pavement. Wenner started the first street art festival in the United States in Santa Barbara; it was the first of many he initiated in America. Added to this, Wenner spent

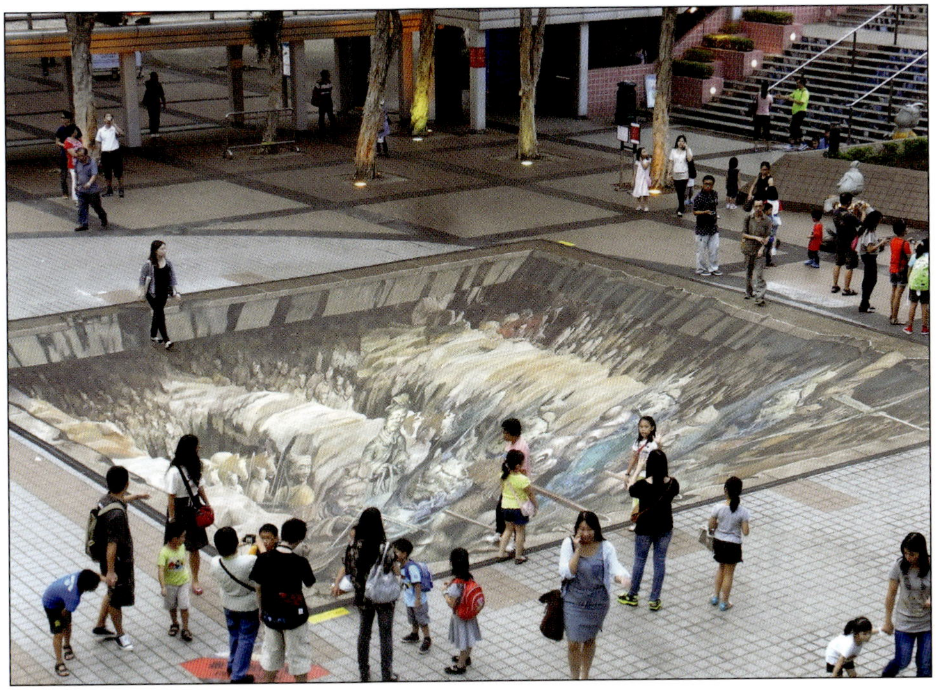

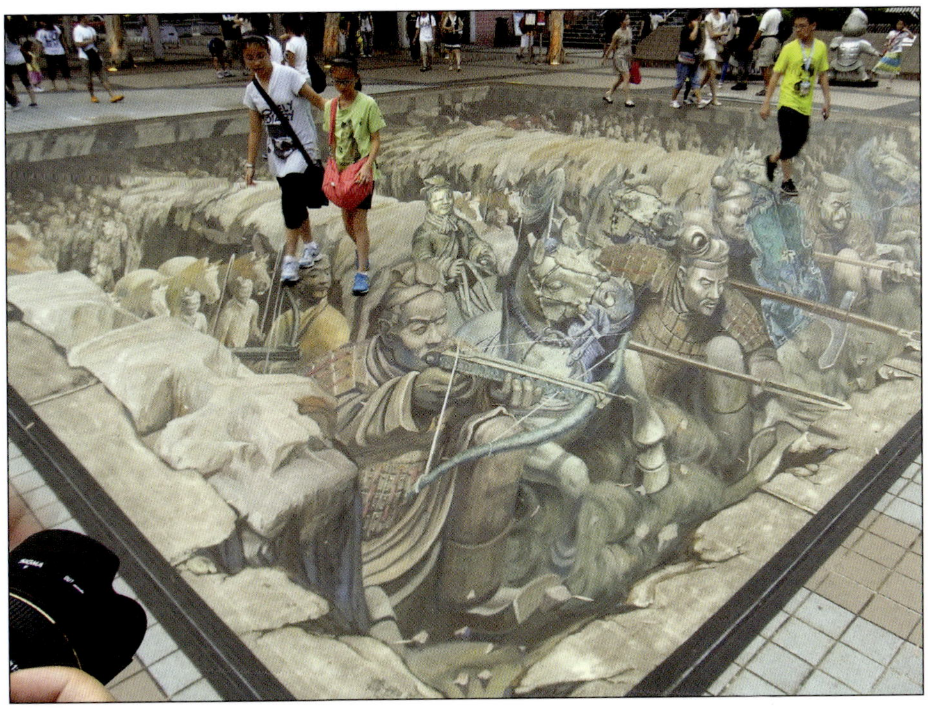

»
Wenner is responsible for the growth in popularity of the illusory 3-D sidewalk art. These large pieces are often done not on the sidewalk, but instead on the road, and are designed so that from one viewpoint the piece looks as though it is rising up from the depths of the world. Cliffs and waterfalls are common subjects because they offer the viewer the thrill of seeing a gaping hole beneath their feet.

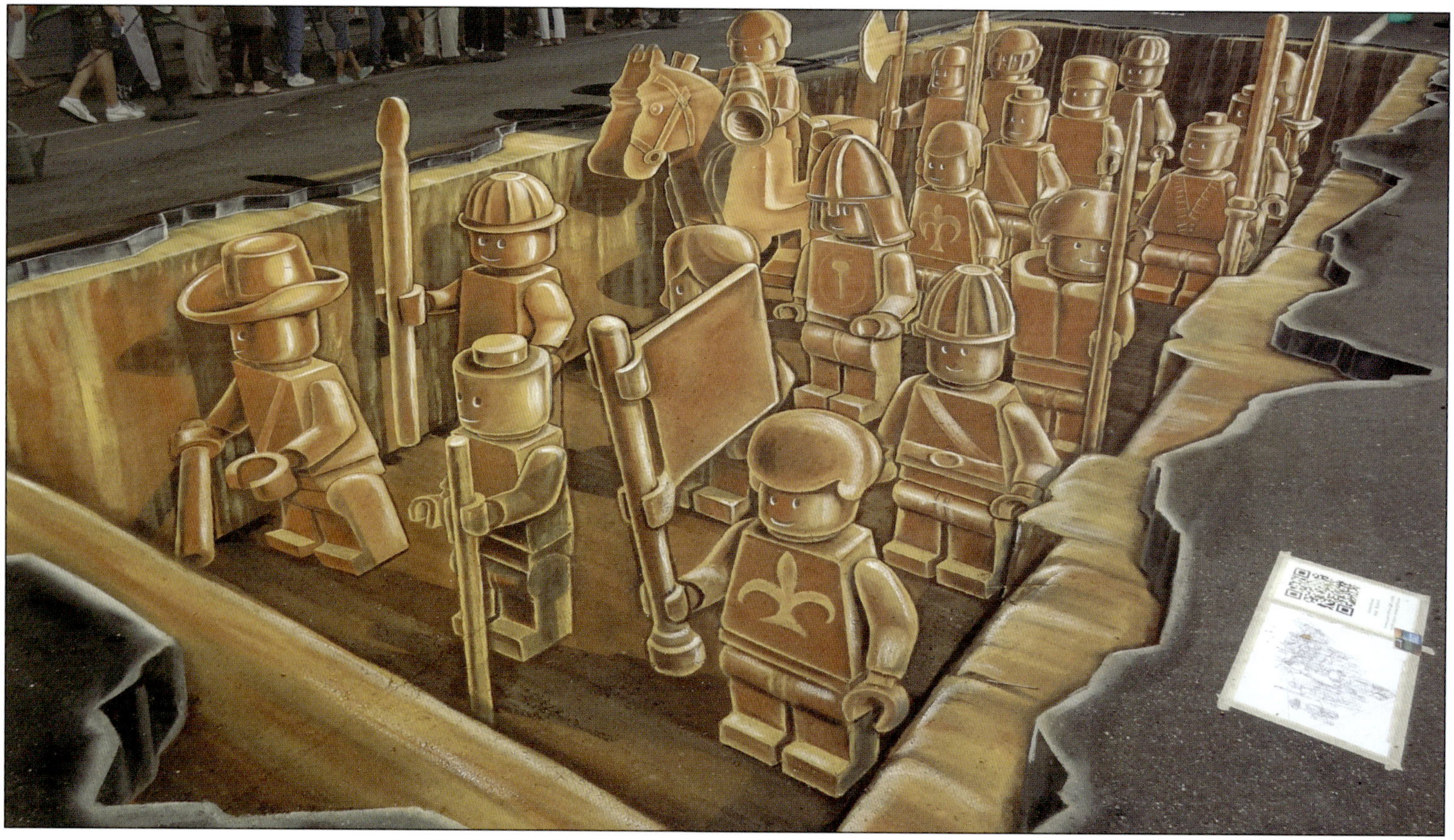

Here is Wenner's parody on the terracotta army unearthed in China, one made of LEGO.

one month a year for ten years teaching his methods of chalk painting to students of all ages, from elementary to university students. He was awarded the Kennedy Center Medallion for outstanding work in arts education. Wenner continues to be involved in chalk painting and has continued to paint on canvas, as well.

Ellis Gallagher

Gallagher produces quite different kinds of sidewalk art than either Wenner or Stum. His work is perhaps more akin with graffiti artists like Richard Hambleton and his Shadowman series and is classified as street/graffiti art. His work consists of drawing simple outlines of the shadows cast by everyday objects: mailboxes, bicycles, fire hydrants, and the like.

Gallagher started his career as a spray can graffiti artist tagging trains on the subway. In the 1990s, he was arrested for graffiti-ing and was assigned to community service and probation. When his friend and fellow graffitist Hector Ramirez was killed by a train during a painting session, Gallagher gave away the spray can and picked up chalk instead, leaving the underground tunnels for the world of light and shadow.

The year 2005 saw his first piece in the new genre; it was the outline of a shadow of a fire hydrant. Gallagher doesn't fill in his outlines with solid color, but instead lets the outline enclose the space. He also does shadows of complex objects such as wire mesh and fencing. Each piece is documented by camera and the resulting photographic prints are signed and numbered. The chalk wears away quickly, so it is surprising to hear that the city tried to sue him for writing with chalk on the sidewalk. The charges did not stick, of course, but the artists spent seventeen hours in jail for one such offense.

YARN BOMBING

Graffiti knitting, more commonly called yarn bombing, is also known as yarn storming or guerilla/urban knitting. This type of graffiti uses knitted or crocheted yarn, wrapped around signposts or bus shelters, hung from trees, or even just left lying around to make dull places colorful. There is no malice or political message behind this practice—just simply the desire to make something beautiful and share it in public. Some crafters have even made toys they leave in areas of high child usage so that they can be picked up and taken home. Yarn bombing is considered an illegal activity as it makes use of public space, but because it is so easily removed, there have not yet been prosecutions for it.

The earliest examples of yarn bombing occurred in the Netherlands in 2004. A year later, the fad had hit the United States. The movement has been credited to Magda Sayeg, who lives in Houston, Texas. She says she covered a door handle with a hand-crocheted doily and that sparked the craze. Another contender for the first yarn bomber is Shanon Schollian, who claims to have been knitting cozies (as in the tea-cozy kind) for tree stumps in Oregon.

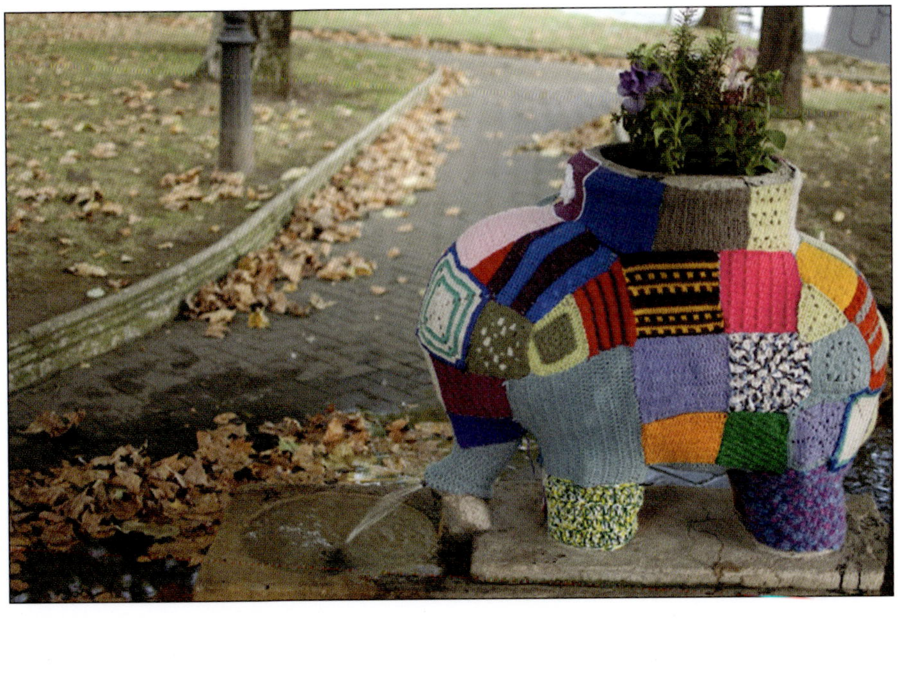

» Yarn bombing found in Aviles, Spain.
Photo courtesy of Rebes.

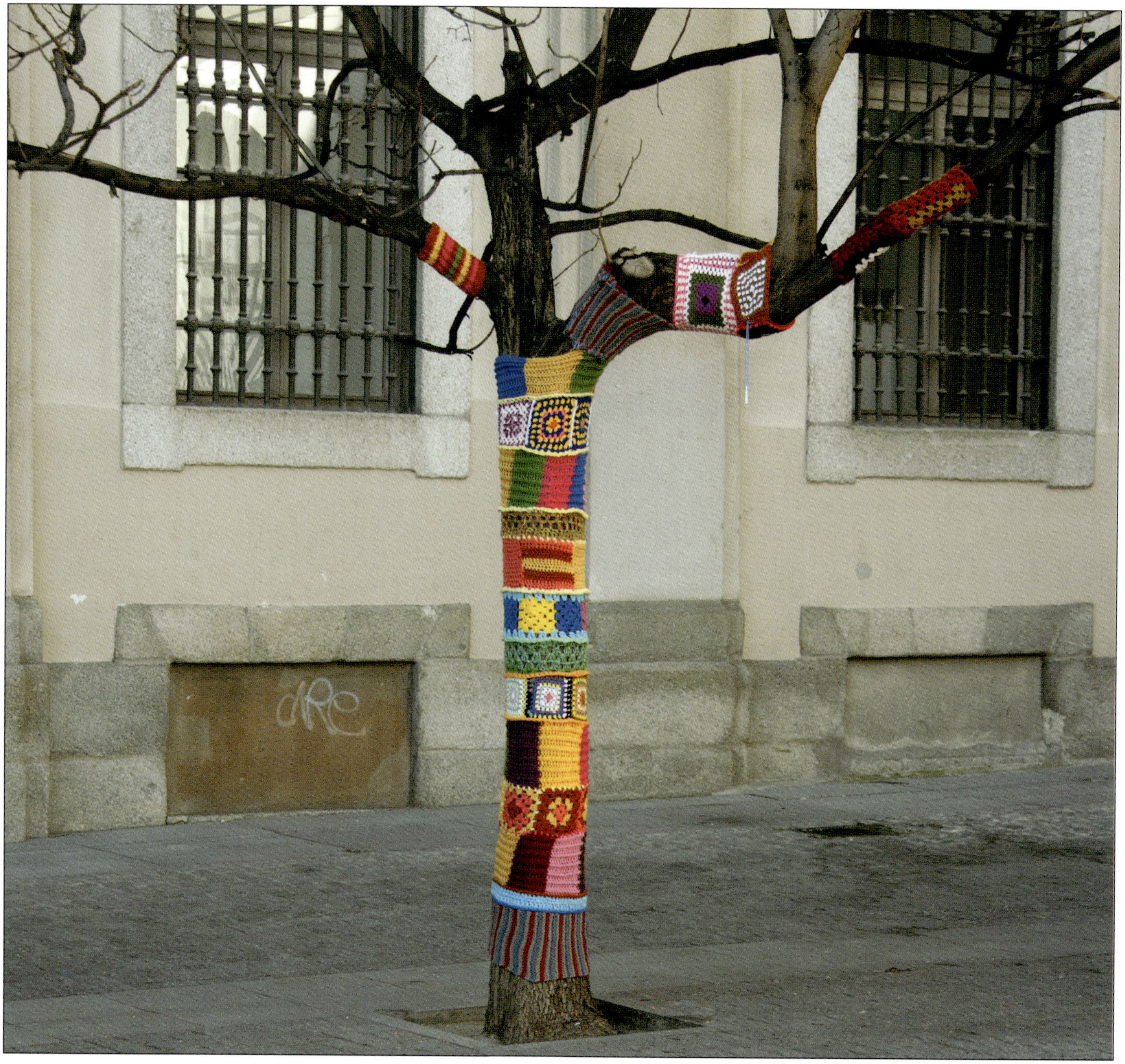

Yarn bombing found in Madrid, Spain.
Photo courtesy of Alvaro Leon.

The "stitched story" is the equivalent of a piece of graffiti in the spray can world (in this way, the cozies are like tags). It uses amigurumi animals placed so that they tell a story.

Yarn bombing has now become a worldwide phenomenon.

GUERILLA GARDENING

This is perhaps moving out of the realms of graffiti, although the legal issues associated with it are quite similar. Guerilla gardening crews target ugly places in towns and cities they think would respond well to some plant life. These crews view their mission as beautifying the space much the same way as socially conscious street artists believe their colorful works have a positive impression on the people of the area where they are painted. Guerilla gardeners often plant fruit trees and vegetables so that all people can have access to fresh food.

An amalgamation of guerilla gardening and street art is the use of moss for making graffiti-like images on walls. The moss is specially grown and then arranged on a prepared surface. It is easily removable, though, and considered less offensive than spray can graffiti.

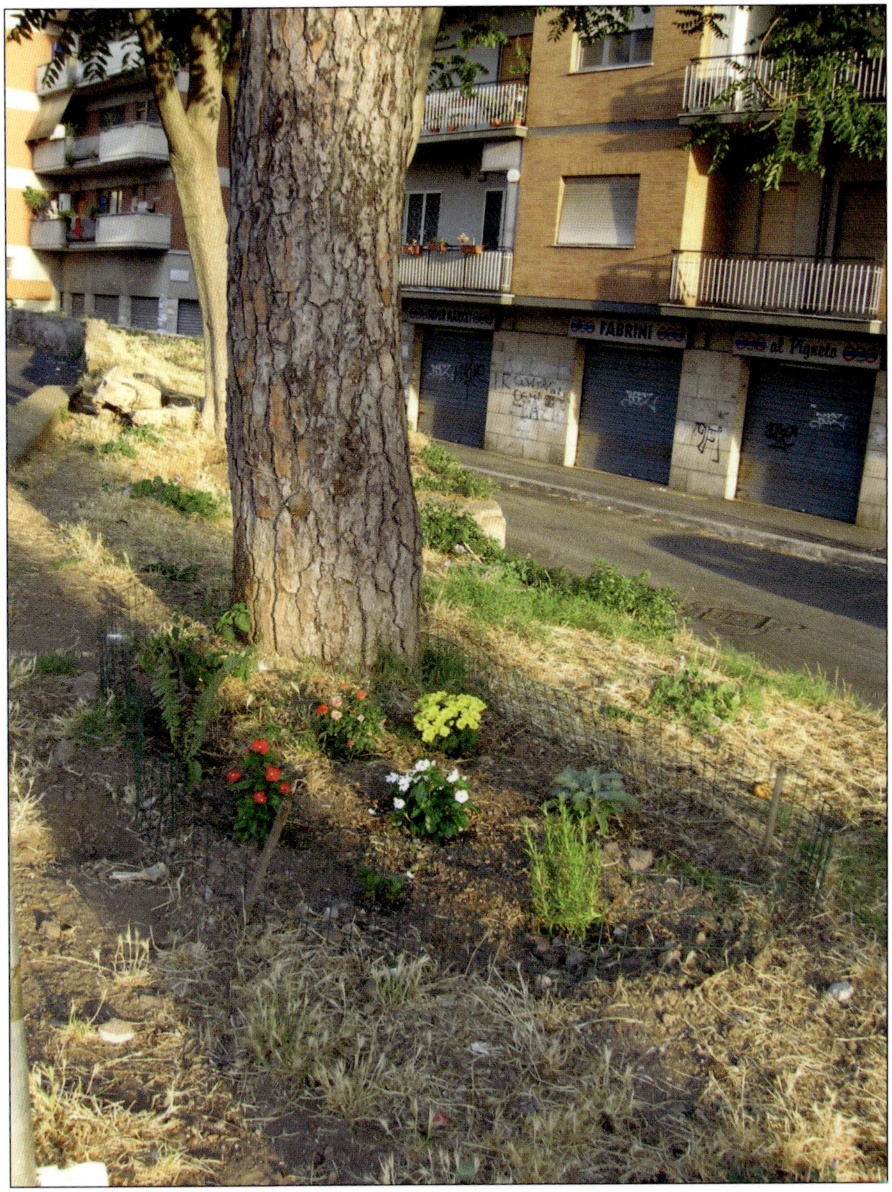

» It is only a handful of flowers, but they bring a spot of color to a less affluent area of Rome, Italy. Note the tag style graffiti on the garage doors in the background.

SOMETHING COMPLETELY DIFFERENT

This is graffiti art at its wackiest, but also most enterprising. Shelley Miller of Montreal uses colored icing mixture to paint her exquisitely decorative graffiti pieces. Her work is very temporary, melting almost as soon as it has been applied.

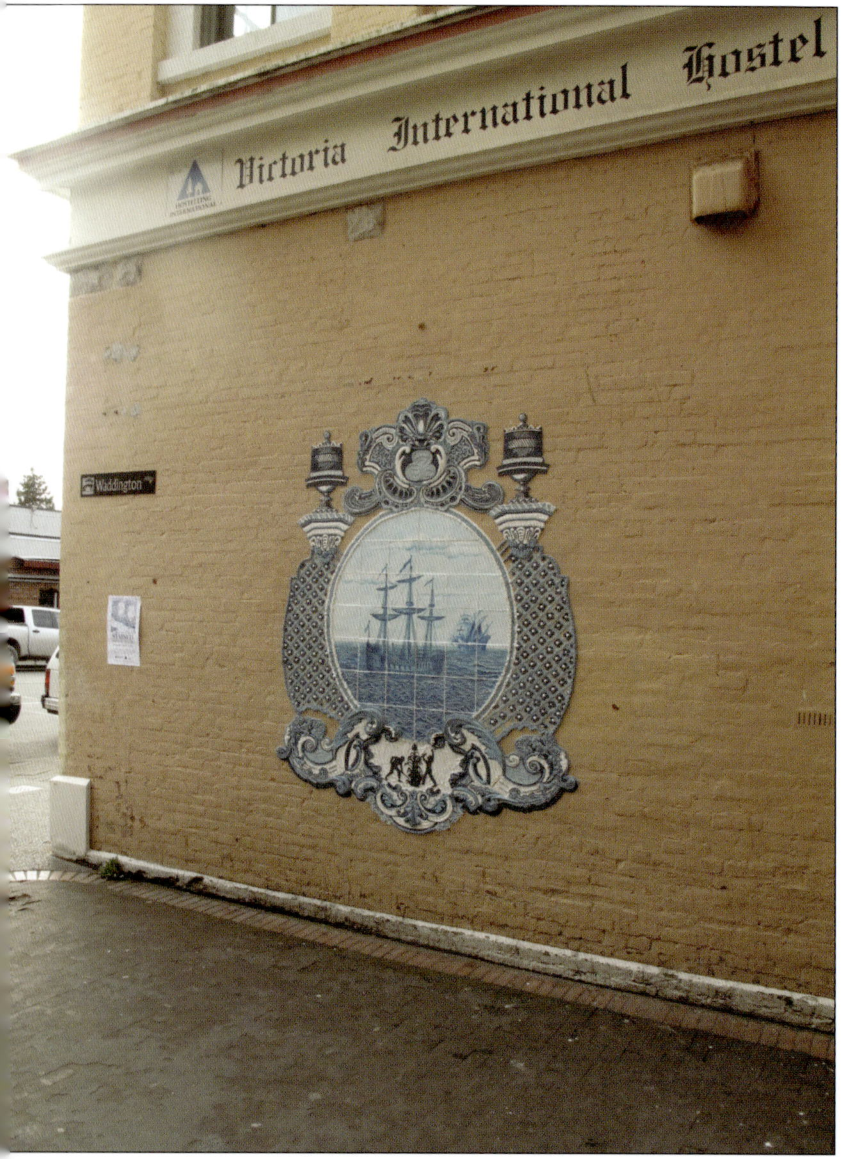

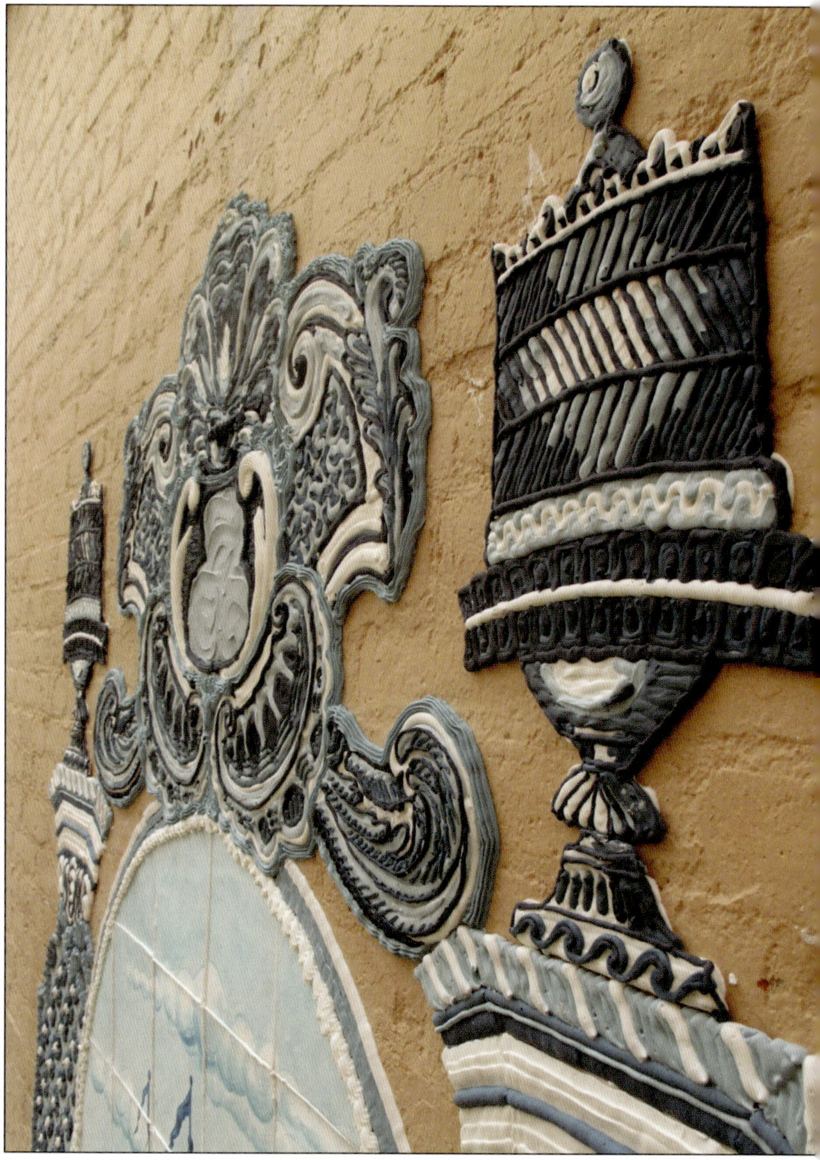

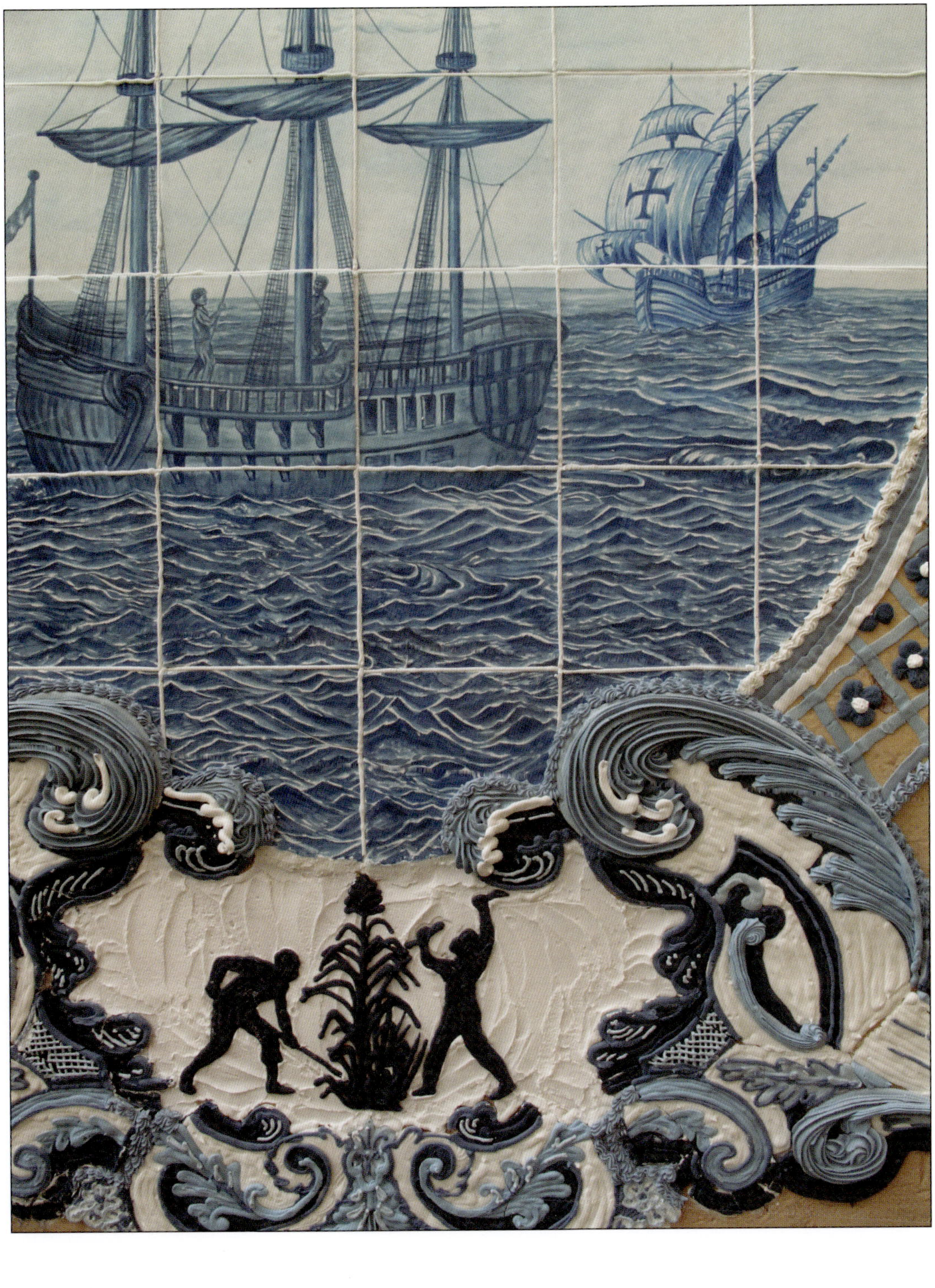

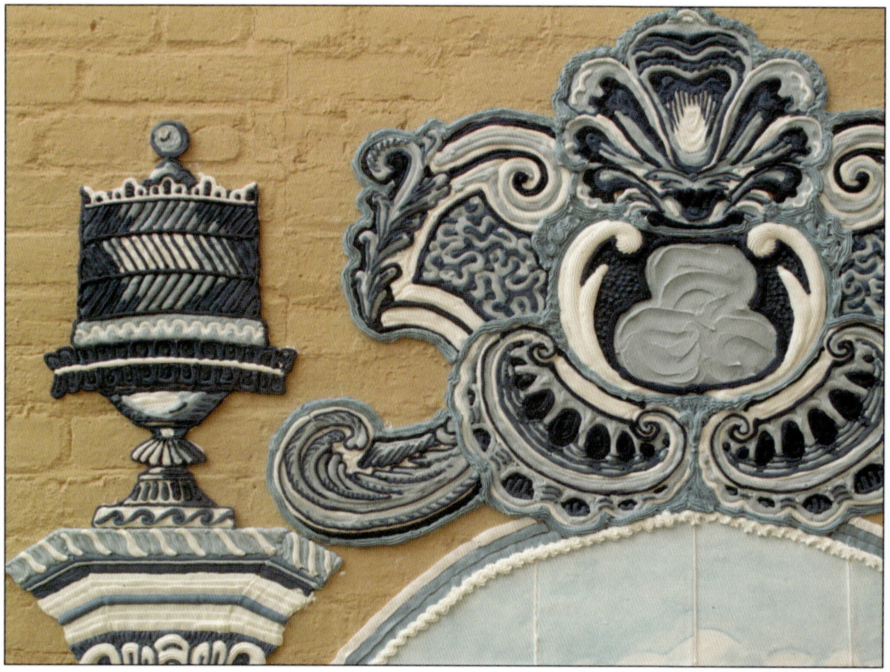

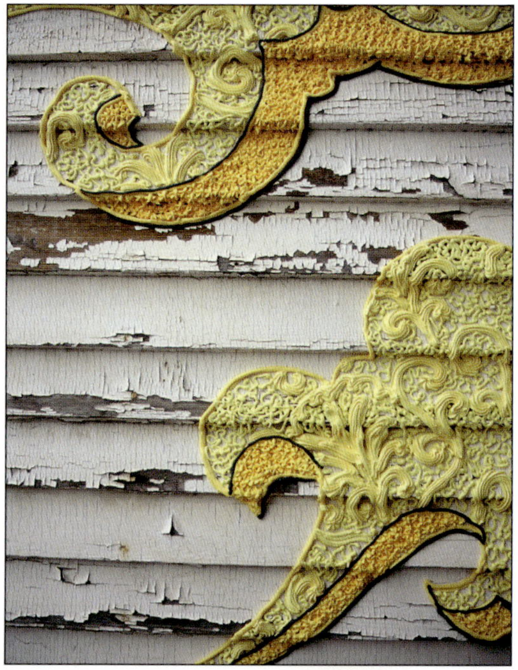

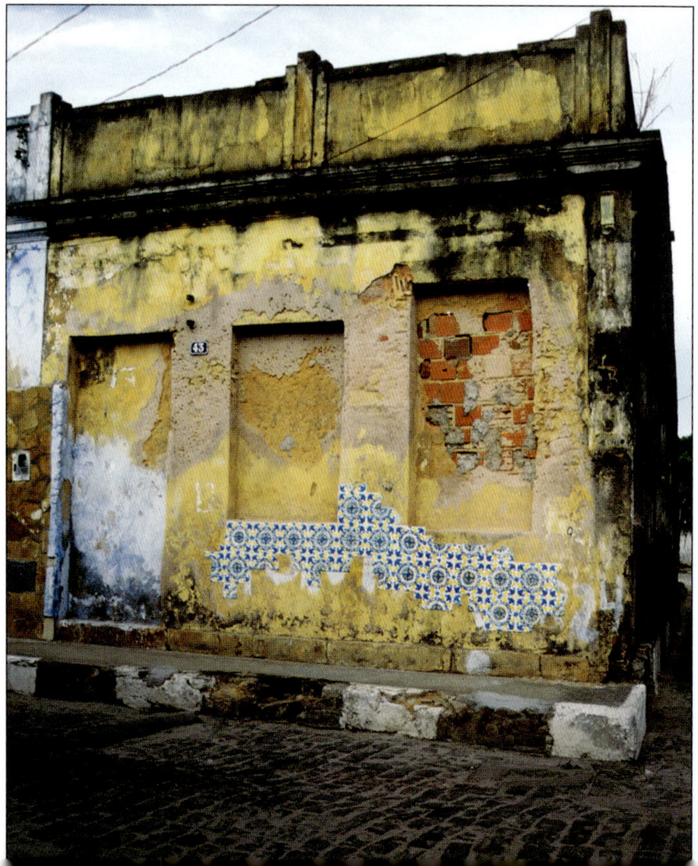

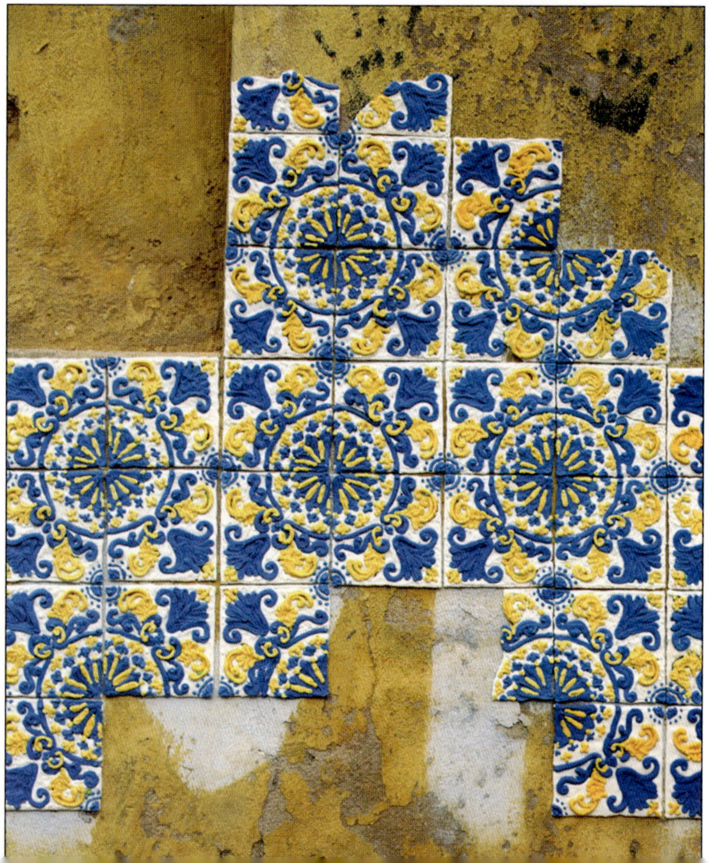

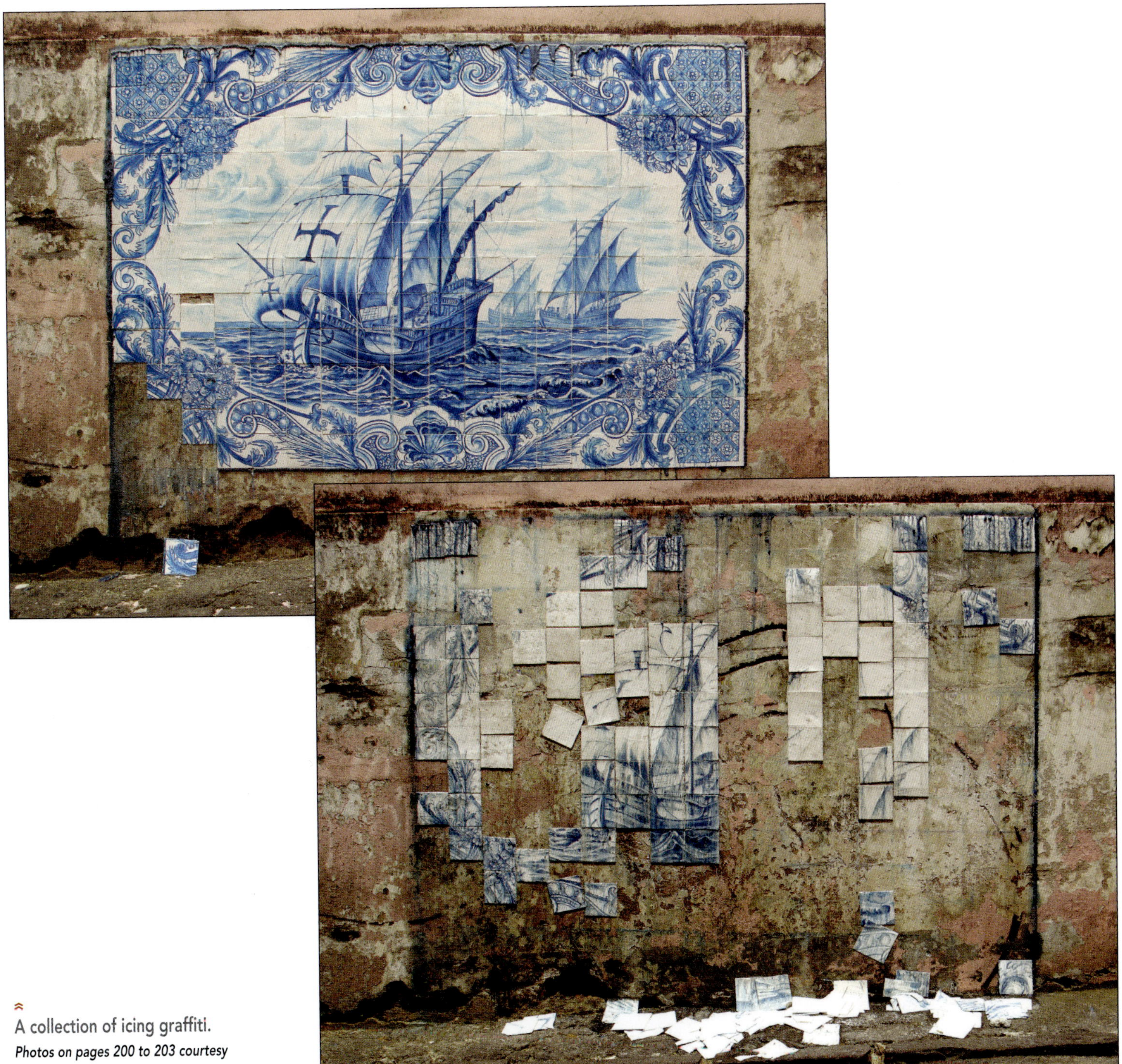

A collection of icing graffiti.
Photos on pages 200 to 203 courtesy of Shelly Miller.

FAKE GRAFFITI

These days, everyone can make their own "fake" graffiti thanks to digital programs like Photoshop. You can use images you have made yourself, photos or drawings, and alter them so that they appear to be placed on any building or place in the world. Of course, they only exist in cyberspace or photographic prints, and apart from copyright issues pertaining to the electronic or print material, there is no worry about prosecution for vandalism.

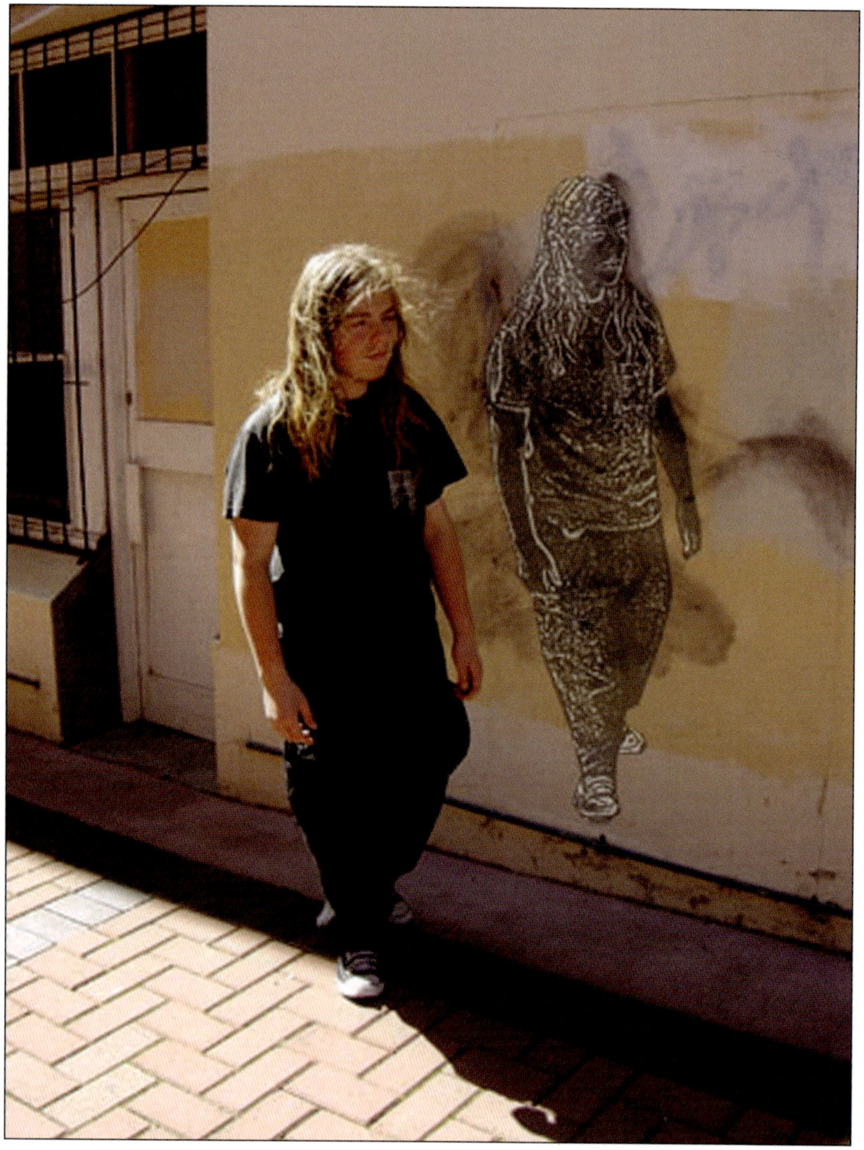

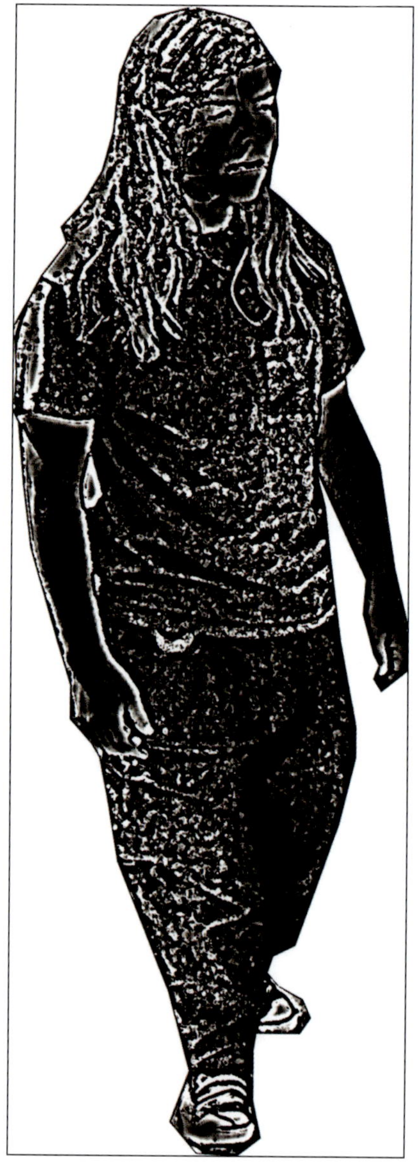

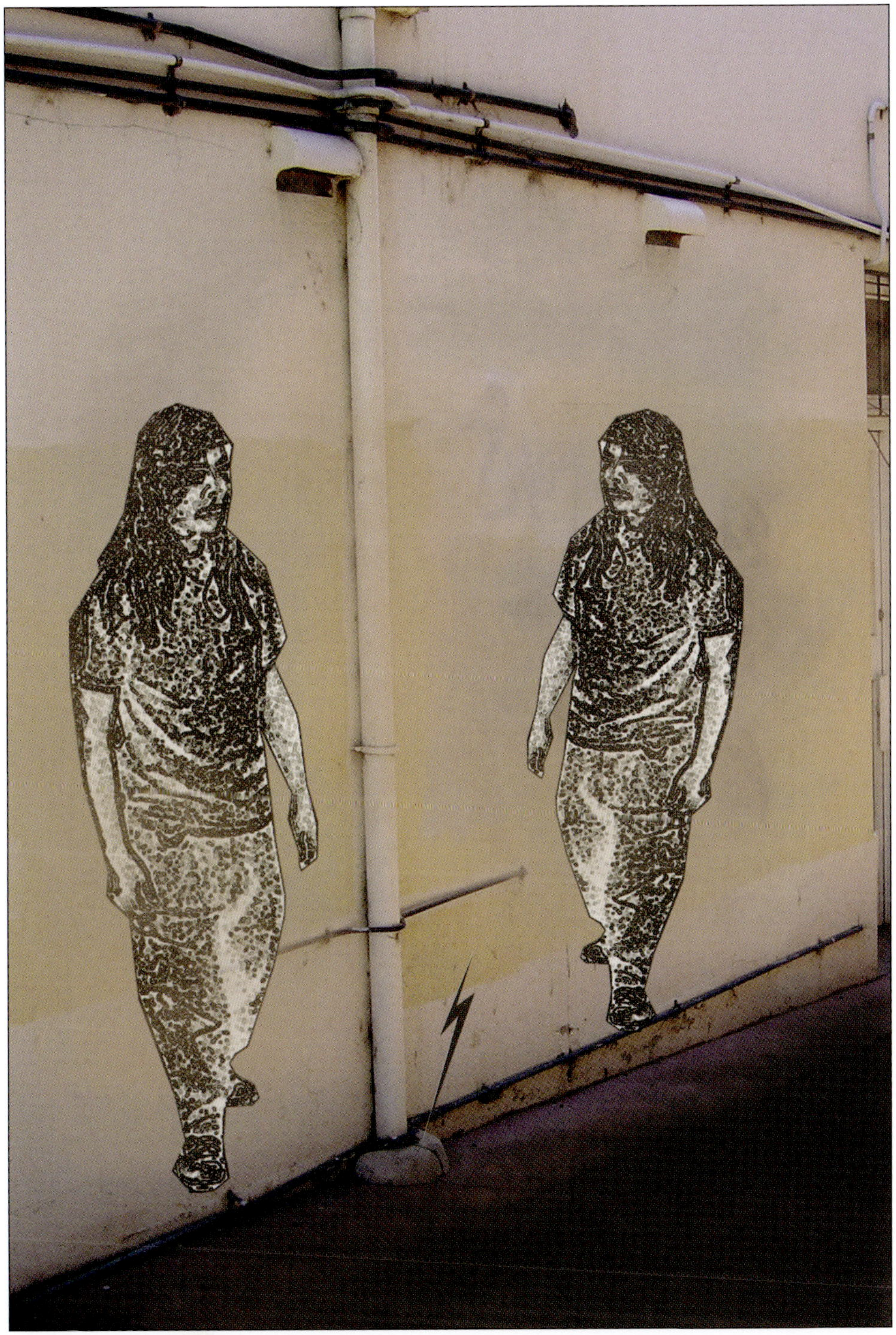

«

I was asked by an author friend to come up with a graffiti figure that was following a young man around a city as if it was his shadow. I used my son as a model and took photographs of him and then applied various Photoshop filters to get a stencil/ wheat paste look to it. With my template ready, I was then able to put it into almost any situation on any city wall anywhere in the world.

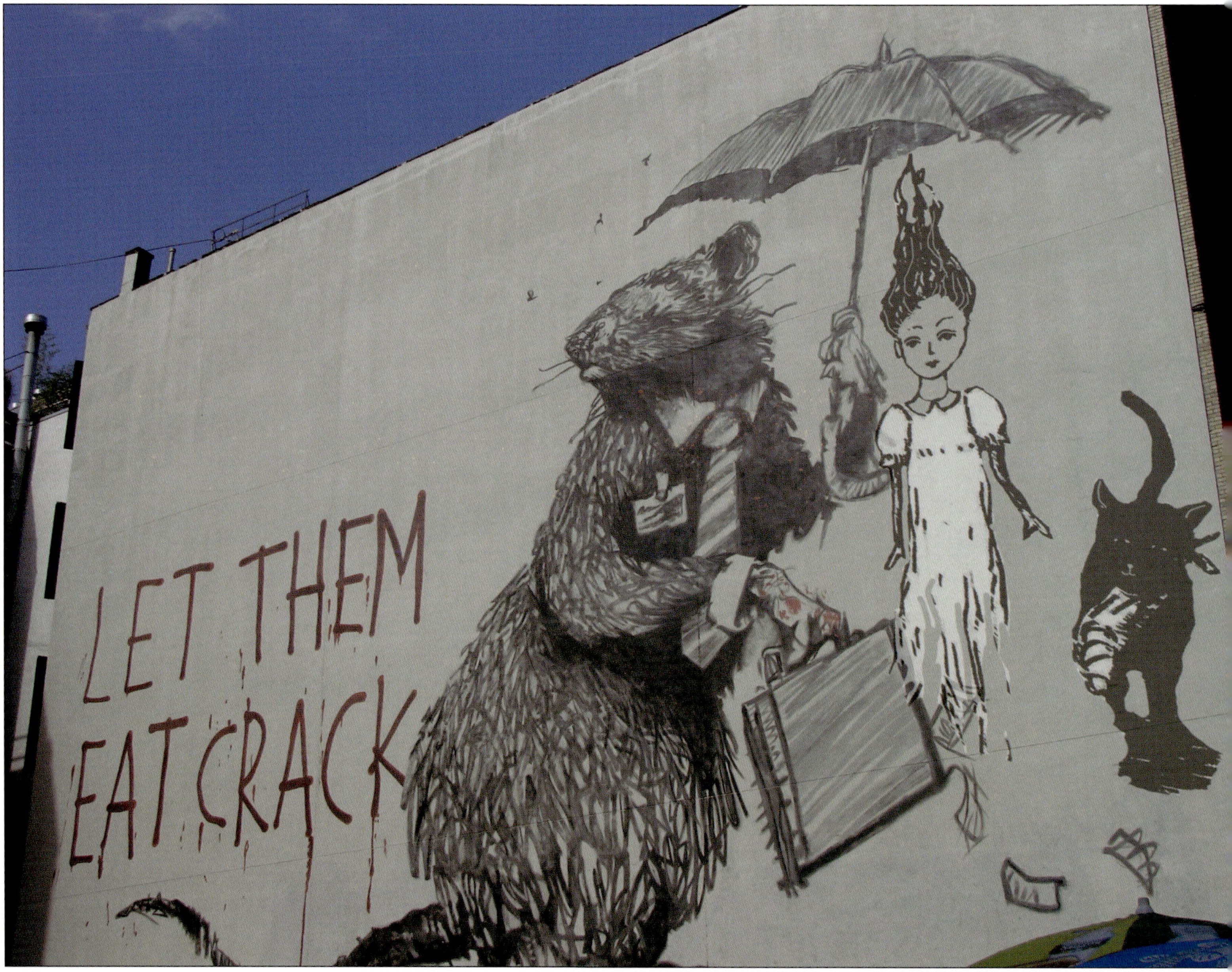

I couldn't resist the temptation to flirt with fame and alter a piece of Banksy graffiti with the addition of my own characters Ghost Doll and Jasper the cat. These two friends come together in an adventure that features many large and vicious rats. I took my own illustration and cut them out on Photoshop to resemble stencils. To get the new work to blend in with the original Banksy, I faded my stencil templates to the same grade of gray.

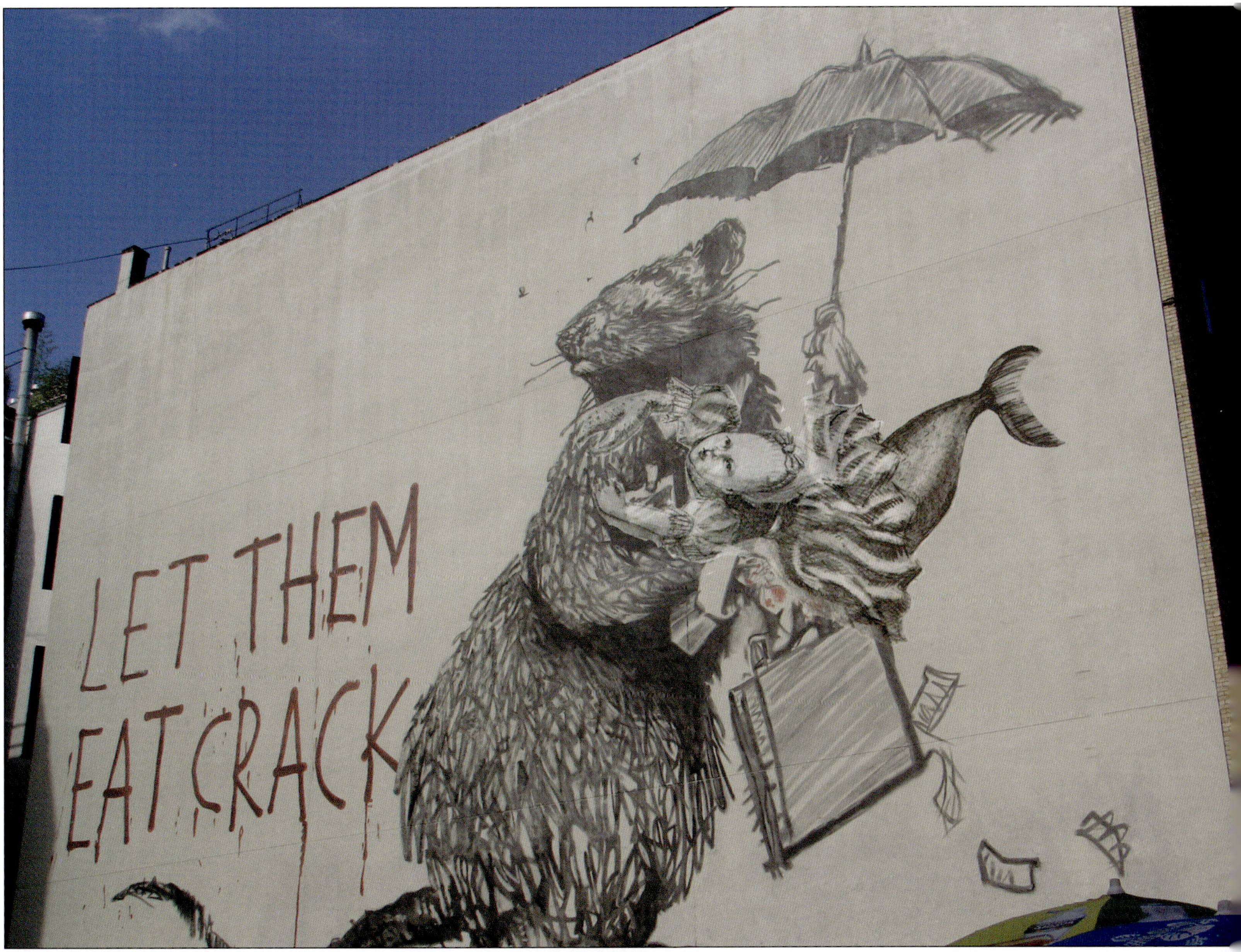

Not content with one fraudulent piece, I found that I needed to try another one. My mermaid with crab claw sat so well in the rat's arms that I felt I had to leave her there.

IN CONCLUSION

It has been difficult to pinpoint exactly what constitutes graffiti throughout our history as a human race. There are the obvious examples, of course: tags, writing in public restrooms, and the names and dates people have scratched onto the walls of famous places. I have tried to be as inclusive as possible, because it is obvious that there are many gray and overlapping areas that may, or may not, be classified as graffiti. When boundaries meet, crossover, and blur, it is by far the safest route to go too far rather than not far enough in this type of popular history investigation.

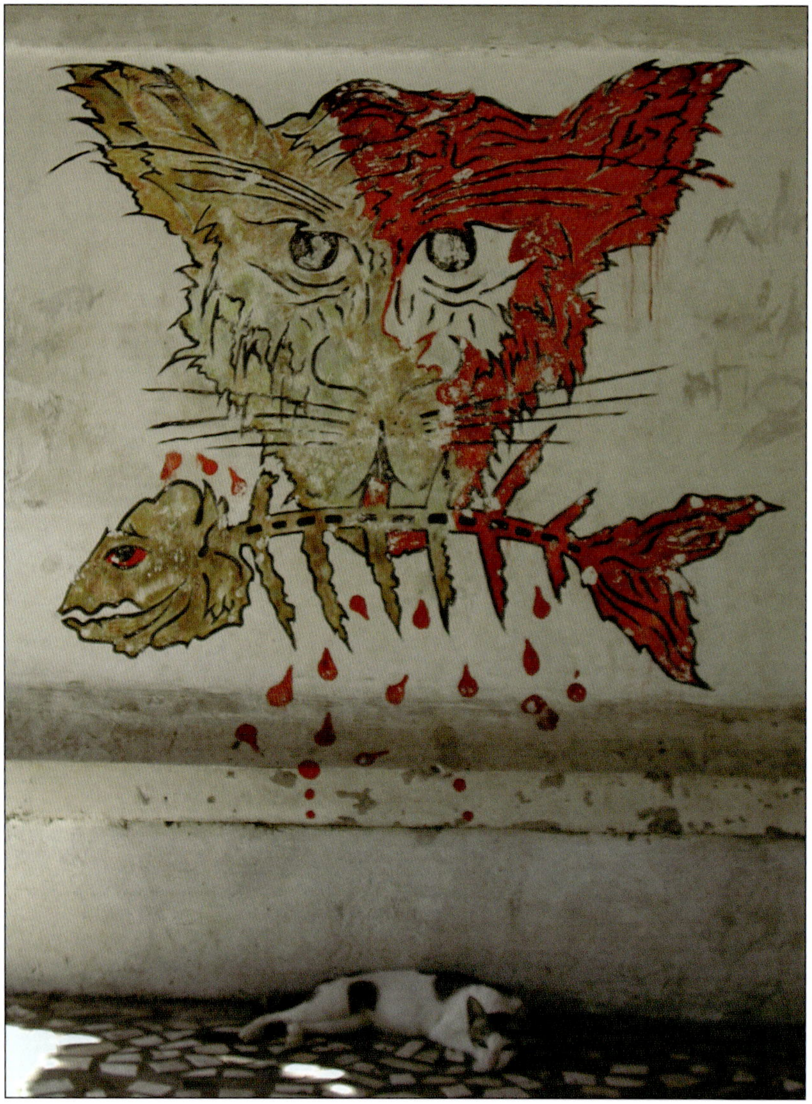

I have tried to show how man's earliest art efforts on cave walls were, according to the strictest sense of the word *graffito*, an important part of this movement. I have also included the beginnings of writing, as it was often preformed on walls and quite often engraved, or scratched, into particular surfaces. Without writing, we would not enjoy the presence of tags or political slogans or those age-old toilet jokes.

As the world organized itself more into cities and towns, with all the accompanying bustle and commerce, it was obvious that leisure time would bring forth idle messages written in a moment of insight or inspiration or pure boredom. When tags and spray can art emerged in the 1970s, we saw the birth of a whole new art movement that we termed "graffiti." This also ushered in the time when tags and throw ups were seen as a method of confronting authority and challenging social mores—which also brought along legal implications of vandalism and urban blight.

Sometimes graffiti has been written to point out the awfulness of slums and the need to clean up; as we've seen, other graffiti was created in an attempt to beautify the environment. The illegality of the activity provides a thrill for the perpetrator and a culture that has evolved around it between law-breaking graffitist and hard-nosed government officials.

Graffiti has also become increasingly sophisticated as art schools trained artists joining the graffiti movement. People made stencils and prints and art history references that they hoped would not only look good, but also provoke thought among those who came into contact with the work. The trouble with identifying graffiti after this point comes when those same artists began to be recognized as legitimate, showing and selling their works in art galleries and earning immense fame. Is it still graffiti if it looks like graffiti but is hanging in a museum and not on an urban building? And is graffiti lifted from city walls still actually graffiti once it is put up for auction and sold to private bidders? These are questions that those in the art world and the general community continue to struggle to answer.

Also arising are issues of copyright and plagiarism. If the works done by graffiti artists are created rather anonymously then surely the artists cannot claim copyright on them. And if they are placed illegally and can be removed at the discretion of a town council or a building owner, then does copyright still apply even if the artist is known? Again, these are complicated questions that don't have an answer yet.

Graffiti often relies on borrowing from popular culture or cartoon characters to fuel images for work. These characters are themselves the subject of copyright and it is actually illegal to copy them for money or to claim them as your own invention. Then again, throughout history artists have borrowed from one another, learning processes and techniques, paying homage, and indulging in century-long conversations with dead artists. If another graffiti writer then borrows from another living graffiti artist, is it really any different? Copying is, after all, the sincerest form of flattery.

If all that we've discussed in this book is graffiti, then perhaps we can also include crop circles, those mysterious patterns formed in crops by unknown artists, often at the expense of the farmer. And what about skywriting—can it fit in the genre, too? It is perhaps the most ephemeral type of writing of all, vanishing within minutes of appearing but visible to the general public. And tattoos often profess similar emotions as graffiti carved into trees by lovers, showing a heart and two names. Is this then a form of graffiti?

I'd like to conclude this look at the popular history of graffiti with a theory of my own. As a journalist suggested, graffiti is so wide spread in time and space that it is almost part of the natural human condition, and this has made me think about what is really behind our fascination with making and viewing graffiti. It has occurred to me as I have sat at a dinner party, or at a café, and watched people idly pick up a pen and begin to doodle on a paper napkin, and this is perhaps one of the reasons behind mankind's propensity for making graffiti: In our fingertips, we hold an innate desire to create, itching to exercise in order to evolve. What, then, will happen to this as we become more reliant on computers for writing? Our pens will fall into disuse and perhaps in time all graffiti will fade from the city walls, leaving it dull and lifeless. But all is not lost as we invade the places opened by new technology: cyberspace provides new canvas and fresh material. We can write, paint, add music, create theater, and insert interactive elements in our new virtual world. It will be hard to police this new form of graffiti, if we can call it that, and who knows where the possibilities will end.

What we have seen through our investigation of the markings people make, from their earliest smudges on cave walls to the sophisticated paintings covering entire train cars, is that the making and the showcasing of art to an audience will always be an important practice for the human race. To leave a mark is a form of immortality. Who knows who will come along in decades or centuries and ponder on the dates, pictures, and names that are left by the viewers' ancestors. But what is even more interesting, and perhaps more frightening, is the deductions made about our lifestyles and cultures from these messages left in relative haste and without much thought to their future impact.

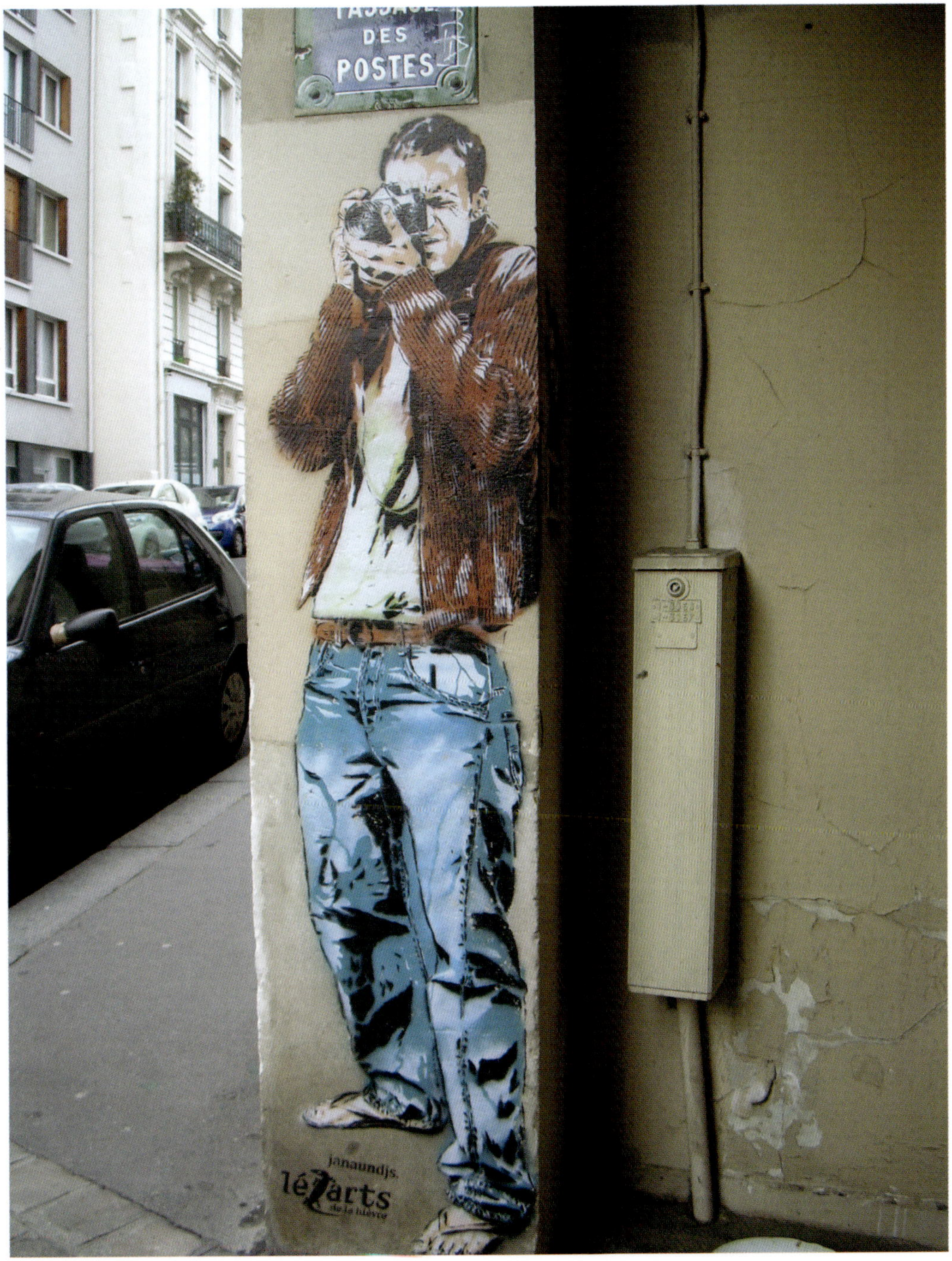

Photo courtesy of Sophie Masson.

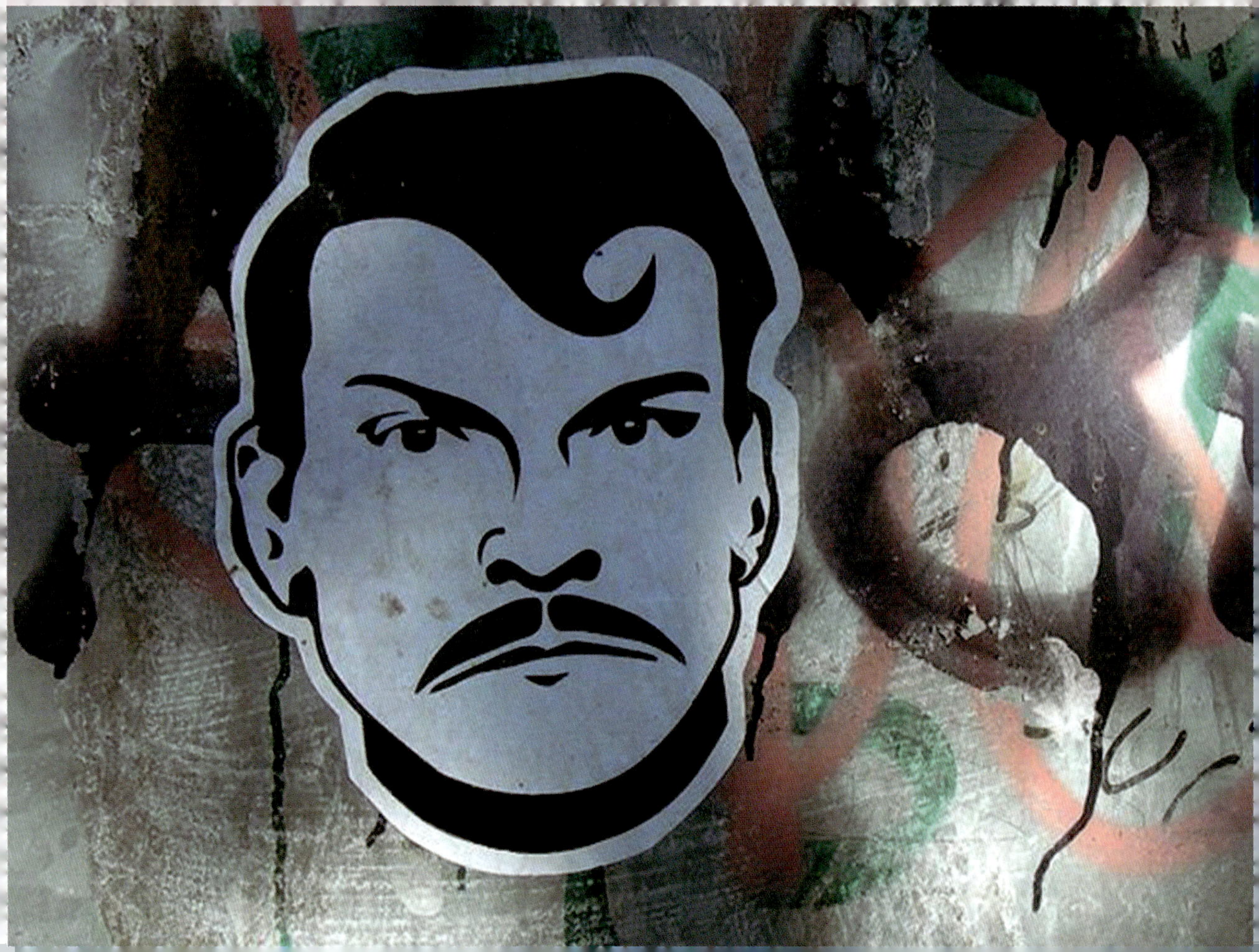

GRAFFITI GLOSSARY

All City: As the name implies, this refers to graffiti by a writer or a crew produced over a large geographical area, such as major subway lines. Originally it specifically meant all of the five boroughs of New York. If a writer or crew is so prolific that they are able to produce a large body of work like this, then they are also considered to be Up—a term conferring status.

Angels: Dead graffiti artists are known as angels, and other artists often put a halo over their work or tags; sometimes birth and death dates are attached.

Back in the Day: Not surprisingly, this term refers to a graffitist's early days of producing graffiti. It is also used to mean graffiti practitioners from the old days and is used in hip-hop culture.

Background: When a "canvas" is already covered with tags and graffiti, it is necessary to make a new piece stand out, so a suitable background color needs to be applied first.

Back Jump: A piece of work quickly executed and often not filled in with color. This type of graffiti is usually found on the sides of trains or other large vehicles.

Back to back: When a whole wall or train car is completely covered with graffiti. It is also used when a series of throw-ups are made in quick succession on one piece of "canvas."

Battle: This is a competition between individual writers or crews. It may involve skill, where both opponents must cover a wall within a given time and produce a high-quality piece, or it might refer to quantity. To judge the contestants, a third party writer or crew is called in. The prize or punishment is open to negotiation between the parties involved, but often involves a supply of paint (also marijuana), a punch up, or that the loser(s) have a ban put on them from writing graffiti for a specified time.

Beef: An argument or other disagreement between writers or crew.

Bench/Benching: A subway station where writers or crews gather and then watch the graffitied trains pass by.

Bite: Copying someone else's work without permission, particularly in regards to tags or writing style. If someone is found guilty of this, they are accused of "dissing" the artist.

Black Book: Although tags and throw-ups might be spontaneous, there are still many graffiti artists who like to plan out their work in a sketchbook. It is seen as an artist's most precious and secret property, especially where the police are involved, as it can be used to identify the artist.

Block Buster: Large writing, usually square in shape, placed under the windows of a train car. The letters stretch, leaning backwards and forwards, along the whole length of the car. It is often used to cover other graffiti. Blade and Comet both claim to having invented this style.

Bomb/Bombing: The act of writing and painting graffiti that implies prolific activity. Possibly comes from the word "bombard."

Bubble Letters: Type of lettering that was big in the 1970s.

Buff /buffed: Refers to the removal of graffiti by authorities such as a transit authority. The MTA (Metropolitan Transit Authority) are called The Buff among graffitists in New York City.

Burn: If you "burn" your rivals, it means you have outdone them in quantity of graffiti, but it also means to wear something out.

Burner: A spectacular piece of work.

Burning: Graffiti that is still in existence—has not been removed—is said to still be burning.

Cannons: Originally this term was used in Brooklyn, New York, and is the name for spray cans.

Caps: Spray-can attachments of different sizes to get different widths of spray. These are also called tips. This term is also used when a piece of graffiti has been crossed out or painted over by someone else's work. The term originated from a graffitist nicknamed Cap who was notorious for doing this.

Character: A cartoon character, usually from popular culture rather than invented by the graffitist. Characters are used to enhance a piece of text and are sometimes used in place of a letter in a word.

China Marker: This is a type of grease-based pencil used in commercial art. They are small but very handy for writing on anything.

Clean Train: Refers to all New York City subway cars. These are hard to paint on and they are not in service when they have graffiti on them.

Cloud: This background style is not very common nowadays but was used a lot in the past on subway cars.

Coal Mine: Subway cars that were taken out of service in the mid-1970s were known as "coal mines." They were a rusty brown color.

Computer Style: As the name suggests, any graffiti that looks computer generated (or digital).

Crazy: Insane, mad, or wildly enthusiastic, as well as a term used to emphasize size.

Crew: A collective of graffiti artists who often work and hang out together. In some cases, but by no means all, graffiti crew members are also members of an associated gang. Crews usually have a name that is only three letters long. The last letter is very often "K," as this means "Kings" or "Kill."

Crossing Out: When someone paints over or disfigures another graffitist's name.

Cutting Lines: Painting inside the outlines of letters to thin those lines down.

Cutting Tips: A method of altering the nozzle of a spray can to alter the spray effect.

DEF: This term is considered so out of date that it is an embarrassment to use it today. It comes from a combination of the words "death" and "definite," which, as everyone knows, means "really good."

Designs: Patterns used in the infill of letters or shapes. They can be stripes, dots, checks, or anything decorative.

D.G.A.: Stands for "Don't Get Around."

Ding Dong: The name given to the new, stainless steel subway cars now in use. Before the doors close, a bell sound is made, which gives this term its name. Ding Dongs were designed with graffiti artists in mind. The smooth steel surface repels paint.

DIS: The first three letters of "disrespect" and refers to an insult. It started as a hip-hop term but has been assimilated into general popular culture.

Dope: Originated out of hip-hop culture to mean "cool."

Down: To be with the group.

Dress up: To completely cover the area surrounding a doorway or window with graffiti.

Drips: Deliberately painted, stylized drips on letters. This style began in the early days of New York subway graffiti practice.

Dropsy: A bribe.

DT: A detective, especially if in plain clothes.

Dubs: This is specific to the United Kingdom and is quickly executed in a metallic paint by a crew. It is normally found on railway walls or in streets.

End to end: Covering a surface, usually of a subway car, from one end to another.

Etch: Just as in traditional etching, acid is used to eat away at a metal surface to form a design. It has been applied to the sides of train cars in Norway and consequently these cars have to be removed from service in the interests of public health.

Fade: When painting colors are subtly blended.

Fame: The aim of an ambitious writer is fame for the number or quality of work. Fame is not necessarily expected outside the subculture of graffiti.

Families: Rows of throw-ups of the same name.

Fan Spray: A nozzle tip on a spray can that makes a fan-shaped mark. It is not good for fine work or writing but is used for filler. These tips are not removable as some others are.

Fanzine: A special interest magazine, such as one about graffiti writing.

Fat: Sometimes refers to the thickness of a line or is a term used to mean "good."

Fat Cap: A nozzle that makes a broad mark.

Female Tips: Traditionally, spray cans have what is called a male tip, with the nozzle protruding. The female tips are the opposite and are not good for graffiti painting.

Fill/Fill-In: The solid color inside the outlines of words or picture.

5-O: Comes from *Hawaii Five-O*, the popular television series. Refers to the police.

Flats: These were the best types of subway cars to paint, offering a large, flat surface. They are an older type of car.

Flicks: The printed photographs of graffiti. The plural is flix.

Floaters: Throw-ups made on subway cars below the windows.

Fly: An early hip-hop term meaning "cool."

Freights: The cars of freight trains.

Fresh: Another early hip-hop term meaning "cool," "new," or "good."

Front: Probably derives from the word "confront." It is a hip-hop term. If someone fronts you, they are asking for a fight.

Gallery: Galleries are often found in places not easily accessible for cleaning. These are often underpasses or under bridges. The space is large and can accommodate a lot of graffiti and so is able to provide a long-term surface for artists to show their work.

German Montana: A brand name for a paint specially designed and marketed to graffiti artists.

Getting Up: The term used for making graffiti. It originally referred only to painting graffiti on a train (possibly a moving one), but now means all sorts of graffiti made anywhere.

Getting Over/Going Over: Both terms are used to mean painting over another's work. Usually this is an insult to the previous writer unless the work has already been vandalized. Certain forms of graffiti rate higher and lower than others. For instance, a tag maybe legitimately painted over by a throw-up or larger work. Less so now, but more common in the early days of graffiti, crossing out was not uncommon with several artists and crew specializing in crossing out (using a red "x") as many graffiti as they could.

Ghost: The mark left on a wall after graffiti has been removed.

Grease Pencil: Used by commercial artists and is ideal for writing on almost any surface. It is not suitable for large scale work, however.

Griffin: A pigment used in homemade markers, with its name deriving from a type of shoe dye.

Grocery Store Ink: The ink specially used in pricing guns at grocery stores. Homemade pens once used this ink. It was supposed to be a good long-life ink.

Hand Style: The tag or handwriting style of a writer.

Hat: An acronym for "Honor among thieves" and relates to the trustworthiness of a writer.

Head: Hierarchical term for a supreme writer.

Head Buff Spot: The area just above where the passenger on a subway sits and where his or her head gently rubs. Graffiti made at this spot will eventually be worn away by the passenger and is therefore not a good place for it.

Heaven/Heaven spots: Places that are difficult to access to either create or remove graffiti. They are often dangerous and people have died in the attempt at writing in such spots and are therefore said to have gone to heaven—hence the name. They also sometimes known as giraffiti, a play on the words "giraffe" and "graffiti" because one needs a long neck to write that high up.

Henry shots: This is a term that applies to a photographic technique for capturing graffiti on a moving train. It was developed by Henry Chalfant and involves setting a fixed-point camera that is set for film advance. The result is a photograph of a single image that is made up of several frames.

Hip Hop: Refers to the culture of the same name that emerged in the 1970s. Early graffiti was strongly linked to it.

Hit/Hit Up: The act of having just executed a piece of writing or tagging.

Hollows: Graffiti, often text, that is made up of outline only.

Homemade: A marker made by the artist using a container such as an old deodorant bottle and filled with an absorbent material (anything from socks to the felt taken from chalkboard erasers) and then filled with ink.

Homemade Ink: Grocery store ink is a favorite ink for the homemade marker, but it can also be made from carbon paper shredded and mixed with alcohol or lighter fluid.

Hot: An inexperienced or incompetent writer

Icy Grape: The name of a color that was made by Krylon. It is no longer made and old cans of it are eagerly sought after.

Insides: The interiors of subway cars.

Invent: Another out-of-date term, used mainly in the 1970s, to mean shoplifting. "Rack" is the current term for theft.

IRT: A subway division called Interborough Rapid Transit, whose flat-sided cars made excellent canvases.

Jungle Green: Another discontinued color from Krylon.

Karak: A shortened form of character.

Kill: To set about a major bombing campaign.

King: To be king is to be top of the range, and the king is looked up to for skill or prolificacy.

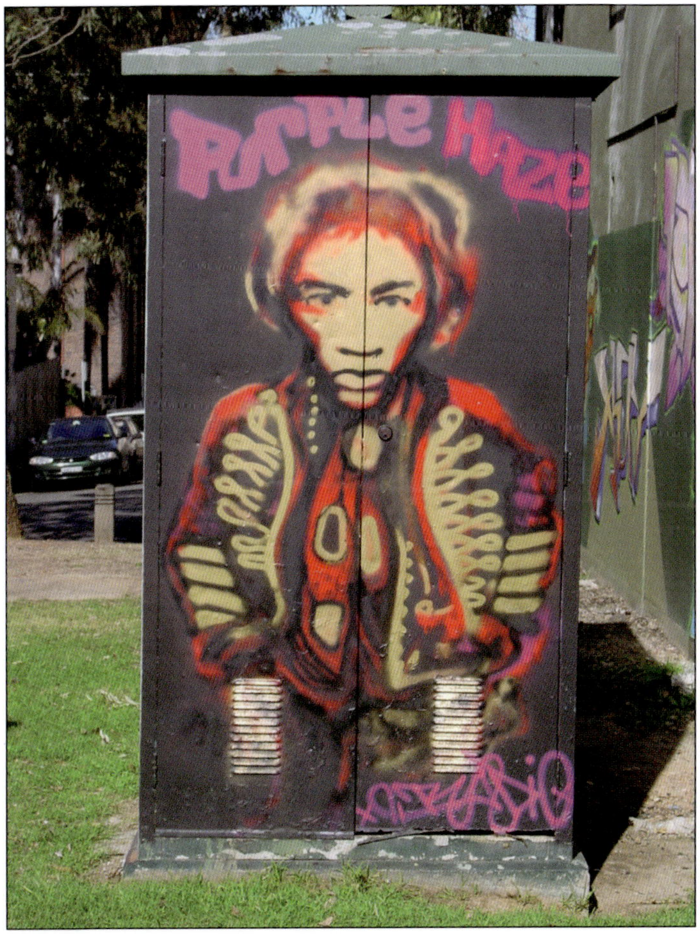

Knight: A writer who is gaining a steady reputation although his style is still developing and so not considered as good as a king's.

Krylon: A popular brand of spray paint that was used for much of the graffiti produced in the 1970s and 1980s. It has now fallen from favor because of the changes made to the nozzle and the quality of paint. It sports a distinctive five spot logo and comes in a large range of colors at a very reasonable price. There are three different groups of Krylon paints, as designated by writers: 360 Krylon, triple Krylon (no runs, no drips, no errors label), and original Krylon, which are now considered highly collectable.

Landmark: A piece of graffiti made in a difficult to access location so that removal is almost impossible or simply not feasible. It means that the graffiti will stay there a long time and become a landmark.

Lay-up: The side tracks where trains are put when not in use, often overnight.

Legal: A piece of work that has permission to be made where it is.

Lock on: Refers to a sculptural, non-commissioned, and therefore illegitimate art piece that has been locked to an immovable object, such as a bench or tree.

Mad: Crazy.

Magnum: A brand of non-refillable fat marker.

Marks-a-lot: Product name for a black magic marker that was standard in the early days of graffiti, but is rarely used now as better products have replaced it.

Married Couple: An older term for two subway cars that are permanently coupled together and provide a long canvas.

Massacre: The mass removal of graffiti by authorities leaving nothing in its place but bare wall.

Mean Streak: The name of a type of paint stick produced by the Sanford Corporation. The solvent base is glycol, which makes graffiti made with it very difficult to remove. It is opaque, waterproof, and comes in white, blue, red, and yellow.

Mop: A homemade graffiti marker that is larger than the usual type.

Motion Tagging: Tagging subway cars while they are in service and requiring a quick response time before the car moves off again.

MTA: Metropolitan Transit Authority of New York City.

Mural: Holds a similar meaning to that of a wall filled with an image or images; in this case, graffiti, although it often has figural elements (they may or may not be characters).

New School: The new wave of graffiti artists from the mid-1980s onwards.

Old School: Graffitists from the dim and distant past of the 1970s and early 1880s. These writers are usually highly respected by the younger generation.

One liner: A piece of writing, often a tag, written in one entire movement without lifting the marker from the surface.

Outline: A sketch made in a book from which a larger piece will be made. It can also refer to the outline drawing made on a wall, which may or may not be filled in later.

Pain eater: An unprimed or raw surface that will absorb paint readily, therefore requiring more and thicker paint to cover it.

Painters Touch: A brand name for a readily available product made by Rust-Olem that has a reputation for quality.

Panel Piece: The area between the doors and below the windows of a subway car and the artwork made there.

Paneling: A term, possibly only used in Australia, to mean painting on a railway car while it is temporarily stationary.

Paste up: A piece of work done on paper and then glued to a structure with wheat or wallpaper paste.

Patch: Where graffiti has been painted over with a neutral color, such as brown or gray.

Pawn: If a King is the top stratum of graffiti hierarchy, then the pawn is at the lowest end. A pawn is one who is inexperienced or just plain inefficient at the art.

Penit: This term is only used in Miami and refers to a structure that is not used and therefore ideal for graffiti. If it is a building, graffiti will appear inside and out.

Pichação: A term only used in Brazil to refer to a type of tagging used there.

Piece: A term derived from "masterpiece"that refers to a significant work. To gain this prestigious moniker at least three colors must be used and it must demonstrate skill and imagination. Sometimes pieces use 3-D effects, subtle shading, and other painterly techniques.

Piecebook: An artist's sketchbook, similar to the black book.

Piece quake: An exaggerated stylization of a writer's name.

Pilot: A fat, refillable marker.

Production: A large, complex piece of graffiti.

Props: Coming from the hip-hop term for a shortened form of proper respect.

PT: Short for "Painters Touch" brand of paint by Rust-Olem.

Pull-in Pull-out: Trains that are waiting in a lay-up for anywhere between five and fifteen minutes until they are due to move out again. The graffitist has to move quickly to get the work done in this time. Usually only throw-ups are managed. It is also highly dangerous.

Racking/Racking Up: Theft, usually in the form of shoplifting, and often of paint or other graffiti-related equipment. In some groups of graffiti culture, it is seen as essential to the art to use only ill gotten materials for work.

Red Devil: A brand of spray can paint that was very popular with the Old School but is not considered very good nowadays.

Ridgy: A type of subway car that was used in Brooklyn and that was made of corrugated iron that made it difficult to paint on. The only type of graffiti done on this type of surface was the two-color and top-to-bottom throw-ups. Often one of the colors was the hard-to-remove silver.

Roll Call: All the tags or names of a crew involved in a piece of graffiti.

Roller: A piece so large that it needs to be executed with a paint roller rather than brushes, spray cans, or markers.

Roller Letters: Letters made with a paint roller.

Rook: A crewmember who is entirely trustworthy.

Run: The time a piece of graffiti lasts before it is removed.

Rustoleum/Rusto: A brand of spray paint that was and still is popular; it a higher priced product than most used by graffitists.

Scribe/Scriber/Scratchiti: A piece of graffiti, as well as the tool used to make it, that has been incised into the surface with a key, knife, drill bit, or something similar. It is very hard to remove this kind of graffiti.

Scrub: A throw-up done in two colors that is filled in using a side-to-side movement (like quick coloring in).

SG-7: Sakura make this very large marker that can be refilled, although it is not designed to do so. It is not as large as Sakura's Pentouch model, which has a mixing ball inside it.

Slam: To execute a piece of graffiti in a very dangerous spot or where it is in a very obvious position.

Slash: Another term for crossing out or painting over someone else's graffiti.

Shoe Dye: A popular paint for making graffiti. It can be bought in a bottle with a sponge on top that soaks up the dye and deposits it when pressed to the surface being marked.

Slants: These are a type of subway car with a slanted side.

Soak up: Looking at other graffiti for inspiration.

Spanish Montana: A company producing paint specifically for graffiti.

Stainer: A marker with a 12- to 20-mm tip used for marking. They are illegal to carry on your person without a good reason in certain countries.

Steel: A term applied to any railway car as opposed to a piece of architecture such as a wall.

Stickers: A pre-tagged label or sticker that can be quickly slapped onto a surface.

Straight Letters: A simple type of lettering using straight lines that is easily read.

Sucker Tips: Spray cans come with a factory-produced stock tip and they are not usually good for making graffiti so are replaced with more suitable tips by the artists. A sucker tip is so called because only a sucker would try to use this tip for doing graffiti. Old School writers had no choice and are excluded from being termed a sucker.

The System: The New York subway system.

Style Wars: A competition between artists.

Tag: A stylized form of the writer's name, similar to a signature.

Tagger: A graffitist who only produces tags and no other type of work.

Tagging Up: The act of writing a tag.

Third Rail: This refers to the third, electrified rail on the railway system. It supplies the power to the trains and will electrocute you if you touch it.

3-D: Three-dimensional-type lettering.

Throwie: A more modern term for a throw-up.

Throw-Up: This is usually an outline-only piece that may be done in one or two colors and must be made very quickly. Sometimes it is used to refer to bubble letters.

Top-to-bottom: A subway car or wall that has been covered completely from top to bottom by one writer or crew.

Toy: This is not a nice term and is applied to inexperienced or incompetent writers. It is thought to stand for "trouble on your system."

Ultra Flat: A matte paint often used by taggers for its easier application properties compared to gloss paint.

Ultra wide: A very wide, refillable marker.

Undersides: Graffiti made underneath the subway cars.

Up: A graffitist whose work is well known or appears in many locations. It is a positive term.

Ups: A way to talk about other people's work referring to pieces as "ups."

Wall Paper: By repeating a name many times on a wall, it will begin to look like a pattern similar to wallpaper.

Wack/wak: Comes from the term "out of whack" and is applied to poor standard graffiti.

Wet Look: The brand name of a discontinued paint.

White Trains: The color of subway cars running in the early 1980s. They were a graffitist's dream car.

Whole Car: A work of graffiti covering the entire car.

Whole Train: As the name implies, this means the covering of a complete train with graffiti.

Wild Style: This term has three distinct meanings. The first is an intricate piece of writing featuring interlocking letters. The second is a reference to a Bronx crew working in the 1970s. The third is a film by Charlie Ahearn about hip-hop culture.

Window Down: Graffiti appearing below the window on a subway car.

Wood block: A piece of graffiti done on a separate piece of wood, such as plywood, and then attached to a street sign or similar.

Work Bum: A track maintenance worker for the New York City Transit Authority.

Writer: A graffitist who does writing only.

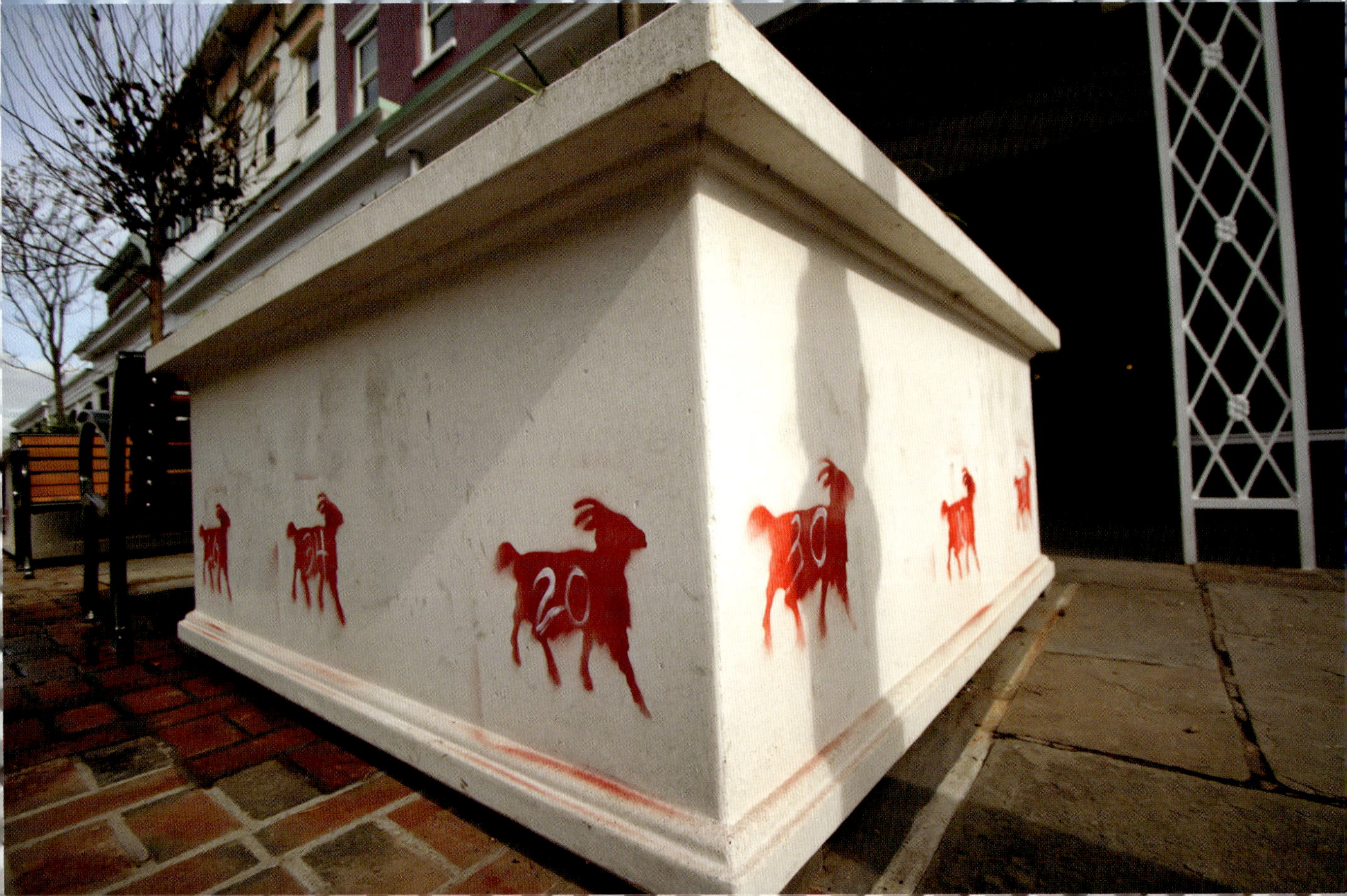
20
30

BIBLIOGRAPHY

BOOKS

Allemand, Michel, and Gérard Laux. *Savanes Urbaines.* Paris: Altern Atives, 2009.

Ganz, Nicholas. *Graffiti World.* London: Thames & Hudson, 2004.

Grévy, Fabienne. *Graffiti Paris*. New York: Abrams, New York, 2008.

Manco, Tristan. *Stencil Graffiti*. London: Thames & Hudson, 2002.

Mesnager, Jérôme. *Maintenant je parle*. Paris: Les Éditions 24x36, 2003.

Miss.Tic. *Parisienne*. Paris: Editions Alternatives, 2006.

Nemo. *Nemo par Pennac*. Paris: Éditions Hoëbeke, 2006.

ARTICLES

Forster, Alan M., Samantha Vettese-Forster, and John Borland. (2012) "Evaluating the cultural significance of historic graffiti." *Structural Survey*, Vol. 30 Iss: 1, 2012: pp.43-64.

Whiting, Sam and Veronika Koller. "*Dialogues in solitude:the discursive structures and social functions of male toilet graffiti.*" *Other*. Centre for Language in Social Life (CLSL), Lancaster University, 2007.

INTERNET

a-french-education.blogspot.com.au/2012_07_01_archive.html
ces53.com
clawmoney.com en.wikipedia.org/wiki/Graffiti
en.wikipedia.org/wiki/Graffito_(archaeology)
en.wikipedia.org/wiki/Sgraffito
knittaporfavor.wordpress.com
medieval-graffiti.co.uk/index.htm
mesnagerjerome.free.fr
swooninprint.com
theartofsmear.com/home.html
www.alexandreorion.com
www.banksy.co.uk
www.basquiat.com
www.bleklerat.free.fr
www.borfyou.com
www.dface.co.uk
www.donleicht.com
www.ericailcane.org
www.goabove.com
www.graffiti.org/nemo/index.html
www.graffitiresearchlab.com
www.gzzglz.com
www.internetjournalofcriminology.com
www.jefaerosol.com
www.jr-art.net
www.internetjournalofcriminology.com 8
www.johnfekner.com
www.haring.com
www.kurtwenner.com
www.leequinones.com

www.missticinparis.com
www.missvan.com
www.mrbrainwash.com
www.ninapandolfo.com.br
www.obeygiant.com
www.richardhambleton.com
www.shelleymillerstudio.com/info.php
www.space-invaders.com
www.stayhigh149.com
www.teamrobbo.org
www.tejnibyen.dk
www.tracyleestum.com
www.xmarkjenkinsx.com

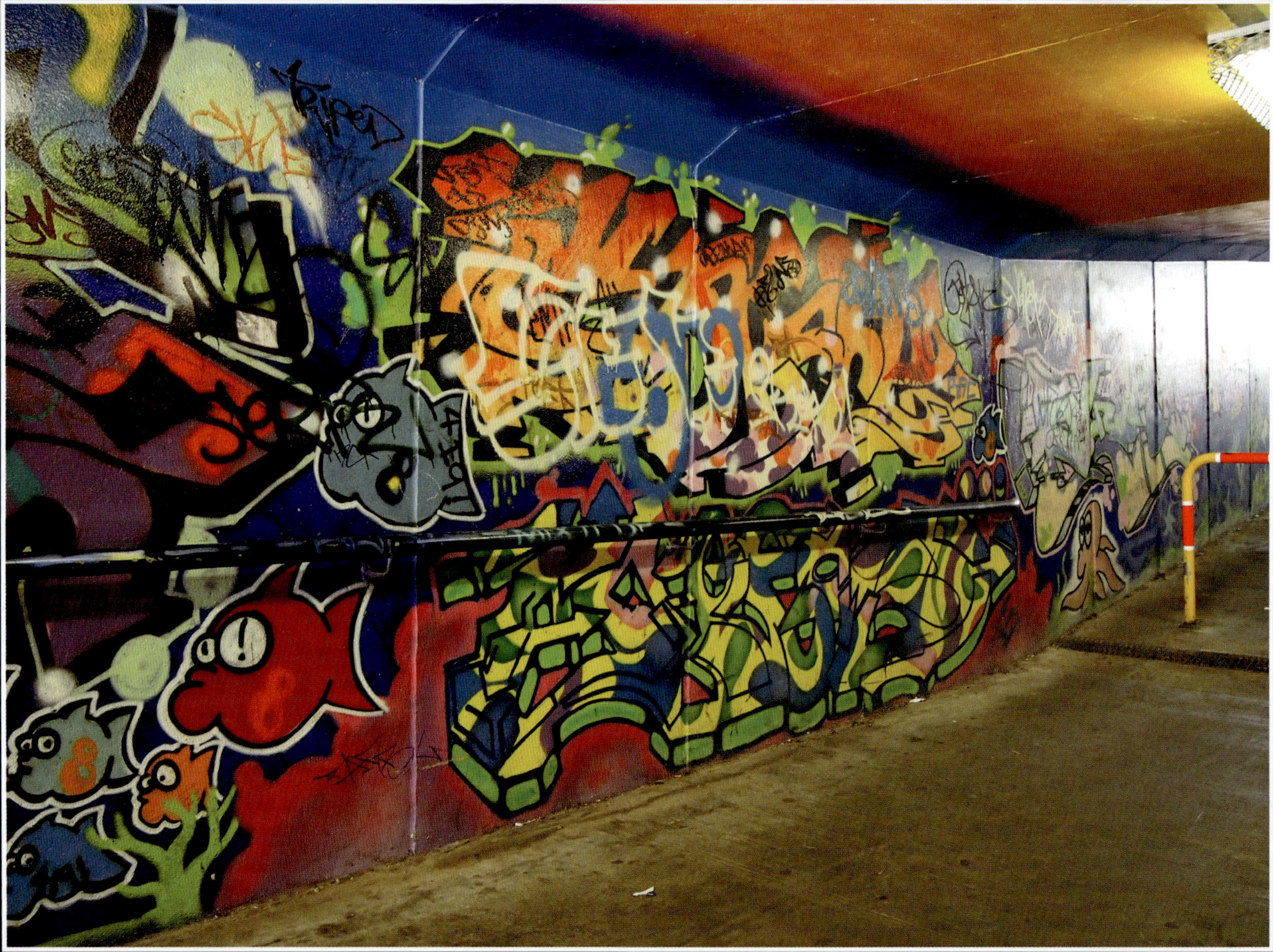

Photo courtesy of Homer Alvarez.

ACKNOWLEDGMENTS

First of all a huge thank-you to Julie Matysik of Skyhorse Publishing; without Julie's brilliant editing, this book would not have happened. Second, thank-you to my ever-wonderful agent Isabel Atherton of Creative Authors, who is always on the lookout for exciting projects for me. Third, I'd like to send my thanks to all those people who have let me use their beautiful photos to illustrate this book. As much as I would love to be able to travel the world and collect images myself, it just isn't feasible. And last, but never least, thank you to all the behind-the-scenes people who slog away putting the book together so it looks fabulous.

INDEX

M

N

O

P

Q

R

S

T

U

V

W

X Y Z